EXPLORING AMERICAN FOLK MUSIC

AMERICAN MADE MUSIC SERIES

David Evans, General Editor
Barry Jean Ancelet
Edward A. Berlin
Joyce J. Bolden
Rob Bowman
Susan C. Cook
Curtis Ellison
William Ferris
John Edward Hasse
Kip Lornell
Bill Malone
Eddie S. Meadows
Manuel H. Peña
David Sanjek
Wayne D. Shirley
Robert Walser

EXPLORING AMERICAN FOLK MUSIC

Ethnic, Grassroots, and Regional Traditions in the United States

Third Edition

KIP LORNELL

University Press of Mississippi • Jackson

www.upress.state.ms.us

The University Press of Mississippi is a member of the Association of American University Presses.

Copyright © 2012 by University Press of Mississippi
All rights reserved

First printing 2012

∞

Library of Congress Cataloging-in-Publication Data

Lornell, Kip, 1953–
Exploring American folk music : ethnic, grassroots, and regional traditions in the United States / Kip Lornell. — 3rd ed.
p. cm. — (American made music series)
Prev. ed. published under title: Introducing American folk music.
Includes bibliographical references and index.
ISBN 978-1-61703-264-6 (pbk. : alk. paper) — ISBN 978-1-61703-265-3 (cloth : alk. paper) — ISBN 978-1-61703-266-0 (ebook) 1. Folk music—United States—History and criticism. 2. Popular music—United States—History and criticism. I. Lornell, Kip, 1953–. Introducing American folk music. II. Title.
ML3551.L67 2012
781.62'13—dc23   2011036451

British Library Cataloging-in-Publication Data available

*To the late Mark T. Tucker,
family man, doubles partner, friend, and scholar,
and to my father, Wally Lornell (1921–2011),
who helped to show me the way*

BOOKS BY KIP LORNELL

2012 *Melody Man: Joe Davis and the New York Music Scene 1916–1972* Bruce Bastin with Kip Lornell (Jackson: University Press of Mississippi)

2012 *Exploring American Folk Music: Grassroots, Ethnic, and Regional Music in the United States* (Jackson: University Press of Mississippi)

2010 *From Jubilee to Hip Hop: African American Music Since Reconstruction* (New York: Prentice- Hall)

2009 *The Beat! Go Go Music from Washington, D.C.* (With Charles Stephenson), (Jackson: University Press of Mississippi)

2008 *Shreveport Sounds in Black & White*, co-edited with Tracey Laird (Jackson: University Press of Mississippi)

2004 *NPR's Curious Listeners Guide to American Folk Music* (New York: Penguin/Perigee Books)

2002 *Introducing American Folk Music: Grassroots and Ethnic Traditions in the United States* (New York: McGraw-Hill)

2001 *The Beat! Go Go's Fusion of Funk and Hip Hop with Charles Stephenson* (New York: Watson Guptil/Billboard Books)

1997 *Musics of Multicultural America*, co-edited with Anne Rasmussen (New York, New York: Schirmer Books/MacMillan Publishing USA).

1995 *African American Vocal Harmony Quartet Singing in Memphis, Tennessee: The Sacred Tradition* (Knoxville, Tennessee: University of Tennessee Press).

1993 *Introducing American Folk Music* (Madison, Wisconsin: Brown & Benchmark/McGraw Hill).

1993 *The Life and Legend of Leadbelly with Charles Wolfe* (New York City: HarperCollins,); published in Great Britain and western Europe by Secker & Warburg in 1993; published as a Harper/Perennial paperback in 1994; published as a paperback by Da Capo Press in 1999).

1989 *Virginia's Blues, Country, and Gospel Records: 1902–1943—An Annotated Discography* (Lexington, Kentucky: University Press of Kentucky).

1988 "*Happy in the Service of the Lord:*" *Afro-American Gospel Quartets in Memphis* (Urbana, Illinois: University of Illinois Press); published in Great Britain and western Europe by Bayou Press, Ltd.).

CONTENTS

Exploring American Folk Music
   A Preamble to the Third Edition   xi
A Prelude to the Second Edition   xv
Preface and Acknowledgments   xix

1. START HERE!   3
Introduction   3
The Roots of Twenty-first-Century Folk Music   6
Music in Our Daily Lives and in the Academy   9
Defining American Folk Music   12
Cultural Geography and Traditions   16
Folk Culture in the United States   17
Bred in the Bone   21
Listening to American Folk Music   25
Instruments   27
   Accordion / Banjo / Dulcimer / Fiddle /
   Fife / Guitar / Harmonica / Mandolin /
   Mouth Bow / One-String / Quills / Washboard
Final Thoughts   36

2. MASS MEDIA   42
Introduction   42
Minstrel and Medicine Shows   43
Recording the Blues   47
Record Companies and Folk Music   51
Country Music over the Airwaves   54
Border Radio   58
The Ancestors of MTV and VH-1   61
Uncle Dave Macon and the Electronic Media   62
Final Thoughts   64

3. FIELDWORK IN TWENTY-FIRST-CENTURY AMERICA   69
Musical Communities and Fieldwork   70
Accomplishing Fieldwork   73
   Topic / Focus / Preparation / Questions /
   Communication / Interview / Ethics

CONTENTS

Some Nuts and Bolts of Fieldwork ... 77
Final Thoughts ... 80

4. ANGLO-AMERICAN SECULAR FOLK MUSIC ... 82
British Ballads ... 83
Broadsides ... 87
Native American Ballads ... 89
Singing Cowboys ... 91
Tin Pan Alley and Country Music Texts ... 96
Ernest Stoneman's Repertoire ... 98
The Father of Bluegrass ... 99
Honky-Tonk ... 106
Western Swing ... 107
Final Thoughts ... 110

5. ANGLO-AMERICAN SACRED MUSIC ... 118
Psalmody ... 119
Shape Notes ... 120
Camp Meetings ... 125
Shakers ... 128
Later Hymnody and Gospel Songs ... 129
Sanctified Styles ... 133
Southern Gospel Boogie ... 135
Final Thoughts ... 138

6. AFRICAN AMERICAN RELIGIOUS FOLK MUSIC ... 143
The Great Awakening and Camp Meetings ... 144
Spirituals ... 146
Ring Shouts ... 150
Gospel ... 153
Pentecostal Singing and Guitar Evangelists ... 158
Preachers on Record ... 162
Gospel Quartets ... 163
Final Thoughts ... 166

7. AFRICAN AMERICAN SECULAR FOLK MUSIC ... 171
Work Songs ... 172
String Bands ... 176
Fife and Drum Bands ... 178
Ragtime and Coon Songs ... 180
Ballads ... 181

Songsters and Rural Music	186
Down-home Blues	189
Modern Blues	191
Final Thoughts	195

8. ETHNIC AND NATIVE AMERICAN TRADITIONS — 202

Jewish American: Klezmer	207
Native American	210
Music and Ceremony Today /	
Musical Characteristics / Instruments / Powwows	
Hawaiian American	220
Franco-American	224
Cajun Country / Zydeco / Northeastern States	
Scandinavian American	234
Ballads / Instrumental Music / Polka and More Polka! /	
Norwegian American Folk Music	
Final Thoughts	241

9. THE HISPANIC AMERICAN DIASPORA — 251

The Southwest	253
Tex-Mex Music / Corridos / Mariachi /	
Native American Influences	
Florida	270
New York City	274
Final Thoughts	276

10. THE FOLK REVIVALS — 281

Red Roots	284
The Mass Media and Popular Culture	288
Field Research	291
The 1960s Folk Revival	292
A British Invasion	306
The Blues Boom	307
Back to the Mountains	309
New Entrepreneurs and Frontiers	314
Final Thoughts	318

11. THE FOLK ROOTS OF CONTEMPORARY POPULAR MUSIC — 323

Black Codes from the Underground	324
Improvisation in Black Musical Culture	325
Rhythm and Blues	332

Rockabilly	334
Early Rock 'n' Roll and Rock	337
Motown and Soul	341
Hip-Hop and Rap	342
Country Music Today	344
Final Thoughts	345

12. URBAN FOLK MUSIC — 350

Introduction	350
Blues and Gospel in Chicago	353
San Antonio's Country and Conjunto Traditions	357
Washington, D.C.	359
Country Music / Bluegrass	
Final Thoughts	375
Selected Song Index	379
General Index	382

EXPLORING AMERICAN FOLK MUSIC

A Preamble to the Third Edition

On consecutive weekends in mid-September 2010, I found myself in Shreveport, Louisiana, and Yarmouthport, Massachusetts, visiting relatives. My father-in-law, Bubba Gandy, insisted that we try Shreveport's newly opened Logan's Roadhouse for their popular Monday evening 2-for-1 catfish dinner. Bubba, as usual, was correct. The fried catfish proved an excellent choice, along with the homemade green tomato relish and hush puppies.

The local music scene also reflected the fact that I was in the Ark-La-Tex; the widely used local shorthand for the intersection of Arkansas, Louisiana, and Texas. In addition to the live music acts (both local and national) heard at the five riverboat casinos anchored on the Red River, a twist of the AM/FM radio dial revealed no less than three radio stations featuring African American gospel music and an equal number focused on southern gospel, which included several groups playing live on Sunday morning.

My three days on Cape Cod provided me with another glimpse of regional America. A mere two blocks from my parents' retirement condo, a flooded bog marked the autumn cranberry harvest and, yes, it sat at the end of Cranberry View Lane. My mother and I twice ate baked codfish, though I eschewed the New England clam chowder because it just doesn't suit me. The weekend's entertainment included the Thirty-third Annual "Eastham Windmill Weekend" featuring The Cape Cod Fiddlers. This group, which has been together for twenty-one years, playing for festivals, dances, and weddings on the Cape, performs not only local fiddle tunes but also draws from other traditions that have long informed New England fiddlers: Irish, Scottish, and French Canadian.

Because my drive home from Baltimore/Washington International Thurgood Marshall Airport following my Cape Cod trip happened to be on Sunday evening, at 9:00 PM I tuned to WKYS-FM for the final hour of "Da Ghetto Prince Show." Hosted by Anwan Glover (the charismatic lead talker for Backyard Band and an actor with roles in both *The Wire* and *Treme*), it's the 2010 equivalent of a down-home D.C. house party with numerous shout-outs to

A PREAMBLE TO THE THIRD EDITION

residents of Trinidad (a section of D.C., not the Carribean nation) as well as to local "go-go heads" who are always identified both by name and their neighborhood. Between 9:00 PM and 10:00 PM Big G spins only go-go, certainly the most localized form of community-based American music; it's African American music that is only heard in the "DMV" (the District of Columbia and its neighboring Maryland and Virginia suburbs). Big G several times reminded listeners that WKYS-FM was sponsoring an upcoming concert by Chuck Brown, the "Godfather of Go-Go," who in 2005 received the prestigious "National Heritage Award" from the National Endowment for the Arts (Folk Arts).

These two brief excursions and my ride home from BWI, along with my work on the third edition of this textbook, underscore that American folk, ethnic, grassroots, and regional music (not to mention food and place names) remains integral to our daily lives. But it's not simply food and music that mark American regionalism. A conversation with Bubba Gandy (who lived in either Shreveport or Bossier City, Louisiana, for eight decades) or my sister-in-law Patty, who has lived on or just off Cape Cod for her entire life, reveals that regional accents and colloquialisms remain alive and thriving in the second decade of the twenty-first century.

Moreover the number of books, essays, and sound recordings in this field continues to grow. I added several dozen new items to the suggested listening, reading, and viewing lists found at the end of each chapter. These additions reveal only the proverbial tip of the iceberg. I sifted through hundreds of possibilities before adding these suggestions to the lists I compiled for the second edition (2002).

Although my students at George Washington University or my own teen-aged daughters disagree at first, not everything that you need to know can be found on the Internet. The Internet is certainly a marvelous tool that brings us closer together and engenders more expedient and diverse communication via options such as e-mail and Facebook. My classes in black American music and ethnomusicology underscore to GWU students that music in their own family, ethnic group, or community (the music of everyday life) is worth studying. Such grassroots music is increasingly found on media available by way of your computer, which provides a wonderful tool for anyone studying folk, ethnic, and regional music in the United States.

The sales of compact discs peaked around 2000, but now only a few of my students actually purchase music on a "hard" format. When the second edition of this book was published you couldn't download the musical examples for this book from Smithsonian Folkways. Now the entire Smithsonian Folkways catalogue can be legitimately downloaded from several sources. Tom Davenport initially incorporated Folkstreams.net in 2002, while youtube.com wouldn't hit the Internet for another three years.

A PREAMBLE TO THE THIRD EDITION

Today, however, you can find video performances of African American banjo players Joe and Odell Thompson, footage of Flatt and Scruggs from the late 1950s or see Lydia Mendoza play and sing a ranchero. Individuals can download not only anything from the vast Smithsonian Folkways catalogue, but also from other important independent companies, most notably Arhoolie Records. Academic institutions can subscribe to a service via Alexander Street Press that allows students to stream selections not only from Smithsonian Folkways, but also from the African American Music Reference Library, the Garland Encyclopedia of World Music Online, and American Song.

Folkstreams.net began in 2002 when independent filmmaker Tom Davenport decided that films about folk culture needed wider distribution. The Web sites describes its purpose as "A National Preserve of Documentary Films about American Roots Cultures streamed with essays about the traditions and filmmaking. The site includes transcriptions, study and teaching guides, suggested readings, and links to related websites." This nonprofit site partners with The University of North Carolina at Chapel Hill School of Information and Library Science (SILS) and BIBLIO.ORG at the University of North Carolina at Chapel Hill. The topics of the documentary films that you can stream from this site are not only music (though music is perhaps its strongest suit) but also religion, family, festival, and foodways.

This edition includes one new chapter, "Urban Folk Music," that discusses traditions found in urban areas but focuses on country music and bluegrass in the District of Columbia. The suggested listening, reading, and viewing has been updated and expanded by about 20 percent. The musical examples discussed in each chapter can be accessed either by way of compact discs purchased from Smithsonian Folkways or (more likely) via downloading or streaming.

Exploring American Folk Music: Ethnic, Grassroots, and Regional Traditions in the United States, third edition, found a new home due to the belief in this project by both the "American Made Music" series editor, David Evans, and University Press of Mississippi editor Craig Gill. Chris Freitag oversaw the first two editions of this book, first for Brown & Benchmark and then for McGraw-Hill. He quietly worked to help move this book to its new home, which I greatly appreciate. Finally, I am grateful—as always—for the love and support of my three "girls": Kim, Cady, and Max.

A PRELUDE TO THE SECOND EDITION

"Mrs. Brown is dead." The topic of Whoopie John Wilfahrt research and his relationship with my own relatives was broached almost immediately after I arrived in central Minnesota during the last week of May 1999. They all knew, of course, of my interest in American vernacular music, and my cousin Tom Esser and Aunt Mickey—my mother's oldest sister—in New Ulm had helped me arrange interviews related to Whoopie John in the middle 1980s. His younger sister, Mrs. Brown, lived (quite literally) across the street from the Essers' liquor store. When we gathered for lunch on the Thursday before Memorial Day weekend my cousin, Tom, informed me that she had passed away two weeks before.

Later that day (following a two-hour drive across the rich and verdant flat farmlands of southern Minnesota) I brought this uneasy news to my uncle, Bob Meffert, who lives in Marshall. Uncle Bob knew her but was better acquainted with her son, Dennis Brown, who lives about an hour south of Marshall. Bob (a high school instrumental music teacher with thirty years of teaching experience and a veteran of amateur polka bands in Milroy, Minnesota) discussed the importance of Whoopie John in American music and spoke about one of the unsung heros of German American (or "Dutchmen") polka music, Leo B. "Pinky" Schroepfer, who is acknowledged locally as *the* man who promoted the clarinet as a key instrument in twentieth-century Dutchmen polka bands.

While riding in the car to the nearby South Dakota border, my uncle observed that we were about to drive through Ivanhoe, Minnesota, which he identified as a "real Polish town." With a little prompting from me about local ethnic celebrations Bob also told me about some of the annual festivals, such as Edgerton's "Dutch Festival," Henderson's "Sauerkraut Days," Ghent's "Belgium-American Days," and, naturally, New Ulm's "Heritage Days." The rivers of European ethnicity run deep in this very rural part of the state.

But what Bob Meffert spoke of in the greatest detail were the changes that have occurred in Marshall since my last visit a decade ago. Since the early 1990s hundreds of Mexicans and Somalians have moved into town, many of them

A PRELUDE TO THE SECOND EDITION

Folk musicians in central Virginia (circa 1936). Courtesy of the Southern Historical Collection, The University of North Carolina at Chapel Hill.

settling there permanently. They are economic and social immigrants to this small town tucked away in the southwest corner of Minnesota, in search of jobs (many in a local turkey-processing factory) and freedom from war. ESL—English as a Second Language—classes are now offered by several local organizations. And, as my aunt Mary observed, their elementary and secondary school concerts look like a "UN on stage" with not only Somalians, Mexicans, and Mexican Americans, but also Vietnamese and African Americans adding to the European American faces that still predominate. This diversity has put a new face on Marshall that would have been unthinkable to me visiting this town of 15,000 people in 1989. And it's even more interesting for the folks who live there.

This trip to Minnesota reminded me about my revisions to *Introducing American Folk Music: Ethnic and Grassroot Traditions in the United States*. Although it's a book dedicated to the study of music, after visiting nearly a score of cousins, aunts, and uncles, I am even more convinced that you can't divorce the music from its historical roots and cultural contexts. Folk, folk-based, traditional, grassroots, and "ethnic" music (these terms are very similar though not precisely synonymous) are intimately tied to family, ethnicity, community, and racial identity. Not surprisingly cultural change, diversity, history, family, and regionalism—all viewed through the lens of music—form the core of this book.

A PRELUDE TO THE SECOND EDITION

This new edition was mostly written in the spring and summer of 1999—just as the millennium crept closer and a decade after I began work on the first edition. The coverage of American folk (and ethnic) music has been enlarged to include a new chapter on Hispanic American traditions, which was addressed in the first edition, but its importance on America's musical landscape has only increased. This edition contains other changes, such as updated and greatly expanded annotated "Suggested Listening," "Suggested Reading," and "Suggested Viewing" sections that close each chapter. I have also rearranged the order in which the chapters are presented. This new order makes sense to me, but you may wish (quite legitimately) to present the chapters in a different sequence.

The careful reader will note that my coverage of genres has also expanded in some subtle ways. Each of the chapters has been revised, some more than others. These changes were prompted by ideas presented by outside readers, most of whom are professors who have used the book in their American music courses. Equally important, I have assigned this book a half dozen times to my students at the George Washington University, who provided me with heartfelt and thoughtful feedback. Their suggestions have also been taken to heart. For example one of the students' best-liked chapters, "The Folk Roots of Contemporary Popular Music," has been greatly expanded, while the "Mass Media" and "Ethnic and Native American Traditions" have also been significantly rewritten.

These changes are also due in part to my own rethinking on certain subjects. For the past decade I have been teaching courses on African American music, popular music, and jazz, which has also helped me to reshape this book. This is especially true when it comes to the interaction of popular and folk music, which was addressed in the first edition, but is emphasized to an even greater degree in this edition. I have come to think that this book rightly contains "folk" in its title but the ties to and interaction with popular music and culture is even more critical than I realized. Much of the music discussed here is called "roots music" in popular magazines as diverse as *Dirty Linen* or *Goldmine*.

Roots music, most notably blues, early country music, and songs associated with the folk revival of the early 1960s, has inspired groups like Wilco (with and without Billy Bragg) and Son Volt, both of which have impinged upon the world of popular music enough that their recordings are regularly reviewed in magazines devoted to contemporary popular music. I have even heard them on for-profit radio stations located above the noncommercial band that ends at 91.9 FM. In other words, they have displayed enough commercial potential to be noticed and are not shy about speaking out about their musical inspirations.

Sadly, the music discussed in this textbook remains largely ignored by most academic scholars who teach in our colleges and universities. Most music departments are undergoing a gradual metamorphosis, inching toward the

A PRELUDE TO THE SECOND EDITION

inclusion of "world music," the vernacular and notated music created in the United States during the twentieth century, and multiculturalism. In these important regards, this textbook sits firmly in the mainstream. It joins the growing number of textbooks on black American music, Latin American music, and multicultural music in the United States—textbooks that did not exist when the first edition of *Introducing American Folk Music* was published in 1993. The times they are (slowly) a-changing!

PREFACE AND ACKNOWLEDGMENTS

This book is for the student possessing a lively interest in our distinctly American vernacular culture and music. Specifically, *Introducing American Folk Music: Ethnic and Grassroot Traditions in the United States* examines folk and closely related grassroots music, such as gospel, western swing, and folk/rock, that developed in the United States. The book covers a wide variety of topics from the geographically discrete Cajun music of Louisiana and the hulas from Hawaii to the more familiar blues and gospel music, which have strong roots in the late-nineteenth-century South. Rock 'n' roll and rock, two important forms of twentieth-century American vernacular music that drew (and still draw) a large portion of their strength and inspiration from folk music, are mentioned throughout the text but largely remain outside our scope.

American folk music, however, retains its close ties to popular trends. Rock as well as other forms of popular music often display direct links to this heritage. Go-Go (a type of urban black popular music pioneered in Washington, D.C., in the middle 1970s) is performed in clubs patronized almost exclusively by younger African Americans. One of the top go-go bands, Trouble Funk, always begins its show with a call and response (antiphony) interlude between the band members and audience that not only recognizes who is "in the house" but helps to establish an intimate atmosphere. Antiphony has graced black American music since slavery and its contemporary use recalls prayer and church services, railroad gandy-dancers (track layers), and blues singers. Without these earlier folk expressions, go-go (as it has evolved today) would not exist. Folk-based styles, such as the folk/rock of the middle 1960s, commercial country music, and contemporary electric blues, that have crossed into popular culture are also part of the book. The folk roots of contemporary popular music, much of it African American, are explored in the final chapter.

The influence of traditional music moves through space as well as over time—a phenomenon studied by cultural geographers as well as folk music scholars. In the first two decades of the twentieth century black migrants carried their love of blues and gospel northward during the "great migration," as they fled from both southern racism and its impoverishing working conditions. The interest in western swing remains quite strong in California despite its Texas roots. This is due to the westward movement of dust bowl residents who looked toward its fertile valleys during the 1930s and 1940s. A strong affinity for bluegrass developed among blue- and white-collar workers in Ohio and Michigan who abandoned Tennessee and West Virginia in search of industrial jobs in the 1940s and 1950s. Be it food, colloquial expressions, or music, we Americans always carry our folk culture with us.

My own approach to this subject is interdisciplinary, drawing from the ideas of scholars in ethnomusicology, cultural geography, anthropology, history, and folklore. Although the emphasis of this book is on our musical and historical culture, it also defines several basic musical concepts to discuss some fundamental aspects of the music itself. Performances by a variety of musicians drawn from the extensive Smithsonian Folkways catalogue constitute the compact disc that accompanies *Introducing American Folk Music: Ethnic and Grassroot Traditions in the United States*. The inquisitive reader may wish to delve further into the subject by exploring the resources described in the annotated bibliography ("Suggested Reading"), discography ("Suggested Listening"), and videotapes ("Suggested Viewing") that close each chapter.

Introducing American Folk Music: Ethnic and Grassroot Traditions in the United States works well in tandem with the sweeping scholarly surveys by Rich Crawford (*An Introduction to America's Music*) and Daniel Kingman (*American Music: A Panorama*). Its main chapters are further divided into discrete sections about blues, ballads, cowboy songs, spirituals, and so forth. This new edition of *Introducing American Folk Music* builds upon the important writings of Bruce Bastin, Harlan Daniels, Arthur Kyle Davis, Serge Denisoff, David Evans, Robert Winslow Gordon, Archie Green, Jim Griffith, Jim Leary, Jose Limon, Alan and John Lomax, Bill Malone, Paul Oliver, Neil Rosenberg, Tony Russell, Henry Sapoznik, Dorothy Scarborough, Nick Spitzer, Dick Spottswood, Jeff Titon, Charles K. Wolfe, and dozens of other scholars and enthusiasts. These individuals scoured homes, juke joints, farms, churches, prisons, bunkhouses, and taverns across the United States to write about and record America's ballads, cowboy tunes, bluegrass, blues, and work songs. To this corpus I add my own idiosyncratic vision, a perspective based on my research, field recording, and writing about black folk music, gospel singing, and hillbilly artists that began in 1969.

I would like to thank the following people and institutions for their help in making this book possible. First of all I wish to acknowledge the assistance of the Smithsonian Institution, which awarded me a postdoctoral fellowship during the majority of the time this book was written. Tony Seeger, curator of the Folkways Collection of the Smithsonian Institution (who is now teaching

PREFACE AND ACKNOWLEDGMENTS

Eleanor Roosevelt at Whitetop. Courtesy of the Southern Historical Collection, The University of North Carolina at Chapel Hill.

at UCLA), served as my advisor during this period. Nick Spitzer, John Hasse, Ralph Rinzler, and Martin Williams of the Smithsonian Institution encouraged this project from its outset and helped to bring it to fruition. And I must also thank Atesh Sonnenborn, Jeff Place, Pete Reiniger, Stephanie Smith, and my other friends at Smithsonian Folkways. Also the encouragement and wise council of the staff of the Blue Ridge Institute of Ferrum College, most notably Vaughan Webb and Roddy Moore, is always appreciated. During the academic year 1999–2000 my departmental and program chairs in Africana Studies, American Studies, and Music at George Washington University helped to rearrange my teaching schedule to accommodate revising and rewriting this book. I wish to thank my friends and colleagues at GWU as well as Mario Reyes, Dale Olsen, and Vaughn Webb, among others, in the fields of American music and ethnomusicology for their assistance.

Special thanks to Phil Martin of the (now-defunct) Wisconsin Folk Museum for his many helpful suggestions in the Scandinavian American section and Bill Vaughan of George Mason University, who helped with maps and photographs. Others who contributed in a variety of ways are Bruce Bastin, Andy Cahan, Sam Charters, Kim Gandy, Jim Griffith, Joe Hickerson, Peter B. Lowry, Ted Mealor, Mike Seeger, Jared Snyder, Nick Spitzer, Mark Tucker, and Charles K. Wolfe.

PREFACE AND ACKNOWLEDGMENTS

I am also deeply indebted to three outside readers—David Evans, Jim Leary, and Anne Rassmusen—who have used this book in the classroom and have shared their thoughts with me. Their suggestions for revisions helped to reshape the book in many small and important ways. The result is a far better book.

I need to acknowledge my debt to those whose work has shaped my thinking and writing in the expanded section on "Ethnic and Native American Traditions" and the Hispanic American section. I am specifically indebted to the research and writings of Jim Griffith, Jose Limon, Peter Manuel, Manuel Pena, Mario Reyes, Brenda Romero, Henry Sapoznik, and Daniel Sheehy.

The music textbook team at McGraw-Hill, especially Chris Freitag, thought highly enough of this project to encourage me to write this second edition. I wish to thank him and Nadia Bidwell, another member of the McGraw-Hill team, who lent her kind assistance at every turn.

Finally, I would like to thank my family (Kim, Cady, and Max) for their cooperation. I would also like to especially acknowledge the encouragement of five outstanding mentors—David Evans (Memphis State University), Frank Keetz (Bethleham Central Senior High School), Wallace and Betty Jane Lornell (also known as Ace and Beagle), and Daniel Patterson (University of North Carolina at Chapel Hill). They inspired me to follow my muse by exploring American vernacular musical history and to challenge conventional educational wisdom. I would not have even attempted to write this book were it not for all of the important American musicians who touched me over the years—David Byrne, John Coltrane, Jimi Hendrix, Robert Johnson, Thelonious Monk, Bill Monroe, Charlie Poole, Cole Porter, Sonny Rollins, They Might Be Giants, Sonny Boy Williamson, and many others. Their music has been a constant source of inspiration.

EXPLORING AMERICAN FOLK MUSIC

Chapter 1

START HERE!

- Introduction
- The Roots of Twenty-first-Century Folk Music
- Music in Our Daily Lives and in the Academy
- Defining American Folk Music
- Cultural Geography and Traditions
- Folk Culture in the United States
- Bred in the Bone
- Listening to American Folk Music
- Instruments
- Final Thoughts

INTRODUCTION

Thanksgiving in Franklin County, Virginia, marks a period of transition. By late November all of the leaves on the trees are carpeting the gentle knolls of the Blue Ridge Mountains, leaving the landscape bleak and quiet. The high school football season is but a memory and reports of the upcoming basketball campaign have begun to appear in local newspapers. People are just starting to think about Christmas plans, while the deer, bear, and squirrels prepare for their annual winter struggle.

Thanksgiving Day in 1987 dawned cloudy and the temperatures remained unusually warm. I was among a half-dozen people gathered for homemade bread, pumpkin pie, roasted chestnuts, mashed potatoes, and turkey. Before supper we lolled casually on the front porch; the 70 degree temperature invited us to sit outside to swap stories and sing. Joni Mitchell, Suzanne Vega, America, and Bob Dylan numbers were popular, but Neil Young and John Prine were the two most requested singer/songwriters that evening.

Just as the yearning words and simple chord progressions of an early Neil Young composition "Sugar Mountain" settled into the air, Rusty's eyes lit up as he picked up his guitar. He sang a ditty that began: "Last night when I got home,

Tommy Jarrell. Courtesy of the Ralph Rinzler Archive, Center for Folklife and Cultural Heritage, Smithsonian Institution.

drunk as I could be. Saw another car parked, where my car ought to be." When he finished I asked Rusty where he had picked up this song. "From an old drunk at a fiddlers' convention in Union Grove, North Carolina. I thought it was fun, so I learned it," came his instant reply. After musing for a few seconds, Rusty launched into John Prine's "Paradise" and the rest of us joined him in singing the chorus about the long-gone, nostalgic days of Prine's Muhlenburg County, Kentucky, youth.

During the course of daily living we rarely intellectualize the differences between the elements of traditional and popular culture in our lives. Nor do we necessarily make the distinction between what we perceive to be old and new. Most of us casually throw these ingredients into a cultural brew without thinking about it. Many self-taught musicians are like Rusty, who learns his songs from commercial phonograph records, friends, the radio, sheet music, and other musicians. Both "Our Goodman," the eighteenth-century British ballad that Rusty casually learned from an anonymous musician, and his well-studied version of John Prine's finely chiseled and sentimental "Muhlenburg County" represent the range of the acoustic music that he enjoys. And both songs reflect Rusty's unaffected proclivity for popular and folk music.

Washington, D.C., my present home, is only 300 miles from bucolic Franklin County, Virginia, but in many ways it's a different world. It is urban, 65 percent nonwhite (largely African American), and many of its young residents are firmly planted in the early-twenty-first-century world of hip-hop culture, music, and speech. Go-go is a form of local expressive black American culture unique to Washington, D.C.—music that developed in the middle 1970s with Chuck Brown (and his Soul Searchers) at its helm. Brown was in his early forties when go-go first hit the District's nightspots, and he remains the "Godfather of Go-Go."

Chuck Brown, however, never left his North Carolina roots entirely behind—the fish fries, down-home blues, and Saturday night parties that were sometimes called "struts." Slug-Go, one of the genre's most cleverly named bands, came under Brown's spell in the late 1980s. One of their show stoppers was "Go-Go Strut," a tune inspired by Brown and one that calls to mind the virtuoso instrumental piano solos by early blues pianists such as Cow Cow Davenport and Cripple Clarence Lofton. These pieces intimate a public display of dancing, to sashay in public, to strut one's "stuff"—an impulse that goes back to the nineteenth-century cakewalk in black American culture. "Display," in the form of recognizing members of the audience, and "crews," representing specific sections of the city as well as highly individualized styles of dancing, are integral to live go-go shows. Even in our postmodern era, certain elements of African American expressive culture associated with the Reconstruction South are not as far from the present day as we might think.

The traditional styles discussed in this book result from the hybridization that keeps traditional American music in constant evolution. Its lyrics are forever in flux and have never been frozen into immutable texts with fixed melodies. Diversity within established aesthetic boundaries, however, is an important key to these musical forms. Traditional songs and the instruments that frequently accompany them are combined in a variety of contexts. The very human sound of a harmonica, for instance, can be heard accompanying the clogging of a Franco-American dancer in northern Vermont, as the heavily amplified lead instrument of a Southside Chicago blues band, or integrated into a small Louisiana Cajun stringband.

"Our Goodman" was recorded in 1929 by Coley Jones, a black Texas singer, and the famous Georgia hillbilly fiddler, Earl Johnson, long before Rusty heard it performed in Union Grove in the 1980s. Rusty's melody is similar to Coley Jones, though less ornate than Johnson's fiddle tune. As early as the 1880s the text for "Our Goodman" began to be "collected" by folklorists and English professors across the entire country. This ballad remains one of the most popular of the British ballads that is still sung in the United States.

In the twenty-first century music that once thrived through face-to-face transmission within small communities was disseminated quite rapidly, largely because CD players, radio, television, jukeboxes, phonographs, and tape players reached into every corner of the United States. The explosion of the Internet in the late 1990s added yet another dimension to the dissemination of music.

Scholars have long suggested that the **mass media** will eventually obliterate today's racial, ethnic, regional, and traditional styles of American music that clearly stem from their eighteenth- and nineteenth-century roots. In other words... that mass communications will result in the "death" of folk music.

This may eventually come to pass, but not anytime soon. The fact remains that the multilayered interaction fostered by the mass media inevitably enriches and expands our musical vocabulary, leading to yet new musical vistas. One example is the steadily building interest in "world music," which increasingly melds with aspects of the American vernacular. In the teens, for instance, many traditional musicians were entranced and influenced by Hawaiian slide guitar styles. Today you are just as likely to see a hybrid like Nigerian juju that draws upon American music, especially funk and soul, for some of its inspiration.

THE ROOTS OF TWENTY-FIRST-CENTURY FOLK MUSIC

Distinctly American music began to emerge almost as soon as the first Europeans and Africans arrived in the New World. Both the European settlers and African slaves brought instruments and musical traditions with them. The Europeans contributed fiddles and pianos, while Africans brought the knowledge of making and performing upon banjolike instruments with them. By the nineteenth century, these three instruments were played by black and white Americans, but often in very different ways. White settlers brought their ballads; transplanted Africans contributed the concept of call and response. While the races may have remained legally separate, legislating the strict segregation of musical ideas and instruments proved impossible. Twenty-first-century American folk music draws from this common background.

The states east of the Mississippi River dominated our country into the early part of the nineteenth century. Outside of New England, the Middle Atlantic states, along with the far Southwest, became the first extensively settled sections of the United States. Scotch, Irish, and German pioneers settled in the mountains and valleys of the Blue Ridge and Appalachian mountains, far from the port cities and slowly growing cities on the Piedmont. In the Southwest, pioneering Spaniards gradually moved into what would become New Mexico and Arizona.

Face-to-face communication among these settlers was the norm. Most people remained illiterate or obtained the most meager formal education. Travel along the rutted, unpaved roads (or along trails) proved difficult at best and impossible during the worst of times; physical and sometimes spiritual isolation was common. As the United States emerged from the shadow of British domination, new hybrids began to emerge. The seeds of syncretization had been planted and the beginnings of distinctly American folk music could be heard in the first few decades of the nineteenth century.

Outside of the major cities most of the United States remained a rural, insular world populated by neighbors and family that one knew almost always from birth until death. Paved roads were unknown, telephones didn't exist, and electricity came to many with "rural electrification" programs of the New Deal 1930s. Musical activity was an important means of entertainment at home, at homes of neighbors, and in church. The fact of isolation combined with slowly developing American idioms ensured that we would be blessed with regional differences in folk music. Not only did we have French-speaking citizens in Louisiana and northern New England in 1800, but the physical separation of Maine lumbermen from Kentucky River roustabouts also led to unique regional differences. The tripart electric and electronic levelers of musical regionalism (phonograph records, radios, and television) lay in the future, poised to forever alter our modern world.

The folk musics of white and Hispanic Americans remains a complex, complicated topic involving a variety of vocal and instrumental traditions. The eighteenth- and early-nineteenth-century musical styles largely followed the lead of their counterparts from the British Isles and Spain, in part because of the ongoing domination by England of the eastern United States and the influence of Spaniards in the Southwest. Churchgoers sang Wesley's hymns, and ballads of British and Spanish origin entertained folks at home, while the old-world fiddle tunes provided dance music on Saturday night.

Our knowledge of early folk music is almost entirely derived from a crazy quilt of primary and secondary printed sources: newspaper and magazine articles, diaries, travel accounts, and fiction. Fascinated by slavery and black people, literate people often wrote of everyday black life. Until the 1820s some writers occasionally noted aspects of African survivals such as drumming, singing, and dancing. Most writers, however, seemed more interested in the contemporary black folk music that surrounded them. Visual evidence, especially paintings of blacks performing music, also suggests the widespread development of black American music. Unfortunately few blacks wrote accounts of their own music until after the Civil War, a true loss to American music history but not a surprising one given the trying conditions under which slaves lived.

Early African American folk music resulted from the synthesis of African music, which often arrived by way of the Caribbean Basin, with European music to create a richly unique blend. Our interest is in the traditional music that developed out of this cultural clash. The majority of the early slaves came to the United States from West Africa, thousands of square miles ranging from beautiful beaches to large expanses of flat, hot savannah. Seventeenth-century West Africa was a huge and complex **multicultural** region that included sophisticated city-states as well as complex social organizations that ruled smaller areas.

The musics of Africa were exceptionally diverse. Religious and public ceremonies, rites of passage, and other types of functions most often called for music making. Because of these inherent links between music and everyday life the contemporary West African musics were difficult to separate from the societies themselves. From formal court ceremonies to the songs chanted by pole-wielding boatmen, music was an integral part of these societies.

Drums of varying sizes and shapes were the primary instruments of West Africans. Often played in ensembles of two or more, drummers sometimes used the palm of their hands or sticks to beat out the complex rhythms. Fingertips created yet more complicated rhythms, and drum ensembles played patterns that crossed meter, pitting duple against triple time. Master drummers of the highest skill became valuable members of any clan or tribe because they added so much to the rituals. Some of these drummers, in fact, were held in very high esteem among their peers and were viewed as specialists. Because percussion was so integral to West African musical culture, younger men—this was the domain of males—aspired to achieve higher status through drumming. We see this legacy as recently as the 1970s when funk, hip-hop, and go-go developed.

Like their African ancestors, black Americans incorporated music into their everyday experience. This was difficult because of the conditions of slavery, in which slave owners attempted to control all vestiges of culture. Nonetheless, black Americans maintained customs and rituals utilizing music. They sang and drummed at Virginia funerals as late as the second decade of the 1800s. Secondary accounts suggest that blacks appropriated the Dutch "Pinkster Day" celebrations, a day free from work during which banjos, enthusiastic dancing, and spirited and complex drumming lasted for many hours.

Precisely how quickly African music became integrated into our musical fabric remains difficult to ascertain. The legal sanctions against African culture—dancing, drumming, language, and so on—were in place before the dawn of the eighteenth century, but to measure the degree to which these actually affected the culture itself is not easy. Because of reports of drumming and African religious practices, it appears that acculturation in the West Indies took much longer.

The sheer number of slaves imported to the southern United States indicates that this was true in the South. Except for South Carolina, where for a short period the number of slaves actually exceeded the white population, Africans brought to the South soon learned of European culture. The South was also home to most of the slowly maturing black American music; it spawned most of the unique forms of American folk music, such as blues, gospel, Cajun, and hillbilly, that have received the greatest worldwide attention.

START HERE!

MUSIC IN OUR DAILY LIVES AND IN THE ACADEMY

Our senses are bombarded daily by music that we hear on the television, in elevators, through speakers in our computers, or at the local shopping mall. Many cars come fully equipped with a radio, an MP3 input, and/or CD player so that we don't miss a beat while we are stuck in traffic. Many younger people walk or jog with an MP3 player or other similar portable device in hand. When we attend a Baptist church service, an (Italian) opera by Puccini, or a concert by a pop group such as Phish, we are exposed to live performances of music. Some of these performances contain more improvisation and are less predictable than others. While most fans of opera are probably familiar with the libretto as well as the opera's plot and the pop music aficionado might know Phish's repertoire, the performance of contemporary popular music not only lacks a program but is also more likely to contain surprise of all sorts.

Whether one prefers Beethoven's compositions over the extended jazz works of Duke Ellington or the guitar artistry of Andre Segovia to Kentucky picker Merle Travis, at least we agree that these people are musical composers or performers. Some might argue that the popular "heavy metal" groups of the 1970s and 1980s, such as Led Zeppelin, KISS, Poison, Anthrax, or AC/DC, made devilish noise that barely qualified as music. Others might suggest that Brittney Spears or the Backstreet Boys are simply too saccharin to be taken seriously. Perhaps you feel that the polka music of Frankie Yankovic or the Six Fat Dutchmen is only good for easy listening while consuming bratwurst and beer, and to suggest that it is music worthy of serious study is laughable.

Furthermore, are rap and hip-hop's highly rhythmic, percussive vocalizing actually music? Others take the stance that opera stars, twentieth-century legends like Beverly Sills or Luciano Pavarotti, merely stand onstage in ludicrous costumes and bellow loudly but that they're not *really* singing. I believe that during our objective moments, each of these detractors would accept the fact that all of these artists are engaged in making music worthy of our attention.

"Music is a healing force in the universe" was the spiritual sentiment sometimes chanted during the late 1960s performances of jazz saxophonist Pharaoh Sanders and vocalized by the late Leon Thomas. This premise was set forth during the close of a decade of exceptional turmoil and change in America and much of the rest of the world. We had struggled through the early stages of the civil rights movement and the dawning of the age of feminism (two struggles that remain ongoing), riots that had blackened many major cities in the United States, and students' protests of the unpopular war in Vietnam. Today Sanders's cry might sound naive, but his thoughts of love and peace directly reflected the hopefulness of its Aquarian age. The concept that music truly is a spiritual force binding us together is quite interesting and bears closer scrutiny. But is music a truly universal language? The easy initial response is yes, music is found across the entire world and in each society.

Despite the differences that cut across cultural lines, music is a part of each human society. And these differences in interpretation, presentation, and meaning are precisely what make the study of music so interesting and provide one of the most vital keys to understanding the varied nature of cultural expressions. Individual concepts of music are inherently tied to one's culture. Just as some cultures embrace octopus, snails, and cow intestines as food for everyday consumption, other (mostly non-Western) societies cannot conceive of the work of avant-garde composer Philip Glass, Moondog's ethereal vocalizing, Ron McCroby's improvised jazz whistling, or the blues guitar of Charlie Patton as music. Our task is less problematic, of course, since *Exploring American Folk Music: Ethnic, Grassroots, and Regional Traditions in the United States* focuses upon what surrounds us.

It's far from simple, because our country of 260 million people is becoming increasingly multicultural due in large measure to in-migration from Asia and Latin America. Within two decades the Hispanic population of the United States will become the largest "minority" population, supplanting African Americans. The Twin Cities (St. Paul and Minneapolis) are home to one of the largest Hmung populations in the United States, most of whom have migrated from Laos or Cambodia since the late 1960s. In Shoreview, Minnesota (a northern suburban community located just outside the Beltway and to the southeast of Coon Rapids), on June 5, 2000, the City Council voted that all of the newspaper ads regarding their biannual "Clean-Up Days" must be published in Hmung in addition to English.

Dictionary definitions of music are not particularly helpful because they tend to overlook the difficulties inherent in describing its complexities. Such definitions typically use phrases like "the ability to pleasantly combine vocal or instrumental sounds" or "tones which incorporate varying melody, harmony, timbre, and a structured form to create an emotionally complete composition." Although music is clearly an aural phenomenon, it simply cannot be defined in terms of sound alone. Most of these definitions fail to take into account the fact that music is a culturally based phenomenon that varies greatly over time and the geographical landscape. Consequently, the definition of music used in this text comes from a slightly different perspective:

> Music is any complex of vocal or instrumental sound that is organized in a manner agreed upon by members of a particular racial, ethnic, or regional group.

But how do we learn about music, music history, and emerging trends? The electronic media, the Internet, our parents' and friends' tastes, and magazines are among the forces that help shape musical conceptions and interests in the United States. So do our teachers and academic institutions. The majority of the scholars affiliated with the academy, however, still look toward the notated music of western Europe as their field of study. Although this emphasis is clearly shifting to become more inclusive, professors with training in **musicology** still teach the majority of "music history" courses at colleges and universities in the United States. They largely concern themselves with the German, French, and Italian music created by educated white males between 1500 and 1900. Historical musicologists "teach" composers ranging from Palestrina, Bach, Mozart, and Beethoven to Wagner, who wrote grand music that well deserves to be performed and studied today. Moreover, this imposing body of choral and chamber works, symphonies, and operas contains thousands of important artistic works invaluable in helping to establish and define Western culture. But what about the music, which encompasses the overwhelming majority of the music performed across the world, that falls outside of these parameters?

Ethnomusicologists, folklorists, anthropologists, and other interdisciplinary scholars are usually the ones who investigate the rest of music across the world and in more recent times: African juju, the tangos of Argentina, blues, Bulgarian women's choruses, India's ragas, calypso, contemporary Japanese popular songs, and American bluegrass. The list is most impressive and seemingly inexhaustible, especially as the investigation of our worlds of music thrives and expands. These allied fields are usually interested in music as culture; consequently, ethnomusicologists study music as one aspect of culture, and much of their work involves placing music in the context of human activity. Ethnomusicologists, in particular, generally receive training in anthropology, folklore, history, sociology, and linguistics in addition to music.

Given their strongly contrasting interests and preparation, it is not surprising that musicologists and ethnomusicologists usually (though not always) spend their careers examining very different bodies of music with dissimilar ends in mind. And these music scholars also usually understand and treat music differently. Nonetheless, as interest in vernacular and world music expands and the scholarly preparation for musicologists ever so gradually shifts to be more inclusive, the differences between historical musicologists and others who study music appears to be diminishing ever so slowly.

To illustrate some of these contrasting perceptions about the nature of music, let us briefly step outside of the United States border into the heart of Africa. Ethnomusicologist Alan Merriam points out that for the Basongye people who live near the Congo River music emanates only from human beings. Therefore birds cannot "sing" nor can electronic instruments produce music. The Basongye are uncertain about whistling. If whistling is used to signal during a hunt, then it is not music; however, the whistling that accompanies dancing is

Laura Bolton—Hudson Bay Research. Courtesy of the Ralph Rinzler Archive, Center for Folklife and Cultural Studies, Smithsonian Institution.

accepted as music. Closer to home, it is interesting to note that the traditional Navajo language has no word for music or musical instruments. The languages of many Native Americans generally lack a word to describe overall musical activity, though the Blackfoot's word for dance describes a religious activity that encompasses ceremony, dance, and music. The Blackfoot also have a word that can be translated as "song," but this excludes any instrumental music without words. It is clear that once we look outside of our own culture, defining music becomes more problematic.

DEFINING AMERICAN FOLK MUSIC

Defining folk music in our **postmodern** world is not an easy task. In the nineteenth century the United States was a less hectic and more rural and agrarian society. But in the early twenty-first century we can watch the latest news about the use of robots in Japanese automobile factories on television and explore Internet sites to learn about genocide in Africa or to find out the latest prices on the French stock market—all in "real" time. Prior to modernization the United

States did not support such a strong and extensive popular music industry nor very many academically trained composers. The ways in which music is performed, sold, and disseminated in the early twenty-first century has become extremely complex, blurring some of the tell-tale attributes of folk music—such as its rural characteristics and its oral transmission. Despite these complicating factors in this text, we focus upon music with strong regional ties or a racial/ethnic identity and direct links with its past.

To expand upon this rather simplistic definition, consider these six general characteristics of folk music:

1. *Folk music varies greatly over space but relatively little over time.* A cowboy song such as "When the Work's All Done This Fall," for example, has been sung in Wyoming since at least the late nineteenth century and in this context its lyrics about ranch/cattle work are timeless. However, its appeal to a third-generation Ukrainian American steelworker in a Gary, Indiana, mill is rather limited. She might well prefer the sounds of her favorite polka band, Li'l Wally (Jagiello). Innovations, however minor, tend to occur slowly because the forms of folk music are largely determined by a conservative musical culture. This is especially true in Euro-American groups, but less so in African American expressive folk culture.
2. *Folk music emanates from a specific, identifiable community, such as coal miners, Louisiana Cajuns, or Native Americans.* Such communities are found throughout the United States and they are associated by way of their occupation, tribal affiliation, ethnic identity, or even physical proximity. These folk communities also share some of the characteristics—such as speech patterns, **foodways**, or family names—that are part of our everyday lives. Folk music often retains well-established associations with functional activities within the **community**: in the workplace, during a religious ceremony, or at a community dance.
3. *The authorship or origins of folk songs and tunes are generally unknown.* We rarely know who writes folk music. The authorship of fiddle tunes such as "Soldier's Joy" or "Old Molly Hare" is unknown and almost certain to remain that way. A specific song, nonetheless, can sometimes be attributed to one region or folk community. For example, "Pony Blues," "Walking Blues," and "Rollin' and Tumblin'" clearly emanate from the Mississippi Delta blues tradition.
4. *Folk songs are usually disseminated by word-of-mouth, aurally, or through informal apprenticeships within a community.* Folk music is learned within a community by people who grow up in or become an integral part of that community. The process rarely entails formal lessons, as one would take for credit at a conservatory or a university. You learn the music that others in

your community play as part of worship, relaxation, or entertainment. Today folk music is also often transmitted by way of mass communication, particularly through radio and recordings.

5. *Folk music is most often performed by nonprofessionals.* Specialists within folk communities often perform music, but only a very small percentage of them actually make their full-time living from music. The majority of these are musicians who arrived on the scene during or after the "folk revival" of the 1960s. Less well known is the network of folk music performers, consisting of primarily unpaid or part-time musicians, who play for others within their community—such as the bluegrass band that regularly provides the music for the Saturday night dance at the Danville, Virginia, Moose Hall. Some exceptions include musicians such as Georgia blues man Blind Willie McTell or bluegrass mandolinist and progenitor Bill Monroe, who eventually made a full-time living from performing a popularized form of folk music.

6. *Short forms and predictable patterns are fundamental for folk music.* Most American folk music falls into repetitive paradigms that are generally familiar to members of the community. Blues, for instance, tends to follow the same, basic harmonic progression based on I, IV, and V chords; however, its form invites individual expression within these boundaries. The short and predictable hula meles from Hawaii may all sound similar to the uninitiated but can be distinguished by the vocal qualities demonstrated by the singers. While the folk music itself is often complex, its general performance "rules" vary little from one presentation to the next.

It might help to also consider folk music in light of popular and classical music. We know that folk songs are not composed, "art" ballads championed by academic institutions. Nor, unlike opera, is it very often heard in formal, often greatly subsidized, concerts. The work of most commercially popular tunesmiths enjoys fleeting, short-lived popularity, which fundamentally owes its dissemination to the mass media. There are exceptions to this generalization; writers of popular songs, such as George Gershwin, Irving Berlin, Randy Newman, and a handful of others has or is likely to endure for many decades to come. And the music of a few rock-oriented groups, like the Beatles and the Grateful Dead, appear headed toward long-term acceptance and study. Folk music tends to be overlooked by "serious" music scholars and often used by the tradesmen of popular culture, many of whom are constantly looking toward their roots for inspiration. Perhaps you can think of it as the forgotten music of America that reflects both our diverse heritage and our everyday lives. An appreciation for community and family traditions and a look at our heritage appear to be increasingly important in our dynamic society, which is becoming increasingly multicultural, fragmented, and complex.

START HERE!

Blues man Sleepy John Estes (1970). Courtesy of the Ralph Rinzler Folklife Archives and Collections, Center for Folklife and Cultural Heritage, Smithsonian Institution.

"Folk" and "traditional" are used interchangeably in this book. In the world of popular culture, however, "traditional" sometimes carries a somewhat different meaning—it is used to describe something that is merely old or simply anything created in the past. In 1991 the National Association of Recorded Arts and Sciences (the body that oversees the annual Grammy Awards) added the seemingly oxymoronic category: "Best Traditional Pop Vocal Performance." They were simply referring to popular songs written in a style that existed prior to the advent of rockabilly and rock 'n' roll in the middle 1950s. Perhaps the next Grammy category should be "Best Traditional Classical Instrumental Performance" to differentiate older classical musicians such as Christoph Gluck from a more modern figure such as Lou Harrison. Maybe they should also distinguish between the "traditional" country music of Uncle Dave Macon or Eva Davis and the "contemporary" sound of Mary Chapin Carpenter or Faith Hill.

The modes of transmission—word of mouth, the Internet, radio, CDs, and so on—underscore the ways in which alterations occur within these traditions and the subsequent creation of new movements. The twin processes of industrialization and urbanization have increased contact with other cultural groups, which causes even greater blending, hybridization, or **creolization**. These terms generally refer to a cross-pollination between two or more different cultures, resulting in a unique hybrid that contains elements from both. Cajun and zydeco music in southwestern Louisiana remain the clearest specific examples of creolized American folk music. Chapter 8 discusses other examples of the varied forces accelerating changes in folk music.

CULTURAL GEOGRAPHY AND TRADITIONS

Cultural geographers are the most familiar with the first two characteristics in our expanded definition of folk music. They study spatial variations in human culture: the differences in human culture from one place to another. Sports, politics, languages, place names, and architecture are among the aspects of culture that have been studied by geographers. Since about 1970 cultural geographers have focused a bit of their attention on music in the United States. Because the attributes of folk music include *regionalization* and *diffusion*, the study of American folk music clearly intersects with geography.

A **cultural region** is an area inhabited by people possessing one or more cultural traits in common. Cultural regions generally reflect shared traits such as ethnic identity and foodways as well as music. For instance, the Navajo cultural region in the Southwest is delineated by language, religion, foodways, architecture, as well as physical proximity. Because culture is fluid, such regions do not have fixed borders. **Vernacular culture regions** are particularly important because they are perceived by their inhabitants to exist. "Dixie," for example, is more than a beer brewed in New Orleans, an anthem associated with the former Confederacy, or a part of a name associated with popular music (i.e., Dixie Chicks or Dixie Dregs); it's also a more generalized term for some sections of the South that is both informed and restrained by its historical connotations.

Earlier in this chapter you read about go-go. This genre represents an extreme example of regional music—its strongest base of support remains in Washington, D.C., and its immediate suburbs. Furthermore, most of its adherents and practitioners are African American; few outside of D.C.'s black community know much about go-go. In these regards, go-go must be the most regional and racially focused music in the United States.

Musical styles like Southern California beach music or southern rock are often informally grouped by cultural regions. American folk music is quite often defined by region or community: Mississippi Delta blues, sea shanties, and the folk songs of northwestern lumberjacks. Regional variation is one of the main attributes of American folk culture and helps to explain the differences in the music, such as blues, produced by members of a specific community.

Every cultural region in the United States evolved through communication and human contact. **Cultural diffusion** describes the spread of ideas, innovation, and attitudes across time and space. Prior to our postmodern era most diffusion was accomplished through the relocation of human beings from one location to another and then communicated face-to-face. This communication spread also throughout the general population like a snowball rolling down a hill or the rippling waves of a rock thrown into a pond.

Today's ideas and innovations are equally likely to result through electronic discourse or the printed media. Although they once had stronger local or regional ties, radio, television, and the Internet now provide instantaneous contact with the entire world. Newspapers and magazines exchange information on a daily or weekly basis. It would be impossible to find an American folk musician in the early 2000s untouched by these forces. Folk music is still widely disseminated through informal means, but records and the radio have both added a new dimension to this process.

FOLK CULTURE IN THE UNITED STATES

It is important to make the distinctions between the levels of culture that touch and shape our daily lives. As a college student you are presently part of the elite, academic world that involves, among other things, attending lectures, doing library research, writing critical essays, performing scientific experiments, doing Internet searches, and reading novels. At the same time you also participate in popular culture by enjoying comic strips such as "Dilbert" eating the occasional hamburger at a McDonald's restaurant, or listening to a top-selling popular music artist by way of the Internet.

Our participation in folk culture seems almost subconscious or second nature. These are the customs and traditions that we learn or assimilate from our family, members of the community, and our ethnic or racial group. Folk culture can be expressed in many ways—how we celebrate our religious holidays, greet one another, or pronounce certain words. It is the "traditional, unofficial, noninstitutional part of culture. It encompasses all knowledge, understandings, values, attitudes, assumptions, feelings, and beliefs transmitted . . . by word of mouth or by customary examples" (Brunvand 1998). Folk culture is circulated when people communicate. Allowing for the inevitable exceptions, this communication is almost always oral, such as the telling of a ghost story, an urban legend about a poodle in the microwave, or a jump-rope rhyme passed along by girls on playgrounds across the country. But it can also be transmitted by example, especially in everyday living. For instance, I learned to make meatballs by watching my second-generation Swedish American mother prepare scores of them for our annual Christmas smorgasbord.

Folklore (the "items" of folk culture) are usually grouped into three categories:

Oral folklore. At its most basic level, an individual word or phrase may qualify as "folk speech." One example is the oft-used pronunciation of the word "chimble" for "chimney" in southwestern Virginia. Because of their speech patterns and pronunciations most residents of "down east" Maine can be easily identified as soon as they open their mouth. At another greater level of complexity are proverbs or proverbial sayings, such as "Red sky at night, sailor's delight." Finally, there are more complicated forms of oral folklore such as narratives—tall tales or cowboy recitations—and ballads.

Customary folklore. These often combine oral communication and example for their transmission. For instance, superstitions can be transmitted orally. As a youngster perhaps your father warned you that black cats mean bad luck. Or it can be promulgated by example—catching the bride's flowers because it means you will be the next to marry. Children's jump-rope games almost demand that one both move and speak properly to participate. Folk dance and drama provide two other examples of customary folklore.

Material folklore. These are the tangible objects created by a craftsperson or by members of a community. For example, the seasonal icehouses found on lakes in the frigid north during the midwinter fishing season. Navajo blankets woven by Native Americans in Colorado or Arizona fall into this category, as do the traditional foods prepared by Greek Americans for Easter.

Significantly, we continue to distinguish the geographical origins of our fellow Americans based on speech patterns and expressions; for example, how we greet one another. "Howdy," a diminutive for "how do you do," is commonly heard in the South but rarely in Idaho. If you ordered a "frappe" (milk shake) or a "grinder" (a submarine sandwich) in a restaurant outside of New England, you would no doubt be asked to explain your request. By the same token, the use of the Scandinavian expletive "Uff-daa!" (a very ethnic/family-specific term) is generally greeted with blank looks in Miami.

Food is perhaps the most common way by which people distinguish their geographic and cultural backgrounds. Hogjowls and greens can be found in northern urban supermarkets largely patronized by black Americans, many with strong southern ties. In New Mexico "eggs rancheros" (essentially an omelet with salsa) is found on many menus, while cheese grits are rarely found on the tables of the hearty residents of Michigan's Upper Peninsula. Restaurants in Rhode Island sometimes offer quail dishes in deference to their Portuguese and Portuguese American patrons. Wherever Swedes, Norwegians, or Danes have settled you are likely to find lutefisk, a very distinctive smelling dried white fish that is reconstituted in alternating baths of lye and water.

START HERE!

Gomez wood carving. Courtesy of the Ralph Rinzler Folklife Archives and Collections, Center for Folklife and Cultural Heritage, Smithsonian Institution.

While the United States is not yet a bland melting pot composed entirely of K-marts, the Fox television network, and General Motors, homogenization increases each year. The "modern" era began early in the twentieth century, transforming America from our fundamentally rural agrarian society into a new age characterized by urbanity and industrialization. Today we live in a postmodern United States linked by instantaneous communication and interstate highways, and informed by almost universal public education. These factors help to make us more like one another in our speech, foodways, music, and other basic aspects of culture. **VH-1** similarly inform viewers from Portland, Maine, to Portland, Oregon, with the same news, videos, and commercials, all of which are related to contemporary popular music.

Regional and ethnic variations remain important keys to understanding twenty-first-century American folk music because they clearly display great variety across the country. The music of a Norwegian American Wisconsin polka band is, for example, easily distinguished from a north Georgia country string band. Think also of the differences between the music of two neighboring churches in Washington, D.C.: Performances of "Amazing Grace" by an African American Primitive Baptist congregation and an Anglo-American Methodist choir present a study in strongly contrasting musical cultures. America's melting pot still steams with a warm and rich brew of Cajun music from Louisiana and southeastern Texas, German and Scandinavian polka music in the upper Midwest, and sacred harp singing in Georgia and Alabama. The regional differences found in American music remain strong. They have been reinforced by a recent resurgence of interest in ethnic traditions and racial roots, which is illustrated in everything from T-shirts ("Coonass and Proud," worn boldly by Louisiana Cajuns) to children's names such as Sven, Bobby Jo, Zelodious, or Anna Maria.

This book focuses upon the traditional music that developed in the United States between the late nineteenth century and today. American folk music co-exists alongside popular and elite music, and frequently interacts with these other levels of musical culture. For the most part, these interactions consist of informing or reminding popular culture of its roots. Folk music is rarely heard over the radio or seen on television today; nonetheless thousands of folk music recordings are available, and folk festivals of every size and description abound in the United States. In the increasingly rare full-service music stores across the country as well as online businesses, the consumer is offered CDs and cassettes in categories such as "polka," "Cajun," "bluegrass," "zydeco," "blues," and other grassroot forms of American music. Furthermore, there are hundreds of Web sites devoted to all of the forms of grassroot American music, and these can be found through the use of any of the Web's many search engines.

The periodic revival of interest in our heritage and ethnicity often expresses itself musically. This occurred most dramatically during the "folk revival" of the early 1960s when many people discovered blues and hillbilly music. Popular musicians such as Neil Young, Bob Dylan, Roger McGuinn, John Lennon, and Janis Joplin drew from the wellspring of folk music to help create the music of the "British Invasion," San Francisco's "psychedelic rock," and folk rock. In a more contemporary vein hip-hop's use of poetic, simple, often obscene, rhymes stems directly from the African American tradition of toasts and the dozens (an insult game often played by males). The chanted/sung lyrics also have strong roots in the sermons performed in many black Baptist churches. The use of syncopation in the bass lines and drum patterns follows a tradition that relates back to early jazz, ragtime, and ultimately to West African drumming. The "swing revival" of the late 1990s and early 2000s, fronted by groups such as Big Voodoo Daddy, the Brian Sezter Orchestra, and Swing Six, looks back to the cool days of the middle twentieth century when the two Louis (Jordan and Prima) reigned. Their music, of course, drew upon the blues, marching brass bands, and other earlier forms of folk and **folk-based music**. And so the cycles continue with the "new" music being informed by its predecessors, many of which are folk or folk-based.

START HERE!

BRED IN THE BONE

In our pastoral vision, folk music emanates from homogeneous, static, rural communities, but the twenty-first-century reality is of increased mobility and **electronic communication**. Nonetheless these ties to a community are essential in any discussion of contemporary American folk music. Robertson Davies wrote a wonderful book, *Bred in the Bone*, which takes its title from an expression meaning that certain traits become culturally ingrained. We follow them almost unconsciously because they are part of our daily lives. Such "breeding" reflects **regionalism**, of course, but it implies something more subtle and possibly profound. These are the traditions and patterns inculcated by way of our immediate surrounding and our families. Highly respected twentieth-century American folk musicians, such as Lydia Mendoza (Tex-Mex), Muddy Waters (blues), Nathan Abshire (Cajun), Bill Monroe (bluegrass), or Roberta Martin (gospel), remained intrinsically tied to the music they inherited. Some people deliberately and very willfully shed their heritage, renouncing family and community to begin anew. Such a transformation reflects conscious choice, sometimes born of necessity or even pure survival. However, we cannot fully escape our pronounced familial influences.

Folk musicians usually come from families or small communities immersed in the music. **Wade Ward**, for example, who grew up in Galax, Virginia, in the late nineteenth century came to embody many of its values and traits in his life and music. Older members of his immediate family played the fiddle and banjo, which Ward also embraced. In short, Wade Ward became a product not only of the Upland South, but more specifically of the Grayson County/Blue Ridge community and his extended families. His music and lifestyle were bred in the bone.

Can you still be a folk musician in the early twenty-first century? It might be increasingly difficult as we become more entangled in technology and as Wal-Marts become even more ubiquitous, but I believe the answer is yes. Look at accordion-playing Santiago Jimenez, Jr., as one example. Born in San Antonio, Texas, in 1944, his father was a highly respected conjunto (Tex-Mex) musician and his older brother, "Flaco," is an internationally recognized master of the accordion. Jimenez performs his jaunting conjunto sounds throughout Texas and has recorded scores of records for small regional labels as well as compact discs for Arhoolie Records and Rounder Records. Although his older rancheros, polkas, and waltzes may sound archaic to ears that are used to Selena or even Ricky Martin, Jimenez has already helped to inspire a generation of musicians born in the 1960s and 1970s. These new kings and queens of conjunto will be carrying on this tradition (albeit always morphing into something slightly different, of course) well into the twenty-first century.

Wade Ward with the Bogtrotters. Courtesy of the Library of Congress.

A distinction needs to be made between a folk musician such as Ward and those from outside of his community who learn to play folk music. Wade himself served as the mentor to dozens of musicians, including many younger people who grew up far from Grayson County, Virginia. The majority of these musicians learned from Ward during the 1960s at folk festival workshops, through visiting his home, or by listening to his numerous recordings. Some of these musicians spent months living near Ward and learned to play highly accomplished renderings of his versions of well-traveled fiddle and banjo tunes such as "Fox Chase" or "Sally Anne."

I view these musicians as interpreters of Ward's music. Similarly, a third-generation Finnish American from Minnesota who visits the Mississippi Delta to learn the work songs of black Americans or a New England–bred Dartmouth-trained WASP who travels to El Paso, Texas, to become a conjunto musician is consciously stepping out of his or her own well-worn shoes to try on something new. These field hollers or polkas might be performed quite well by accomplished musicians; nonetheless, these remain interpretations. There is nothing wrong with this. Nor is there anything improper with a black woman such as Jessye Norman singing Italian opera or German lieder. These choices reflect options that we are (fortunately) able to make.

START HERE!

MUSICAL EXAMPLE

Wade Ward (banjo) and Glen Smith (fiddle) played together for many years around Galax, Virginia. This well-known piece is often performed for square dancing and displays Ward's virtuoso clawhammer banjo technique. "Clawhammer" refers to a style of brushing the banjo strings with the back of one's fingers on the downstroke, which predates the better-known bluegrass style. This performance was recorded on location in the middle 1960s.

Title "Sally Goodin'"
Performers Glen Smith, fiddle; Wade Ward, banjo
Instruments fiddle and banjo
Length 1:11

Musical Characteristics
1. The lead melody is played on both the fiddle and banjo.
2. It is cast in a simple *ab* song form that repeats throughout.
3. They perform this piece at a rapid tempo.
4. Neither instrument takes a solo break.
5. "Sally Goodin'" is in a major tonality.

This performance was originally issued on Smithsonian Folkways 3802.

But if we take a culturally based view of music and music making, then hearing a non-Mexican playing conjunto back home in Milford, New Hampshire, is simply not the same experience as listening to Santiago Jimenez, Jr., performing at a San Antonio cantina. It's similar to the intangible but distinctive difference between pouring my father-in-law's homemade muskadine syrup over pancakes in his Bossier City, Louisiana, home and watching my own Swedish American mother struggle to replicate the same event in her Cape Cod home. The pancake and syrup may taste similar but the experience (the location, the smells—its essence) is very different.

The aural differences between Ward's music and that of his students may be slight; however, the master's music reflects subtle, sometimes intangible, cultural and family attributes missing from his students' interpretations. Qualities tangential to the music itself (expressions that easily roll off of one's tongue, racial attitudes, stories about local musicians, shared references that you don't need to explain, even diet) encompass a lifestyle and breeding that one cannot learn merely by listening to Ward's recordings or even by living in Grayson County,

The Harps of Melody (1980). Courtesy of Clara Anderson.

Virginia, for several years. Had Wade Ward lived into the 2000s, he would have been surprised by some of the changes in his home county. Not only have the local roads been improved but also many of the local furniture factories have been closed or retooled. However, the biggest change is the notable influx of Hispanic Americans who have arrived since the early 1990s to work on local farms and in factories. The result is daily Spanish-language broadcasting on the local radio station and bilingual signs now found in many stores in Galax.

You can think of Wade Ward's music students as expatriates or visitors. No matter how fluently they learn to speak the (musical) language and how well they fit into the culture, they remain "outsiders." Musicians occupying this category may play folk music well, but they cannot be considered folk musicians. In short, they play folk music but are not themselves folk musicians. Such interpreters of folk music are often called **revivalists**, and their role will be discussed later in this book.

Let me relate another personal example to illustrate this concept. I spent four years researching and interviewing black American gospel quartet singers in Memphis for my doctoral dissertation and would occasionally sit in and sing with the groups. I can tell you the history of the genre, talk about its important figures, and relate anecdotes about gospel quartet contests, but I can never tell you what it was like to be an African American quartet singer during the genre's golden age of the 1940s. In many regards I became a very well informed observer who now understands this musical community in ways that certainly eluded the singers themselves. But because I didn't live and perform in the same ways that Clara Anderson, James Darling, and Elijah Jones did for decades, I can only interpret what I learned. For many musicians learning folk music this participant-observer role is critical, but such musicians should never be mistaken for the genuine item.

It is clear that the importance of American folk music extends well beyond its immediate communities. Folk music has influenced the work of American composers such as Aaron Copland—his well-known "Appalachian Spring" provides a prime example—and Charles Ives as well as rock musicians on the order of the Rolling Stones, the Cowboy Junkies, the Allman Brothers Band, and Wilco. Such musicians are not "folk," but they sound closer to their folk roots because of their appreciation of Lead Belly, Robert Johnson, Uncle Dave Macon, Howlin' Wolf, Riley Puckett, and Patsy Montana. These earlier musicians grew up in a society closer to the ones found in idealized rural folk communities, albeit during four decades (1900–1940) of startling transitions.

In addition to describing the genres of traditional music, this book discusses the impact of the folk revivals and some of their strongest and most influential personalities, such as Bob Dylan, Judy Collins, and Pete Seeger. I endorse Dick Weissman's term "folk-based" to describe these professional and semiprofessional musicians with a strong interest in various types of traditional music (see Sandberg and Weissman 1989). Folk-based performers form an important part of the story because of their strong impact on our national consciousness, their commercialization of the more traditional styles, and their clear, unwavering respect for their own musical heritages.

LISTENING TO AMERICAN FOLK MUSIC

A formal background in music theory, ear-training, and harmony is not necessary to use this textbook, nor will you have to be able to read notated musical transcriptions. However, you will be required to listen carefully to the musical examples that illustrate this book and that are discussed in detail. These basic listening skills are not difficult to obtain, though this is an active process that is critical in appreciating any kind of music. They can be applied to nearly any form of music from punk rock, Bill Monroe, and blues to hip-hop.

Here are some of the key terms that are useful in listening to and describing music:

> **Pitch** is a single tone or note, which is produced by vibrating air. The faster the air vibrates, the higher the pitch; a slower rate of vibration causes a lower pitch. Pitches fall into three basic *registers*: low, middle, and high.

START HERE!

A **tone** describes a sound with a definite pitch.

The notes on a piano are organized into systems that are usually referred to as **scales**. Some are a simple series of five notes, which constitute a *pentatonic* scale. The organization of most notes fall into the category of *major* and *minor* scales.

The first and last names of the eight pitches in a scale have the same name, which is known as its **tonic**.

An **interval** measures the distance in pitch between two tones.

Two simultaneous tones create an interval, but three or more simultaneous pitches are perceived as a **chord**. In this book we will most often refer to the *tonic* chord (built upon the first tone of a scale), the *subdominant* chord (built on the fourth tone), and the *dominant* chord (built upon the fifth scale tone).

The system of combining chords is known as **harmony** and it forms the basis for our folk and popular music.

A series of individual tones makes up a **melody**. If a melody is derived from a series of close intervals, usually a second or whole step in a major scale, it is referred to as *conjunctive*. American folk songs tend to be conjunctive. Tunes that contain larger intervals, more than a third, are *disjunctive*.

Rhythm refers to the long and short patterns of duration, which can be simple or complex, regular or irregular. The rhythm generates an energy, an impulse that drives the music forward in interesting ways.

Meter is what organizes the rhythm of music, just as it orders the reading of poetry. American folk music is almost always organized in measured beat patterns of *duple* (two) meter or *triple* (three) meter.

One way to create rhythmic interest is to accent beats unexpectedly. This is called **syncopation**, and it is a fundamental rhythmic element of African American music from ragtime master Scott Joplin to the "funk" music of Bootsy Collins, Parliament Psychedelic, and George Clinton.

Dynamics refer to the degree of loudness or softness of music.

The unique tonal quality that can be attributed to all voices and instruments is its **timbre**. Today's electronic synthesizers are able to reproduce the sound of a harmonica, a clarinet, even a piano with uncanny accuracy.

Texture is another important musical concept that refers to the density of sound. It is directly related to the number of musical lines sounding at a particular time during a musical performance. Music can be texturally rich and full at one extreme or spare and thin at the other. A *monophonic* texture means a single, unaccompanied melodic line. A melody that is in the foreground and supported by harmonic underpinning results in a *homophonic* texture, which is most common in American folk music.

All of our folk genres are cast into **forms**—the basic structure or shape of a piece of music. *Binary* (two-part or *ab*) and *ternary* (three-part or *aba*) are the most common forms you will encounter in American folk music. Ballads are often performed in *strophic* form—the same music is used for each stanza.

Let's close with two other useful concepts: **genre** and **style**. A genre refers to a specific category of music, such as blues, bluegrass, and ragtime. Style refers to a subset within the genre. In blues, for example, Piedmont, Delta, and Chicago exemplify some of the regional styles that constitute the blues tradition.

INSTRUMENTS

Many different instruments are utilized by musicians throughout the United States. The use of these instruments is rarely limited to one genre of music; violins/fiddles are heard in symphony orchestras, Ukrainian American bands, bluegrass quintets, and rock bands. On the other hand, accordions are rarely heard in contemporary popular music or in chamber music groups.

Folk musicians use well-known instruments, including pianos, string bass, and drums. They also perform on such less orthodox instruments as the kazoo, one-string bass, and jugs. The use of particular instruments, however, frequently depends partially on regional or ethnic background as well as personal preference and family traditions. Some of them have surprisingly long histories that sometimes cross continents and many decades. Most of these instruments are acoustic models, although electrification and amplification have become increasingly common since World War II.

Accordion

The accordion enjoyed a late-twentieth-century renaissance among folk musicians from the bayous of Louisiana directly northward to the Nebraska plains. "Squeeze boxes" were originally promoted by the waves of European immigrants, usually German, Irish, French, and Italian, who commonly used this instrument. Because of its durability, volume, and portability the accordion makes an ideal instrument for dance music.

Accordions, a European invention, come in several distinctive variations. Some are free reed instruments that use a keyboard similar to those found on a piano and have a range of up to five octaves. The smaller accordion is one-half to one-third the size of the piano style and its reeds are activated by depressing a corresponding small button. Both piano and button accordions require that the performer squeeze the instrument, forcing air in and out of the bellows.

The more versatile piano accordion is favored by many of the African American zydeco musicians like Clifton Chenier and Buckwheat Zydeco from the Texas/Louisiana border country. Polka musicians like Frankie Yankovic or Li'l Wally Jagiello (who are both of central European background) favor a button-style accordion, specifically the German concertina. Marc Savoy, Ally Young, and other French Louisianans also prefer the smaller accordions.

These modern accordions were developed in Germany and Austria in the 1820s and 1830s. They were particularly popular in France in the middle nineteenth century, which perhaps accounts for their widespread use among French-speaking Americans. Monarch and Hohner models have long been favored by Cajun musicians, though a younger generation (most notably Marc Savoy of Eunice, Louisiana) now makes a "Cajun accordion." This model improves the timbre of the upper range, and its bellows are easier to use.

Banjo

What began as an African instrument migrated to the United States by way of West Africans brought as slaves. Despite its origins, the banjo is closely identified with country music. As early as the late seventeenth century banjolike instruments made from gourds and called names like banzas, bandores, or banjas were being played by New World slaves. Contemporary accounts of life in the Middle Atlantic states from around the time of the American Revolutionary War suggest that the banjo was the most common instrument used by slaves and freed blacks. The number of strings on early banjos varied anywhere from three to eight, although by the 1820s these homemade instruments usually had four strings.

The size and shape of banjos began to be regularized by the middle of the nineteenth century. Joel Walker Sweeney and other minstrel show entertainers brought banjos to the attention of urban white Americans at about the same time that they began to be made commercially. Within thirty years white musicians in the rural South and, to a lesser degree the Northeast, had embraced the banjo as their own instrument. During Reconstruction the banjo gradually became more closely associated with Anglo-American music and began losing its African American identity. By the 1950s most blacks had lost interest in the instrument.

Pre–Civil War banjo playing was often done with a down stroke of the thumb and back nail of the index or middle finger. This style is often called "clawhammer" or "frailing." A new style of finger picking developed and gained rapid acceptance during the late nineteenth century and it closely resembles the guitar picking upon which it was modeled. By 1900 many folk musicians were using this two-finger style, although in the 1940s the three-finger "bluegrass roll" began to gain wide favor.

Around the turn of the twentieth century, banjos flirted with popular acceptance. Transcriptions of light classical and popular music were marketed to the innumerable banjo, mandolin, and guitar orchestras that sprang up on college campuses and in cities across the United States. During the 1920s commercially produced four-string tenor banjos were coming into vogue. They were preferred by the musicians who performed with popular dance and jazz bands.

Slovenian polka bands and Norwegian old-time string bands also utilized them in their ensembles around the same time. However, the five-string banjo made its comeback following World War II because of bluegrass, the folk revival, and its continued use in commercial country music.

Dulcimer

The best-known dulcimer is the Appalachian mountain or lap dulcimer, which developed from the German zither, known as a scheitholt, that came with immigrants to Pennsylvania. Developed in the southern Appalachian mountains, the American version is narrow and usually between two and three feet long. Dulcimers date from the early nineteenth century, though the "modern" shape did not emerge for another one hundred years. Today's dulcimers feature an extended fretboard and four strings. The melody is played on the first string, with the other strings serving as drones. Dulcimers are usually placed across the performer's knee and plucked with some type of pick. Dulcimers are used to accompany both dances and singing.

A hammer dulcimer is an entirely different instrument. It is also a member of the zither family, but it is always played with small mallets that are handheld in order to strike the sixty or so strings. Hammer dulcimers are shaped like a trapezoid that is between 2.5 and 4 feet in length, 1 to 2 feet in height, and 3 to 6 inches in depth. These instruments were introduced by English settlers sometime prior to 1700. Nineteenth-century dulcimers were made both commercially and by folk artisans. The tradition has remained largely in New England and upstate New York, although it diffused to Piedmont, North Carolina, and the Great Lakes region during the early twentieth century.

Some quaint and perhaps unique 1920s string band recordings by the Perry County Music Makers (Tennessee) feature the hammer dulcimer. In some of the Moravian Czech and Volga German settlements in Texas, Colorado, and Nebraska, a few musicians still play the cymbalum and hackbrett, which are hammer dulcimers by another name. By and large, however, most twenty-first-century hammer dulcimer players began playing as the result of a revival of interest that began in the late 1960s.

Fiddle

Violins and other closely related instruments, such as a viola, were first used by European musicians during the sixteenth century. The size and precise shape of fiddles, as they are called by American folk musicians, became standardized by the seventeenth century. With only a few minor alterations, violins look almost exactly like they did three hundred years ago. The highly skilled craftsmanship of early Italian makers like Stradivari and Guarneri has resulted in instruments the rich sound of which is hard to match today.

START HERE!

Unique fiddle. Courtesy of the Southern Historical Collection, The University of North Carolina at Chapel Hill.

These instruments have been among the mainstays of European art music, and fiddles were among the first instruments to arrive in the New World. They were not only popular but highly portable and versatile, too, for they could be used for performing music in all idioms. Within a few decades Americans were making their own violins. Some people crafted their instruments with great skill and reference for European craftsmanship. Others, particularly African Americans, were forced to use whatever materials and means they could muster.

Since the late eighteenth century, fiddles have been among the most prominent folk instruments in the United States. Some Anglo-American fiddlers have repertoires that include scores of tunes, some of them brought over from the British Isles. Genres such as early hillbilly and bluegrass feature fiddles as one of their principal lead instruments. Most of these fiddlers hold the instrument against their chin, though a minority of players nestle the instrument against their chest.

Fife

A fife is a wind instrument similar to a flute. Long associated with military marching bands, these fife and drum band corps first formed in late seventeenth-century England and eventually in other European countries. Fife and drum bands were heard in the United States during the Revolutionary and Civil wars and remain part of New England's musical landscape.

This same ensemble, consisting of multiple drummers and fifers, became part of African American folk culture in the Deep South during Reconstruction. Black Americans eventually began to use the local cane to make their own twelve- to fifteen-inch fifes, most of which have six fingering holes in them. In the early twenty-first century African American fifers, accompanied by two or three drummers, continue performing in the Mississippi hill country, though at least one band from western Georgia was located and recorded around 1970.

Guitar

Although now commonly associated with folk and rock music, the six-string guitar was developed in southern Europe in the late eighteenth century. It was regularly imported to the East Coast by 1800, though the first American-made instruments did not appear until the 1830s. These early models were plucked by the fingers, smaller than contemporary acoustic guitars, and strung with gut or silk strings. The C. F. Martin Company became the first American company to manufacture guitars, but it was not until Reconstruction that they were joined by Ephiphone (1873), Harmony (1892), and Gibson (1894).

During the 1890s steel-string guitars, which were commonly found in Central America, began to be mass produced in the United States. Both Montgomery Ward and Sears, Roebuck & Company sold mail-order guitars for under $10. Within thirty years the production of guitars had risen to approximately 150,000 annually. This same period witnessed two important innovations. Gibson's "arch-top" instruments, with their f-shaped sound hole and arched body, came into vogue during the 1920s. They gave some competition to the slightly softer Martin flattop models, which remained popular. Slightly earlier both Hawaiian guitars and dobro resonator guitars, which are primarily made from steel and are usually played with a slide or bottleneck rather than finger-picked, became popular. They found a ready audience because of the volume they generated with little effort.

Gibson experimented with electronic pickups for guitars in the middle 1920s, but the first amplified guitars were not introduced for another ten years. These hollow-body models did not gain prominence until after World War II, however. Solid-body electric guitars, developed primarily by Leo Fender and Les Paul, became affixed on the scene by the middle 1950s.

Rather than eschew technology, today's folk musicians play both electric and acoustic instruments. Those who play electric guitars generally use hollow-body instruments, although many African American blues performers use the solid-body models. Since the 1950s flattop acoustic models have been the instrument of choice among American folk musicians.

START HERE!

Harmonica

This is a free reed instrument of German descent and is related to the accordion. It was perfected by Christian Friedreich Ludwig Buschman about 1828, whose first prototype was successful because it was easy to play and to control its dynamics. The instrument slowly caught on in central Europe, where its manufacture constituted a cottage industry for several decades. By the 1860s harmonicas caught the eye and imagination of Mathias Hohner. He spent several years hand making harmonicas before he discovered a method to mass produce them. His annual output skyrocketed to almost a million harmonicas by 1885, and nearly two-thirds of these were exported to the United States. Today Hohner remains the predominant name in the manufacturing of harmonicas.

There are two types of harmonica: diatonic and chromatic. With the exception of a few "Chicago-style" blues musicians, folk harmonica players almost always use diatonic harps. This ten-hole instrument is tuned to a tonic chord, which is attained by alternating exhaling and inhaling. Chromatic harmonicas are larger and consist of twelve holes with a slide on one end. You depress the slide to attain the accidentals needed to complete a major scale. These instruments have a three-octave range.

Diatonic harmonicas are played by all types of American folk musicians. They are quite important in the blues idiom, where they are one of its essential instruments. Early-twentieth-century country musicians also used them to accompany singing or as a lead instrument in a small string band.

Mandolin

This stringed instrument came to the United States by way of Italian immigrants beginning in the late eighteenth century. It is small bodied and features a double set of four strings, which causes it to ring out loudly. Mandolins are almost always played with a flat pick, permitting a tremolo effect.

For over one hundred years it was used almost exclusively within the Italian community. The mandolin's popularity increased during the 1880s because of touring European string ensembles that featured it. By the turn of the century it was not unusual to find mandolin orchestras or societies in small towns and colleges across America. Such groups played contemporary rags, marches, jigs, and so on that they learned from other musicians or from one of the many specialty periodicals that sprang up to serve these musicians. During this same period, hybrid instruments such as mandolas and mandocellos were developed but never gained widespread acceptance.

By World War I the craze had slowed down, supplanted by a mania for Hawaiian music and jazz. More folk musicians picked up the mandolin and it could be heard on some of the string band recordings of the 1920s. During the

Homemade instruments. Courtesy of the Library of Congress.

1930s fraternal groups such as the Mainers (J. E. and Wade) and Bill and Earl Bolick (the Blue Sky Boys) were using it in tandem with the guitar. By the middle 1940s, Bill Monroe had made it the centerpiece of his first bluegrass band. Today mandolins are still primarily associated with bluegrass music, though country music and some rock groups have used them since the early 1960s.

Mouth Bow

This is a single-string instrument that is shaped like a bow for shooting an arrow. Commonly found in Africa and South Africa, mouth bows are relatively rare in the United States. They resemble and sound like large Jew's harps and are played in similar fashion. A mouth bow's range and timbre is somewhat limited. It is played by resting the bow itself on one's slightly parted lips and then plucking the strings with the fingers. The pitch that it produces is enhanced by the player who changes the size and shape of his or her mouth to achieve overtones. These harmonic overtones create a tune. Mouth bow playing is found in both black and white traditions.

START HERE!

MUSICAL EXAMPLE

Joe Patterson lived in Ashford, Alabama, and Ralph Rinzler came upon him while researching southern folk traditions for the Newport Foundation in 1964. This selection was recorded in May 1964 at Patterson's home. It is a unique performance that combines playing with vocalizing. This is one of the very few examples of African American quill playing that has ever been made.

Title Untitled
Performer Joe Patterson
Instruments percussion, quills, voice
Length 1:30

Musical Characteristics
1. Patterson maintains a steady underlying duple meter with his homemade percussion instrument.
2. The quills have a limited range of about five notes.
3. A feeling of syncopation is established by the tension between the steady percussion and the quills' mixed rhythmic patterns.
4. This performance roughly follows an *ab* song form.

This selection comes from the Smithsonian Folkways Archive.

One-String

This instrument—also known as a diddley-bow or monochord zither—is most often associated in American folk music with blacks born in the Deep South. Well into the twentieth century, musicians from the Mississippi Delta often fashioned diddley-bows as their first instrument. They take a single strand of wire or a guitar string and nail it to the wall of a house, which serves as a resonator. They raise either end away from the wall with a block of wood and use a slide or bottle neck to fret the diddley-bow. The picking is done with a finger, a guitar pick, a metal nail, or some other similar object. Diddley-bows, which are almost always played by children, foreshadow the bottleneck guitar style. Mississippi blues men Muddy Waters and Big Joe Williams both first learned music on a diddley-bow.

Quills

These are a simple wind instrument, also known as panpipes, which are found across the entire world. Most quills consist of between four and eight tubes of

START HERE!

Joe Patterson, Alabama quill player (1964). Bob Yellin photo, courtesy of the Ralph Rinzler Folklife Archives and Collections, Center for Folklife and Cultural Heritage, Smithsonian Institution.

increasing lengths bundled together; the longer the tube, the lower the pitch. Quills are most often made by the person playing them and are usually made of cane. A tone is produced by blowing across the top of each pipe. Blowing across the top of a partially filled bottle of soda pop produces a similar effect.

Panpipes were played by the ancient Greeks, who called them syrinx. They were also found in fifth-century China. Today panpipes are a folk instrument that is often heard from Burma eastward to western Latin America, especially in the mountainous sections of Peru and Ecuador. Panpipes are also found in many sections of Africa, and the technique of alternating between blowing and whooping is distinctly African. In the United States they were rarely found in twentieth-century American folk music, usually in the Deep South among African Americans.

Washboard

Many decades ago—before the invention of the washing machine—many people in the United States scrubbed their clothes clean on a washboard before hanging them up to dry. A washboard is simply a rectangular corrugated piece of metal framed by wood on all four sides. Folk musicians use spoons, nails, thimbles, or even metal guitar picks to provide rhythmic accompaniment for other musicians. Some washboard players also attach cowbells, shakers, tambourines, or woodblocks to their instruments to add tonal variation to their repertoire. Black American musicians playing blues and zydeco in small ensembles are among the leading proponents of washboards.

FINAL THOUGHTS

Even though America's distinctive regional and ethnic characteristics remain strong, the differences are slowly (and perhaps inevitably) dissipating. The rapid changes in how American music is disseminated illustrate this process. Before the era of instant electronic communication (television, radio, telephones, and computers), improved long-distance transportation, and literacy for the masses, people spoke face-to-face. Most folk music was also transmitted directly from neighbor to neighbor or from a mother to her daughter or nephew. Because this music was passed along orally/aurally, most types of American folk music remained within small groups, relatively narrow geographic regions, or small communities. Today's students of American folk music stand on a fulcrum glancing back toward our antecedents while on the other side are more contemporary developments brought on by increased acculturation.

KEY FIGURES AND TERMS

chord
community
creolization
cultural diffusion
cultural region
dynamics
electronic communication
ethnic
ethnomusicologists
folk-based music
foodways
forms
genre
harmony
interval
mass media
melody
meter

MTV
multicultural
musicology
pitch
postmodern
regionalism
revivalists
rhythm
scales
style
syncopation
texture
timbre
tone
tonic
vernacular culture regions
VH-1
Wade Ward

START HERE!

SUGGESTED LISTENING

Various. *Anthology of American Folk Music,* edited by Harry Smith. Smithsonian Folkways 40090. This Grammy-Award-winning, multi-CD set, originally issued in 1952, covers almost every important style of American folk music found in the South and is taken from commercial recordings originally issued during the 1920s through the early 1930s. This 1997 reissue includes an interactive CD devoted to the eclectic Harry Smith.

Various. *Arhoolie Records 40th Anniversary Collection: The Journey of Chris Strachwitz 1960–2000.* Arhoolie CD 491. This five-compact disc set and lavish booklet celebrates the label and the work of its founder, Chris Strachwitz, with a well-rounded anthology of his field recordings of blues, conjunto, string bands, etc., presented in chronological order.

Various. *Classic Folk From Smithsonian Folkways.* SFW40110. This single compact disc provides a nice overview of the Smithsonian Folkways' huge catalogue.

Various. *Folk Masters: Great Performances Recorded Live at the Barns of Wolf Trap.* Smithsonian Folkways 40047. A compilation from the public radio series of the same name; these performances came from the 1992 season and include such stalwarts as Dewey Balfa, the Texas Playboys, Cephas & Wiggins, and Boozoo Chavis.

Various. *Mississippi: River of Song.* Smithsonian Folkways 40086. A musical tour of the Mississippi River and its contemporary musical traditions, such as blues, gospel, and Native American, are showcased on this two-CD set.

Various. *My Rough and Rowdy Ways,* Volumes 1 & 2. Yazoo 2039–40. These two compact discs survey songs about "badmen and hellraisers." These forty-six selections were originally recorded during the 1920s and 1930s by artists such as Uncle Dave Macon, Tommy Johnson, the Fruit Jar Guzzlers, and Ken Maynard.

Various. *Roots of American Music.* Arhoolie 2001/2. This double set includes a fine cross-section of black and white folk music from across the United States. Most of the selections were recorded between 1960 and 1970.

Various. *Smithsonian Folkways American Roots Collection.* Smithsonian Folkways 40062. These twenty-six tracks cover a wide range of folk and folk-based artists, from Lead Belly to Lucinda Williams.

Various. *The Alan Lomax Collection Sampler.* Rounder CD 1700. This 1997 release inaugurates a breath-taking reissue series devoted to the work of Alan Lomax on several continents and over fifty years. "The Southern Journey Series" (a thirteen-volume set) revisits the late 1950s recordings by Lomax in the American South. *The Alan Lomax Collection* is—quite literally—all over the map. This set of over one hundred well-annotated compact discs looks at his work with folk and vernacular music not only in the United States but in the Caribbean and Europe as well.

Various. *Times Ain't Like They Used to Be: Early American Rural Music*, Volumes 1 & 2. Yazoo 2028–29. A collection of some of the best recordings of blues, rags, fiddle tunes, ballads, etc., from the 1920s and 1930s by artists as diverse as Henry Thomas, Fiddlin' John Carson, Rev. D. C. Rice, and the Shelor Family.

Various. *The Young Fogies*. Rounder 0319. This 2009 compact disc surveys the diversity of regional and grassroots music found across the United States through a mixture of younger and more veteran musicians performing fiddle tunes, blues, old-time dance tunes, and other forms of traditional music.

SUGGESTED READING

Philip Bohlman. *The Study of Folk Music in the Modern World*. Bloomington: Indiana University Press, 1988. A scholarly and thoughtful approach to the problems of defining folk music in our postmodern world.

Jan Brunvand. *The Study of American Folklore: An Introduction*, 4th edition. New York: Norton, 1998. A solid introduction to folklore and folklife, including a good section on music.

George O. Carney, ed. *The Sounds of People and Places—Readings in the Geography of American Folk and Popular Music*, 3rd edition. Lanham, MD: Roman & Littlefield, 1994. A series of essays about the geographical implications of American folk and popular music in the twentieth century. Includes an extensive and helpful bibliography.

Norm Cohen. *Folk Music: A Regional Exploration*. Lanham, MD: Greenwood Press, 2005. This nicely balanced book addresses the topic by geographical regions rather than by genre or personality or chronology.

Ron Cohen. *A History of Folk Music Festivals in the United States: Feasts of Musical Celebration*. Lanham, MD: Scarecrow Press, 2008. Folk music expert chronicles the development of festivals from as early as 1912 into the twenty-first century.

Oxford Music Online, N.D. Many biographies and topics related to folk music are found as part of this ongoing project to update and revise the most recent (2002) print version of this extensive project.

START HERE!

Daniel Kingman and Lorenzo Candelaria. *American Music: A Panorama, Concise Edition,* 4th edition. New York: Cengage/Wadsworth, 2012. Even the slimmed-down version of this survey includes several lengthy sections titled "Folk and Ethnic Musics," "The Blues," and "The Native American Tradition" related to the broad spectrum of American traditional music.

Ellen Koskoff, ed. *The United States and Canada (Garland Encyclopedia of World Music,* Vol. 3). New York: Garland Press, 2000. This very ambitious volume encompasses a wide variety of vernacular music, including most of the folk and ethnic traditions covered in this book.

Stephanie Ledgin. *Discovering Folk Music.* New York: Praeger Press, 2010. A nicely written introduction to this broad field of music and culture, with a focus on the period since World War II.

Kip Lornell. *The NPR Curious Listener's Guide To American Folk Music.* New York: Penguin/Perigee Books, 2004. The title says it all, a primer that provides an overview of the topic.

Greil Marcus. *Invisible Empire: Bob Dylan's Basement Tapes.* New York: Henry Holt, 1997. A very personal and revisionist look back at the music of Bob Dylan but equally importantly at various individuals, such as Dock Boggs, who helped to shape twentieth-century folk and folk-based music.

William McNeil. *Encyclopedia of American Gospel Music.* New York: Routledge, 2008. A landmark book that includes both black and white artists and topics in the same volume.

Terry Miller. *Folk Music in America: A Reference Guide.* New York: Garland, 1987. Miller provides a valuable guide to articles, books, and other studies of American grassroots music published through the middle 1980s.

Theo Pelletier (photographer), John Funkerman, and Elijah Wald. *River of Song.* New York: St. Martin's Press, 1999. A companion to the PBS-broadcast film, and multi-CD set about vernacular, folk, and folk-based music found along the Mississippi River from Minnesota to Louisiana.

Larry Sandberg and Dick Weissman. *The Folk Music Sourcebook*, 2nd edition. New York: Da Capo Press, 1989. With sections titled "Listening," "Learning," "Playing," and "Hanging Out," this book covers nearly everything in contemporary American folk music.

START HERE!

Jeff Titon and Robert Carlin. *American Musical Traditions,* Volumes 1–5. New York: Gale Group/Thompson Learning, 2002. These volumes reprint a wide range of articles, liner notes, and essays that cover a tremendous range of genres and styles from Native American to blues to Asian American musics.

Michael Ann Williams. *Staging Tradition: John Lair and Sarah Gertrude Knott.* Urbana: University of Illinois Press, 2006. This book contrasts how the Renfro Valley Barn Dance and the National Folk Festival produced and promoted folk music for audiences beginning in the late 1930s.

SUGGESTED VIEWING

Various. *A Musical Journey.* Vestapol. This low-tech but compelling video consists of "home movies" of Big Bill Broonzy, The McPeake Family, Pete Steele, and others filmed by Pete Seeger between 1957 and 1964.

Various. "Dreams and Songs of the Noble Old." Vestapol. As part of the *Alan Lomax Collection,* this anthology includes interviews and brief performances by half a dozen of America's best folk singers, such as blues man Sam Chatmon, fiddler Tommy Jarrell, and balladeer Nimrod Workman.

Various. *Free Show Tonight.* CARTS (Cutlural Arts Resources for Teachers and Students)/Folkstreams.net. An old-time traveling medicine show visits a small town in North Carolina, bringing with it a doctor, comedians, and plenty of music.

Various. *Homemade American Music.* Agrinsky Productions/Folkstreams.net. Follow Mike Seeger and Alice Gerrard in the late 1970s as they perform and visit other influential folk musicians on a journey throughout the southeastern United States.

Various. *The Mississippi River of Song.* Acorn Media Publishing. This lengthy journey from New Orleans northward to Minnesota was originally aired on PBS early 1999. The 4 one-hour programs are now available separately for home viewing.

Various. *Mouth Music.* Blaine Dunlap/PRESERIVSTA/Folkstreams.net This playful documentary demonstrates the distinctive modes of the human voice in daily life from jump-rope rhymes to the calls of auctioneers.

SUGGESTED WEB SITES

More and more traditional music can be found on the World Wide Web. There are various list serves, chatrooms, and sites for blues, old-time music, bluegrass, Cajun, klezmer,

START HERE!

and so forth. In fact nearly all forms of American folk and grassroots music now enjoy a presence on the Internet. Its tempting to list all of the current urls for many of these groups, but the Web changes so quickly that this would be folly.

Instead, I have listed the well-established organizations or companies presently on the Internet. These should be on the Web for many years to come and will no doubt serve as resources not only for information but also as handy links to other related sites. Their precise location can be found using the search engine of your choice:

American Folklore Society
Arhoolie Records/Flower Films
College Music Society
Folklife Center of the Library of Congress
Folkstreams
Roots and Rhythm
Rounder Records
Shanachie Entertainment
Smithsonian Folkways
Society for American Music
Society for Ethnomusicology

Chapter 2

MASS MEDIA

- Introduction
- Minstrel and Medicine Shows
- Recording the Blues
- Record Companies and Folk Music
- Country Music over the Airwaves
- Border Radio
- The Ancestors of MTV and VH-1
- Uncle Dave Macon and the Electronic Media
- Final Thoughts

INTRODUCTION

The **commercialization** and popularization of American folk music have taken many paths over the decades. During the eighteenth century, folk music relied almost entirely on **aural transmission**. Low literacy rates in the United States meant that newspapers reached a small percentage of citizens, few people could read books, and even fewer could read printed sheet music.

By the middle 1800s, however, shape note hymnals and ballad chapbooks emerged as two early examples of the confluence of the printed media, commerce, and traditional music. Minstrel songbooks also contained much folk material. Most of these were published by small and regional presses, so their dissemination was usually quite limited. The trend to publish folk and folk-based material became more pronounced in the late nineteenth century and reached a new level of importance with the development of the electronic media in the early twentieth century.

Nearly all types of folk music have gained some measure of commercial attention through established, small groups of consumers already familiar with the traditions. Despite the burgeoning interest in Cajun music across the United States that began in the 1970s, its popularity remains strongest in southwestern Louisiana and southeastern Texas, the area settled by the Arcadians in the eighteenth century. Cajun music can be heard locally on the radio (and sometimes seen on local television stations) and has been recorded by major and local record labels. But its primary appeal remains within its initial hearth area largely because of the language barrier (many Cajuns still speak a creolized, heavily accented French) and its propensity to perform easygoing two-steps and waltzes. A similar situation exists for Norwegian American folk music in the northern Midwest (especially in Wisconsin) and Native American music in selected reservations across the United States. For example, the blend of country western, Pima Indian (Tohono O'odom), and Mexican music known as waila (or "Chicken scratch") is popular only in southern Arizona.

We've also discovered that music and musical styles migrate across regional boundaries, both due to human movement and the influence of the electronic media. Although cowboy music and its 1930s counterpart, western swing, originated on the lone prairies, its impact was not confined to the plains. The musicians of the Blue Ridge Mountains were deeply impressed by the Sons of the Pioneers, Roy Rogers, and Bob Wills. This occurred not because of the movement back east of musicians from Oklahoma and Texas but rather because easterners heard this music over their radios and on their phonographs and were captivated by western music's genuine appeal and its intrinsic nostalgia. The image and myth of the West was further reinforced by matinee idols, such as Tom Mix, Gene Autry, and Roy Rogers, who appeared in dozens of films during the late 1930s and 1940s. In the Midwest, groups such as the Modern Mountaineers (Missouri) along with the Prairie Ramblers and Hoosier Hot Shots (Illinois and Kentucky) performed in a style closely allied with western swing.

This chapter discusses several ways in which the electronic mass media and popular culture have interacted with folk music. These changes, especially during the twentieth century with the advent of sound recordings and radio, have been profound, encouraging interesting hybrids such as western swing. The creation of such musical styles also further blurs the lines between the constructs of "folk" and "popular," which are likely to change further as mass communication—particularly the Internet—becomes even more pervasive and as record companies large and small seek out even more discrete niche markets.

MINSTREL AND MEDICINE SHOWS

By the 1840s black folk performance practices were well known enough across the United States to be represented or reinterpreted in **minstrel shows**, the first distinctly American form of popular entertainment. Minstrel shows represent the country's first major exploitation of folk culture through its presentation of black music and entertainment on the popular stage. An amalgamation of racial stereotypes and elements of actual black American vernacular culture, the minstrel stage brought a vision of southern plantation life to audiences throughout the country. Early minstrels rarely featured African American performers; rather they embraced white entertainers sporting blackened faces and playing their own interpretations of African American music. This **blackface** tradition provided Anglo-American performers with a mask of safety, removing them from the daily reality of the life that they portrayed. "Blacking up" became a staple vernacular entertainment, appearing later in medicine shows and the twentieth-century **vaudeville** stage.

Blackface white performers singing and telling stories in "Negro" dialect first gained prominence shortly after 1800. Within thirty years popular white performers such as George Washington Dixon, J. W. Sweeney, and Thomas Rice captivated audiences with their interpretations of emerging black culture. Their models were both British and Afro-American. The tunes they sang often followed well-known Irish and Scottish melodies, while the lyrics relied upon images of American lore of the black man as a shuffling comic dandy in songs like "Zip Coon" and **"Jump Jim Crow."** Thomas Rice popularized "Jump Jim Crow" in the late 1820s, taking it to the stages of America and to Europe by the middle 1830s. Some songs that we think of as "folk" and are often performed by traditional musicians, like "Oh, Dem Golden Slippers," were actually composed by professional musicians touring on the minstrel circuit.

New York City is the birthplace of the minstrel show; it also served as its lexus during the classic period—1840 through 1870. Sometime in the early 1840s blackface entertainers joined together on the same stage to delight white audiences with their songs and stories about Sambo and other stereotyped black performers. Minstrel shows were actually born when small bands of blackface interpreters added new elements to their acts that helped to broaden their appeal. Short skits about southern black culture featuring stock black characters merely reinforced stereotypical views for northern audiences eager to learn more about the curious "Ethiopians" of the South. This combination of oral traditions and visual lampoons proved irresistible and audiences flocked to hear this new entertainment form. For the first time, on the stage at least, Americans paid to look at a reflection of themselves and of the development of their own vernacular culture.

The Virginia Minstrels, as Bill Whitlock, Frank Pelham, Dan Emmett, and Frank Bower billed themselves in early 1843, became the first group to popularize their format. Complete with ragged costumes, negro dialects, and the "curious gait" of the southern colored people, the Virginia Minstrels literally set the stage for America's first unique form of popular entertainment. By 1850 minstrels were seen across the United States, and through the beginning of the Civil

War Anglo-American performers dominated the minstrel stage. Blacks did not become minstrel performers in significant numbers until the decades following emancipation.

The underlying importance of minstrel shows extends beyond the appropriation of black culture by whites, a pattern that will repeat itself many times in this book. When people flocked to the minstrel stage, they reaffirmed America's slow emergence from the domination of European culture. Minstrels presented a stereotypical vision of America's common people: illiterate but hardworking Afro-Americans who toiled in the fields, frolicked to the sounds of banjos, and then shuffled off to the church on Sunday to sing spirituals. It also acknowledged our country's agrarian roots, particularly for northern audiences who themselves labored in urban settings very unlike the laconic southerners portrayed in minstrels. Despite the oftentimes crude images and presentation, at least minstrel shows helped to prepare northerners for their eventual glimpse of the "real life" of southern blacks.

Many northerners, and even some southerners, got their first taste of black folk music through minstrel shows. The highly rhythmic and often lightly syncopated minstrel songs clearly prepared audiences across the country for the ragtime, blues, and jazz styles that began emerging in the early 1890s. But minstrel shows also introduced music that ultimately filtered back to become a part of the folk musicians' repertoire; "Turkey in the Straw" and "Buffalo Gals" are two fine examples of fiddle tunes that were introduced by traveling minstrels. Popular songs that have become part of the American consciousness, such as James Bland's "Carry Me Back to Old Virginny," were often originally disseminated by way of minstrels and sheet music publication. Ironically, the unofficial anthem of the South, "Dixie," betrays its minstrel and African American origins.

Traveling medicine shows proved to be another source of steady income for black and white musicians alike. From 1870s into the era of rock 'n' roll these shows crisscrossed the United States. They were similar to minstrel shows in some respects, but instead of charging admission they sold medicine, salves, and tonics. While minstrels sold themselves as purveyors of southern black plantation life, medicine shows often played up the Indian theme with their sales of herbal and medicinal products. Medicine shows traveled under names both eye-catching and grandiose: The Great Mac Ian's Mastodon Medicine Company, The Jack Roach Indian Medicine Show, The Kickapoo Indian Medicine Company, and Dr. Lou Turner's Shaker Medicine Company. Most were operated by alleged doctors who promoted their shows as clean, medically sound, and family oriented. The shows themselves abounded with entertainment: theatrical performances, magicians, ventriloquists, contortionists, trapeze artists, blackface comedians, jugglers, and of course the pitches of the doctors

Alabama Minstrel Show Poster (1930s). Courtesy of the Library of Congress.

themselves. Important American popular singers/entertainers such as Billy Golden and William Hughes worked medicine shows. Naturally, the door was also open to black folk musicians with a sense of adventure.

Black singers found employment as songsters with other types of road shows, too. The nineteenth-century traveling troupes expanded to include tent shows by the turn of the century. The mobile equivalent of vaudeville, tent shows provided audiences with a variety of entertainment for one modest admission fee. Often touring in conjunction with carnivals and circuses, tent shows of the oughts and teens featured some of the singers who went on to be the recording blues stars of the 1920s. One show in particular, the F. S. Wolcott Carnival, toured with a lineup of future impact artists: Bessie Smith, Ethel Waters, Butterbeans and Susie, Ida Cox, and Ma Rainey.

In addition to offering black musicians steady employment, these shows brought various types of music to audiences across the South. Because of traveling shows rural folks were exposed not only to the familiar minstrel and ragtime songs but also to the ballads and popular songs of the day. You can be certain that the posters announcing the arrival of traveling shows and the advance work of the buskers (entertainers who arrived in advance of the show to advertise it) had an easy time drawing a large opening-night crowd.

MASS MEDIA

RECORDING THE BLUES

At the turn of the twentieth century most blacks still lived in the South; however, many others were new arrivals to the urban North. In the years following the close of World War I, the great migration north began as hundreds of thousands of African Americans caught the Dixie Flyer and other trains to New York, Toledo, Chicago, Buffalo, Detroit, Milwaukee, Philadelphia, Minneapolis, and Hartford. They were searching for a new life away from the South, the Ku Klux Klan, humid and oppressive summers, and limited job opportunities.

The migrating black population did not leave their traditions behind; **down-home** ways moved northward, too. This relocation diffusion is also illustrated by way of southern foodways. Barbecue restaurants and rib joints quickly appeared and proliferated along the streets of northern "black bottoms." Moreover, the availability of collard greens and pigs' feet in grocery stores illustrate these changes. Southern cuisine was celebrated in song as well as in stomachs, perhaps most notably by Bessie Smith in "Gimme a Pigfoot (and a Bottle of Beer)." Such songs signified not only the relationship between food and music but also a strong link with down home.

These early commercial blues and jazz performers shared another trait, their choice of "royal" names. This flush era of commercial success provided opportunities for local and regional performers to tour and record, some of whom wished to aggrandize their status. Bessie Smith and Ma Rainey were billed as the "Empress" and "Queen" of the blues, respectively; they were sometimes accompanied by the likes of New Orleans–born trumpeter "King" Oliver. Such self-importance not only betrays their commercial orientation toward the stage and the promotion it requires but also their pride as a well-recognized member "of the race" and as a purveyor of black music in a racist, segregated society. African American gospel groups often promoted a similar image through names such as the Royal Crown Quartet (Hampton Roads, Virginia), the Five Kings of Harmony (Birmingham, Alabama), and the Majestic Soft Singers (Memphis, Tennessee).

"Country" blues was the first down-home style documented by the record companies as they explored ways to expand their "race" series and sell product. Ed Andrews, recorded by OKeh in Atlanta in April 1924, became the first country blues artists to record. His performance of "Time Ain't Gonna Make Me Stay" and "Barrel House Blues" typifies the southeastern blues artists: a relaxed vocal accompanied by a nicely syncopated ragtime-styled guitar.

This music appealed not only to northern immigrants but also to southern record buyers. Many record buyers came to local furniture stores (where both phonographs and records were sold) to purchase the latest disks or they checked the newspaper advertisements to see about the most recent Paramount,

Columbia, and Victor releases. In addition to news and gossip, each weekly issue of the *Amsterdam News* (New York City), *Chicago Defender*, or the *Norfolk Journal and Guide* (Virginia) contained advertisements for the newest **race records** for the current country blues releases by Blind Lemon Jefferson, "Daddy" Stovepipe, Frank Stokes, "Long Cleve" Reed, and Lonnie Johnson.

Beginning in the 1920s and continuing for approximately thirty years, blues simultaneously functioned as folk and popular music within the black community. One key to understanding this process is cultural integration, which points out that "folk groups" retain their unique character while remaining part of the larger popular culture. This relationship has resulted in an ongoing dialogue: an interchange in which ideas and innovations move back and forth between folk and popular culture. The result is an integration or coexistence of the two. This is a natural synthesis in a world united by instant communication and easy interregional movement. The "ideal" isolated folk community or folk group no longer exists in the United States today. Nearly everyone is touched by the news, editorials, information, and music brought to us by our computers, radio, and television ... and has been for decades.

Before the 1920s blues was primarily a folk music propelled by the oral tradition. W. C. Handy and a handful of others published sheet music in the mid-teens that had furthered interest in the tradition, but the folk blues remained in the realm of African American performers. The media's sudden explosion intruded into the lives of many people, interesting them in new musical styles. Inside the black community an even greater appetite developed for blues, its inherent popularity enhanced by the attention it received. The status of blues changed because this down-home folk music that people previously associated with the South, beer gardens, and black-bottom dancing quickly became commercial property. People from Boston to Los Angeles could now order recordings of down-home and vaudeville blues performances without ever seeing these performers in person. The absolute need for personal contact with black folk musicians was obliterated.

One by-product of the increasing popularity of blues during the 1920s was the standardization of the form. Early blues songs were of varying lengths and did not always follow the same scheme of rhyming in the lyrics. Again, some of the more down-home musicians adhered to their musical sensibilities that had developed over years of playing. Musicians such as Sam Collins, Joe Callicot, or Bo-Weevil Jackson were so heavily steeped in early-twentieth-century rural black vernacular music that they paid little attention to popular trends. They continued to play songs with eleven or thirteen bars, wordless moans, and to markedly speed up during the course of their performances—sometimes as much as 20 percent. By the middle 1920s the blues form—twelve bars, *aab* verse form—had been standardized by way of sheet music as well as through

"Daddy" Stovepipe. Courtesy of Kip Lornell.

the recordings of the popular classic female blues singers who almost always adhered to this format. This standardization can largely be attributed to the growing professionalization of blues and, in the case of female vaudeville blues performers, the need for a larger ensemble to follow a more predictable song form.

Innovations occurred more quickly as a result of these alterations in dissemination. The single-string solo work of the innovative popular black blues guitarist Lonnie Johnson's numerous OKeh recordings touched musicians and listeners alike. Johnson's music influenced his black recording contemporaries, including such obscure blues musicians as Gene Campbell and George Jefferson. In 1929 Johnson also waxed a stunning series of guitar duets with white jazz guitarist Eddie Lang that are regarded as masterpieces of the genre. Lonnie Johnson's recordings, along with Texas blues man Blind Lemon Jefferson, clearly foreshadow the postwar blues guitar work of B. B. King, Eric Clapton, Otis Rush, Duane Allman, and others. His guitar playing illustrates how folk music is able to spread beyond regional and racial boundaries to penetrate into popular culture.

Neither was blues impervious to the impact of popular culture. Some of the hard-core, Deep South, down-home blues recording artists of the 1920s, such as Six Cylinder Smith, Jim Tompkins, Edward Thompson, or Willie Brown, apparently remained untouched by popular trends. Their handful of recordings

Lonnie Johnson, Disc Recording Artist. Courtesy of the Ralph Rinzler Folklife Archives and Collections, Center for Folklife and Cultural Heritage, Smithsonian Institution.

are "pure" examples of black American folk music; some are considered masterpieces of the genres. But many other blues recording artists whose careers began during the "first wave"—Leroy Carr, Big Bill, Tampa Red—unveiled repertoires that touched upon popular music. Urbane and sophisticated Leroy Carr performed many songs that extended the blues idiom beyond its inherent harmonic language into different song forms. His versions of "Think of Me, Thinking of You," "Love Hides All Faults," "Let's Make Up and Be Friends Again," or "Longing for My Sugar" owe more to Cole Porter and the Gershwins than they do to down-home blues. In his later career Tampa Red showed a distinct fondness for sentimental ballads, as did Lonnie Johnson.

Even though blues no longer enjoys a strong support base within the African American community, white-owned record companies continue to produce this music because it sells. But it is consumed more by a white American and international audience. Alligator, a small, **independent record company** based in Chicago, has built a substantial catalogue by recording electric blues artists. The United Kingdom is home to Document Records, which has reissued the greatest number of blues records from the 1920s and 1930s. Even Japanese-owned Sony, through its Columbia operation in the United States, had a smash blues reissue with its Robert Johnson (no relation to Lonnie Johnson) compact disc set. This set (originally recorded in 1936/7) is the biggest single-selling down-home blues release of the 2000s, most of which no doubt have ended up in the homes of white enthusiasts.

RECORD COMPANIES AND FOLK MUSIC

Commercial record companies began seriously recording regional country, blues, and gospel artists simultaneous to radio's first days. Although cylinder phonograph records had been marketed early in the 1890s, performers of grass-root American music were largely ignored. A meager number of black gospel groups—the Dinwiddie Colored Quartet of Dinwiddie, Virginia; Old South Quartette of Richmond, Virginia; and the Fisk (University) Jubilee Singers—recorded prior to World War I. In 1920 the General Phonograph Company's OKeh label recorded cabaret singer Mamie Smith performing "Crazy Blues," which quickly lit the way for blues and other forms of black secular music appearances on disk.

After a general recording slump in 1921 and 1922, blues, gospel, and country music finally caught the attention of record company officials. Victor took a chance with Texas fiddler Eck Robertson, who was accompanied by Henry Gilliland, in the summer of 1922. His pre-electric recording of the old dance tune "Sallie Goodin'" is widely acknowledged as the first country music recording. But the commercial country music industry really got started in 1923 with Fiddlin' John Carson, an older musician from Atlanta, Georgia. By 1925 this market enjoyed a steady stream of releases by banjo pickers, string bands, and fiddle/guitar duets. Victor, OKeh, Paramount, Columbia, Brunswick, Vocalion, Gennett, and Black Patti recorded thousands of blues, country, and gospel performances.

In addition to being distributed across the country and sold in furniture stores, the fragile 78 rpm recordings were also available through mail order. Newspapers and magazines advertised the most recent monthly releases in a series of stylized ads. The companies themselves distinguished between black and white artists by segregating the series. All of the selections by African American artists were issued as part of the "race" catalogue, while the white artists were labeled "old-time," "hillbilly," or "country." For instance, Columbia Records reserved its 13/14,000 series exclusively for black performers, while secular and sacred country music appeared on its 15,000 Old-Time series.

A & R (Artists & Repertoire) **men** supervised all of the recording sessions; their aesthetic and commercial sensibilities helped to shape the direction of American music. Ralph Peer, Art Saitherly, and Frank Walker worked with hundreds of musicians, relying upon a network of musicians, local furniture dealers, and even newspaper advertisements to locate talent. Musicians whose records sold well came back to the studios on numerous occasions. The openness of early talent scouting led to the recording of poor-selling and obscure but exceptionally interesting folk music talent like the Weems String Band (Arkansas), Blind Willie Reynolds (Louisiana), and the Memphis Sanctified Singers.

While the best-regarded artists generally sold no more than 50,000 copies of a record, these regional lightweights were lucky to sell several hundred copies of one of their disks.

Although the "hillbilly" and "race" folk traditions were the most widely documented by the commercial record industry, it did not entirely overlook the ethnic or "foreign" market. With the exception of a handful of musicians such as Irish artists like the Flannagan Brothers or Michael Coleman, who recorded extensively and whose disks often sold in the thousands, most ethnic recording artists remained utterly obscure outside of their own communities. The ethnic record market was as highly segmented as the communities in which the first- and second-generation Poles, Finns, Germans, and Ukrainians lived. As early as the turn of the twentieth century Victor, Edison, and Columbia began recording music to serve our large and diverse "foreign-speaking population" that was already being courted by hundreds of specialty daily newspapers that reached millions of people.

By the time they started selling race records, the companies were already in the market with releases aimed at the ethnic market. As early as 1908 Columbia had began segregating its specialty series by ethnicity, followed by Victor some four years later. They primarily targeted their record series by country, marketing series for nearly every country in central Europe. The companies did not forget the rest of our immigrant population, as they also released selections designated to appeal to the Albanian American, Indian American, and Chinese American audiences. By the late 1920s, the record industry had documented such important styles of unique American ethnic music as Hawaiian meles and klezmer.

According to Dick Spottswood (*Ethnic Music on Record*), "Most record companies, major and minor, eventually developed ethnic series." Although Victor and Columbia dominated the entire record industry, even smaller companies such as Banner, Brunswick, Cardinal, Gennett, and Pathe also maintained ethnic series. Some examples include Bluebird B-2000 through B-2092 (Cajun), Columbia 7000-F through 7304-F (Greek), and OKeh 17001 through 17373 (Bohemian).

Unlike today, the companies were not above serving very small, niche markets. For example, the highly accomplished Finnish singer and fiddler Erik Kivi recorded four selections for Victor in August 1926. These records were issued on their general ethnic 77000–79499 (1923–27) series during a period of unprecedented growth and interest among companies in American vernacular music, yet these two records counted sales in the hundreds. Nonetheless Victor invited him to record three more times (over a three-month period!) in either New York City or Camden, New Jersey, before the Depression sent the industry reeling.

A & R man and music publisher, Ralph Peer, in the mid-1930s. Courtesy of the Peer-Southern Organization.

The Depression struck the entire country, altering the record industry. A conservative pallor settled over the business of selling records, and comparatively little out-of-the-way talent was recorded. Instead the companies relied upon proven artists with a formula for selling records, such as blues man Big Bill (Broonzy), country music legends the Carter Family, and Bohemian concertina master Whoopie John Wilfahrt. Just as World War II began pulling record companies out of their prolonged slump, two things occurred. First, a shortage of shellac (the material from which 78s were then pressed) and then the **Petrillo Ban** (a contract dispute between the record companies and the American Federation of Musicians Union) combined to virtually shut down the entire industry for eighteen months, from the fall of 1942 into the spring of 1944.

By war's end a new breed of record entrepreneurs slowly infiltrated the industry, challenging the way the major companies did business. While the major companies looked more toward popular music and displayed less interest in blues, country, and gospel, new labels began taking up the slack. The Chess Brothers in Chicago, Bernie Bessman (Apollo) in New York City, and Houston's Don Robey (Duke/Peacock) explored the grassroots of American music. Significantly, Sam Phillips's small Memphis operation helped to launch the rock 'n' roll revolution when Elvis Presley walked into his studio in 1954 looking for an opportunity. Within a few years many of the small labels looked toward rock 'n' roll and its permutations for their livelihood.

Nonetheless, traditional music continues to sell to a select audience. Since the folk boom of the early to middle 1960s the number of small labels devoted to grassroots music has increased. Arhoolie, Rounder, and Flyright (England) helped to ensure an outlet for contemporary performers of folk and folk-based music. These and other companies also devote part of their catalogue to reissuing vintage performances. Although such companies do not have the financial backing or distribution of major labels, they do offer opportunities for artists who would otherwise be overlooked and unheard.

COUNTRY MUSIC OVER THE AIRWAVES

The history of modern American folk music remains inseparably tied to the evolution of the radio and phonograph industries. Although the commercial recording industry began in the late 1800s, their strong, symbiotic relationship began in 1920 when the first commercial radio station, **KDKA** in Pittsburgh, Pennsylvania, initiated its regular broadcasts. Within a matter of months stations erected by entrepreneurs in other major cities began broadcasting. By 1924 scores of radio stations beamed their virtually unregulated signals throughout the United States. These early radio stations relied almost exclusively upon local talent to entertain their audiences with music, drama, comedy, recitations, and news.

Almost as quickly as commercial radio stations sprang up, country music became part of their regularly scheduled daily broadcasts. Weekly "barn dance" shows featuring country music were established by broadcasters eager to serve their rural listeners. **Barn dance radio shows** were by no means a uniquely southern phenomenon. As early as 1925 the powerful 50,000-watt signal of WLS in Chicago presented hillbilly talent to its vast midwestern audience. Small-town uppermidwestern radio stations from Yankton, South Dakota, to Rice Lake, Wisconsin, featured daily radio programs spotlighting local talent performing music that ranged from polka to country. Nonetheless, the most famous of these shows, **"The Grand Ole Opry,"** has been a Nashville, WSM, and country music institution since its 1924 debut.

Radio was very tentative and exploratory during its first ten years of existence—1920 through 1930—because nobody was certain what would work. By the mid-1920s there were regular country music jamboree broadcasts over WBAP in Fort Worth and WLS in Chicago. By the Depression's onset, radio stations were found across the entire United States and they proliferated during the 1930s. What began as a big-city phenomenon spread to small cities and towns, which proudly boasted of their own radio stations. This meant that even more talent was needed to fill the demand created by the spread of local radio. Traditional music, especially country music, filled part of this void. The centralized radio networks brought national talent to local stations. Sometimes local grassroots talent came to the broadcast headquarters to go nationwide.

Reno & Smiley EP Cover. Courtesy of Kip Lornell.

The Roanoke Entertainers (Virginia), for example, were recommended to the CBS network by their hometown station, WDBJ. Their appearance was such a novelty that the *Roanoke Times & World News* sent a reporter along on their February 1931 trip to New York City, who wrote:

It isn't often the diners of the Memphis Special have a real old time string band to furnish "music with their meals," but that's what happened last week when the Roanoke Entertainers, radio performers from WDBJ, and Hayden Huddleston, the red headed announcer, left here for New York. There were six in the party, five musicians with their banjos, guitars, and fiddles, and the announcer who drawls and slurs his R's. They had a drawing room, for this gang of Roanokers was traveling in style.

They were on their way to the Big Town to play before the Columbia Broadcasting System audition board . . . At 2 o'clock John Mayo, Columbia announcer, introduced the band with "Ladies and Gentlemen, presenting a program of unusual entertainment, the Roanoke Entertainers under the personal direction of Hayden Huddleston . . ." With that, the Roanoke Entertainers went on the air, playing "Lights in the Valley." The band played six numbers, including the popular tune, "Smokey Mountain Bill," and it was not long before the telegrams began coming in. The Entertainers went over with a bang. But, like everything else, there is an end to all good things. The Entertainers remembered that Roanoke awaited them, so Saturday night they again boarded the train. The boys played for about an hour, then came sleep—welcome after two wild and hectic days in the Big City.

The Roanoke Entertainers, first of the local musicians to play over a national network, are back home today carrying on in their everyday life. For this band is made up of men who work every day. They are not professional musicians . . . A lot of folks heard about Roanoke, Virginia, Saturday that never heard it mentioned before. Such is the power of radio.

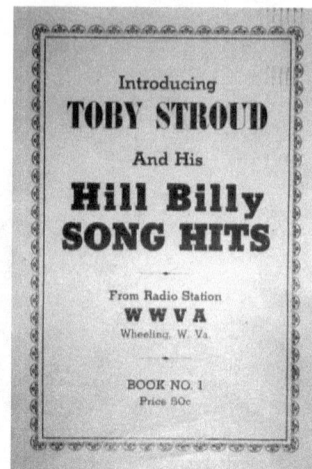

WWVA (Toby Stroud) program booklet. Courtesy of Kip Lornell.

WDBJ is typical in its use of local hillbilly groups like the McCray Family, N & W Stringband, Blue Ridge Fox Chasers, and Floyd County Ramblers. By the 1930s cowboy music and western swing by groups such as the Texas Troubadours (a Roanoke-based group who came up with the moniker at least two years before Ernest Tubb gave his band the same name!) became part of its daily schedule. The biggest names on Roanoke country radio, Roy Hall and the Blue Ridge Entertainers (1939–1943) and Flatt and Scruggs (1947), comforted Roanoke Valley listeners with their own blend of humor, string band music, and informal commercials.

For many country musicians radio became more than a performance vehicle. The radio broadcasts themselves paid rather poorly (or not at all), but they allowed the musicians to announce their live **show dates** and personal appearances. Thus radio became their most effective source for advertising the true financial basis for their musical careers—lucrative live appearances at which they sold autographed pictures and songbooks. An immediate, intimate link between performer and audience helped these fifteen- to thirty-minute shows develop into more than a musical event. They responded to the musical requests that came by way of the telephone, mail, and telegraph wires; talked about the weather; and poked fun at one another. Once country artists worked an area dry and the requests for show dates slowed down, they either moved on to more fertile ground or temporarily retired from music as a full-time occupation.

The bias of country music broadcasting is clearly toward the South and the border regions of the Midwest and Middle Atlantic states. The truth is that country music, with roots tied to traditional Anglo-American styles, existed in all parts of the United States. Very little has been written about country music outside of the South, though its impact proved to be nationwide. Even the cold northern climate of upstate New York was not impervious to the charms of **hillbilly music**. This southern emphasis underscores the inescapable importance of regionalism in folk music; Americans expect hillbilly music to be from the South where it is bred in the bone.

Consequently, we are more hard-pressed to describe the broadcasting of early country music outside of the South. The recording industry also largely ignored white country music north of the Mason-Dixon line, and the statewide collecting projects were largely initiated by scholarly types in search of ballads: British, American, and occupational. The books they published in the first half of the twentieth century focus on these aspects of the northern Anglo tradition. Comparably few commercial and **field recordings** of nonsouthern folk music were made prior to the advent of easily portable equipment in the 1950s. In the halcyon days before the Depression, the commercial companies themselves did not go out of their way to scout nonsouthern hillbilly talent. Most of their recordings were done at studios in New York City or Chicago. Victor used its Camden, New Jersey, facilities for recordings and made field trips to a variety of southern cities in search of vernacular music talent. With the exception of several trips to the West Coast and one brief session in Butte, Montana, their vision turned ever southward.

But not even all southern-born "rural" talent heard over the airwaves and produced by the northern-based record companies was factually represented. **Vernon Dalhart**, born Marion Try Slaughter on April 6, 1883, in northeastern Texas, received conservatory vocal training in Dallas before moving to New York City early in the twentieth century. Dalhart went on to become one of the era's most prolific recording artists whose talents knew no arbitrary musical boundaries. Some of his records were marketed as country, most notably those on the Columbia's 15,000 Old-Time series. In reality Dalhart's country records foreshadowed the "citybilly" sound heard in the early 1960s. His Tin Pan Alley songs also appealed to the rapidly developing country music clientele, who flocked to purchase his versions of the contemporary ballads "Wreck of the Old '97" and "The Death of Floyd Collins." This music was far removed from Dalhart's rural roots; nonetheless, Dalhart literally coined the genre of **pop country**, a term that would not come into general currency for several decades.

Throughout the 1940s country music radio was largely southern based. Some radio stations in rural areas outside of the South featured country music early in the morning and surrounding the daily farm reports and grain prices. Live broadcasts remained the rule of the day for most radio stations until well after the close of World War II. By the early 1950s, however, the radio industry was undergoing an evolutionary upheaval caused partially by television. Established radio stars like Arthur Godfrey and Art Linkletter jumped ship and

MASS MEDIA

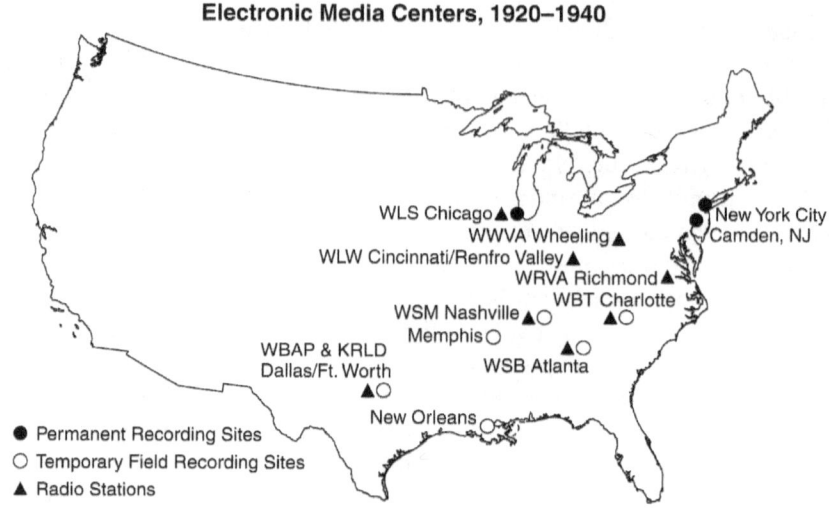

Electronic media map. Courtesy of William Vaughan.

moved into television's more glamorized spotlight. Networks also proliferated and an even greater demand for national talent caused radio stations to move away from their local identity, resulting in an ever-diminishing number of "live" slots for local grassroots and country musicians. For all practical purposes in-studio musical performances became passe when the nation was engulfed by the rock 'n' roll revolution. The most notable exception is the highly successful Garrison Keillor's and American Public Media's "A Prairie Home Companion," a distinctive anachronism in today's world of Arbitron ratings and inflexible playlists on commercial radio stations.

BORDER RADIO

Border radio stations provided another wonderfully unconventional opportunity for some of America's early country musicians—Slim Rheinhart and Patsy Montana, Asher Sizemore and Little Jimmie, the Pickard Family, Bob Wills, and one-time Texas senator W. Lee O'Daniel and the Hillbilly Boys—to reach a wider audience. Beginning in the early 1930s, these unregulated stations located just inside the Mexican border blasted their northern neighbors with signals that ranged from 250,000 to 500,000 watts. A handful of stations blasted out an unprecedented 1,000,000 watts of sound that regularly reached listeners in southern Canada, though they could regularly be heard as far away as western Europe and the southern tip of South America.

By way of contrast most of the radio stations based in the United States transmitted at between 1,000 to 10,000 watts of power, except for several dozen "clear-channel" stations—including WGY in Schenectady, New York; WOI in Des Moines, Iowa; WOWO in Fort Wayne, Indiana; WBZ in Boston, Massachusetts; and KOA in Denver, Colorado. These stations broadcast at the highest allowable power (50,000 watts) day and night and didn't share their frequency with any other station—a common practice in the early days of radio before the creation of the Federal Radio Commission (FRC; later the Federal Communications Commission, FCC) and its expansion of the AM radio band.

Because FRC regulations did not restrict power and content, these behemoths operated with impunity and immunity from prosecution by the U.S. Government. And these dozen or so stations were strung all along the borderland, from XEFW in Tampico, Mexico (just south of Brownsville, Texas) to XELO in Tijuana, Mexico, on the Pacific Coast. For all intents and purposes border radio stations could broadcast whatever they wanted, and for the most part they did. And the charge was led by a very engaging and bright character, John Romulus Brinkley.

Dr. J. R. Brinkley, a North Carolina native born in 1885, became the most famous wildcat broadcaster, pitching the notorious goat gland transplant for men whose sex drive had diminished. In pursuing his dream of becoming a medical doctor, Brinkley was booted out of Johns Hopkins University and left the Bennett Eclectic Medical School in Chicago under curious circumstances before earning a degree from the Kansas City–based Eclectic Medical University ... after less than one month of study! "Dr." Brinkley worked in rural Kansas for several years, which is where he ran into the "goat gland cure" that was to become his road to infamy and financial success. Eager to share his cure for impotency and sexual dysfunction with the entire world, Brinkley first took to the airwaves in the United States over KFKB in Milford, Kansas, which he eventually purchased. Not only did his medical practices cost him his ability to practice medicine but the FRC also forbade him from owning a radio station.

It was the sage observation that radio waves knew no political boundaries that brought Brinkley to the northern Mexican border. He had become wealthy enough during his decade of prosperity to build a 75,000-watt station (XER) in Villa Acuna, which opened for business in the fall of 1931. In addition to Dr. Brinkley's own programs, the station featured a potpourri of talent as part of its daily programming: the Bluebird Trio (a female singing group), psychologist/astrologer Mel Ray, the Studio Mexican Orchestra, and Roy Faulkner ("The Singing Cowboy"). Within six months, this eclectic mixture of talent, which was peppered by Brinkley's own pitches for all types of medical cures, ointments, and products that were not available through outlets in the United States, was bringing in between 25,000 and 30,000 pieces of mail each week.

This healthy response rejuvenated Brinkley's medical and communciations agenda. As his business increased dramatically, he wanted to dramatically increase the power of the station. First he suggested that 150,000 watts would be enough, but by the middle of 1932 he was so successful that half a million watts became his new target. In the meantime, however, some of the American radio stations located near his frequency were becoming increasingly nervous about his plans. Even such important stations, most notably WGN in Chicago and Atlanta's WSB, were complaining to the FRC about the interference from XER, and the thought of 5.5 times as much power was simply too much. They began to pressure the U.S. Government, which in turn turned up the heat on their Mexican counterparts.

A protracted series of lawsuits by Mexican officials related to Brinkley's broadcasts from remote facilities in the United States finally shut down XER in the fall of 1933. After the Mexican Supreme Court ruled in Brinkley's favor in the summer of 1935, he quickly bought the lower-power XEAW in nearby Reynosa, Mexico, and was back in business in a matter of months. But all of this was the prelude to going back on the air in Villa Acuna, where he prepared XERA to replace XER. And just before the close of 1935, his new operation went on the air with an unprecedented and astonishing 1 million watts of power. For the next six years Brinkley prospered, but a new lawsuit finally forced XERA off the air early in 1941 and Brinkley himself died on May 26, 1942, without ever facing the mail-fraud charges that ultimately caused his station to be closed by Mexican officials.

Brinkley's pioneering efforts opened the door to other like-minded entrepreneurs. Dozens of colorful pitchmen touted themselves as radio seers, spiritual healers of the airwaves, or medical men with astonishing cures. They hosted shows such as "The Bible Institute of the Air," "Good Neighbor Get-Together," "The Brother Human Hour," and "Helping Hand." Their product was sold on a "P.I." (per inquiry) basis with the hosts and the radio stations sharing in the profits. Nearly all of these men and women were most certainly quacks, but they offered hope, solace, and entertainment to millions of listeners living both north and south of the rather porous border that divides Mexico from the United States.

The border stations featured not only Anglo-American music but Mexican popular and folk music including stars such as Lydia Mendoza. Even the famous Carter Family made a move from southwestern Virginia to broadcast over border radio stations from 1938 to 1942, mostly on the "Good Neighbor Get-Together" radio program. They were joined by other prominent folk-based groups—the Pickard Family, for instance—who had also performed at the Grand Ole Opry or had been previously sponsored by Harry O'Neil and the Consolidated Royal Chemical Company. Border radio provided a forum for musicians—many of them American folk artists—to broadcast to a large and widespread audience;

hundreds of thousands more than they could have reached through any other means.

Border radio reigned virtually unchecked for more than twenty years, well into the rock 'n' roll era. Its influence diminished in the 1950s as the FCC and Mexican government began a series of legal actions to limit them. As late as 1960 Wolfman Jack launched his broadcasting career as a disc jockey on XERF in Del Rio. Changing tastes in radio and even more stringent regulations have all but shut down these powerful stations. Well into the 1980s rock groups like Z.Z. Top and Wall of Voodoo continued to celebrate the zaniness and power of border radio: "I wish I was in Tijuana, eating barbecued iguana . . . I'm on a Mexican radio" ("Mexican Radio" by Wall of Voodoo, 1982).

THE ANCESTORS OF MTV AND VH-1

Postmodern television history would have you believe that such cable outlets as MTV (Musical Television) and VH-1 (Video Hits-1) pioneered the integration of musical themes with visuals, which became known as music videos. In essence, music videos are three- to ten-minute short films that illustrate a song. MTV in particular initially relied heavily on the same format as found on most radio stations: the intermixing of short musical selections with an interlocutor and commercial messages. In the early part of the twenty-first century, the MTV format has expanded to include half-hour programs, documentaries, and retrospective programming.

The truth is that filming musicians is not new, nor is filming vernacular music particularly innovative. It is part of a lineage that can be traced back for decades. Because music videos have exploded in popularity since the middle 1980s, it is worth examining their origins—a legacy that extends back to just before the Great Depression.

As early as 1928, shortly after the advent of "talking pictures," American folk musicians were captured on film. These short pieces played at commercial theaters, permitting the viewers to watch and hear two to three minutes of contemporary folk music artists. Bela Lam (Stanardsville, Virginia), Whistler's Jug Band (Louisville, Kentucky), and the Rust College Jubilee Group (Mississippi) were among the groups documented during the first few years of this new wave of technology. The closest parallel to MTV from this period is "St. Louis Blues," a twelve-minute film starring Bessie Smith that chronicles the love problems that entangle the legendary blues singer. It closes with Smith and a group of singers in a beer joint singing the theme song.

At least two well-known folk artists from the 1920s and 1930s, Lead Belly and Charlie Poole, made trips to Hollywood to star in feature-length films that were never completed. Of course some of the singing cowboys of the silver screen, most notably Gene Autry and Roy Rogers, began their careers as folk singers. The early recordings of both men display the distinctive flavor of the blues-influenced country yodeler Jimmie Rodgers, whose Victor recordings were highly influential. But most folk performers were limited to short clips that appeared on movie screens as a prelude to a feature film. In the late 1940s some jukebox operators distributed machines that for a dime would play a two- to three-minute musical short called a soundie. The intent of soundies is identical to a music video on MTV: a thematic musical short designed to get you to purchase their product.

UNCLE DAVE MACON AND THE ELECTRONIC MEDIA

To exemplify the relationship between folk artists and the mass media in its infancy, let's turn to **Uncle Dave Macon**—one of country music's most influential and colorful characters. Born in 1870 in central Tennessee, Uncle Dave Macon first entered a recording studio at the age of fifty-four. For many years Macon farmed and operated the Macon Midway Mule and Wagon Transportation Company, hauling freight between Murfreesboro and Woodbury, Tennessee. He also learned banjo picking under the expert tutelage of minstrel and circus veteran Joel Davidson, who exposed Uncle Dave to his own repertoire and taught him the importance of raconteurship. In 1920 Macon quit the hauling trade and soon after turned to music full time. He played locally but quickly joined the vaudeville circuit, bringing his considerable skills to engagements arranged by the Loew's organization.

From 1923 until his death in 1952 Uncle Dave Macon entertained people with his music and stories. Inspired by the success of Fiddlin' John Carson, Sterchi Brothers Furniture Company (Nashville's Vocalion Record distributors) arranged for Macon and his fiddling partner, Sid Harkreader, to record in New York City. Macon's first session in July 1924 suggests the breadth of his experiences, interests, and tastes all tempered by what he knew the people wanted. He combined elements of his stage act, including his popular comic piece "Chewing Gum," with traditional material, "The Fox Chase," and his own version of William Shakespeare Hays's composition "Little Old Log Cabin in the Lane." Future sessions were equally broad in their interpretation of country music for the masses. One of his most famous sessions came in May 1927, with his Fruit Jar Drinkers performing classic renditions of Anglo-American fiddle tunes and lyric songs: "Sail Away Ladies," "Carve That Possum," and "Tommy and Jerry" as well as eight sacred numbers. "Carve That Possum," written by black minstrel performer Sam Lucas and published in the middle 1870s, underscores Macon's own minstrel roots. Its humor relies on racial and rural stereotypes that seem far removed from those living in an urban, high-tech world. This performance is sung in "negro dialect" and features a response by the band, which is shown in parentheses:

My dog treed, I went to see (Carve him to the heart).
Dar was a possum up dat tree (Carve him to the heart).
And dat possum begin to grin (Carve him to the heart).
I reached up and took a pin (Carve him to the heart).

Chorus: Oh, carve that possum, carve that possum, children.
Carve that possum, children, oh carve him to his heart.

Carried him home and dressed him off (Carve . . .).
Hung him out that night in the frost (Carve . . .).
But the way to cook the possum sound (Carve . . .).
First parboil, then bake him brown (Carve . . .).

Chorus

Possum meat am good to eat (Carve . . .).
Always fat and good and sweet (Carve . . .).
Grease potatoes in the pan (Carve . . .).
Sweetest eating in the land (Carve . . .).

Chorus

Some eat early and some eat soon (Carve . . .).
Some like possum and some like coon (Carve . . .).
That possum just the thing for me (Carve . . .).
Old Rattler's got another one up a tree (Carve . . .).

Chorus

Macon recorded nearly 180 songs during his lengthy commercial recording career that stretched well into the 1930s. His final, rather informal recordings were done by folklorist Charles Faulkner Bryant in 1950, shortly before Macon's death.

Not only did Macon sell records and appear on the stage, he became one of hillbilly music's early radio artists. His debut came late in 1925 over Nashville's WSM, home of the recently established Grand Ole Opry, where he remained a

Uncle Dave Macon late in life. Courtesy of Ralph Rinzler Folklife Archives and Collections, Center for Folklife and Cultural Heritage, Smithsonian Institution.

fixture for fifteen years and regular performer until his death. Macon was not limited to the three- to five-minute confines of the contemporary Opry; he often had fifteen- to thirty-minute blocks of improvisatory time permitting him to stretch out by telling jokes, comic tales, and music. Over his nearly thirty-year radio career Macon reached the ears and hearts of millions of Americans.

Uncle Dave Macon's career stretched from the age of minstrelsy to the year before Elvis Presley first walked into Sam Phillips's Memphis Sun studio. He very clearly recognized the vital impact of radio and records as forces in disseminating his music to an audience far more vast than touring could ever hope to reach. Unlike Ernest V. Stoneman, who all but boycotted radio and rarely toured until the renaissance of his musical career in the mid-1950s, Macon embraced both aspects of the new technology to further his professional career. By the end of his life Uncle Dave was a true anachronism. He remained true to his creative muse. As a fiercely individualistic, perhaps eccentric, man, Macon brought his nineteenth-century musical vision to people across modern-day America.

FINAL THOUGHTS

The electronic media has shaped postmodern America in many and varied ways. It helps to define and promulgate popular trends in fashion, language, dance, and music. American folk music has been intrinsically linked with radio and the recording industry since their inception, both of which have assisted in the breakdown of the cultural traits that delineate regional American culture and music. But traditional music is far from dead. It continues to lurk just beneath the commercial underbelly, infusing younger musicians who seemingly annually discover the old records of Robert Johnson, Gid Tanner and the Skillet Lickers, Elmore James, the Carter Family, Jimmie Rodgers, and the Golden Gate Quartet—truly American originals.

KEY FIGURES AND TERMS

- A & R Men
- aural transmission
- barn dance radio shows
- blackface
- commercialization
- Vernon Dalhart
- down-home
- field recordings
- Grand Ole Opry
- hillbilly music
- independent record company
- "Jump Jim Crow"
- KDKA
- Uncle Dave Macon
- minstrel show
- Petrillo Ban
- popcountry
- race records
- show dates
- vaudeville

SUGGESTED LISTENING

Carter Family. *The Carter Family on Border Radio*. Arhoolie CD 411-13. These three compact discs contain a cross-section of songs and talking taken from 1939 border radio transcriptions.

Adolph Hofner. *South Texas Swing*. Arhoolie 7029. The master of "Czechstern Swing" from the 1930s, including a brief radio broadcast.

Louvin Brothers. *Radio Favorites '51-'57*. Country Music Foundation 009. The title sums up the contents of this release by one of the best of the "brother groups."

Maddox Brothers & Rose. *On the Air*. Arhoolie 222. These performances are from live radio broadcasts that originally aired during the 1940s, including two songs from the Grand Ole Opry.

Emmett Miller. *The Minstrel Man From Georgia*. Columbia/Blues & Roots CK 66999. The "missing link" between minstrelsy and country music recorded twenty wonderful selections, including "Lovesick Blues" and "Big Bad Bill Is Sweet William Now" for OKeh in the late 1920s and they are all here.

Dewey Phillips. *Red Hot & Blue*. Memphis Archive MA 7016. A collection of "airshots" by this truly wild Memphis disc jockey taken from 1952 to 1964 when he was pioneering the broadcasting of rockabilly and rock 'n' roll in the mid-South.

Merle Travis. "Unreleased Radio Transcriptions 1944–1949." Country Routes RFD 09. Excerpts from California radio broadcasts, many of them from the Hollywood Barn Dance, that place Travis in several musical contexts.

Hank Williams. *Health and Happiness Shows*. Mercury 314-517862. A double CD set brings you eight complete twelve-minute radio shows recorded and broadcast in the fall of 1949. Colin Escott's essay greatly helps to contextualize these programs in light of William's career.

Various. *Early Roanoke Country Radio*. Global Village/BRI 010. A lengthy monograph accompanies this compact disc, which encompasses the period between 1925 and 1955.

SUGGESTED READING

Bill Barlow. *Making Waves*. Philadelphia, PA: Temple University Press, 1998. A well-researched and broad introduction to the history of black radio personalities (primarily disc jockeys) from the middle 1920s through the mid-1990s.

Chad Berry. *The Hayloft Gang: The Story of the National Barn Dance*. Urbana: University of Illinois Press, 2008. This edited volume contains essays about radio broadcasting in the 1930s and 1940s and Chicago as a center for country music as well as writings about the National Barn Dance itself.

John Broven. *Record Makers and Breakers: Voices of the Independent Rock 'n' Roll Pioneers*. Urbana: University of Illinois Press, 2009. Please don't let the title fool you, as Broven underscores in this excellent book, these independent record companies also recorded a great range of blues, country, and gospel music.

Louis Cantor. *Dewey and Elvis: The Life and Times of a Rock 'n' Roll Deejay*. Urbana: University of Illinois Press, 2005. One of the wildest of all mid-century disc jockeys, Dewey Phillips (the creative voice who helped to integrate the airways in Memphis) is a key figure in this entertaining book.

Dale Cockrell. *Demons of Disorder: Early Blackface Minstrels and Their World*. Cambridge: Cambridge University Press, 1997. Cockrell provides a new look at the importance and significance of the "blacking up" tradition and its underlying meanings.

MASS MEDIA

Bill Crawford and Gene Fowler. *Border Radio*. Austin: Texas Monthly Press, 1987. An entertaining and informative account of Mexican border radio.

Jonathan Hartley Fox. *King of the Queen City: The Story of King Records*. Urbana: University of Illinois Press, 2009. A comprehensive look at the development and history of King Records, which brought artists ranging from Grandpa Jones and the Stanley Brothers to Ike Turner and James Brown.

Craig Havighurst. *Air Castle of the South: WSM and the Making of Music City*. Urbana: University of Illinois Press, 2007. The author examines the intersection of radio and the development of Nashville as "(country) music city."

Rick Kennedy. *Jelly Roll, Bix, And Hoafy: Gennett Studios and The Birth Of Recorded Jazz*. Bloomington: Indiana University Press, 1995. Kennedy documents the history of the Richmond, Indiana, based Gennett label, which made the first recordings of Jelly Roll Morton, Bix Beiderbeck, and scores of other blues, gospel, hillbilly, and jazz performers for a just over a decade beginning in the early 1920s.

Rick Kennedy and Randy McNutt. *Little Labels—Big Sounds: Small Record Companies and the Rise of American Music*. Bloomington: Indiana University Press, 1999. Unevenly written profiles of ten independent record companies, ranging from Gennett to Sun, that helped to document American vernacular music from the 1920s through the 1960s.

Eric Lott. *Love and Theft: Blackface Minstrelsy and the American Working Class*. New York: Oxford University Press, 1993. A revisionist look at the meaning and uses of minstrel shows and blackface minstrelsy in American culture.

Brooks McNamara. *Step Right Up*. New York: Doubleday & Company, 1976. Despite its publication date, this remains the best account about the development and history of medicine shows from the mid-nineteenth through the early twentieth century.

John Minton. *78 Blues: Folksongs and Phonographs in the American South*. Jackson: University Press of Mississippi, 2010. Minton has written an in-depth study of southern folk-derived music on phonograph records before World War II and their impact on artists and audiences.

Dick Spottswood. *Ethnic Music on Record*. Urbana: University of Illinois Press, 1990. This seven-volume discography documents all of the "ethnic" recordings done in the United States between 1893 and 1942. It is a monumental work.

Robert Toll. *Blacking Up: The Minstrel Show in Nineteenth-Century America*. New York: Oxford University Press, 1974. Toll's work exams the history of nineteenth and early twentieth century minstrelsy during its heyday.

Ethnic Recordings in America: A Neglected Heritage. Washington, D.C.: American Folklife Center—Library of Congress, 1982. This book of essays remains the best source of information regarding the recording of ethnic music in the United States.

SUGGESTED VIEWING

The Life and Times of Rose Maddox. Produced by Gail Waldron, this 1983 documentary recounts Ms. Maddox's career (including her work on radio) through interviews, photographs, and a live performance.

Various. *Cradle of the Stars: The Story of the Louisiana Hayride.* This production of Louisiana Public Television chronicles the development and impact of this barn dance program, which was broadcast over clear channel KWKH during the 1940s and 1950s and that helped to launch the careers of Johnny Horton and Elvis Presley.

Various. *On Air Country.* Blue Ridge Institute, Ferrum College. This 1988 documentary is about country radio in Roanoke, Virginia, from the early 1920s through the late 1950s, which complements BRI 010, *Early Roanoke Country Radio*.

Chapter 3

FIELDWORK IN TWENTY-FIRST-CENTURY AMERICA

- Musical Communities and Fieldwork
- Accomplishing Fieldwork
- Some Nuts and Bolts of Fieldwork
- Final Thoughts

Exploring American Folk Music: Ethnic, Grassroots, and Regional Traditions in the United States has described the rich history and development of our roots music, an aspect of our expressive culture deserving of far more historical and contemporary research. This work can be undertaken with relative ease because we are quite literally surrounded by and often immersed in our own musical culture. American folk music touches everyone's lives at some juncture: overhearing the jump-rope songs of children as we walk down the street, watching B. B. King and Lucille (his guitar) perform a blues number as part of the annual Grammy Awards ceremony, listening to a documentary on Polish American music on public radio, recalling the lullabies sung to us by our mothers, or hearing a string band play an old-time fiddle tune at the local music festival. Despite its reputation as old-time or conservative music, American folk music has always been characterized by innovation within artistic and culturally defined norms. After more than 235 years of development it remains abundantly clear that our own rich musical worlds demand serious attention. In my opinion field research is the most important and timely path that one can take to study these genres.

This chapter encourages and helps to prepare you to explore the musical world around you with an open, more informed ear and mind. Libraries, archives, and private collections contain invaluable, irreplaceable, and rich caches of printed and aural material. There are a number of noteworthy repositories across the United States. The Archive of Folk Culture at the Library of Congress, the Southern Archive at the University of North Carolina, the Wisconsin Music Archive at the University of Wisconsin, the Ralph Rinzler Archives at Smithsonian Folkways, the Blues Archive at the University of Mississippi, and the Archives of Traditional Music at Indiana University each contain unique material: manuscripts, field recordings, videotapes, photographs, and interviews.

Held in perpetuity this material will always be available for researchers. Fieldwork, however, is equally energizing, rewarding, frustrating, enlightening, and capricious. It also adds valuable material to the very archives that people explore for their primary research. If accomplishing your own original fieldwork sounds like a daunting prospect, it need not be. The opportunities for fieldwork abound; it can be as simple as stepping out your door to speak with some children playing outside or as complicated as relocating across the country for an ill-defined period of time. You may venture into a church to speak with members of a gospel choir or even interview members of your own family. No matter the project, your basic task remains the same: to select and document some aspect of a musical community directly tied with American folk or folk-based music. (Specific research topics within a musical community are suggested later in this chapter.)

MUSICAL COMMUNITIES AND FIELDWORK

Communities represent one way to examine musical phenomena. Musical communities are a generally loose-knit, often eclectic group of people coalescing around a shared, specific musical interest. Such communities can be found in any genre of American music—jazz, blues, rock, old-time, alternative, classical, or bluegrass. Many of our musical communities are casual and ephemeral, while others (such as those that coalesce around a symphony orchestra) are generally more stolid and well organized.

The community of black gospel quartet singers in Memphis, Tennessee, for instance, has evolved over more than eighty years into a truly extended family through birth, marriage, religious beliefs, proximity, and shared values. In addition to the musicians themselves, disc jockeys, record company officials, promoters, and enthusiasts can be included among the members of such a "family." I spent three years documenting this rich, complex community and wrote an ethnographic study, *Happy in the Service of the Lord: African American Sacred Vocal Harmony Quartets in Memphis* (2nd ed., University of Tennessee Press, 1995) based almost entirely on my fieldwork.

A *family*, quite possibly your own or one of your friends, is another place upon which you might concentrate your research. Our families are often the first place that we encounter music. For example, Bessie Jones's (with John Stewart) book *For the Ancestors: Autobiographical Memories* (University of Georgia

Ralph Rinzler conducting fieldwork in Louisiana for the Smithsonian Institution in 1964. Courtesy of Ralph Rinzler Folklife Archives and Collections, Center for Folklife and Cultural Heritage, Smithsonian Institution.

Press, 1990) talks about the religious and folk music found within her own family, who for many years lived on the Georgia Sea Islands. We can look at families through many lenses and in different contexts, such as a record collection, radio, church services, or family musical sessions. Just as all of us have family folklore (when to open Christmas presents, how birthdays are celebrated, nicknames, or the name for automobiles with one headlight), there is often music that we learned within our family. Many parents sing lullabies to their children; perhaps you sing them to your own. Summer camp songs are often transmitted within families, among siblings, or between parents and their children, in addition to being perpetuated in context. Perhaps you learn Christmas or Kwanza songs from your parents, reaffirmed each year during the early winter holiday season. Someone in your family may have informally taught you simple instrumental tunes—"Go Tell Aunt Rhody," "Red Wing," "Chopsticks," or "Turkey in the Straw"—on the piano, guitar, or another instrument.

Secular *organizations* of all descriptions incorporate some type of musical activity associated with them. Sports teams, for example, often have pep or marching bands taking part in each game or match. All of the branches of the United States military support ensembles that perform many types of music for a variety of occasions. Educational institutions on all levels sanction many musical groups such as choral singers, wind and jazz ensembles, and orchestras.

FIELDWORK IN TWENTY-FIRST-CENTURY AMERICA

Willie "Red" Smith, East Bend, Alabama (circa 1954.) Courtesy Ralph Rinzler Archive, Center for Folklife and Cultural Studies, Smithsonian Institution.

University-level conservatories are the focus of ethnomusicologist Henry Kingsbury's fascinating book *Music, Talent, and Performance: A Conservatory Culture System* (Temple University Press, 2001). Fraternal lodges (VFW, American Legion, Elks, or Moose) sometimes include bands as part of their organizations. Some service groups hold musical competitions as a means of fundraising or for disseminating scholarship money to promising young musicians.

Many of us are exposed to music through *religious affiliations*. There are many examples of musical communities in the context of religion. Music, of course, is part of nearly every sect's weekly services. The music of the Church of Jesus Christ of Latter-Day Saints (Mormons) has a distinctly American tradition that goes back to the 1880s. Methodists prefer the grandeur of hymns written in the eighteenth and nineteenth centuries, often set to the music of masters such as Bach. Glenn Hinson's *Fire in My Bones: Transcendence and the Holy Spirit in African American Gospel* (University of Pennsylvania Press, 2000), for example, focuses on one church in central North Carolina. Those brought up in the Pentecostal faith recognize the camp meeting songs of the nineteenth century and more recently composed gospel songs, which are often performed by family groups or other ensembles. Similarly, people belonging to African American Baptist churches are familiar with the twentieth-century gospel songs that predominate in the Sunday services and Wednesday evening prayer meetings.

Musical communities also spring up around *commercial enterprises*. Charles K. Wolfe took one such organization—powerful radio station WSM and their Grand Ole Opry program—and wrote *A Good Natured Riot: The Birth of the Grand Ole Opry* (Vanderbilt University Press/Country Music Foundation Press, 1999). Much of the music that we consume on a daily basis—in elevators, on most radio stations, by way of television theme songs, or on our CDs or MP3 players—is performed by paid professionals. Commercial music frequently bombards our senses through means outside our control such as in grocery stores, some of which even have their own "stations" that praise the quality and goodness of their operation. In other contexts, like concerts or in our own homes or automobiles, we can choose the types of music to which we listen. The commercial music industry in America is enormous, multifaceted, and, for most of us, pervasive. And here in the early twenty-first century, the Internet has become an important means of disseminating popular music, either through Web broadcasting or down-loading for personal consumption.

ACCOMPLISHING FIELDWORK

Fieldwork is rarely the overwhelming hurdle that people, especially those with no experience, expect it to be, but it is difficult to do well, especially in the beginning. With a lively interest, careful preparation, and experience, timidity decreases while the quality of the results increases. A persistent fieldworker who is genuinely interested in a topic and the people whom he or she meets often uncovers information and documents material that simply does not exist in libraries and archives. Your field research can often be combined with previously published articles or information into an original paper that really adds something new. Fieldwork rarely stands alone; it almost always needs to be placed into the context of our existing knowledge.

The key to successful fieldwork includes these following steps:

1. Select a subject.
2. Focus on your topic.
3. Research and listen to related materials.
4. Prepare questions for your interview.
5. Communicate your intent.
6. Interview attentively.

Topic

Your fieldwork situation should relate to some aspect of American folk music. I suggest that you investigate one of the genres covered in this book. Because you are likely to be neophytes in this arena, or simply shy, you may wish to select a more familiar musical style. Above all pick a musical style that truly appeals to you or with which you have had personal experience. Here are seven possible subjects that involve fieldwork: the folk revival in your area, an ethnic music group, members of an occupational group (cowboys, miners, railroad workers, etc.), the organizers of a coffeehouse or folk music festival, a folk instrument maker, traditional songs or elements in the repertoire of a contemporary rock music group, or a blues performer. Many state and a few local arts councils have folklorists on their staff who can sometimes offer suggestions for fieldwork.

Focus

Once you have selected a topic, be aware that its focus may change as you ask questions and learn more. Focus is an important key to fieldwork. You may begin with a general line of inquiry or interest, such as Bohemian American polka music, but you need to refine your research to ask a more specific question. Studying the development of Bohemian American polka music in central Minnesota, for example, refines your subject further. With even greater research you may decide that a focus upon the importance of Whoopie John Wilfahrt in the development of Bohemian American polka music in New Ulm, Minnesota, specifies precisely what you wish to know. Now you have a manageable core topic, arrived at by a refinement process that began with a general interest. Don't be afraid to let the topic lead you into new areas of inquiry about which you knew nothing or for which your background research did not prepare you. The troika of an open mind, library and listening preparation, and the process of refinement leads to the best fieldwork.

Preparation

Successful fieldwork begins with careful preparation before you go into the field. After you select a topic that interests you, check what literature has been written on the subject. Your search may prove futile because so many areas of American music await the scrutiny of intelligent writers. However, if you select the folk revival, blues, cowboy songs, or gospel music, then a wealth of published information is at your disposal. An informed fieldworker needs to be familiar with the important figures in the music, its historical development, and, above all, with the sound of the music itself. Listen to the music! The suggested readings that close the chapters in this book list the important literature and musical selections in American traditional music. Use them as a steppingstone for further inquiry, but you need not try to read everything on a subject. A library or archive provides you with the background tools necessary for work in the field; your true mission lies outside its walls.

Questions

Fieldwork involves asking the right questions ... of the right people. The identity of "right people" is sometimes obvious from the beginning of a project. If you have decided to study an individual—a dulcimer maker, blues singer, ballad singer, or disc jockey—your focus will almost certainly lead you in the correct direction. But gaining entrees to other communities may not be so easy. Fieldwork can be hindered by the researcher's gender, age, ethnic background, or race. On the other side of the coin, being an in-group member often facilitates fieldwork because of the known contacts and immediate acceptability.

Your questions should cover such basic information as the date and location of the interview; the full name of the interviewer; date and location of the interviewer's birth; and the previous places he or she lived. You will probably want to include some of these general questions:

How long have you been involved in this activity?
From whom did you learn?
Where have you traveled to perform your music?
Was this tradition within your family?
Who first exposed you to this type of music?
What role have books or the mass media played in your learning of music?
Who else do you know that I should talk to about this?

Communication

Once you have located someone of interest, a straight-ahead approach works best to assuage fears and suspicions or simply as a matter of courtesy to explain your research. You must clearly identify yourself and your own role as a student and delineate the nature of your project as well as your interest in the music. This can be done quickly and efficiently, and such candor often places people at ease. Always tell people who referred you or how you came to speak with them. Initial inquiries about a musical community frequently lead to the head of an organization—barbershop quartet, folk music festival, musicians' union, or gospel group. Such contacts may not immediately yield results, but a formal introduction helps to sanction or legitimize your work and will probably lead you in the right direction.

Interview

The interview itself is a critical part of fieldwork. A written list of questions or topics for discussion is often a good idea, but don't be dogmatic about using this list. They are merely guideposts; let the interview proceed into new or unexpected areas if they seem fruitful or interesting. Remember that your interviewees know more about the subject than do you, which is why you are seeking their knowledge and perspective. You may start with simple factual questions. As the situation relaxes and the questions flow more easily (hopefully they will), then move on to more complex issues. Use your intuition. If a subject appears too difficult or painful to discuss, then move on. A poorly conducted interview may be better than no interview at all, but if it is not going well, do not be afraid to take a break or suggest that you come back at a better time.

Rarely will you want to interview people as soon as you meet them. It takes a while to ascertain their actual position within the musical community and what might be important to discuss. With an intricate or more detailed research project you will probably find that a single interview is insufficient. With further reflection on your part and often on the part of the subject, you will often gain new insights or information with multiple interviews. These are also often accomplished by letting the interviewee lead the way and by your tacit encouragement—simply nodding your head or a quick verbal affirmation. Most people enjoy talking about themselves and providing their viewpoints.

Here are some other tips: Verify the correct spellings of names; ask if you are not sure. Clarify dates as precisely as possible; "the summer of 1971" is more helpful than "in the early 1970s." Ask for specific locations; Reno, Nevada, is more precise than "somewhere out West," or even Nevada. Ask about older photographs or written materials, such as a diary, that might stimulate their thoughts. If undertaken in the right spirit and within a nurturing context, the interview can yield an immense amount of valuable information. Rules, so goes the cliché, are meant to be broken or at least bent. If you are unable to easily interview someone again, then it may be necessary to push certain issues or topics. You also might need to interview someone the first time you meet. Use your intuition, good judgment, and you may profit by breaking the generally accepted maxims.

I wish that I had violated them on several instances. In the fall of 1979, while working within the community of black gospel quartet singers in Memphis, I conducted a brief interview with Elijah Jones. I knew only that Jones trained gospel quartets and that he was not in the best of health. Within two months it became abundantly clear that he was one of the important keys to my entire project, so I called for another appointment. During the intervening eight weeks Jones had died of a heart attack and his wife had thrown out all of his personal effects related to his fifty-year musical career—hundreds of photographs, placards, contracts, and newspaper clippings! My short initial interview is the only account of Jones's place in musical history. In 1970 I was searching with good success for down-home blues singers in Albany, New York. I came across an elderly black man who played the fiddle and used to work with medicine shows, but he didn't interest me because he was not directly part of the blues tradition. Three years later, after I became more aware of African American string band music and had met several medicine show performers, I went back to visit this gentleman. I could not even recall his name, but remembered the house. He, too, had passed away, another potential treasure of information irrevocably lost. These anecdotes are another way of reminding you of fieldwork's timeliness and that you can add to our knowledge of American music history, too.

Ethics

Much space has been devoted to the ethics and the morality of fieldwork in the literature of anthropology, folklore, and ethnomusicology. These questions become more problematic in cultures outside of our own, but American fieldwork is usually much less cloudy. Honesty and clarity of communication are the fundamental keys to confronting these occasionally sticky issues. There are sometimes legal issues regarding the ownership and rights of musical performances captured on tape and stored in an archive, but these are more often overshadowed by the researcher's extralegal responsibilities. Be sure to ask if the interviewee wishes to place restrictions, for whatever reasons, on the material.

Your responsibilities as an active and ethical fieldworker might someday include keeping folks informed about the release of recordings, giving them copies of your own work (if they desire), arranging for public performances, or gaining newspaper, television, or radio publicity for musicians within the larger community. This list implies a level of activity and commitment that may transcend your initial research project. Nonetheless such work is often on the agenda of many ethnomusicologists, folklorists, and American music scholars. These scholars are taking an increasingly avocational role in their work, particularly in helping the music reach a larger audience or to underscore the music's importance within its own community base. Others take a more benign, hands-off role, arguing that objectivity and distance must be maintained to preserve scholarly integrity. Each fieldwork situation comes with its own organic problems and rewards. Some lend themselves to public presentation or tend to place the fieldworker in the role of a social or musical advocate, while this may be wholly inappropriate in other contexts. Fieldwork within a musical community presents new opportunities, challenges, and research possibilities each time you go out. If field research were wholly predictable or too easy, then the thrill would be gone.

SOME NUTS AND BOLTS OF FIELDWORK

Fieldwork involves technology as well as the human touch. In our modern world nearly everyone who formally interviews people, be it an anthropologist, newspaper reporter, Internal Revenue Service field agent, or ethnomusicologist,

The famed novelist and folklorist Zora Neale Hurston collecting folk songs in Florida, circa 1936. Courtesy of the Library of Congress.

takes electronic "notes" of the meeting. Field notes used to be handwritten, but digital or video recorders are becoming nearly ubiquitous. The advantages of using recorders nearly always outweigh the problems they present (e.g., cost, availability, or the hassle of setting up the equipment).

If you are not able to or do not wish to tape-record an interview, then by all means do not rely solely upon your memory. The memories of human beings are often faulty and never 100 percent reliable. A small notebook is an invaluable tool, for it allows us to write down factual information, such as a name, address, or phone number, that would require tedious tracking down on the recorder. It can also be useful for quietly recording your own impressions regarding the situation, especially if the session includes or is a performance. These notes often prove to be important later because they can refresh your memory in recalling its ambiance, flavor, or details. In retrospect, trivial events sometimes loom more important as we become more intimately familiar with our subject. Notebooks also gather this information in one place, rather than having things written on small separate slips of paper.

With the affordability of digital equipment, you will probably use a digital recorder of some type. The major uncertainty with today's digital equipment is its long-term value as a storage medium; will DAT tapes last as long as, for instance, a well-preserved 78 rpm record? Only the passage of time can answer that question. Given the problems with Ampex reel-to-reel tape manufactured during the mid-to-late 1970s (a plague known to sound archives across the United States), one must always be weary of unforeseeable problems.

Digital video recorders have become more prevalent and decreasingly expensive since their introduction to the general public in the middle 1990s. For interviews their main value is as a visual record of the person. Video recording interviews usually results in a static visual documentation with little use beyond archival storage. Musical performances inherently lend themselves more kindly to video recording. They allow us to review a performance in a format more closely related to its natural context. Video recording (both analogue and digital) often capture nuances—gestures, posturing, performance styles—that are not always easy to remember and permit the researcher to transcribe the words of songs, anointed speech, or other oral information.

Still cameras remain among our most valuable tools and have been for many decades. They freeze images for us to savor in print—an important detail in itself. A digital camera is a versatile tool that can capture a simple, effective portrait of a musician or the broad panorama of a musical performance. It is easy to use, preferable in most fieldwork, and useful in a variety of situations. The results of a still camera can be utilized in a final class report, an exhibit of photographs, on the cover of a phonograph record, or to illustrate a magazine article. Which type of camera to use, or whether to shoot black-and-white or color images, depend on the specific ends of your project. Choosing the best media for visual documentation is also part and parcel of your budget.

Written forms can also be useful for obtaining certain information. They facilitate the gathering of repetitive data and are particularly valuable for survey studies that sample many people. A survey form can also document basic factual information, such as names, instruments played, transmission of musical knowledge, and telephone numbers. A survey of musicians within a county, for example, is perhaps best undertaken by using a form or questionnaire. Such a form can also supplement a series of more intensive interviews within a specific musical community.

Conducting fieldwork related to folk music is also partially determined by your goals. For a college student using this book as a text, the goal is probably handing in a final project for a class grade. You may wish to innovate and ask your instructor if a carefully edited video or audio documentary can be submitted as your class project. You might write a publishable article or mount a photographic exhibition in lieu of a term paper. Or you could simply submit photographs, taped interviews, or video material as an addendum to your written paper.

Those with grander ambitions (college student or otherwise) might want to think about wider dissemination along the lines that I've already suggested. If the musician or musical group is talented enough, there may be commercial

The Ardoin Family (1969) has been involved with zydeco music for several generations. Courtesy of the Ralph Rinzler Archive, Center for Folklife and Cultural Studies, Smithsonian Institution.

interest in the music. You might approach a public radio station about a series of documentary programs related to regional music. The local art museum may be receptive to a series of concerts by the musicians with whom you are involved. The explosion of cable networks and local access channels could lead to the visual presentation of the music you have explored. Or you may wish to post the material on a Web site and to take advantage of its multimedia capabilities.

FINAL THOUGHTS

Fieldwork requires innovation, exploration, and a sense of carpe diem (seize the day). Students don't always want to be (nor should they be) force-fed information. This kind of musical fieldwork underscores the fact that you are capable of adding to our body of knowledge through original efforts. Such work not only serves as an adjunct to library resources but also as a vital pathway to primary resources that are all too often missing from our knowledge of American vernacular music. A well-executed field project is also challenging and fun because it reveals a musical world that has been awaiting discovery.

FIELDWORK IN TWENTY-FIRST-CENTURY AMERICA

SUGGESTED READING

Peter Bartis. *Folklife and Fieldwork,* rev. edition. Washington, D.C.: American Folklife Center, Library of Congress, 1990. This is a valuable and free (!) monograph devoted to fieldwork and folk culture, including musical traditions. It is available by mail through the Library of Congress and is also posted on their Web site: WWW.LCWEBB.LOC.GOV/FOLKLIFE/.

Gregory Barz and Timothy Cooley, eds. *Shadows in the Field: New Perspectives For Fieldwork in Ethnomusicology.* New York: Oxford University Press, 1996. Barz and Cooley have edited a valuable series of essays by various authors on conducting fieldwork on folk and vernacular music across the world.

Sandy Ives. *The Tape-Recorded Interviews: A Manual for Field Workers in Folklore and Oral History,* 2nd edition. Knoxville: University of Tennessee Press, 1995. Although Ives does not focus on music, he carefully discusses fieldwork in light of oral histories that are documented with tape recorders, photographs, and field notes.

Bruce Jackson and Sandy Ives, eds. *The World Observed: Reflections on the Fieldwork Process.* Urbana: University of Illinois Press, 1996. The sixteen contributors to this volume reflect upon their own fieldwork experiences—most of which are quite interesting—but not all of which are directly related to music. Despite this caveat, it remains a valuable book.

Bruce Jackson. *Fieldwork.* Urbana: University of Illinois Press, 1987. A pragmatic and theoretical guide to fieldwork based on the author's own classroom and worldly experience, divided into four parts: "Human Matters," "Doing It," "Mechanical Matters," and "Ethics."

George H. Shoemaker, ed. *The Emergence of Folklore in Everyday Life: A Field Guide and Sourcebook.* Bloomington, IN: Trickster Press, 1990. A series of essays about folklore and folklife research, some of which are specifically on music, but there are some useful words about fieldwork in general.

Martha C. Sims: *Living Folklore: An Introduction to the Study of People and Their Traditions.* Logan: Utah University Press, 2005. Although not about music, per se, this handy volume addresses relevant issues such as the importance of rituals, the context of performance, and ethics.

Jeff Titon, ed. *Worlds of Music: An Introduction to the Music of The World's People, Shorter Version,* 3rd edition. New York: Schirmer/Cengage Learning, 2009. An introductory textbook on ethnomusicology that covers music from Africa, eastern Europe, and the United States, which concludes with a fine chapter, "Discovering and Documenting a World of Music," on musical fieldwork and accompanying CDs of music.

Chapter 4

ANGLO-AMERICAN SECULAR FOLK MUSIC

- British Ballads
- Broadsides
- Native American Ballads
- Singing Cowboys
- Tin Pan Alley and Country Music Texts
- Ernest Stoneman's Repertoire
- The Father of Bluegrass
- Honky-Tonk
- Western Swing
- Final Thoughts

Exploring American Folk Music: Ethnic, Grassroots, and Regional Traditions in the United States gradually exposes you to a wide variety of styles, some of which you've probably never before encountered. This chapter, however, focuses upon genres, such as bluegrass, that should be more familiar. Many of the figures discussed here are obscure, others are quite well known because of their exposure in the commercial media: Gene Autry, Bill Monroe, and Bob Wills, among others. Their music, ranging from cowboy songs to the Native American ballads celebrating train wrecks, are discussed in the following pages.

This music largely developed here via emigrants from the English-speaking British Isles. Typically, the subject of ballads arises in discussions of Anglo-American folk song, and a small number of British ballads remain part of our culture. Even a few songs, such as the ballad "The Unfortunate Rake" (better known as the "The Streets of Laredo" or "St. James Infirmary") and the fiddle tune "Paddy on the Turnpike," are still played and sung by musicians on both continents. Much of this music eventually went into the brew that evolved into two commercially oriented strains: the "Nashville" sound and rock music in the post–World War II era.

Mary McClain and her fiddle. Courtesy of the Library of Congress.

BRITISH BALLADS

Ballads, frequently considered a "purer" literary folk tradition, exerted an important influence upon early Anglo-American music. These are the older British ballads, songs with a clear, usually linear story line. Certainly the later Tin Pan Alley writers were interested in storytelling, but the classic Old World ballads belong in a separate category because their antiquity and intent differs so greatly from the professional authors. The ballads in Francis James Child's canon, for instance, generally migrated to the United States during our settlement. Child, an English professor at Harvard University, categorized these ballads of British origins in the late nineteenth century. He idealized these oral stories purely as products of the unsullied "folk" who preserved these songs as part of an ongoing oral process that was passed down from one generation of semiliterate (at best) folk to another. Many of these songs were transmitted by written means: texts printed in rough chapbooks, or copied by the singers themselves in notebooks.

The early ballad singers generally performed alone and with no instrumental accompaniment. Scholars beginning with Francis James Child have generally been intent upon merely collecting the words to these songs. In recent years a more holistic approach has prevailed, with not only the text but also the tune and the context gaining more status among collectors of folk songs. Bill McNeil's compilations, Southern Ballads, exemplify this trend as does Simon Bronner's regional study. Bertrand Bronson's important work with the tunes of **Child ballads** further adds greatly to our knowledge of the music associated with these venerable songs.

By definition ballads tell a story, but they also contain other characteristics that make them different from other forms of narrative songs. Ballads are impersonal in tone and compress their action to focus upon the story's highlights, usually the ones with plenty of drama, romance, and melodrama. They are usually told without commenting upon the event itself. In these regards a ballad is similar to a newspaper story, particularly a tabloid bannered with headlines about aliens, Elvis Presley, and wonder diets. Several well-known British ballads imported to this country would make impressive headline fodder: "Farmer Sells Wife's Soul to Devil" ("Farmer's Curst Wife—Child 278), "Cuckold Husband Mistakes Wife's Lover for a Cabbagehead" ("Our Goodman"—Child 274), "Lover Wins Last-Minute Reprieve with Gold Offer" ("The Maid Freed from the Gallows"—Child 95), or "Enemy Ship Sunk by Greedy, Love-Crazed Cabin Boy" ("The Golden Vanity"—Child 286).

Ballads invariably use plotted action. Typically there is an unsettled situation and its resolution, which makes for suspenseful drama. They tend to gloss over the unsettled early situation and concentrate on the more consequential action of the second section. Ballad scholars have labeled this **leaping and lingering**: leaping over the background details to linger on the powerful and dramatic scenes. But even the most climactic action unfolds in objective prose, while the most gruesome or emotional scenes are revealed dispassionately and without critical comment. They often unfold as though they are being recounted by a jaded, veteran court reporter who has seen it all dozens of times before.

Lyric songs don't present the same well-developed narrative as do ballads, but they share many of the same themes. These humorous, sad, or satirical songs often deal with love, work, death, and tragedy. Blues, many commercial country tunes, and most rock 'n' roll songs provide good examples of lyric songs.

While the British ballads in Francis James Child's canon contain stories about Robin Hood, Northumbria, and England's battles with European countries, such tales are not encountered in the United States. The Child ballads that survived into twentieth-century America contain more universal themes with generalized plots: the love of Barbara Allen, tragic events between two sisters, or the roguish charm of the Black Jack Davie. The basic appeal of such stories is apparent, especially in eighteenth- and nineteenth-century America where so many people were closer to British culture and lacked the formal education to read and write. It is important to remember that ballads are not perpetuated only among the rural, illiterate poor.

MUSICAL EXAMPLE

Ms. Ritchie comes from an exceptionally musical family in Kentucky. She has made many recordings of ballads, including this version of "The House Carpenter" from the middle 1950s. This popular British ballad easily jumped the Atlantic Ocean into the repertoire of American singers because of its treatment of romance and drama. The American edition displays many of the traits described above: (1) it leaps over superfluous details, concentrating instead upon action; (2) the narrative makes emotional sense; (3) the story moves briskly along; and (4) listeners are left wondering about details—What are the names of the people involved? Where in Italy were they bound? What caused the ship to spring a leak?

Title "The House Carpenter" (Child 243)
Performer Jean Ritchie
Instrument one voice
Length 4:16

Musical Characteristics
1. The a cappella singing creates a monophonic texture.
2. The form of this ballad is strophic.
3. You can hear very minor variations in melody and the occasional rhythmic inflections.
4. Her voice is at ease and falls into the lower middle register.
5. Ritchie uses a pentatonic (five-note) scale for this song.

Well met, well met, my own true love,
Well met, well met, said he,
I've come from far across the sea
And it's all for the sake of thee.

I could have married the King's daughter fair,
And she would have married me,
But I have forsaken the crowns of gold
And it's all for the sake of thee.

If you could've married a king's daughter fair,
I'm sure I'm not to blame,
For I have married me a house carpenter
For I'm sure he's a fine young man.

Oh will you leave your house carpenter,
And sail away with me?
I'll take you where the grass grows green
Down in sweet Italy.

Oh if I leave my house carpenter,
And sail away with ye,
What will ye have to maintain me upon
When we are far away?

Oh I have seven ships upon the sea
Seven ships upon the land
Four hundred and fifty bold sailor men
To be at your command.

She turned herself three times around
She kissed her babies three;
Farewell, farewell, you sweet little babes
Keep your father sweet company.

They hadn't been sailin' but about two weeks,
I'm sure it was not three;
When this fair lady begin for to weep
And she wept most bitterly.

Are you weepin' for your house carpenter
Are you weepin' for your store,
Or are you weepin' for your sweet little babes,
That you never shall see anymore?
Not a-weepin' for my house carpenter
Not a-weepin' for my store,
Yes, I'm weepin' for my sweet little babes
That I never will see anymore.

They hadn't been sailin' but about three weeks,
I'm sure it was not four,
When the ship sprung a leak and down she sank,
And she sank to rise no more.

What hills, what hills so fair and so bright,
What hills so white and fair?

Oh those be the hills of heaven, my dear,
But you won't never go there.

What hills, what hills down in yonder sea,
What hills so black as coal?
Oh those be the hills of hell, my dear,
Where we must surely go.

This selection was originally released on Smithsonian Folkways 2301.

Well into the twentieth century Edwin Kirkland collected and recorded some fine versions of British ballads from his colleagues and peers at the University of Tennessee in Knoxville. Most of the mid-to-late-twentieth-century ballad singers documented by collectors tend to be from the South, particularly from the Appalachian or Blue Ridge mountains. A few outstanding ballad singers, such as Sarah Cleveland (New York), have been "discovered" in the Midwest and the Northeast. Some of the best of them, Horton Barker (Virginia) or Aunt Molly Jackson (Kentucky), continued the old-fashioned style by singing without musical accompaniment, but their performance style tended to be formal, rather emotionally detached in delivery. Other singers of older ballads, such as Frank Proffitt (North Carolina) and Jean Ritchie (Kentucky), often used their own stringed instrumental accompaniment despite the fact that a cappella singing permits greater freedom from both meter and strict phrasing.

BROADSIDES

Not all of the ballads with British roots are contained in Child's collection, which was subjective, selective, and labeled "popular." Another category of non-American, English ballads are called **broadsides** because they were printed pieces with strong journalistic ties. Broadside ballads are ephemeral by their very nature and few survived into oral circulation, particularly in the United States. Such ballads tend to be topical, placing immediate temporal limitations on them.

Broadside ballads are usually considered inferior to the classic Child ballads by scholars who suggest that they lack the refinements and polish of good poetry. Formulas are an important feature of broadside ballads, most often through the use of stock phrases such as the **come-ye-all** salutation that opens "When the Battle It Was Won" (J 23):

ANGLO-AMERICAN SECULAR FOLK MUSIC

Willard Watson and his nephew Doc Watson in Deep Gap, North Carolina, circa 1962. Ralph Rinzler photo courtesy of the Ralph Rinzler Folklife Archives and Collections, Center for Folklife and Cultural Heritage, Smithsonian Institution.

> Come all you aged people, I pray you lend an ear,
> You'll hear my feeling story, you can't but shed a tear.
> 'Twas of an aged couple that had one only son;
> He was shot as a deserter when the battle it was won.

Broadside ballads often take the first-person perspective, rely upon stereotyped characters, and frequently lack the objectivity of Child ballads. These ballads are also more often subject to recomposition, often with condensation of plot and sometimes with not so subtle shifts in details.

Because they are largely part of an oral tradition, ballads are subject to alterations in time, place, or other details. If the ballad is immediately recognizable and changed only in minor ways, it is said to be a version of some older, usually printed, text. Major changes can be fashioned, but if the fundamental plot is unaltered it is considered a **variant**. **G. Malcolm Laws** (1957) undertook the most intensive study of broadside ballads, classifying them thematically and assigning them an alphabetical symbol: War (J), Sailors and the Sea (K), Crimes and Criminals (L), Family Opposition to Lovers (M), Lovers' Disguises and Tricks (N), Faithful Lovers (O), Unfaithful Lovers (P), Humorous and Miscellaneous Ballads (Q). The categories themselves underscore the types of themes most often found in broadside ballads and reflect the interests of the people who sang them.

Though they sound very distant from postmodern America, some broadside ballads survived well into the twentieth century. Ballads about war, sailors, and crime were not as well preserved as those related to love and its consequences. Many versions and variants of broadside ballads about love were collected up through World War II by English professors and others interested in ballads. Broadsides such as "The Drowsy Sleeper" (M 4), "The Banks of Dundee" (M 25), "The Girl I Left Behind" (P 1), and "The Butcher Boy" (P 24) are found from Maine to California. Broadside ballads have circulated through the medium of commercial recordings, too.

In the middle 1960s California folk/rock group The Byrds recorded "John Riley" (N 36), about a soldier who returns from war in disguise so that he can test his love's fidelity. Not surprisingly early hillbilly recordings reflect the importance of broadsides, with Gid Tanner and his Skillet Lickers, Kelly Harrell, and the Dixon Brothers, among the many who dipped into this well. Perhaps the most famous broadside ballad related to the problems of love, "The Bad Girl's Lament" (Q 26), is related to another broadside, "The Unfortunate Rake." In America it is known as "St. James' Hospital (or Infirmary)," "The Streets of Laredo," "The Young Girl Cut Down in her Prime," or "Cowboy's Lament." It has been recorded many times since the 1920s and relates, in very oblique language, the consequence of contracting a venereal disease.

NATIVE AMERICAN BALLADS

With the strong ballad tradition in folk music from the British Isles, the emergence of indigenous American ballads seems inevitable. As soon as the Puritans settled in New England, the process began in the United States; however, nearly all of the best-known Native American ballads, such as "John Henry," "The Titanic," and "Casey Jones," come from the second half of the nineteenth or the early twentieth century. Ballad making in the United States was not dissimilar to the British broadside tradition, especially in its stereotyping of character and situation. The authorship of Native American ballads is almost always anonymous; until the twentieth century their dissemination was by way of oral or written means. Not surprisingly their topics encompass the same human impulses that have attracted ballad singers for decades: love, violence, scandals, and tragic events or disasters.

American ballads are often categorized according to a genre or are attributed to an occupational or folk group such as miners, sailors, cowboys, or African Americans. Many early ballad scholars such as James Francis Child, Phillips Barry, or Gordon Hall Gerould tended to downplay Native American ballads because they lacked both the antiquity and the poetic qualities of their British counterparts. Eventually, when compiling the state and regional collections that began in the 1920s and continued through the 1950s, collectors slowly recognized the importance and unique qualities of Native American ballads. This trend was driven both by waves of nationalism that swept the country and the championing spirit of popularizers like Alan Lomax, Carl Sandburg, and Ben Botkin. By the 1950s most such collections gave similar weight to Child, broadsides, and Native American ballads.

In 1964 G. Malcolm Laws published a revision of Native American Balladry, the major collection in this field. Laws divides **Native American ballads** into nine primary categories:

A. War Ballads
B. Ballads of Cowboys and Pioneers
C. Ballads of Lumberjacks
D. Ballads of Sailors and the Sea
E. Ballads about Criminals and Outlaws
F. Murder Ballads
G. Ballads of Tragedies and Disasters
H. Ballads on Various Topics
I. Ballads of the Negro

The qualities found in Native American ballads are similar to British oral poetry, especially the broadsides. They also leap and linger, downplay detail, and concentrate on the overtly dramatic. Like broadsides, Native American ballads are often recounted in the first person or from a less objective perspective. The events, though, are distinctly American in their origin.

The murder of Pearl Bryant by two dental students was disseminated to the entire nation through newspaper coverage. During the early years of the twentieth century a ballad about this murder circulated across the country and later appeared on country music recordings of the 1920s. Notice the typical greeting, a variant of "come ye all," that opens this ballad and its somber, warning tone:

1. Young ladies if you'll listen, a story I'll relate,
   Which happened near St. Thomas in the old Kentucky state.
   It was January the 31st, that awful deed was done,
   By Jackson and Walling. How cold Pearl's blood did run!
2. But little did Pearl Bryant think when she left her happy home,
   That the grip she carried in her hand would hide her head away.
   She thought it was a lover's hand she could trust both night and day.
   But alas! it was a lover's hand that took her life away.

3. But little did Pearl's parents think when she left her happy home,
   That their darling child in you would never more return.
   Her aged parents, you know well, a fortune they would give,
   If Pearl could but return to them a natural life to live.
4. Now all young girls take warning, for all men are unjust.
   It may be your truest lover; you know not whom to trust.
   Pearl Bryant died away from home on a dark and lonely spot.
   My God, believe me girls, don't let this be your lot.

These ballads touched not only the general population but also singers. They were especially important to the new generation of aspiring hillbilly musicians, who recognized their immediate appeal to a mass audience and suspected that the fledgling country music audience would enjoy such tragic ballads. These singers apparently did not make strong distinctions among the ballad types, certainly not like the contemporary scholars who carefully pigeonholed each specimen, searching for examples in other printed collections and listing the possible variants. Many circulated orally, but their printed version would do just as well.

It is ironic indeed that phonograph records from the 1920s helped to keep some Native American ballads in our minds and hearts. The fact is that many traditional American ballads were documented and disseminated by way of phonograph records. The Columbia Old-Time country series of the middle 1920s through the early 1930s, for example, included the cowboy ballads "Bandit Cole Younger" and "On the Old Chisholm Trail" among its releases.

SINGING COWBOYS

Ballads are also found far to the west and as an integral part of the cowboy tradition. Cowboy songs describe their life and, quite often, their work. The early (late-nineteenth-century and early-twentieth-century) **cowboy singers** represent a distinctive musical genre. Montana, Idaho, Wyoming, New Mexico, and the other western states were largely the domain of first- or second-generation settlers who lived, worked, and performed music in a world quite separate from the country music that developed in the Southeast and Midwest.

Although we frequently refer to commercial country music as country and western, this moniker did not develop until the middle 1930s. Tex Ritter, Roy Rogers, Rex Allen, Jimmie Wakely, and all of the other movie cowboys literally rode the cowboy image onto movie screens across the United States. But it was **Gene Autry**, with songs that he popularized on the silver screen, such as "Back

ANGLO-AMERICAN SECULAR FOLK MUSIC

MUSICAL EXAMPLE

Harry Jackson was a cowboy who worked the western plains during the 1930s and 1940s. He learned many songs and poems during his life, many of which were recorded in the 1950s and released by Moe Asch. This selection was well known to cowboy singers and bears the unmistakable influence of a rather maudlin Tin Pan Alley composition.

Title "When the Work's All Done This Fall"
Performer Harry Jackson
Instrument one voice
Length 2:24

Musical Characteristics
1. Jackson's solo voice is in the middle register.
2. The form of this piece is strophic.
3. He uses a major scale.
4. Several times during the song he uses a distinctive leap of a major fourth.
5. "When the Work's All Done This Fall" has a monophonic texture.

A group of jolly cowboys discussing plans at ease,
Says one "I'll tell you something, boys, if you will listen please;
I am an old cow-puncher, and here I'm dressed in rags,
I used to be a good one, boys, and go on them great jags."

"Well, I have got a home, boys, a good one you all know,
Although I have not seen it since long, long ago;
And I have got a mother who's waiting for me, that's all,
And I shall see my mother when the work's all done this fall."

That very night this cowboy went out to stand his guard,
The night was very dreary and stormin' very hard;
Them cattle they got frightened and rushed in wild stampede,
And he was a-tryin' to head them and turn them at full speed.

While ridin' in the darkness, and givin' the cattle call,
His saddle horse did stumble, boys, and on him he did fall;
Next morning we did find him, no hat upon his head,
We picked him up so gently, we thought the poor boy dead.

We carried him to the wagon and put him on his bed,
He opened wide his blue eyes, and this is what he said;
"I'll ne'er again go ridin', nor give the cattle call,
And I'll not go see my mother, when the work's all done this fall."

This selection was originally issued on Smithsonian Folkways 5723.

in the Saddle Again" and "Riding Down the Canyon," who initially mythologized and romanticized cowboys by way of the electronic media.

Autry's early career included a stint as a musician and comedian with Fields Brothers Marvelous Medicine Show and a relief telegraph operator. In 1929 he traveled to New York City and recorded for RCA Victor, Champion, and several other companies. Determined to stay in music, Autry returned to Tulsa and broadcast over KVOO as "Oklahoma's Singing Cowboy." His local popularity brought him to the attention of the American Record Company, which enabled him to move to the "National Barn Dance" on Chicago's WLS. On the strength of Autry's puckish good looks, the radio broadcasts, and his first hit record, *That Silver Haired Daddy of Mine*, Republic Pictures signed him to the movies. Gene Autry eventually made a fortune exploiting this image in films and on records and the radio. He eventually became the owner of the California Angels baseball team and a real estate magnate in the Los Angeles metropolitan area. In his final years Autry established a cowboy museum in Pasadena, California, which has emerged as a destination for fans of the Old West who come from across the world.

Autry's success in *Tumbling Tumbleweeds* and other grade B westerns helped to open the gates for others to follow and helped to solidify the connection between country music and a western image. This image remained strong for over twenty years. From Massachusetts to Oregon local country performers adopted names like "Tex" and wore bolo ties and cowboy boots. His or her backup musicians were likely to be called something like "the Lonesome Cowpunchers." The "western" conception in country music faded in the 1950s as Nashville's dominance of commercial country music rose. Nonetheless it was a powerful symbol that has not entirely dissipated.

Before Gene Autry and the other celluloid heroes, singing cowboys were really closer to the reality of rural life in the West, rather than the image of the West. Such songs were first written and sung by cowboys as they drove cattle, mended fences, branded calves, and did other related ranch work. By the 1890s cowboy songs began showing up in newspapers and magazines, often as a poem or a broadside, or in songbooks. They often appeared as ballads whose structure and melodies owed much to contemporary folk and popular tunes. In 1908 the

Gene Autry, circa 1940. Courtesy of the Southern Folklife Collection, The University of North Carolina at Chapel Hill.

first important printed collection, *Songs of the Cowboy*, by N. H. Thorp was published, which was followed almost immediately by John A. Lomax's seminal *Cowboy Songs and Other Frontier Ballads* (1910).

Some cowboy songs began life as printed poems that were eventually put to a familiar tune. Cowboy poetry, a related genre of oral folklore, has enjoyed a renaissance since the 1980s. Cowboy poetry gatherings have grown in size and now attract participants and audiences from around the country. Some cowboy poets are also singers, further blurring the lines between music and the spoken word.

Many cowboy songs, some of which are also Native American ballads, were composed between about 1880 and 1930. The genre became so well known that Tin Pan Alley composers (who are discussed in the next section) also began writing songs with cowboy motifs at the turn of the century. Some of the best-known cowboy songs, "Bury Me Not on the Lone Prairie," "The Dying Ranger," and "Home on the Range" were first heard in the middle nineteenth century. One of the classic cowboy songs, "Western Pioneer," apparently originated in the 1870s. Notice the opening lines, which use the standard formula so often heard in broadside and Native American ballads:

Come, give me your attention and see the right and the wrong.
It is a simple story and it won't detain you long;
I'll try to tell the reason why we are bound to roam,
And why we are so friendless and never have a home.

My home is in the saddle, upon a pony's back,
I am a roving cowboy and find the hostile track;
They say I am a sure shot, and danger I never knew;
But I often heard a story which I'll relate to you.

In eighteen hundred and sixty-three a little emigrant band
Was massacred by Indians, bound West by overland;
They scalped our noble soldiers, and the emigrants had to die,
And the living captives were two small girls and I.

We were rescued from the Indians by a brave and noble man,
Who trailed the thieving Indians and fought them hand to hand;
He was noted for his bravery while on an enemy's track;
He had a noble history, his name is Texas Jack.

Old Jack could tell a story, if he was only here,
Of the trouble and the hardships of the Western pioneer.
He would tell you how your fathers and mothers lost their lives.
And how our aged parents were scalped before our eyes.

I am a roving cowboy, I've worked upon the trail,
I've shot the shaggy buffalo and heard the coyote's wail;
I have slept upon my saddle, all covered by the moon;
I expect to keep it up, dear friends, until I meet my doom.

I am a roving cowboy, my saddle is my home,
And I'll always be a cowboy, no difference where I roam;
And like our noble heroes my help I'll volunteer,
And try to be of service to the Western pioneer.

Cowboy songs were among the first folk songs to be recorded in the 1920s. **Carl T. Sprague**, the "Original Singing Cowboy," was born near Houston in 1895 and grew up working on the family ranch. Sprague learned his music firsthand, although he later supplemented his repertoire through songs learned from *Cowboy Songs and Other Frontier Ballads*. At the age of thirty, after graduating from Texas A & M University, Sprague traveled to Camden, New Jersey, where he had arranged an audition with the Victor Company. These northern record executives were so impressed by Sprague that they immediately released "When the Work's All Done This Fall," which sold well over 100,000 copies in 1925/26. Sprague went on to record other popular cowboy songs for Victor, including "Utah Carroll," "The Last Great Round-up," "The Dying Cowboy," and "The Mormon Cowboy." Before long other "real" (i.e., working) cowboy singers such as the Cartwright Brothers, Goebel Reeves, Jules Verne Allen, J. D. Farley, and Billie Maxwell were also recording for Victor and Columbia.

There are still cowboy songs in the early twenty-first century. For some of today's fans, country music is cowboy music, but the older traditions can still be heard. Younger cowboys still learn some of their songs from older musicians and records, though the impact of Nashville songwriters must be given its due. A generation of western songsters born in the 1930s and 1940s, notably Michael Martin Murphy, Guy Clark, and Mike Williams, have helped to keep western themes in commercial country music.

There are even a small number of performers, such as ex-rodeo champion Chris Le Doux and Canadian Ian Tyson, who really worked as full-time cowboys in addition to their careers as singers. The legacy of the cowboy image in country music can also be seen in the almost ubiquitous use of western attire still worn by many country singers, few of whom have ever wrestled a calf to the ground or even been on a horse in their entire life. This public image, however, remains paramount to the reality of commercial country music in postmodern America.

TIN PAN ALLEY AND COUNTRY MUSIC TEXTS

The songs written by a group of late-nineteenth-century American composers touched the repertoires of many Americans, including those rural musicians who pioneered the country music industry. By the last two decades of the nineteenth century popular music had become a big business fueled by a new and aggressive cadre of publishers. Some of the songwriters also published their own material; others hired performers to plug their songs to a mass market. In this age just before the dawn of the commercial record industry, sheet-music sales not only affected the dissemination of new popular songs but were also the measure of a song's success. Sheet music was the main product of the music industry and its goal was sales. These songwriters become known as **Tin Pan Alley** craftsmen, named after a mythical New York City back alley where these songs were cranked out.

The songs of the Tin Pan Alley composers deeply affected the first generation of commercial country artists, born near the close of the nineteenth century

"Wednesday Night Waltz." Courtesy of Kip Lornell.

and recorded before the Depression. These included Ernest V. Stoneman, the Carter Family, and Vernon Dalhart. The Tin Pan Alley songs of writers like Bob Miller, who composed new pseudo-country disaster ballads like "The Crime of Harry Powers," "1930 Drought," and "Wreck of the N & W Cannon Ball," became part of their everyday repertoire. Such singers emerged from the first generation to grow up with Tin Pan Alley songs. These sentimental, innocent, often heart-touching stories flowed from the pens of professional songwriters and touched Americans from all classes and regional lines.

Paul Dresser, brother of the highly regarded novelist Theodore Dreiser, qualifies as an important early member of this songwriting fraternity. A failure in the music publishing business, Dresser began his show business career with a minstrel show stint during Reconstruction. He settled in New York City, eventually writing such successes as "The Letter that Never Came," "Just Tell Them That You Saw Me," and "My Gal Sal." The words and music for dozens of patriotic, funny, and topical ditties flowed from his pen before his death in 1906 at the age of forty-nine.

Charles K. Harris (1867–1930) remains one of the most prolific and well-respected members of the early Tin Pan Alley writers. In 1885 he plunged into the songwriting profession in Milwaukee after boldly hanging out the shingle "Songs Written to Order." His first major success, "After the Ball," arrived after the song was included in the hit musical revue, "A Trip to Chinatown." "After the Ball" eventually brought thousands of dollars into the coffers of Harris's publishing firm, which went on to open New York and Chicago offices. Harris's prolific pen produced "'Mid the Green Fields of Virginia," "Hello Central, Give Me Heaven," "Break the News to Mother," and scores of others.

These songs, along with the work of **Harry von Tilzer**, who wrote "Goodbye Liza Jane" and "I Want a Girl Just Like the One that Married Dear Old Dad," later turned up in the repertoires of hillbilly groups—the Carter Family, the Delmore Brothers, Walter "Kid" Smith, and countless others. This early generation of recording artists venerated the innocence, pastoral vision, and maudlin simplicity of "Little Old Log Cabin in the Lane," "Nobody's Darling on Earth," "I'll Remember You, Love, in My Prayers," "The Little Rosewood Casket," "In the Baggage Coach Ahead," and "The Letter Edged in Black." Their importance to white audiences is underscored by the frequency with which these songs appeared in the early record catalogs of the hillbilly artists. It is no accident, I suspect, that the first acknowledged country music recording, "Little Log Cabin in the Lane" by Fiddlin' John Carson in 1923, fits into this category. The song itself was published by William Shakespeare Hays in 1871, only three years after Carson's birth.

ERNEST STONEMAN'S REPERTOIRE

Ernest V. Stoneman, one of the pioneering commercial country music artists, was born in Carroll County, Virginia, in 1888. A musician such as Stoneman certainly enjoyed these songs, which had been circulated by way of sheet music and cylinders for better than twenty-five years before his own recording debut in 1924. Not surprisingly he chose a topical disaster ballad, "The Titanic," for his debut. A retelling of the famous sinking of the world-class ocean liner that occurred one dozen years before, it is deliciously ironic that this famous "folk artist" learned his version from a published source. In later years Stoneman recalls that he obtained the words for "The Titanic" from a poem published in a newspaper. But he then told American music expert Dick Spottswood that the lyrics came from a contemporaneous folk song collection, *Folk-Songs of the South*, published by West Virginia folklorist John Cox. The truth remains unclear.

The fact remains that this early country music artist from the backwoods of the Blue Ridge Mountains was clearly moved by the sentimental songs that he heard all around him. Stoneman truly enjoyed these songs, and his early recorded repertoire is peppered with nostalgic, gently ironic songs. During the first few months of his recording career he waxed versions of "Give My Love to Nell" (William Gray, 1894), "The Lightning Express" (Helf and Moran, 1898), and "The Dying Girl's Farewell" (J. D. Patton, 1894). He also recorded another topical ballad, "Wreck on the C & O"; it too came from the pages of Professor Cox's book.

Stoneman's 1920s repertoire is filled with these older songs from written and oral tradition. His second Asheville, North Carolina, session (April 1926) illustrates these influences. He included a cowboy ballad, "The Texas Ranger," learned from two neighbors, Bertha and Myrtle Hawks, who may have ultimately picked it up from John Lomax's cowboy song collection (Lomax, 1910). "The Religious Critic," a gently sardonic song about religious hypocrisy, later became better known as "S-A-V-E-D," while the comic Tin Pan Alley ditty "When Will My Wife Return to Me" came from the pen of Charles D. Vann in 1889. Two pieces of sentimental American Victoriana, "Sweet Kitty Wells" (1860) and "In the Shadow of the Pine" (1895), were sandwiched between a turn-of-the-century lament "The Orphan Girl" and a railroad song "Asleep at the Switch." Evidence of the impact of the rapidly growing record industry is illustrated by Stoneman's "covering" of popular disks by other artists. He waxed his version of Charlie Poole's commercially and artistically successful "Don't Let Your Deal Go Down," several month's after Columbia released the original. This trend portended the future, for in his next session Stoneman reworked two of Texas artist Carl T. Sprague's popular Victor recordings, "Bad Companions" and "When the Work's All Done This Fall."

Despite this varied repertoire, Stoneman's performance style was fairly conservative. His family was steeped in a tradition of playing stringed instruments for themselves and at local parties. The importance of string band music in this social fabric is underscored by Burton Stoneman's (born 1881) comments during a 1941 Library of Congress interview:

> We'd go to places, gatherin's, have a good time, all play music; people'd all go home, everybody'd be satisfied, friendly . . . I recollect you'd go to a party and they'd bring it [whiskey] in a bucket with a dipper in it, set it on a table. People'd come in with their music—banjo and fiddle—that was mostly all they had in that day and time.
>
> I never seen a guitar till I was about twelve years old, I reckon. Just a fiddle and banjo was all we had . . . They'd dance, they'd fiddle, they'd dance, every-body'd go peaceable . . . never have no disturbances at all in them days when I was a small boy. (Tribe 1993, 28)

THE FATHER OF BLUEGRASS

But by far the most influential brothers group, **Bill Monroe** (born September 13, 1911) and his older brothers Charlie and Birch, began playing together as children in western Kentucky. They heard the traditional fiddle tunes, learned shape note hymns, came under the sway of local old-time musicians, and purchased the latest hillbilly records by Jimmie Rodgers and the Carter Family. One of Bill's earliest direct mentors, Arnold Schultz, an African American fiddle and guitar player, left a deep impression on the fledgling mandolin player. Monroe's father died when Bill was young so he went to live with his uncle Pen Vandiver, who profoundly affected Bill as a role model for life and secondarily for his fiddle playing. The well-known "Uncle Pen" is named for Vandiver, who himself passed away in 1933.

By the late 1920s all three brothers had migrated to Detroit in search of more lucrative employment. Their love of music moved north, too. Birch, Charlie, and Bill slid into a semiprofessional musical career in the early 1930s as an adjunct to jobs in the ailing industrial plants. Unlike Stoneman, the Monroes found and thrived on radio work. Between 1932 and 1934 they played a string of radio jobs and show dates in metropolitan Chicago. The trio's music reached large audiences during this tenure; their 1932 WLS (the Sears-owned, Worlds Largest Station) broadcasts reached much of the United States at night because of its 50,000-watt signal.

By 1934 they had left Chicago and turned to full-time music making on radio and the vaudeville stage. This grim time of unemployment, migration to the land of "milk and honey" (California), and its resulting social upheaval proved relatively easy for the Monroes because of their steady work on radio stations in Shennandoah, Iowa, and Omaha, Nebraska. The sponsorship of a cathartic formula, Texas Crystals, underwrote most of their midwestern radio air time. By this time the brothers were reduced by one when Birch decided to stay at a newly found refinery job that brought in steady income to help support the rest of the family.

The year 1935 found them closer to home, wandering among radio stations in North and South Carolina. Bill and Charlie worked as a brother duet, with a sound akin to the Blue Sky Boys (Bill and Earl Bolick). The Bolicks, too, played guitar and mandolin, emphasized empathetic harmony singing, and favored sentimental and sacred songs. But the Monroes were innovators—they played at faster tempos, while Bill's exciting mandolin style demonstrated that it could handle the chores as a lead instrument. Their tight harmonies featuring Charlie's high, piercing lead and Bill's tenor voice supported by a highly integrated mandolin/guitar backup didn't sound quite like anyone else. Their repertoire was not nearly as creative—a durable mixture of religious tunes or already established favorites. Nonetheless, they imbued "Roll in My Sweet Baby's Arms," "He Will Set Your Fields on Fire," "Weeping Willow Tree," "The Saints Go Marching In," and "Darling Corey" with a unique fervor and tenderness.

Some of these Carolina Piedmont and Appalachian mountain bands also included a three-finger picked banjo, an element critical to the development of **bluegrass**. This basic regional style was first documented in the middle to late 1920s on country music records by Charlie Poole and the North Carolina Ramblers and Jack Reedy and his Walker Mountain Stringband. During the middle

1930s "Snuffy" Jenkins was the acknowledged king of the modern Carolina banjo pickers, due in large part to his appearances on the "Crazy Water Crystals Barn Dance" radio shows broadcast over Charlotte's WBT. Jenkin's forward-looking banjo work was often paired with the fiddle of Homer "Pappy" Sherrill during broadcasts and on show dates. These musicians, along with other modernists like J. E. Mainer's Mountaineers (Asheville) and the Washboard Wonders (Charlotte), influenced musicians throughout the Carolinas. They helped to reshape the older string band tradition into a new form that slowly inched its way toward bluegrass. Bill and Charlie Monroe soon integrated themselves into this same circuit; their music quickly became assimilated by local musicians and fans.

Their first encounter with the twentieth century's other important electronic medium occurred on February 17, 1936, when veteran A & R man Eli Oberstein interrupted a Charlotte, North Carolina, recording session by Fiddlin' Arthur Smith and the Delmore Brothers to fit in Bill and Charlie. Busy with radio work and unexcited by the prospect of lackluster record sales, the Monroe Brothers first turned Oberstein down. A telephone call finally convinced the duo to try, and every five or six months thereafter Victor brought them into the studio for a Bluebird session that came out like clockwork. These highly successful records concertized the Monroe Brothers sound, enabling fans and musicians to study their musical vision.

Only a breakup of the duet in 1938 stopped their successful recording string. Both men were proud, creative, and stubborn. Possessed by mercurial tempers, they clashed once too often and Bill went off on his own in search of an expanded musical vision that he could not achieve with Charlie. Bill's peripatetic search lead him across the South: Little Rock, Atlanta, and back to the Carolinas. In 1939 Bill found himself in Greenville, South Carolina, with Cleo Davis (guitar) and Art Wooden (fiddle), carefully remolding his sound. Bill calculatingly and unceasingly instructed both musicians. For many weeks they worked to perfect their instrumental roles to coincide with Monroe's vision of a small string music ensemble.

With the addition of Amos Garen as a lead singer for sacred quartet singing, Monroe covered the religious field as well. This part of his repertoire was inspired by popular black Carolina-based gospel quartets such as the Heavenly Gospel Singers and the Golden Gate Jubilee Quartet as well as their white counterparts like the numerous groups sponsored by the Stamps-Baxter Publishing Company. The bluegrass gospel that developed also owes an obvious debt to revival hymns and the shape note tradition. It is a unique synthesis that exploits the unconventional (for common-practice western art music theory) harmonies found in shape note books and utilizes the syncopation, ornamented slides, and tonal possibilities suggested by black singers to create a tense, high-pitched vocal quartet. In the middle 1980s bluegrass gospel quartets underwent a moderate renaissance due in part to the renewed interest in black gospel quartets. Inspired by a cappella black quartets such as the Harps of Melody and the Gospel Writers and their own reverence for the early Monroe recordings, contemporary groups like Doyle Lawson and Quicksilver and the Nashville Bluegrass Band included even more quartet selections as part of their everyday repertoire.

Just as the leaves turned golden and red in 1939 Bill felt his new band was ready. Armed with the new Blue Grass Boys moniker they traveled west, headed for Nashville and a Grand Ole Opry audition. The Blue Grass Boys caused an instant sensation in Nashville, winning immediate acclaim. Their WSM broadcasts brought in a veritable flood of show date requests; soon they were performing across the entire South. Based in Nashville, the band went through several personnel changes prior to its first recording session in October 1940. Georgia native Tommy Magness joined as the fiddler, Clyde Moody replaced Davis, and comedian Cousin Wilbur (Willie Westbrooks) joined the Blue Grass Boys as its bass player. Such personnel alterations became standard for the Blue Grass Boys, for its grueling travel schedule and Monroe's often temperamental leadership resulted in frequent changes.

Despite Bill Monroe's prominence and innovation in the field, several other bands were also on the cutting edge in the earliest days of bluegrass. Significantly, all of these groups had strong roots or ties to western North Carolina. Roy Hall and the Blue Ridge Entertainers and J. E. Mainer's Mountaineers had each worked on WWNC in Asheville, North Carolina, before moving on to new territory. Their sound on 1940 recordings was not too far removed from Monroe's, though it was clearly not bluegrass in the classic sense.

In 1941 the Blue Grass Boys returned to Atlanta for an important session, very close to the music that Monroe would be playing in ten years. Tuned a half-step above standard pitch, Monroe's band sounded flashier and brighter than even one year before. His standard repertoire shaped the session, which included one certifiable classic, "The Orange Blossom Special." It is a masterful performance with elements of comedy in its dialogue, duet singing, and the precise, flashy fiddling of Art Wooten. The lack of a five-string banjo is the only missing element from the standard instrumentation.

In an effort to get as many people under one roof at a time (due to gas rationing and other related constraints), the war years were spent touring as packaged tent shows with other Opry performers. Monroe's band soon split off on its own with a small, well-rounded tent show featuring comedy, religious quartet singing, fiddle tunes, and even a baseball game with members of the Blue Grass Boys challenging local clubs. Monroe's musical life continued to prosper following the cessation of World War II. The sheer volume of live performances soared with dates as far flung as northern Florida, Ontario, Canada, and Tulsa,

ANGLO-AMERICAN SECULAR FOLK MUSIC

Bill Monroe performing on the "Grand Old Opry," circa 1947. Courtesy of the Ralph Rinzler Folklife Archives and Collections, Center for Folklife and Cultural Heritage, Smithsonian Institution.

Oklahoma. Records for Columbia and Decca kept the Blue Grass Boys in the public's ear.

Late in 1946 Earl Scruggs joined the band, bringing his three-finger banjo roll to the Blue Grass Boys. This final link provided the Blue Grass Boys with the quintessential bluegrass instrumentation and performance styles. Their Columbia records from the early Scruggs and Lester Flatt period are the first instantly recognizable bluegrass records: "Mother's Only Sleeping" and "Blue Moon of Kentucky" remain two of the finest examples. In the ensuing five years, Monroe went on to record many fine examples of traditional bluegrass that are now recognized as classic performances of American music.

Monroe's dynamic new sound proclaimed a bold move into new musical territory. Partly because he sought individual variety within the band itself, the Blue Grass Boys occasionally echoed the ensemble sound of classic New Orleans jazz ensembles like King Oliver's Creole Jazz Band. The Blue Grass Boys' rhythmic feeling also reflected a black influence, especially in the up-tempo 2/4 tunes that at times sound dangerously close to the popular swing bands of the

Flatt and Scruggs poster, circa 1960. Courtesy of the Ralph Rinzler Folklife Archives and Collections, Center for Folklife and Cultural Heritage, Smithsonian Institution.

day. Unlike the other hillbilly bands at that time, Monroe allowed (even encouraged) his musicians to solo. Robert Cantwell describes taped performances of Monroe's first true bluegrass band as they appeared on the Grand Ole Opry in 1945 and 1946:

> [It was] a wildly accelerated, almost violently high-pitched frenzy of mountain music, one which while treading very close to the edge of the bizarre displays an incredible virtuosity which audiences in those days saw, and were plainly encouraged to see, as a prodigy. With Monroe's voice blasting like an air-raid siren and Scruggs' banjo hurrying forward on ten thousand wheels, that band came at you like the Normandy invasion. (Cantwell 1984, 76)

Some of the other first-generation bluegrass artists were not far behind the Blue Grass Boys, both in artistic and commercial terms. The fertile tri-state area where Tennessee, Virginia, and North Carolina meet produced many of the best early bluegrass bands. Curly King and the Tennessee Hilltoppers and the Stanley Brothers and the Clinch Mountain Boys worked this area, gaining prominence by way of their broadcasts over Bristol, Tennessee's, WCYB. They were also assisted by the emergence of the postwar independent record companies. Mr. King worked with King Records of Cincinnati, Ohio, while Rich-R-Tone (Kingsport, Tennessee) helped bolster the Stanleys' career. The Briarhopper's

MUSICAL EXAMPLE

Red Allen is one of the many bluegrass musicians who was born and raised in the heart of bluegrass country, Kentucky. He started played this music following World War II and has enjoyed a long professional and semiprofessional career, recording on numerous occasions. This version of Flatt and Scruggs's classic "Darlin' Corey" was recorded in the middle 1970s with a strong group that included several relatives and the ace fiddler, Vassar Clements.

Title "Dig a Hole in the Meadow" (or "Darlin' Corey")
Performers Red Allen & Friends
Instruments Red Allen, guitar and vocals; Marty Stuart, mandolin; Vassar Clements, fiddle; Terry Smith, bass; Harley Allen, vocals; Greg Allen, vocals
Length 2:20

Musical Characteristics
1. The instrumentation is for a "classic" bluegrass band.
2. Note the high-pitched vocals, especially the "high" tenor vocal on the chorus.
3. Its texture is basically homophonic and becomes richer as the various instruments are added near the beginning.
4. This song is performed in a minor key.
5. On several occasions improvised "breaks" or "leads" are taken by fiddle and mandolin.
6. It is performed in highly regular, duple meter (2/4) time.

This version initially came out on Smithsonian Folkways 31088. Copyright issues do not permit the reproduction of the song lyrics here.

Band in Charlotte pioneered bluegrass in Piedmont, North Carolina, by way of WBT's 50,000 watts of power and the Cowboy Record Company. Lester Flatt and Earl Scruggs left Monroe and by 1948 quickly landed a Columbia contract that led to many strong recordings.

By 1950 this music could be heard across the South. It remained a genre of country music without a clear identity of its own. Country music itself was becoming increasingly bland as Nashville emerged as the potent force in driving country music to its present polished, rather homogenized, state. The Blue Grass Boys were the only group exploiting the Kentucky nickname and "bluegrass" was not widely applied to the genre. Nonetheless this first generation of bluegrass musicians left a marked impact upon Anglo-American traditions and, consequently, commercial country music. Hundreds of bands were playing this music, and its impact had spread far beyond its hearth area, spilling across the entire South and into the Midwest. Surprisingly, the word "bluegrass" does not seem to have gained favor until the early to middle 1950s when it began to be applied to this music. No one knows exactly when this occurred, but by 1956 it was used in print.

Today bluegrass musicians are found across the world. They play at festivals, record for both major and independent labels, and have spawned creative forms. Other musicians who began in bluegrass eventually proved to be innovators in country music. By the early 1960s Bill Keith and Bobby Thompson had begun playing intricate, chromatic melodies on the banjo, while Tony Rice and Clarence White's single-string, lead guitar work inspired a new generation of bluegrass musicians. Some bluegrass groups added a dobro to their band. These creative musicians kept many of the basic elements of bluegrass, but they spawned groups that played "New Grass," "Progressive Bluegrass," and even "Dawg" music—a jazz/bluegrass fusion pioneered by David Grisman in the middle 1970s. Despite these changes all bluegrass performers pay homage to its progenitor, the late Bill Monroe, acknowledging his role as its king. See the final chapter of this book for a study of bluegrass music in Washington, D.C.

HONKY-TONK

Just as bluegrass began a slow rise to nationwide acceptance outside of its southern hearth area, the last two grassroots forms of twentieth century Anglo-American country music (honky-tonk and rockabilly) emerged. Bluegrass has basically remained conservative in its instrumentation, repertoire, and worldview. Hard-core bluegrass musicians eschew amplified instruments, revere Bill Monroe's pioneering work, and are loath to add instruments beyond the basic five—guitar, banjo, mandolin, fiddle, and string bass.

In contrast, **honky-tonk** rose out of the fecund Lone Star State with an unfettered view toward the commercial marketplace. Honky-tonk updated the values found in earlier commercial country music and reflected the slow merging of regional styles into the national, anonymous country music sound churned out in today's Nashville studios. Its roots lie in the western swing bands of the mid- to late 1930s whose noisy beerhall workplaces invited musicians like Rex Griffin, Floyd Tillman, Moon Mullican, and Ernest Tubb to write songs about drinking, extramarital love, and divorce. Similar themes could be found in both black and white rural music, but honky-tonk songs almost celebrated the dissolution of the family unit and the strains on traditional American values. Honky-tonk's beat was as well defined as its working-class values: live hard and get your pleasure where you can.

The quintessential honky-tonk hit of the early 1940s, Al Dexter's "Pistol Packin' Mama," stayed on jukeboxes throughout the country for several years. Beer-drinking music lovers might then drop their nickels in the slot to hear Merle Travis's "Divorce Me COD" or Ted Daffen's "Born to Lose." These musicians paved the road for **Hank Williams** and the Drifting Cowboys, whose music often topped the country music charts between 1949 and 1952. Williams's fidelity to a honky-tonk lifestyle is reflected in his own turbulent marriages, chronic bouts with alcoholism, frequent emotional upheavals, and his tempestuous relationships with the management of the Grand Ole Opry and an important Shreveport radio program, "Louisiana Hayride." Honky-tonk music continued to roll through the 1950s with Texans Ray Price and George Jones carrying the torch, while more recent exponents include Buck Owens, Gary Stewart, and Joe Ely. In the late 1990s, Garth Brooks, another neotraditionalist with strong roots in honky-tonk, revitalized the world of country music and also enjoyed widespread commercial exposure as his music crossed over to the pop field as well. George Strait is another commercially successful artist with a strong sense of history.

WESTERN SWING

Honky-tonk drew much of its strength from another southwestern phenomenon, **western swing**, one of the most interesting and diverse American musical hybrids. Long a cultural crossroads, Texas birthed western swing in the early 1930s. It looked toward the string bands and Norteno music of Mexico as well as the German American communities of the hill country near Austin and San Antonio. The blues and jazz influence came from black musicians and the popular swing bands. Combine these influences with cowboy songs and fiddle tunes and you get western swing.

Bob Wills remains the undisputed king of this genre. He pioneered western swing, and his first band was a small late-1920s hillbilly outfit, the Wills Fiddle Band. By 1931 they became known as the Light Crust Doughboys, named in honor of their radio sponsor Light Crust Flour. The band slowly expanded its size and scope, along with its local popularity. In 1933 the band became known as Bob Wills and his Texas Playboys, complete with string bass, tenor banjo, and piano. This expansion reflects their affinity for swing music and a desire for increased musical flexibility. Shortly thereafter the Wills band shifted from Waco, Texas, to Tulsa, Oklahoma, where they remained until 1941.

About 1933 Milton Brown and his Musical Brownies emerged from a minor schism in the Bob Wills band. Using Fort Worth as his base, Brown toured Texas playing for dances. Fiddler Cliff Bruner, steel player Bob Dunn, and tenor banjoist Ocie Stockard emerged as the band's leading instrumentalists with improvised solos that impressed their fellow musicians. Their broadcasts and Decca records reached a large audience before the group disbanded following a traffic accident that killed Milton Brown in April of 1936.

The mid-1930s repertoire of Bob Wills and his Texas Playboys reveals the breadth of western swing's most influential band. Their 1935 and 1936 ARC (Columbia) records demonstrate their catholic approach to music: "I Can't Give You Anything but Love," "Oklahoma Rag," "Just Friends," "Mexicali Rose," "There's a Quaker Girl in Old Quaker Town," and "Get Along Home Cindy." But above all were their interpretations of black blues, especially the light-hearted double-entendre songs taken from records by Tampa Red, Big Bill, Frankie Jaxon, Memphis Minnie, and others: "Fan It," "No Matter How She Done It," "What's the Matter with the Mill?" and "Sitting on Top of the World." This strong dose of the blues underscores not only the influence of the mass media upon Wills but also his love for black music.

By the late 1930s the more free-spirited western swing bands included a complement of horn and reed players in the groups. Inspired by the success of Tommy Dorsey, Benny Goodman, and Glen Miller, western swing bands began using jazz-influenced musicians who soloed over the pulsing 2/4 meter provided by the rhythm section. The orchestras led by African American band leaders like Duke Ellington, Count Basie, Jimmie Lunceford, and Fletcher Henderson also informed Wills. Their vocalist, Tommy Duncan, could croon with the best of the big band singers.

Only Texas in the 1930s could produce bands such as Adolph Hofner's, led by an accordion-playing Czech American. Another San Antonio band, the Tune Wranglers, recorded popular tunes such as "Texas Sand" that further underscore the identification these musicians hold with the Lone Star State. Dallas was home to Roy Newman and his Boys, another jazz-influenced group that woodshedded with black jazz records before recording "Tin Roof Blues," "Sadie Green, the Vamp from New Orleans," and "Tiger Rag." Gene Sullivan, Newman's prized singer, later teamed with Wiley Walker to form one of the more enduring pop/country vocal teams of the 1940s.

East Texas western swing groups mingled with other artists who combined Cajun music with country sounds. Cliff Bruner played out of Beaumont, Texas, on the edge of Cajun country. He helped bring country swing into Louisiana, inspiring Leo Soileau to form his Cajun swing band, the Four Aces. The Rayne-Bo and Hackberry Ramblers followed Soileau in mixing blues, swing, and hillbilly with Cajun two-steps.

ANGLO-AMERICAN SECULAR FOLK MUSIC

Clarence Ashley, one of the tri-state's best old-time banjo players and singers (1961). Bob Yellin photo courtesy of the Ralph Rinzler Folklife Archives and Collections, Center for Folklife and Cultural Heritage, Smithsonian Institution.

Bob Wills's impact was felt nationwide, but the Sons of the Pioneers (a swing-influenced cowboy singing band) proved to be nearly as influential. This small ensemble brought cowboy swing to the entire country by way of their syndicated radio programs and an extensive recording career that began in the middle 1930s. The Farr Brothers (Hugh and Karl) and Bob Nolan forged a unique string band that eschewed horns in favor of virtuoso musicianship and nostalgic songs about cowboy life. This irresistible blend also helped to establish a movie career that saw them on the screen with Tom Mix, Hopalong Cassidy, and Gene Autry. The Sons of the Pioneers—who often performed with Roy Rogers—were moved by the duets by the French gypsy guitarist Django Rheinhart and his fiddle-playing partner Stephan Grappelli. These wonderful improvised swing recordings are still regarded as jazz classics. It is ironic that French musicians playing swing music should exert such a strong influence over a group of western singers—a global musical village decades before the concept became fashionable.

Western swing continued as a strong regional tradition well into the early 1950s, when rock 'n' roll hit the Texas airways. This music undergoes periodic revivals, and Wills's name remains magical in Texas despite his death in 1975. The eventual dissemination of western swing beyond its Texas/Oklahoma

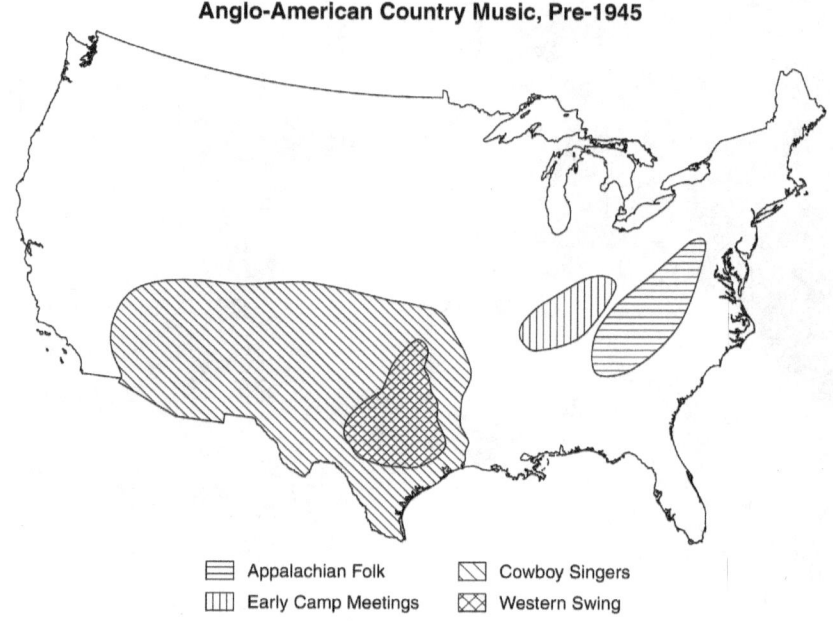

Anglo-American Country Music, Pre-1945

- Appalachian Folk
- Early Camp Meetings
- Cowboy Singers
- Western Swing

birthplace suggests the importance of cultural geography in understanding American vernacular music. Both western swing and bluegrass rather quickly emerged from their hearth areas, moving out across the entire country. Bob Wills, along with other western swing band leaders like Spade Cooley, found enough transplanted Texans in California to relocate his band there in 1946. Significantly, he did not move to Marquette, Michigan, or Miami, Florida, in search of an audience to support his music. When people move, their love of regional music, food, and expressions migrates with them.

FINAL THOUGHTS

Anglo-American folk music forms the basis for today's commercial country music. British and Native American balladry paved the way for the storytelling aspect of Nashville's songwriters. The evolution of folk music into commercial music is illustrated by the popularity of western swing and honky-tonk in the 1940s and 1950s. Some musicians, such as Ernest Stoneman, who began as "folk," ended up as part of the world of commercial country music. This process underscores the ongoing interaction between popular and folk music that marks our postmodern world.

ANGLO-AMERICAN SECULAR FOLK MUSIC

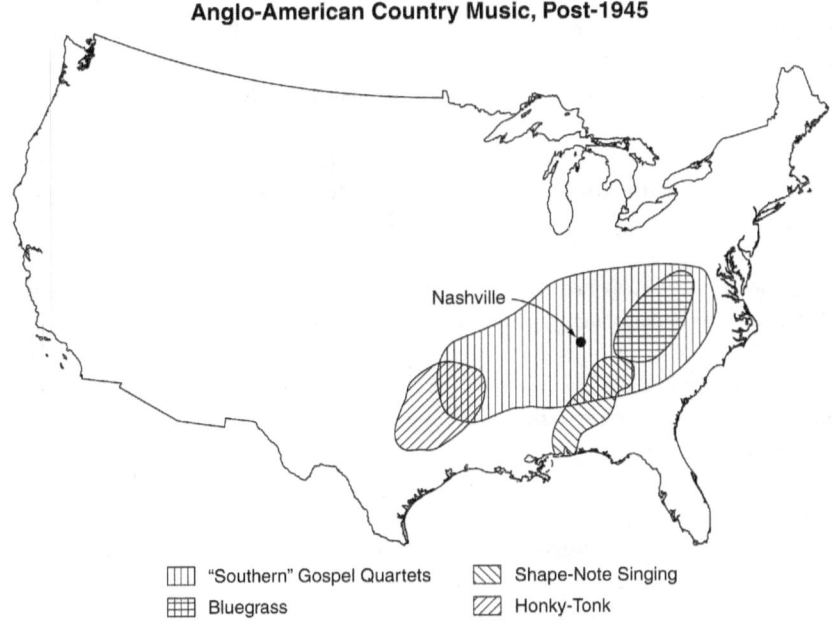

KEY FIGURES AND TERMS

Gene Autry
bluegrass
broadsides
Child ballads
"come ye all"
cowboy singers
honky-tonk
G. Malcolm Laws
leaping and lingering
lyric songs

Bill Monroe
Native American ballads
Carl T. Sprague
Ernest V. Stoneman
Harry von Tilzer
Tin Pan Alley
variant
western swing
Hank Williams
Bob Wills

SUGGESTED LISTENING

Dock Boggs. *His Folkways Years, 1963–1968*. Smithsonian Folkways 40108. These two compact discs contain all of the 1960s performances by this staunchly iconoclastic, important southwestern Virginia banjo-playing songster.

ANGLO-AMERICAN SECULAR FOLK MUSIC

Woody Guthrie. *The Asch Recordings*, 4 vols. Smithsonian Folkways 40100-03. These four compact discs contain some of Guthrie's best-known and rollicking performances, such as "This Land Is Your Land" and "Hard Travelin'," from the late 1930s through the 1940s—the prime of his career. Each disc comes with a detailed booklet.

The Lilly Brothers and Don Stover. *Bluegrass at the Roots, 1961*. Smithsonian Folkways SFW40158. Particularly strong recordings by one of the best second generation bluegrass bands.

Uncle Dave Macon. *Early Recordings*. County 521. This set includes some of Macon's finest solo and group performances from the 1920s and 1930s.

Bill Monroe. *The Music of Bill Monroe from 1936-1944*. MCA MCAD4-11048. This set of four compact discs, along with the fine booklet, offers the best and most affordable view of Monroe's early career.

Almeda Riddle. *Ballads and Hymns from the Ozarks*. Rounder 0017. This album surveys Riddle's vast repertoire of Native American and British ballads.

Jimmie Rodgers. *First Sessions—1927/28*. Rounder 1056. The first in a comprehensive series that reissues all of the recordings by America's "blue yodeler."

Pete Seeger. *Darling Corey and Goofing off Suite*. Smithsonian Folkways 40018. Two of Seeger's earliest (and important) 10" albums are found here on one compact disc.

Bob Wills. *Anthology: 1935-1976*. Rhino 70744. A first-rate sampling of Wills's important and influential western swing.

Various. 16 *Down Home Country Classics*. Arhoolie CD 110. This sampler of the Arhoolie catalogue includes Rose Maddox, Sam McGee, Del McCoury, and the Carter Family.

Various. *Back in the Saddle Again*. New World 80314. This nicely conceived, two-compact-disc package includes early recordings by Gene Autry, Patsy Montana, Carl T. Sprague, Jimmie Rodgers, Girls of the Golden West, and others.

Various. *Brave Boys: New England Traditions in Folk Music*. New World 80239. A well-balanced selection of instrumental selections, ballads, and lyric folk songs, many of which can be traced directly to the British Isles.

Various. *Classic Bluegrass from Smithsonian Folkways*. Smithsonian Folkways SFW40092. A very nice sampling of the Folkways catalogue, which is particularly strong for the 1960s performances by Red Allen, the Friendly City Playboys, and Roger Sprung.

Various. *Classic Mountain Songs from Smithsonian Folkways*. Smithsonian Folkways SFW40094. Another solid release in the "Classic" series that includes the usual suspects, including Pop Stoneman, Wade Ward, Olla Belle Reed, and Dock Boggs.

Various. *Cowboy Songs on Folkways*. Smithsonian Folkways 40043. An anthology that encompasses some of the best performances from its vast catalogue, including older-style ballads.

Various. Native Virginia Ballads. Global Village/BRI 004. This fine collection of Native American/native Virginia ballads taken from early commercial as well as field recordings comes from a comprehensive booklet.

Various. *Old Love Songs and Ballads from the Big Laurel, North Carolina*. Smithsonian Folkways 2309. These solo, a cappella vocals cover a wide range of material, including both Native American and British ballads.

SUGGESTED READING

Simon Bronner. *Old-Time Music Makers of New York State*. New York: Syracuse University Press, 1987. A folklorist's view of the varied musical culture of twentieth-century hillbilly music in up-state New York.

Bertrand Bronson. *The Ballad As Song*. Berkeley and Los Angeles: University of California Press, 1969. The regional collection of Frank C. Brown (North Carolina), Cecil Sharpe's southern explorations, and others are the subjects of Bronson's insightful essays.

T. P. Coffin (with Roger Renwick). *The British Traditional Ballad in North America*, 3rd edition. Philadelphia: University of Pennsylvania Press, 1977. The classic study of this genre.

Norm Cohen. *Long Steel Rail*. Urbana: University of Illinois Press, 1981. The book's subtitle, "The Railroad in American Folksong," sums up the focus of this exhaustive study, which contains many Native American ballads.

Diane Dugaw, ed. *The Anglo-American Ballad: A Folklore Casebook*. New York: Garland, 1995. A lengthy study of the development of balladry and the study of ballads in the United States.

Carl Fleischhauer and Neil V. Rosenberg. *Bluegrass Odyssey: A Documentary in Pictures and Words, 1966-86*. Urbana: University of Illinois Press, 2007. A lovely blend of great photos and insightful writings about this distinctive musical form.

Cary Ginnell (with Roy Lee Brown). *Milton Brown and the Founding of Western Swing*. Urbana: University of Illinois Press, 1993. Ginnell focuses on the beginnings of western swing in central Texas during the early to middle 1930s.

Thomas Goldsmith. *The Bluegrass Reader*. Urbana: University of Illinois Press, 2004. Editor Goldsmith has assembled an excellent sampling of the writings about bluegrass and presents them in roughly chronological order.

Archie Green. *Only a Miner*. Urbana: University of Illinois Press, 1972. The approaches of musicology, literary studies, anthropology, and folklore inform this unique study of mining songs.

Guy Logsdon. *"The Whorehouse Bells Were Ringing" and Other Songs Cowboys Sing*. Urbana: University of Illinois Press, 1990. A very personal yet scholarly view of cowboy songs in the early to mid-twentieth century.

Bill Malone. *Country Music, U.S.A.*, rev. edition. Austin: University of Texas Press, 1985. The breadth of this genre is covered in this broad and masterly survey.

Kristine M. McCusker. *Lonesome Cowgirls and Honky-Tonk Angels*. Urbana: University of Illinois Press, 2008. The author profiles five artists, including the Girls of the Golden West and Rosa Lee Maphis, who helped shape the sound of country music in the 1930s through the 1950s.

Marty McGee. *Traditional Musicians of the Central Blue Ridge: Old Time, Early Country, Folk and Bluegrass Label Recording Artists, With Discographies*. Jefferson, NC: McFarland Press, 2000. Another of those titles that summarizes the book's scope and content.

W. K. McNeil. *Southern Folk Ballads*, 2 vols. Little Rock, AR: August House, 1987, 1988. These two volumes constitute a fine overview of this field, including Cajun and Tex-Mex material.

Nolan Porterfield. *Jimmie Rodgers: The Life and Times of America's Blue Yodler*. Urbana: University of Illinois Press, 1979). A richly rewarding study of this influential country singer.

Neil V. Rosenberg. *Bluegrass: A History* (20th Anniversary Edition). Urbana: University of Illinois Press, 2005. The most complete and well-balanced history of the genre.

Neil V. Rosenberg and Charles K. Wolfe. *The Music of Bill Monroe*. Urbana: University of Illinois Press, 2007. This masterful examination of the recorded legacy left to us by the founder of bluegrass was written by two of the best in the field.

ANGLO-AMERICAN SECULAR FOLK MUSIC

Dick Spottswood. *Banjo on the Mountain: Wade Mainer's First Hundred Years*. Jackson: University Press of Mississippi, 2010. Chockful of photographs and illustrations, the author provides a biography of this important banjo player based on Mainer's own words.

Ivan Tribe. *The Stonemans*. Urbana: Unviersity of Illinois Press, 1993. A solidly researched history of this important musical family, which helped introduce bluegrass to our nation's capital.

John Wright. *Traveling This Highway Home: Ralph Stanley and the World of Traditional Bluegrass Music*. Urbana: University of Illinois Press, 1992. Not a history, per se, but an idiosyncratic view of the life and career of one of the genre's earliest and most powerful performers.

SUGGESTED VIEWING

Flatt and Scruggs. *Best of the Flatt & Scruggs TV Show*, Vol. 10. Shanachie SH-DV. This is the most recent multi-DVD series (all of which are worthwhile and orginally aired as *Flatt and Scruggs Grand Ole Opry*) devoted to the bluegrass and traditional country artists, such as Mother Maybelle Carter and Hylo Brown, who appeared on these shows from the middle 1950s through the early 1960s.

Tommy Jarrell. *Sprout Wings & Fly*. Flower Films. One in a series of strong ethnographic/music films by Les Blank; this one focusing on this North Carolina fiddler whose music influenced not only local musicians but those who came south to study with him.

Jimmy Martin. *King Of Bluegrass: Life & Times Of Jimmy Martin*. George Goehl Films. Martin always wanted to be a regular on the Grand Ole Opry and this film documents not only his quest but his life through footage of Jimmy at home, out coon hunting with his dogs, and playing music on stage.

Bill Monroe. *Father of Bluegrass Music*. Steve Gebhardt/Folkstreams.net. This 1991 film offers a detailed musical biography of the father of bluegrass.

Lawrence Older. *Adirondack Minstrel*. New Pacific Productions/Folkstreams.net. A portrait of a fiddler and singer who lived in the southern Adirondacks for his entire life, playing mostly for friends and neighbors.

Patoka Valley Boys. *Tough, Pretty, or Smart: A Portrait of the Patoka Valley Boys*. Kane-Lewis Productions/Folkstreams.net. The life and music of a semiprofessional old-time and bluegrass group from rural Indiana.

ANGLO-AMERICAN SECULAR FOLK MUSIC

Almeda Riddle. *Now Let's Talk About Singing*. Talking Traditions/Folkstreams.net. Riddle (a lifelong resident of north-central Arkansas) learned scores of English and American ballads, which she sang mostly locally until the folk revival brought her to Boston and New York to sing and record.

Morgan Sexton. *Bull Creek Banjo Player*. Appalshop/Folkstreams.net. Eastern Kentucky banjo player and singer is the focus of this film.

Doc Watson. *Doc Watson*. CMNS. Watson is joined by his older neighbors and mentors Clint Howard and Fred Price in the performance of folk songs from western North Carolina.

Various. *Appalachian Journey*. Association for Cultural Equity/Folkstreams.net. A sampler of performers ranging from fiddler Tommy Jarrell to storytellers/singers Ray and Stanley Hicks.

Various. *Banjo Spirits*. John Paulson Productions/Folkstreams.net. This film explores the roles of the banjo in the lives of bluegrass legend Don Stover and raconteur, musician, scholar Stephen Wade.

Various. *Billy in the Lowground*. Vetapol. This film, another featuring Alan Lomax-shot footage, features performances by Clark Kessinger, Kilby Snow, the Coon Creek Girls, and ten other performers who appeared at the 1966 Newport Folk Festival's "Old Time Music" stage.

Various. *High Lonesome Sound*. Schanachie. Arguably the best video documentary of the genre with performances by and interviews with the best of the old-time musicians encountered by filmmaker/musician John Cohen.

Various. *Legends of Old Time Music*. Vestapol. There are some truly legendary artists, such as Sam McGhee, Clarence Ashley, and Roscoe Holcomb, featured on this documentary film. Nearly a dozen singers or groups can be heard and seen in performances shot mostly in the 1960s.

Various. *Legends of Western Swing Guitar*. Vestapol. Composed of short, delightful clips—mostly from the 1940s and 1950s—this anthology ranges from the well known (Eldon Shamblin) to the unsung (Art Greenshaw).

Various. *Madison County Project: Documenting the Sound*. Martha King & Rob Roberts/Folkstreams.net. This film documents the tradition of unaccompanied ballad singing in Madison County, North Carolina.

ANGLO-AMERICAN SECULAR FOLK MUSIC

Various. "New England Fiddles." Media Generation/Folkstreams.net. A 1983 film that presents seven, highly varied (from Irish American to Quebecois) traditional musicians playing in their homes and at dances and contests.

Various. *Texas Style*. Documentary Arts/Folkstreams.net. Three generations of Westmoreland family fiddlers can be heard and seen here.

Various. *Shady Grove: Old Time Music From North Carolina, Kentucky, & Virginia*. Vestapol. Filmed between 1966 and 1970, this anthology focuses upon autoharp player Kilby Snow and the legendary Tommy Jarrell. One of the highlights are three brief songs by Dock Boggs, the only extant footage of this fine performer.

Various. *Why The Cowboy Sings*. Western Folklife Center/Folkstreams.net. This 2002 film explores this intriguing question.

Chapter 5

ANGLO-AMERICAN SACRED MUSIC

- Psalmody
- Shape Notes
- Camp Meetings
- Shakers
- Later Hymnody and Gospel Songs
- Sanctified Styles
- Southern Gospel Boogie
- Final Thoughts

Religious beliefs and spiritual concerns of all kinds are core issues for many Americans. And religious music remains a vitally important, often underappreciated aspect of traditional music. The early English-speaking settlers brought their own church songs with them, most notably psalms, so it is very likely that psalms were the first European music sung here. For the first few decades of the establishment of the New World, psalm singing was the only form of music generally allowed in colonial churches. Within one hundred years singing schools had developed throughout the colonies, helping to teach religious singing to the musically illiterate. This method of teaching gradually cultivated the shape note tradition that flourished in the South following the early-nineteenth-century Great Awakening.

As the United States expanded westward following Reconstruction, folk and folklike styles of religious music continued to evolve and flourish. Revival hymns, spiritual songs (both black and white), and gospel hymns emerged by the later part of the nineteenth century, disseminated by way of printed sources as well as oral tradition. These styles helped to shape postindustrial religious music. Despite all of the nineteenth- and twentieth-century innovations Anglo-American religious folk song practices tend to be fairly conservative, but, as we shall see, many distinctly American folk styles of religious singing gradually developed out of these essentially European practices.

PSALMODY

Psalmody, or psalm singing, grew out of the practice of chanting psalms from the Bible and it was eventually replaced by composed hymns. The chanting tradition came over with the first English settlers and was promoted through books such as Thomas Ravenscroft's *Whole Booke of Psalms*, published in London in 1621. In fact Ravenscroft's tome eventually inspired the first book published in the American colonies, the **Bay Psalm Book** (1640). Its texts are largely unique, though the musical notation was not added for another sixty years when it was reprinted with some of Ravenscroft's own four-part settings. Early white Americans were also likely to have used the *Ainsworth Psalter*, which had also been brought over by very early settlers. Calvinist theology suggested that this music be sung without instrumental accompaniment and in keeping with the congregation's abilities. Some New Englanders learned the melodies and words from books, but for most seventeenth-century white residents, psalm singing was an oral tradition.

Gradually the Old World ties to religious singing grew weaker and more tenuous as the initial settlers' formal musical skills decreased. This led to the use of a greater number of oral elements, such as slides and other related embellishments, and antiphonal singing. A lack of literacy effected the lining out style, which encouraged more ornate singing from the congregation. All of these factors contributed to a unique, identifiable Anglo-American style of religious folk singing by the early eighteenth century.

This new way of singing did not suit everyone. Cotton Mather and several other important New England clergymen complained that this newly developed style was improper. They called for a reform, which led to the establishment of **singing schools**. Such schools offered instructions under a "trained" musician who could teach vocal techniques and how to read standard Western notation. People taught at singing schools were supposed to return to their congregation and reinforce the "regular singing" of their forebears.

But the Anglo-American style had such strong adherents that graduates of singing schools met with only limited success. Many enjoyed the new freedom to partially improvise and express oneself. But the idea of printed songbooks with a preface, instructions on singing, and a collection of well-known psalms eventually caught on. The first of these, John Tuft's *A Very Plain and Easy Introduction to the Singing of Psalm Tunes* (1721), went through eleven editions in twenty-three years. Most of the subsequent 350 or so songbooks published over the next eighty years were aimed at the singing-school market. One of the most significant of these, *A Collection of Psalms and Hymns*, printed in Charleston, South Carolina, was the first book by John and Charles Wesley, two brothers whose names are now inseparably linked with the Methodist church.

Singing schools and songbooks helped to encourage a few individuals to became part-time singing-school teachers. These men were among the first professional musicians in North America. They taught that a nice blend of voices and vocal production were important traits for congregational singing. These factors later constituted the basis of the Protestant church choirs that emerged in New England.

By the close of the eighteenth century a small school of men writing psalms for American consumption had emerged in New England. *Urania*, a 198-page opus published by James Lyons in 1761, helped to set the standard for later collections. Lyons included not only contemporary English psalms but truly American creations as well. His landmark compilation was followed in short order by Josiah Flagg's *A Collection of the Best Psalm Tunes* and Aaron Williams's *Universal Psalmodist*. Shortly after the Revolution, the number of new American songbooks had increased tenfold over a fifty-year period.

William Billings emerged as the most important composer and singing teacher in New England during the last three decades of the eighteenth century. He began his career as a singing teacher in 1869 near Boston and continued teaching until shortly before his death in 1800. He composed nearly 350 psalms or hymns, nearly all of them written for four voices. He also published six tunebooks, beginning with *The New-England Psalm-singer* (1790) and concluding with *The Continental Harmony* (1794). "Amherst," "Brookfield," and "Lebanon" are among his most popular and enduring tunes.

SHAPE NOTES

The first widely recognized form of white religious folk music was found in the shape note tunebooks first published in the wake of the Second Great Awakening after 1800. The shapes themselves represent a simplified system to help people who were not conversant with standard Western notation. This system is known widely as fasola, referring to the last three syllables used in sight singing—fa, sol, and la. It is also known as **sacred harp singing** because of the very popular book, *The Sacred Harp*. These southern and eastern tunesmiths (an encompassing term that refers to compilers, composers, and singing-school teachers) carried on a tradition that is considered here because it is so often maintained through oral tradition. The late-eighteenth- and early-nineteenth-century shape note books of New England and New York contain many musical examples that appear in later tunebooks from other parts of the United States. They also established the practice of including a pedagogical section to assist singing-school teachers with their craft. The first widely used book with all of

"Wondrous Love." Courtesy of Kip Lornell.

these components, *The Easy Instructor*, by William Little and William Smith, was initially published in 1798.

The vernacular roots of these tunebooks are evident in their utilization of a system based on four to seven shapes. This system initially used four shapes, while the seven-shape method came into use in the mid-nineteenth century. These shapes help the inexperienced to quickly sing without a working knowledge of key signatures or an ability to recognize pitches. The appearance of anthems and fuguing tunes by American composers drawn from oral tradition further establishes its folk roots. These facets are readily apparent in the first southern tunebook *Kentucky Harmony*, compiled by Ananias Davidson and published in Harrisonburg, Virginia, in 1816. A singing-school master, Davidson used the book to help teach his classes in the Shenandoah Valley of Virginia.

The tunes are presented in four-part harmony with the main melody given to the tenor voices. The voices are unusually independent for this time, marking a move away from the harmonizing so commonly found during this time. The tunes themselves (the melody lines) often came from broadside ballads, fiddle pieces, or popular songs of the day, which the tunebook compilers reworked rather than created. They are written in a mixture of major and minor keys, with some modal tunes occurring also. Some of the most stringent rules of Western music composition are routinely broken in these tunes: parallel fifths, octaves, and unisons abound, while inner voices cross to higher and lower

MUSICAL EXAMPLE

This group of older singers was recorded by George Pullen Jackson in northeastern Tennessee in the early 1950s. Most of the singers were older because at this time relatively few younger people were involved with shape note singing in this section of Tennessee. "Wondrous Love" is found in a variety of seven-note books from across the southern United States and is a very popular, beloved song that is universally sung at a slow, deliberate tempo. At the beginning of the song you can hear the names of the shapes being sung before they launch into the words themselves.

Title "Wondrous Love"
Performers Old Harp Singers of Eastern Tennessee
Instruments eight voices
Length 2:05

Musical Characteristics
1. The singers weave the four lines into a polyphonic texture.
2. Its melody is conjunctive and you hear a minor key.
3. The tempo is slow and quite deliberately somber.
4. The song uses a simple *ab* form.

What wondrous love is this, oh my soul, oh my soul.
What wondrous love is this, oh my soul.
What wondrous love is this, that cause the Lord of bliss,
To lend a dreadful curse for my soul, for my soul.
To lend a dreadful curse for my soul.

This song was originally released on Smithsonian Folkways 2356.

---

levels. In these tunes alone the arrangers proved themselves to be American originals. Although such tunes did have some parallels in eighteenth- and nineteenth-century hymnody, these writers undeniably created a distinctive sound that would seem a bit unruly to those trained in the standard European classical music.

Because they proved so popular and practical, many people eventually followed Davidson's lead. In 1831 Reverend James Carroll of Lebanon, Virginia, published *The Virginia Harmony*. William Moore of Wilson County, Tennessee, brought out the *Columbian Harmony* in 1825, while another Tennessean, William Caldwell of Maryville, presented the *Union Harmony* in 1837. Perhaps the

Old Harp Singers of eastern Tennessee, circa 1953. Eugene Kerr photo, courtesy of the Ralph Rinzler Folklife Archives and Collections, Center for Folklife and Cultural Heritage, Smithsonian Institution.

second most popular shape note book, after *The Sacred Harp* by B. F. White, came out in 1835 and went through five editions. *The Southern Harmony* by William Walker of Spartanburg, South Carolina, touched the consciousness of religious singers throughout the South. Like *The Sacred Harp*, Walker's book was set almost entirely in three parts.

"Singin' Billy" Walker was part of the social and economic class of people who used such books. *The Southern Harmony* presented itself as "A Choice Collection of Tunes, Hymns, Psalms, Odes, and Anthems; Selected from the Most Eminent Authors in the United States," though its authors did include a European composer named George Frederick Handel. Some very familiar songs, most notably "Amazing Grace," appear in these shape note collections as did two other popular compositions: "Sherburne" and "The Good Old Way."

In the 1840s, a slow shift from books of four to books of seven shape notes began. They argued that since there were seven distinctive tones in the major and minor scales, each one should have its own name: mi, fa, sol, la, ti, do, re. This was viewed as progressive by younger singers, and publishers eventually moved to fill the need for new books. Jesse Aiken's *The Christian Minstrel* (1846) was perhaps the first popular book to use seven shapes, but it was quickly followed by others. Many of these publishers were once more concentrated in the Shenandoah Valley of Virginia. Joseph Funk was the most notable, and his seven-shape *Harmonia Sacra* (1851) was so successful that it went through six editions in nine years.

These books all contained a wide variety of material. Their texts came from English hymnody, anthems composed by New Englanders, southern spirituals, and camp meeting songs, among others. The music is from equally eclectic sources, with only the tunes from spirituals and camp meeting songs being closely related to the ballads and fiddle tunes that were so often used to accompany folk songs and dancing. Shape note singing contains elements of our aural and elite culture; thus, it is at least partly tied to folk music.

Shape note singing is, above all, a social form of religious music. The singing-school teachers brought people together to instruct them in the rudiments of music theory. People also gathered in small and large groups for the express purpose of singing this music. By the late 1800s formal singing conventions were being held across the South. These lasted from an afternoon to several days, depending on the gathering's size and the distance people had to travel.

Contemporary singing conventions (most of which are found in Georgia and Alabama) are held not only at churches but also in other public buildings. The singers sit in sections arranged by the distribution of the four voices. A different singer often leads each song, which is first sung with the syllables to familiarize everyone and then with the words. The leaders often choose their favorites, leading the same tune or tunes at each convention; sometimes they are identified with these tunes. The singers participate for the spiritual movement of the singing itself and secondarily the fellowship afforded to the singers as they greet old friends. These conventions often also involve food, usually potlucks, and frequently a religious service. The sessions themselves open and close with a prayer.

Contemporary shape note singing continues not only in the Deep South but also among younger revivalists across the country. With song leaders and singing-school teachers such as Hugh McGraw of northern Georgia and Mrs. Helen Nance Church of Yadkin County, North Carolina, spreading the word, the tradition has remained alive. Although it has never disappeared from our cultural landscape, this style of singing has undergone something of a renaissance since the 1990s. I first encountered shape note singing while a student at the University of North Carolina at Chapel Hill in the middle 1970s; our singings involved a mixture of local folks and students. There are now many other revival groups across the country, including in New England, where this type of singing went largely unheard during its days of greatest popularity. Nonetheless, traditional shape note singing remains almost entirely within the borders of the South, and *The Sacred Harp* remains in enough demand that a new edition came out in 1991.

The Phipps Family gospel group. Courtesy of the Ralph Rinzler Folklife Archives and Collections, Center for Folklife and Cultural Heritage, Smithsonian Institution.

CAMP MEETINGS

During the first decade of the nineteenth century a revival of hymns and spiritual songs swept across the United States. The Methodism of John Wesley was behind this movement; circuit-riding ministers rode their horses across the frontier to meet with the widely scattered settlements. **Camp meetings** developed in the early nineteenth century as it became clear that the word of God could be spread more effectively when large numbers of people gathered together in worship. Caught up in a grassroots movement, the first camp meeting adjourned in July of 1800 in Logan County, Kentucky.

Baptist and Presbyterian preachers soon became part of the camp meeting revival, promoting salvation through conversation and unfettered contact with God through the acceptance of Jesus Christ. Methodists predominated the early camp meetings because of their body of popular, familiar revival hymns, many of which appeared in the often-reprinted *The Pocket Hymn Book* of 1797. By the early 1800s several camp meeting songbook collections had appeared, such as John Totten's *A Collection of the Most Admired Hymns and Spiritual Songs, With*

MUSICAL EXAMPLE

The Phipps Family of eastern Kentucky blends a secular and sacred repertoire; they are heavily influenced by the pioneering country music group, the Carter Family, who came from nearby Maces Spring, Virginia. This selection is structured like many other camp meeting songs and its verse/chorus structure is very easy to learn. The incremental textual substitutions of "father," "brother," and so on help to increase the song's length and enables it to encompass more segments of the family.

Title "Away Over in the Promised Land"
Performers The Phipps Family
Instruments autoharp, two guitars, three voices
Length 2:15

Musical Characteristics
1. Its texture is homophonic.
2. The vocals are quite relaxed and in the middle range.
3. A 2/4 duple meter is heard throughout the song.
4. The dynamic range is limited and moderate.
5. The chorus is sung in unison.

I've got a father in the promised land (repeat)
I hope someday we'll all get there
Away over in the promised land

Chorus: Away over in the promised land (repeat)
   I hope someday we'll all get there
   Away over in the promised land

I've got a mother in the promised land (repeat)
I hope someday we'll all get there
Away over in the promised land.

Chorus

I've got a brother in the promised land (repeat)
I hope someday we'll all get there
Away over in the promised land

Chorus

Sister is a-waiting in the promised land (repeat)
I hope we'll all get there
Away over in the promised land

Chorus

Gonna see my savior in the promised land (repeat)
I hope someday we'll all get there
Away over in the promised land

Chorus

This selection was originally issued on Smithsonian Folkways 2375.

Choruses Affixed as Usually Sung at Camp-Meetings (1809) and Lorenzo and Peggy Dow's *A Collection of Camp-Meeting Hymns* (1816).

The camp meetings themselves were lively and spirited religious events. Imagine several thousand frontier women, children, and men camped together for worship; African Americans, though segregated, often participated, too. These uplifting gatherings often lasted several days with people witnessing their faith, reaffirmed by preachers shouting about hell while fires from the nearby campfires roared brightly. Perhaps most striking were the "jerking" masses of humanity caught up in their holy whirling with visions of heaven dancing through their brains. Their happy frenzy was oft described by contemporary witnesses struck by the unlikely sight of the nightly contortions, replete with wild gesticulations, leaping, and shouting. Not surprisingly the term "holy roller" came from this fervent period, though today it is more often applied to adherents of the Pentecostal faiths. Such happy, willing, and photogenic congregations would no doubt be admired and coveted by today's **televangelists**.

At the edge of this new frontier the older methods of Christian education were strained by a lack of trained ministers and a low level of literacy. The major Protestant denominations turned to revivals as a means of reaching a great number of people who would otherwise go unserved by ministers of God. Methodists became particularly successful at revivals. One of the main reasons was their new songs that reached directly for the spirit and soul of each individual.

Camp meeting singing appears to have taken the mid- to late-eighteenth-century New England revival hymns one step closer to the masses. Many of the camp meeting hymns were constructed from the verses of already familiar religious songs by using a simple strophic structure—verse and chorus—that permitted almost unlimited improvisation within a theme. "Satan's Kingdom," first published in *Revival Hymns* (Boston: H. W. Day, 1842), provides a good example of this style. No one knows, of course, exactly what such hymns actually sounded like, but contemporary written accounts suggest that most camp meeting songs might have been sung in a major key in a spirited, simple duple meter. Repetition is one of the keys to the success of camp meeting songs, for this strategy serves to reinforce the fervor and message as well as the lyrics. This type of thematic recombination adheres on an emotional level similar to that of the blues.

Camp meetings continued to grow in popularity during the first four decades of the nineteenth century. They spread from their mid-South hearth by way of direct personal contact (cultural geographers refer to this as *contagious diffusion*) that disregarded social and economic status in favor of religious conviction. The powerful message of direct communication with God swayed many people to join the ranks of the saved, a process no doubt assisted by the beauty and directness of the a cappella hymns. By the 1850s camp meetings were commonplace throughout the South and were not unknown in the Midwest and back East. Just as any manifestation of popular culture must slowly lose its power, the camp meeting revivals had lost much of their punch by the beginning of the Civil War. The songs, however, continued to be sung throughout the country, but most especially in the South.

SHAKERS

Shakerism is one minor and unique offshoot of the camp meeting movement. Started by Mother Ann, who came to the United States at the beginning of the Revolution, the **Shakers** were always a small, self-contained religious movement whose music has been related to their rituals or laboring exercises. Although there were some 8,000 to 10,000 songs in surviving Shaker manuscripts—an astounding number of them were written between 1837 and 1847—very few have survived to the present day. Playful and simple by nature, Shakers believe that life should combine hard, clean work with a spiritual vision that is sometimes manifested by "gift" songs. The best known Shaker song is "Simple Gifts," which Aaron Copland used as part of "Appalachian Spring" and Judy Collins and others—have recorded since the middle 1960s. Other important Shaker folk songs that are still sung today include the quick dance tune "Come Life, Shaker Life" and "Willow Tree":

> I will bow and be simple, I will bow and be free
> I will bow and be humble, Yea bow like the willow tree.

I will be, this is a token, I will wear the easy yoke
I will lie low and be broken, I will fall upon the rock.

Unfortunately there will be no more Shaker songs, for it is truly a moribund religion with only a handful of members living in Sabbath Day Lake, Maine. By the second decade of the twenty-first century, the Shaker religion will almost certainly have joined the ranks of sects that no longer exist.

LATER HYMNODY AND GOSPEL SONGS

These revival hymns and camp meeting songs set the stage for the final third of the nineteenth century. A new wave of evangelism, which emphasized revival "song-services" with sweet lyrical compositions, flourished after the close of the War Between the States. **Ira D. Sanky** and **Dwight Moody**, two of the key figures in this movement, collaborated on a number of **gospel song** collections between 1874 and 1894. This duo helped to popularize gospel hymns, such as "Sweet Hour of Prayer," that proved fashionable among both black and white Christians. They delivered an evangelical message that was as simple and direct as their advertising slogan: "Mr. Moody will preach the gospel and Mr. Sanky will sing the gospel."

Singers, evangelists, and publishers began forming new alliances. Normal singing schools, intensive music education courses that taught all of the rudiments of music by using religious texts and songs, began replacing the shorter singing schools. The Ruebush-Kieffer Publishers of New Market, Virginia, conducted the first such school in 1874. Ten years later, A. J. Showalter, manager of Ruebush-Kieffer's southern office, formed his own company at Dalton, Georgia, and also began teaching normal singing schools. These songbook publishers also printed monthly or quarterly newspapers that expedited communication between singers and teachers. *The Musical Millions*, published by Ruebush-Kieffer, began in 1870 and continued for forty-five years.

The new hymnals appealed to a wide audience because of their catchy melodies and their often strophic form, which made them easy to remember. Some of the tunes came from well-known secular songs. *Gospel Hymns and Sacred Songs by P. P. Bliss and Ira D. Sanky as used by Them in Gospel Meetings* (1875) achieved such immediate and widespread use that it went through four versions within sixteen years. Such books were used across the country, but they gained particular favor in the South.

The singings themselves were becoming more organized, first on a regional basis within a state. Statewide "conventions," however, did not occur for many years. Alabama, for example, held its first statewide singing in 1918. Larger

Rainbow record label from the mid-1920s. Courtesy of Kip Lornell.

conventions met once or twice a year, while local sings often transpired on a monthly basis. The repertoire became so well known that many people knew the songs by heart; new songs were sometimes introduced aurally. But the demand for new books was constant and a handful of new publishers sprang up to meet this demand.

Vaughan Publishers of Lawrenceburg, Tennessee, and **Stamps-Baxter** of Jacksonville, Texas, emerged at the forefront of these new houses. Beginning with the founding of the **James D. Vaughan** Publishing Company in 1902, a small number of publishing businesses promoted gospel songbooks out of which people sang and which were also used for normal singing schools. They printed many of the early gospel songs that are today considered classics within the genre and that many people mistakenly believe come from aural tradition. Songs that have passed into oral tradition, such as "The Sweetest Gift a Mother's Smile" and "I'll Fly Away" are actually composed pieces that first appeared in Vaughan or Stamps-Baxter songbooks early in the twentieth century.

By the early 1900s these publishers began sponsoring their own small groups, usually quartets, to sing out of and promote their songbooks. They were actually placed on a salary, which the publishers could afford because their books were selling so well. Vaughan, for instance, sold in excess of 100,000 songbooks in 1915, a fact that could be attributed in part to touring quartets that had gone on the road about five years previously. Stamps-Baxter soon followed this lead and both companies maintained quartets for several decades. These groups kept up a regular routine of performing and by the middle 1920s had added radio appearances and record dates to their schedule.

The history of publishing southern gospel music, as it later became known, is encapsulated in the life of Luther Presley, who spent nearly five decades writing sacred songs and working for the Stamps-Baxter Music and Printing Company. Presley, born in 1887, began writing hymns and teaching at singing schools in his middle teens. Near the beginning of the Depression, in February of 1930, the

Stamps-Baxter Music and Printing Company (founded in 1926) hired Presley, and he worked for them for almost fifty years. He composed scores of songs, many with themes of eternal life in heaven, that were published in Stamps-Baxter books such as *Thankful Hearts* or *Heavenly Highway*. The success of the Stamps-Baxter organization was sealed in 1927 with the astonishing success of "Give the World a Smile," which was first recorded by the Stamps Quartet in the fall of 1927 for RCA Victor Records and then reprinted numerous times in Stamps-Baxter songbooks. "Give the World a Smile" is the best known song from this era and is still associated with the Stamps Quartet. During the height of gospel songbook publishing—roughly 1925 through 1950—the Stamps-Baxter organization maintained two auxiliary offices in Pangburn, Arkansas, and Chattanooga, Tennessee.

Folk hymns and gospel music were also favored by evangelists because they had become so well known. Homer Rodeheaver and Billy Sunday were two of the most influential early-twentieth-century evangelists who wanted to reach the common folk through this type of music. Rodeheaver worked throughout the United States from his midwestern base. He even began a publishing company in 1910 and a record company (Rainbow) in the early 1920s. Once more, songs such as "The Old Rugged Cross" and "His Eye Is on the Sparrow" that we assume are "folk" really began as composed turn-of-the century hymns.

Charles H. Gabriel's "Brighten the Corner Where You Are" is typical of these songs. Its *ab* (verse/chorus) with its "Brighten the corner where you are; Some one far from harbor may guide across the bar; Brighten the corner where you are" refrain helped to strengthen its popularity. The song is usually performed in duple meter (4/4) with an easy-to-recall nearly stepwise melody. Its rhythm is predominated by quarter notes, though the occasional dotted half note or eighth note can be found.

The performance of early-twentieth-century white religious folk music lacks the emotional intensity of the pre–Civil War revivals. Except in Pentecostal churches, such emotionalism was discouraged and the music emphasized nicely blended voices and well-controlled performances. These trends have a parallel in the Tin Pan Alley school of popular songwriting that flourished in the last two decades of the nineteenth century. Both segments produced sentimental songs that were widely disseminated by way of commercial publications and that eventually passed into tradition. They are most evident on the commercial phonograph records by some of the family groups of the 1920s and 1930s.

Sacred singing, in fact, is often the province of family ensembles. This holds true for Ernest V. Stoneman's religious recordings, the first of which came almost exactly two years after his 1924 debut. He, several friends, and neighbors journeyed to New York City for a three-day Victor session, where the Dixie Mountaineers joined voices to produce "The Resurrection," "Sinless Summer," and "The Great Reaping Day," among others. The strongest religious sides were three songs first published in the late nineteenth century: "Are You Washed in the Blood of the Lamb," "I am Sweeping Through the Gates," and "Going Down the Valley." The latter was composed by Jessie Brown and J. H. Fillmore about 1890. Stoneman's version utilizes a less complex melody and more simple harmony, though its words are very close to printed texts:

> We are going down the valley one by one.
> With our faces toward the setting of the sun.
> Down the valley where the mournful cypress grows.
> Where the stream of death in silence onward flows.
>
> *Chorus:*
> We are going down the valley, going down the valley.
> Going toward the setting of the sun.
> We are going down the valley, going down the valley,
> Going down the valley one by one.
>
> We are going down the valley one by one.
> When the labors of the weary day are done.
> One by one, the cares of earth forever past,
> We shall stand upon the river bank at last.
>
> *Chorus*
>
> We are going down the valley one by one.
> Human comrade you or I will there have none,
> But a tender hand will guide us lest we fall.
> Christ is going down the valley with us all.
>
> *Chorus*

These songs featured a parlor-hall style instrumentation underpinned by Irma Frost's organ, Stoneman's rhythm guitar, and the modest ornamentation of fiddlers Kahle Brewer or Uncle Eck Dunford.

An example such as this is considered folk, or at least folk based, because of a process it goes through from the composer's pen to its performance by Stoneman and his group. First, the origins of the song may be obscured to the singers by time: an old song they heard sung in their church for many years. Second, their rendition makes no conscious attempt to replicate the original published version. Stoneman's version eliminates the accidentals and most chromatic

The Revival, an early-twentieth-century songbook. Courtesy of Charles K. Wolfe.

notes and considerably simplifies the rather elaborate melodies. Third, this rendition adapts the piece to folk performance practices found among Carroll County, Virginia, singers by assigning the lead male and female voices in octaves. Finally, the singers use a somewhat nasal tone that would have been shunned by contemporary popular singers and abhorred by classically trained vocalists.

Other early country music recording artists also mixed a similar sacred and secular repertoire. The Monroe Brothers' (Bill and Charlie) first recording session for Bluebird in 1936 featured a number of late-nineteenth-century hymns including "What Would You Give in Exchange?" and "God Holds the Future in His Hands." The Blue Sky Boys and other brother groups also often utilized similar sacred numbers on their radio shows and records. Many of these mainly southern groups grew up in homes where Sunday church attendance was mandatory, which greatly affected their musical interests. Some northern duos, such as Gardner and McFarland, mined similar territory during the late 1920s and into the 1930s. When bluegrass emerged in the middle 1940s, many of these groups also included religious numbers. Some even worked up four-part harmony gospel songs that they performed as part of their live performances.

SANCTIFIED STYLES

The Pentecostal movement is the largest religious movement to originate in the United States. The movement began in Topeka, Kansas, in 1901 within a small Bible study group organized by Charles Fox Parham, a former Methodist preacher. In the early twenty-first century, Pentecostal churches claim over 200 million members worldwide, making them the largest Protestant religion. The sensational growth of Pentecostal (also known as Holiness or Sanctified) sects suggests that this is an important movement worthy of attention to uncover its musical and cultural impact.

Although it began in the United States, the Pentecostal movement looked toward England for its roots in the charismatic and "perfectionistics" movements. During the middle nineteenth century, an orientation toward holiness or spiritual power developed in the Methodist church. The National Holiness Camp Meeting Association, for example, drew tens of thousands of people over a week-long event in Vineland, New Jersey, in 1867. By the turn of the century the scene for the widespread interest in Pentecostalism was set.

Glossolalia, speaking in tongues, immediately became one of the first issues that set the budding Pentecostal movement apart from other recently established Methodist/Holiness sects. Parham quickly stated that speaking in tongues provided evidence that Pentecostals were baptized in the Holy Spirit. He further suggested that this means of communication would facilitate evangelization through the world. Along with glossolalia, the early Pentecostal Christians believed that they were anointed by the Holy Spirit, they could communicate directly with God, and improvisation—such as shouting and dancing—within the service glorified the Spirit within them.

Some of these aspects of Pentecostalism came to the fore in 1906 during the Azusa Street Revival in Los Angeles, which was led by the black American preacher William Joseph Seymour. This revival is particularly noteworthy because it focused nationwide attention on this movement and its interracial constituency. The fact that blacks and whites worshiped together and their leader was African American was remarkable enough, but the Azusa Street Apostolic Faith Mission continued for nearly three years, seven days a week. Between the summers of 1906 and 1909 tens of thousands of converts received the baptism of the Holy Spirit, spoke in tongues, and danced through the power of the Spirit. This remarkable period not only focused attention on Pentecostalism, but it also helped to disseminate these beliefs throughout the United Sates.

By the teens churches like the Pentecostal Free-Will Baptist Church, the Fire Baptized Holiness Church, the Church of God, and the Pentecostal Holiness Church proliferated. Slowly, perhaps inevitably, the churches began to become racially separated—a trend that has become even more strident today. In the early twenty-first century, the Assemblies of God is the largest predominately white Pentecostal church, while the Church of God in Christ holds the same position in the African American community.

The music and performance practices of white Pentecostal musicians is far removed from the Catholic and the more conventional Methodist churches. Bearing the marks of its early interaction with black religious practices, early Pentecostal music was very expressive and had strong folk roots. There were no recordings of Pentecostal musicians until the late 1920s when groups such as McVay & Johnson and Ernest Phipps's Holiness Singers recorded. These recordings demonstrate that (in the South at least) Pentecostal music was closely tied with old-time (string band) tradition. Their music was performed to the accompaniment of banjos and guitars, their voices were pitched high, and their tone was nasal. The ensemble singing heard on the Phipps recordings were not only highly spirited but also featured loose unison singing. In other words, their music shared traits with and was meant to appeal to people who already listened to country artists such as Gid Tanner and the Skillet Lickers, Jimmie Rodgers, and the Carter Family.

Pentecostalism (and its music) is meant to appeal to everyday folks. The repertoire of many early Pentecostal musicians reflect their evangelical spirit; songs such as "Clouds of Glory," "We Shall All Be United," "If the Light Has Gone Out in Your Soul," and "I Know That Jesus Has Set Me Free" underscore this impulse. Although the music of contemporary Pentecostal musicians has changed to reflect more recent trends, this impulse and spirit remains undiminished.

SOUTHERN GOSPEL BOOGIE

The rise to prominence of gospel performances on the radio and records as well as in live performances helped to change the face of white religious folk music. Here we shift from music that can be considered largely folk to music that is popular but clearly folk based. The tradition of singing out of shape note books declined gradually and the communal spirit of the old-fashioned camp meetings and friendly singing conventions was being lost. Fewer touring singers were directly linked to and supported by publishers because the groups could support themselves. White religious music, specifically the new gospel music that emerged during the 1930s, was quickly becoming a full-time professional business that could sustain a community of singers, songwriters, promoters, publishers, and broadcasters.

The commercialization of southern gospel music had its parallel in the black musical community. And it's significant to note that, especially from the middle 1930s through the present, gospel music has remained stolidly and unabashedly segregated. While other forms of American vernacular, most notably jazz and soul, enjoy multiracial and crossover audiences, gospel music is performed and consumed in terms of black or white.

For example, the Grammy Awards distinguish between "soul gospel" (African American) and "southern gospel" (Anglo-American) in distinctly racial terms not found elsewhere in their categories. This distinction is mirrored in the real world in almost every way. Gospel concerts are promoted to either a white or a black audience and sound recordings are marketed the same way. There are numerous magazines devoted to southern gospel, such as *Singing News*, *Country Gospel News*, and *Gospel Voice Magazine*, while a relatively smaller number focuses on its black counterpart. The only magazine that tried to bridge the racial gap, *Rejoice!*, was published by the Center for Southern Studies at the University of Mississippi and ceased operations in 1994, following six years of uneven sales. Even Web sites devoted to gospel music are neatly divided along racial lines.

Nonetheless, segregation did not stop the crossover of stylistic elements as well as songs that were performed by both black and white groups. Gospel quartets of both races were at the forefront of the commercialization of gospel music. In the southern gospel tradition, some of these pioneering quartets enjoyed the support of songbook publishers. By the late 1930s several Stamps-Baxter–associated quartets were holding regular **all-night sings** over Dallas radio station KRLD and were popular enough to hold a successful all-night sing that all but filled the Cotton Bowl stadium in Dallas. But changes were coming, which became clear in 1941 when one of Vaughan's most popular groups (led by Claude Sharpe) resigned in order to join the Grand Ole Opry as the Old Hickory Singers.

Following World War II, the popularity of white gospel quartets rose to even greater heights. Grand Ole Opry star **Wally Fowler** left his band to concentrate on his gospel quartet career. By 1948 he was a full-time quartet singer and a busy promoter who occasionally set up as many as five programs on a single night! Every Friday night he staged an all-night sing at the home of the Grand Ole Opry, the Ryman Auditorium in Nashville. About the same time the Blackwood Brothers quartet used their Shenandoah, Iowa, base to launch a career in gospel music. They started out on their own small record label and with broadcasts over local radio stations. By the early 1950s the **Blackwood Brothers** realized that the South offered them more professional opportunities, so they moved to Memphis and began recording for the RCA-Victor Company.

Anglo-American gospel music was moving into the mainstream of American music. This type of gospel music quickly echoed some of the themes exploited in popular songs. "Gospel Boogie," copywritten in November 1947 and first recorded by the Homeland Harmony Quartet in early 1948, became an instant sensation. It was quickly covered by nearly a dozen black and white artists, some of whom recorded it under the alternate title "A Wonderful Time Up There." The popularity of "Gospel Boogie" created a controversy within the gospel community. Despite the fact that the Chuck Wagon Gang had been around since the middle 1930s and the Johnson Family since the early 1940s, some of the older, more conservative singers felt that the popularity of these groups—along with the Speer Family and the Statesmen Quartet—was built upon an

An old-fashioned hymn songbook from 1937. Courtesy of Kip Lornell.

ephemeral foundation. Fowler and his cohorts suggested that nothing but good could result from spreading the message of the gospel to more people. The battle took place on all types of grounds: backstage at programs, in churches, at all-night sings, and in newspaper letters to the editor. Ultimately the argument became moot as the younger gospel singers reached a larger audience and the quartets became stronger.

Some of the best and most popular songs performed by these singers were authored by **Albert E. Brumley**, whose "I'll Fly Away" has been recorded more than six hundred times. Brumley was born on October 29, 1905, in rural eastern Oklahoma. Attending his first singing school in 1922, he was struck by the power and beauty of what he heard and continued to study at the Hartford Music Company (Arkansas). This small, regional publisher issued one or two songbooks annually, which were based on the seven-shape system. By the late 1920s he began composing songs for Hartford, including "I'll Fly Away" in 1932.

Over the next twelve years, Brumley unleashed some of his best compositions upon the gospel world: "Jesus Hold My Hand" (1932), "I'll Meet You in the Morning" (1936), "Turn Your Radio On" (1938), and "If We Ever Meet Again" (1945). Most of these early compositions were promoted at conventions, over radio broadcasts, and via other live contexts. The first songbook dedicated specifically to his work, Albert E. Brumley's *Book of Radio Favorites* (1937), helped to spread his fame. But it was not until he switched to Stamps-Baxter in 1937 that his written songs reached a nationwide audience.

Within ten years Brumley had bought out the old Hartford Music Company to form Brumley-Hartford, which his family still operates in southern Missouri. He continued to write songs and run his publishing company until his death in 1977. Groups as diverse as the Chuck Wagon Gang, Elvis Presley, and Hank Williams have recorded his songs, which are firmly in the early-twentieth-century gospel mold. "I'll Fly Away," for example, opens with the same melody as the well-known "Prisoner's Song" and it begins with the catchy line "If I had the wings of an angel."

If this music was being exploited by the mass media and reaching millions of people, can it be considered "folk"? In many of these performances we can find folk elements similar to those used by Ernest Stoneman's version of late-nineteenth-century hymnody, which leads to a qualified yes. These elements include a nasal vocal technique; a repertoire that encompassed not only new compositions but also older gospel hymns and spirituals; simple harmonic structures that were readily accessible to any piano or guitar player; and easily remembered melodies. The message of these songs was equally straightforward: help your neighbors, live a "clean" life, worship God regularly, and then find eternal bliss in heaven.

FINAL THOUGHTS

Since the English brought their psalmody tradition across the Atlantic Ocean, sacred music has been part of white American music. But many decades passed before American religious folk songs developed. The last two hundred years, however, have witnessed the gradual evolution of uniquely American styles from the rejuvenating camp meeting songs to the gospel boogie of the late 1940s. Since the middle of the twentieth century, there has been an expanding relationship and interaction between folk and popular forms of religious music. Despite the commercialization of Anglo-American sacred folk songs, the shape note tradition and gospel hymnody remain a part of life in the South and parts of the Midwest.

KEY FIGURES AND TERMS

all-night sings	Albert E. Brumley
Bay Psalm Book	camp meetings
Blackwood Brothers	Wally Fowler

ANGLO-AMERICAN SACRED MUSIC

gospel song
Dwight Moody
psalmody
sacred harp singing
Ira D. Sanky
Shakers

singing schools
Stamps-Baxter
televangelist
James D. Vaughan
Singin' Billy Walker

SUGGESTED LISTENING

Lester Flatt & Earl Scruggs with the Foggy Mountain Quartet. County 111. Flatt, Scruggs, and their quartet explore a selection of bluegrass gospel numbers.

Primitive Quartet. *20th Anniversary.* PQ CD 362192. A strong concert by one of the best of the southern gospel groups.

Various. *Brighten the Corner Where You Are.* New World NW-224. Both black and white hymnody and gospel songs are heard on this collection.

Various. *Classic Southern Gospel from Smithsonian Folkways.* SFW 40137. This release samples the broad Asch/Folkways catalogue and includes performances of sacred harp, Primitive Baptist, and gospel bluegrass.

Various. *Early Shaker Spirituals.* Rounder 0078. Mildred Barker and other members of the United Society of Shakers perform spirituals from the nineteenth and twentieth century.

Various. *Favorite Sacred Songs.* King CD 556. A nice sampler of country gospel songs recorded by the Delmore Brothers, Grandpa Jones, Wayne Rainey, and others in the late 1940s and early 1950s.

Various. *The Gospel Ship: Baptist Hymns & White Spirituals from the Southern Mountains.* New World 80294. Alan Lomax assembled this fine sample of selections, which focuses on performances recorded after World War II.

Various. *Old Harp Singers.* Smithsonian Folkways 2356. This compilation presents some strong examples of sacred harp singing recorded in Tennessee during the 1950s.

Various. *Old Regular Baptists.* Smithsonian Folkways 40106. A fine set compiled from field recordings from the 1990s by Jeff Titon. These thirteen tracks contain some outstanding examples of contemporary hymnody. The booklet is equally important.

ANGLO-AMERICAN SACRED MUSIC

Various. *Social Harp: American Shape Note Singing*. Rounder 0094. The tunes from this recording from Georgia in the 1970s are found in the *Social Harp* tunebook.

Various. *Southern Journey V. 4: Brethren, We Meet Again—Southern White Spirituals*. Rounder CD 011661170421. Culled from his extensive field trips in 1959 and 1960, these Alan Lomax recordings documented a wide range of genres, including selections from sacred harp to the equally a cappella-performing Primitive Baptist, as well as southern gospel.

Various. *True Gospel Bluegrass*. Rebel Records REB 8002. Fine and varied performances by stalwarts such as Ralph Stanley, Rhonda Vincent, Larry Sparks, and the Seldom Scene.

Various. *White Dove: The Bluegrass Gospel Collection*. Rounder CD 011661052321. A nicely paced collection of the various gospel bluegrass performances found on Rounder's large bluegrass catalogue.

Various. *White Spirituals From the Sacred Harp*. New World 80205. Taken from recordings made during the Alabama Sacred Harp Convention, Alan Lomax captures some powerful examples of the genre.

SUGGESTED READING

Dickson Bruce, Jr. *And They All Sang Hallelujah: Plain-Folk Camp Meeting Religion 1800-1845*. Knoxville: University of Tennessee Press, 1974. A straightforward accounting of the Anglo-American camp meeting movement.

Bill Gaither (with Jerry B. Jenkins). *Homecoming: The Story of Southern Gospel Music Through The Eyes of Its Best Loved Performers*. Nashville, TN: Zondervan Publishing, 1997. This longtime gospel music performer provides informal and short sketches of some of the music's most widely known singers and groups.

James R. Goff. *Close Harmony: A History of Southern Gospel*. Chapel Hill: University of North Carolina Press, 2001. The best and most balanced study of southern gospel yet written.

Kay Hively and Albert Brumley, Jr. *I'll Fly Away: The Life Story of Albert E. Brumley*. Branson, MO: Mountaineer Books, 1990. An entertaining, insiders view of one of the most important twentieth-century gospel composers.

Kenneth M. Johnson. *The Johnson Family Singers: We Sang For Our Suppers*. Jackson: University Press of Mississippi, 1997. One of the most respected of the family gospel ensembles in the decade following the close of WW II, this book details their story.

ANGLO-AMERICAN SACRED MUSIC

Kiri Miller. *Traveling Home: Sacred Harp Singing and American Pluralism*. Urbana: University of Illinois Press, 2007. A contemporary, ethnographic study of this music and the complex communities that support it today.

Lynwood Montell. *Singing the Glory Down*. Lexington: University Press of Kentucky, 1991. A detailed study of amateur gospel singing in south-central Kentucky.

Beverly Patterson. *The Sound of the Dove: Singing in Appalachian Primitive Baptist Churches*. Urbana: University of Illinois Press, 1994. A contemporary and close examination of the down-home, decidedly noncommercial, world of sacred singing in the highly conservative Primitive Baptist Church.

Glen Payne and George Younce (with Ace Collins). *The Cathedrals: The Story of America's Best-Loved Gospel Quartet*. Nashville, TN: Zondervan Publishing, 1998. Another in a new series, these two insiders relate the story of one of the most popular and long-lived southern gospel quartets.

Sandra Sizer. *Gospel Hymns and Social Religion: The Rhetoric of Nineteenth-Century Revivalism*. Philadelphia, PA: Temple University Press, 1978. This book covers the development of gospel hymns and describes its social context during the post-Reconstruction era.

David Warren Steele with Richard H. Hulan. *The Makers of the Sacred Harp*. Urbana: University of Illinois Press, 2010. Primarily a historical study, this important book takes a hard and close look at the nineteenth-century southern culture that spawned this compelling tradition.

Jeff Titon. *Powerhouse for God: Speech, Chant, and Song in an Appalachian Baptist Church*. Austin: University of Texas Press, 1988. A historical, musical, and ethnographic study of the Fellowship Independent Baptist Church in the Shenandoah Valley of Virignia.

SUGGESTED VIEWING

Masters Five. *The Original Masters Five*. Gaither Music Video. A performance video by this all-star group of veteran singers, which includes Jake Hess, Hovie Lister, J. D. Sumner et al.

Statesmen. *An American Classic*. Gaither Music Video. Fine live performance by this group, which is now in its fifth decade of singing.

ANGLO-AMERICAN SACRED MUSIC

Various. *Chase the Devil: Religious Music of the Appalachians.* Shanachie. This BBC documentary was shot in the early 1980s and features holiness singing and preaching, along with other local styles.

Various. *Joy Unspeakable.* Indiana University Television/Folkstreams.net. An ethnographic film that examines Pentecostalism through the documentation of three types of Oneness Pentecostal services in southern Indiana: a gospel-rock concert, a regular Sunday service, and a camp meeting.

Various. *I'll Keep On Singing.* Stephen Shearson/Middle Tennessee State University/School of Music. This film documents the contemporary southern gospel convention tradition, an amateur Christian music-making and educational tradition that developed in rural America following the Civil War.

Various. *Powerhouse for God.* Documentary Educational Resources/Folkstreams.net. An hour-long film by Jeff Titon, Tom Rankin, and Barry Dornfeld, that compliments the book by the same name.

Various. *The Shakers.* Davenport Films/Folkstreams.net. Focused on surviving members of this sect in New England, this 1974 film explores the history, culture, and music of the Shakers.

Various. *Sweet Is the Day: A Sacred Harp Family Portrait.* The Alabama Folklife Association/Folkstreams.net. The story of the Wootens, an Alabama family involved with sacred harp singing since the 1850s.

Chapter 6

AFRICAN AMERICAN RELIGIOUS FOLK MUSIC

- The Great Awakening and Camp Meetings
- Spirituals
- Ring Shouts
- Gospel
- Pentecostal Singing and Guitar Evangelists
- Preachers on Record
- Gospel Quartets
- Final Thoughts

The cliché that churches form the backbone of black American life contains a great deal of truth. This need for social cohesiveness and leadership was particularly pressing in the eighteenth and nineteenth centuries during the decades of legalized slavery. Even following Reconstruction churches served as social services networks, rallying points for civil rights, and public spokespersons, among other functions. Although the federal government sanctioned full civil and legal rights for African Americans by the mid-1960s, black churches remain at the core of life for many people in the United States.

It is abundantly true that religious music remains *the* clear stronghold for traditional music in the African American community. Because the music of most mainstream black churches tends to be conservative, this is not surprising. Technological innovations, such as the adaptation of electric bass guitars or electronic organs, can be heard in many churches. The core framework of black sacred music, however, remains more closely tied to its roots. This is most evident in important elements such as repertoire, training techniques, and vocal styles.

A strong symbiotic relationship between secular and sacred black music has existed since the beginning of the United States. Some singers and instrumentalists have always been devoted exclusively to their religious calling, but many others have mediated between both worlds. By the early twentieth century rural black musicians with varied musical interests played for Saturday night square

AFRICAN AMERICAN RELIGIOUS FOLK MUSIC

Dewey Williams, a revered leader of Sacred Harp Singing in Alabama. Courtesy of the Ralph Rinzler Folklife Archives and Collections, Center for Folklife and Cultural Heritage, Smithsonian Institution.

dances and then got up the next morning to provide music for their church. Since the "golden age of gospel" music in the late 1940s, the monetary opportunites for sacred music performers have sometimes been raised to extraordinary heights. These enticements have lured traditionally trained sacred singers such as Aretha Franklin and Sam Cooke from their churches to pursue careers on the popular stage. As we shall see in chapter 11, there are many elements of folk music in contemporary African American popular music.

THE GREAT AWAKENING AND CAMP MEETINGS

The **Great Awakening** of the 1730s brought several important changes to American religious life, one of which was the enlivening of the tunes and words sung during services. Hymns based on religiously inspired poems rather than the psalms taken from biblical scripture gained favor. The popularity of Dr. Isaac Watts's books, *Hymns and Spiritual Songs* (1707) and *The Psalms of David, Imitated in the Language of the New Testament and Apply'd to the Christian State and Worship* (1717) was so strong that Protestants soon came to prefer **Dr. Watts's hymns**. By the 1740s both whites and blacks who attended church were singing hymns as part of each worship service.

AFRICAN AMERICAN RELIGIOUS FOLK MUSIC

The Second Great Awakening was the next religious movement to greatly impact America. A frontier revival phenomenon, its greatest force was felt between 1790 and 1830. **Camp meetings** where great numbers of people lived and worshiped for at least several days in temporary tents became the norm. Methodists slowly came to dominate camp meetings, and Methodist hymns were sung in meetings that by the early nineteenth century had spread across all of the Middle Atlantic states into the Deep South. Unlike most aspects of contemporary American life, camp meetings were not entirely segregated. Groups upward of 3,000 gathered to sing and hear preaching, with blacks and whites keeping separate quarters on the grounds. Whether standing or seated, blacks attended camp meetings, sometimes participating as preachers. Such modest integration resulted in mutual influences and the emergence of spiritual songs that found favor among both black and white singers.

Camp meeting singing was congregational. Contemporary accounts suggest that blacks often sang louder than whites and that blacks often stayed up singing long after their counterparts had retired for the night. These late-night gatherings provided black singers a forum for experimentation not previously available to them. Away from the watching eyes of their Anglo counterparts, blacks began to shift their singing away from the camp meeting hymns. They improvised by adding lines from biblical verses and prayers to the well-known Watts hymns, which became solidified by the frequent addition of choruses and refrains. The tunes, too, veered from the acceptable European melodies toward the banjo and fiddle dance tunes favored in folk music. These new songs contained enough familiar elements to gain swift and widespread acceptance as a new genre, *spiritual songs*.

In New England, where blacks constituted a vastly smaller number and percentage of the population, slaves became part of the worship service held by whites. Seated in segregated pews (a precursor of the "separate but equal" doctrine), blacks were exposed to the religious practices of northern Europeans, an experience steeped in ritual that possibly reminded them of the importance of their own ceremonies. The music itself, however, must have seemed wildly tame by comparison with their own background. The white religious music, usually Dutch Reformed, Congregational, Methodist, or other related sects, lacked the fervor and rhythmic punch of (the increasingly distant) West African music. Drums, often playing improvisational patterns and indispensable to their rituals, were simply not found in these churches.

But, any black attending a church with strong connections to England would have recognized the lining out performance practice so often found in black African music. Lining out a psalm provided an easy way for white and black churchgoers to learn the song's text, along with the basic melody, with the song leader providing a line or two and the congregation repeating the line(s). This practice proved to be one of the few early direct links between Anglo and African music and was a common practice among blacks singing work songs. African American antiphony, however, often overlaps, creating a more complex and rhythmically interesting style that resonates in today's hip-hop culture.

In the South some whites even became involved with the religious instruction of blacks. On large plantations slaves were kept in relative cultural and social isolation, a practice reflected in the slaves' religious training. Blacks were allowed to attend all-black weekly religious services and could ocassionally participate at a white church by standing in a separate section in the back of the church. Clergymen were sometimes brought in to lead slaves in their own religious worship. Southern colonies in general were not as strict about the Sabbath as their northern counterparts. Indeed there was far less religious instruction for southern blacks and much greater social and economic segregation.

SPIRITUALS

Although their precise origins remain obscure, **spirituals** are among the earliest sacred folk songs attributable to black culture. "Spiritual" is a general term for nineteenth-century black American religious folk songs that are sometimes called anthems, jubilees, or gospel songs. White origins for African American spirituals have been argued, but the considerable interchange between white and black musical traditions prior to the Civil War makes such discussions moot.

The term itself was not used in print prior to the 1860s, but descriptions in travel accounts and diaries of songs that sound like spirituals exist as early as 1819. These descriptions by whites speak of traits such as syncopated hand clapping and foot stamping that provided the rhythmic fervor absent from Anglo-American music. Contemporary accounts also list call and response, group participation, and improvised texts as the other notable characteristics of these spirituals. The form of spirituals tended to be similar with an alternating line and refrain that encouraged the textual improvisation that impressed so many eighteenth-century observers. "In That Great Getting-Up Morning" is a traditional song containing many of the textual elements found in nineteenth-century spirituals. Note how its structure encourages the singer to improvise new lines to further the story:

I'm a-going to tell you about the coming of the savior

Refrain: In that great getting-up morning, fare you well, fare you well!

The Lord spoke to Gabriel.

Refrain

Go look behind the altar.

Refrain

Take down the silver trumpet.

Refrain

Blow your trumpet, Gabriel.

Refrain

Lord, how loud shall I blow it?

Refrain

Blow it right and easy.

Refrain

Do not alarm my people.

Refrain

Tell 'em to come to judgment.

Refrain
Gabriel, blow your trumpet.

Refrain

Lord, how loud shall I blow it?

Refrain

Loud as seven peals of thunder.

Refrain

Wake up the living nations.

Refrain

MUSICAL EXAMPLE

Livingstone, Alabama, was home to Dock Reed, an exceptionally powerful singer with a vast storehouse of African American folk songs who was born late in the nineteenth century. Reed had first recorded for the Library of Congress several times between 1937 and 1941. In the middle 1950s folk songs collector Harold Courlander "rediscovered" Reed while he was surveying black folk music in central Alabama. Courlander recorded Reed in great depth, further documenting his stories as well as Reed's magnificent voice and his nineteenth-century spirituals.

Title "Jesus Goin' to Make Up My Dying Bed"
Performer Dock Reed
Instrument one voice
Length 1:15

Musical Characteristics
1. His a cappella voice means this piece has a monophonic texture.
2. The melody is conjunctive and quite smooth.
3. Reed displays a marvelous control over the vibratto in his voice.
4. A "rise" in his voice of a fifth can be heard at the beginning of the first phrase of the first verse (the extended "Oh . . .") and at several other points.
5. The song is in an *aaab* form.

Oh, don't you worry 'bout me dyin'!
Oh, don't worry 'bout me dyin'!
Oh, worry 'bout me dying'!
Jesus goin' to make up my dyin' bed.

Oh, I been in this valley! (repeat twice)
Jesus goin' to make up my dyin' bed.

Ah, when you see me dyin'
I don't want you to cry.
All I want you to do for me
Just low my dyin' head.

Ah, I'm sleepin' on Jesus!
Ah, sleepin' on Jesus!
Oh, I'm sleepin' on Jesus!
Jesus goin' to make up my dyin' bed!

This selection is from Smithsonian Folkways 4418.

Spiritual texts are often characterized as sad or even sorrowful. They usually lament the trials and difficulties of a life that was made doubly difficult by slavery. Songs such as "Nobody Knows the Trouble I've Seen" and "Roll Jordan" are two well-known spirituals. The refrain "Motherless children have hard time when their mother's dead" exemplifies the motifs of loss and separation. Death and escape are two other recurring themes found in spirituals, and it is often suggested that such themes serve a dual purpose. One purpose is to lament earthly hardships and the peace of dying and eternal life, while the other is a code or a phrase with a double or hidden meaning. They could also express the hope of stealing away from slavery and the freedom of the North. In later years, particularly during the most recent civil rights movement that began in the 1950s, spirituals were sung to protest economic and social conditions in the South with refrains about "crossing the River of Jordan" and creating a new vision of America.

The earliest spiritual collection *Slave Songs of the United States* (1867) by William Francis Allen, Charles Pickard Ware, and Lucy McKim Garrison includes some well-known spirituals that continue to be sung: "Old Ship of Zion," "Michael, Row the Boat Ashore," and "Get on Board, Children." Their transcriptions only hint at the complex rhythms and vocal qualities of the songs, while suggesting that early black spirituals used slightly flattened notes, generally the third, fifth, and seventh. The authors readily admit that they could not reduce to standard Western notation all of the various shadings, anticipations, and slurs that they heard, but their admission clearly underscores that some of the vocal techniques heard in gospel music and work songs were present in the spirituals of the 1860s.

Spirituals were most often performed by a small group that accompanied and supported its leader. In addition to call and response, some of these hymns were lined out. By the late nineteenth century, however, spirituals were commonly found in hymnals and in other printed sources. Their arrangements grew more elaborate, were written in four-part harmony, and moved further from the folk practices. The "jubilee" groups sent out by Fisk, Hampton, Tuskegee, and other pioneering colleges for black and Native Americans included singers trained in Western musical practices. They were also concertizing, rather than performing for a group of peers in a sacred setting. These factors helped set jubilee singing groups apart from their sacred counterparts, both in context and performance style.

Still occasionally performed, spirituals have been an important part of black folk culture for approximately 150 years and are still found in the repertoire of many small black church groups and choirs. Even African American singers trained in the European tradition, such as Leontyne Price, occasionally perform and record spirituals. Rising from the musical culture of camp meetings and other evangelical forums, spirituals helped to guide the way for the gospel songs that developed at the dawn of the twentieth century.

RING SHOUTS

A **ring shout**, one of the earliest forms of African American religious practice, combines physical movement with song. These songs are almost always spirituals. A ring shout is reminiscent of some West African religious ceremonies and remains one of the closest and clearest connections between black American and African folk culture. Arguably the oldest form of Afro-American folk music to be heard today, ring shouts are one way that participants have of communicating directly with God through spontaneous movement and singing.

The concept of divine communication links those who take part in a ring shout with adherents to **Pentecostal beliefs** in many ways. First, both services are of indeterminate length—they last as long as the spirit of the Holy Ghost is present. Second, physical movement (sometimes called a holy dance) is an integral part of a ring shout and a Pentecostal church service. Third, rhythm is at the heart of both services: men and women use body percussion at a ring shout, while a band (usually augmented by syncopated clapping, tambourines, and other handheld percussion) holds forth at a Pentecostal church. Finally, these spontaneous events eschew printed programs that tell you the service's precise order.

Once found across much of the South, ring shouts are now geographically limited and remain part of religious services in a few islands just off the coast where Georgia and South Carolina meet. These islands have only been easily accessible to the mainland since about 1930 when the first bridges and causeways were built. With a black population that once constituted 90 percent of the local population, the people of the sea islands are almost all descendants of cotton plantation slaves. This combination of factors has made the sea islands a stronghold for folk culture including Gullah (a creolized language that retains ties with its African roots) speech, folk tales, and ring shouts.

Contemporary ring shouts are held in special "praise houses" where the faithful regularly gather. The "watch meetings" that draw the greatest number of attendees are held at Christmas and Easter. Most participants have moved past middle age; very few are under the age of forty. These are primarily song services without a sermon or separate choir to sing. The singing is done by a "band" of vocalists—a lead singer and respondents whose songs are almost always antiphonal. The songs themselves are perhaps best characterized as spirituals. Vocal bands, by the way, are still found today in some southern and

The Southern Wonders, a Memphis gospel quartet, broadcast over WDIA in the early 1950s. Courtesy of Kip Lornell.

northern Pentecostal churches. After a long period of singing spirituals such as "Savior Do Not Pass Me By," the ring shout begins.

Although not all of the worshipers actually get up and move, some shuffle around. Their feet are not supposed to cross nor be lifted from the ground—just as the worshipers are in direct contact with God, their contact with the earth is equally constant. During the shout people are singing, speaking ecstatically (in tongues), and clapping polyrhythmically. Most of the participants are able to carry on three different rhythms simultaneously with their feet, hands, and voice. Ring shouts can last for hours and the important ones often last all night.

The following description of a Christmas shout from an elementary school in 1865 illustrates that this religious practice has changed little in over one hundred years:

> The children move around in a circle, backwards, or sideways, with their feet and arms keeping energetic time, and their whole bodies undergoing most extraordinary contortions, while they sing at the top of their voice the refrain. (*Pearson Letters from Port Royal*, 292–93, quoted in Epstein)

AFRICAN AMERICAN RELIGIOUS FOLK MUSIC

MUSICAL EXAMPLE

This ring shout was recorded at a workshop in Mississippi, but it captures the atmosphere and passion of a sea islands prayer service. Singers from the Moving Star Hall on John's Island near Charleston, South Carolina, have kept this very emotional singing alive for many decades. During the 1960s, when this performance was recorded, the group toured the United States, appearing at the Newport Folk Festival and many other smaller events. This tradition and the singers face a new challange as their islands are developed for the tourist and retirement trade, which is exemplified by the Hilton Head Resort; today the sea islands are mostly white.

Title "Talking 'bout a Good Time"
Performer Benjamin Bligen (leader)
Instruments four voices
Length 1:11

Musical Characteristics
1. You hear a cappella singing accompanied by syncopated hand clapping.
2. There is an acceleration in tempo during the final third of the performance.
3. It is an antiphonal arrangement with unison singing in the chorus.
4. There is a crescendo in dynamic level toward the middle of the performance.

Call: Good time, a good time
Response: We gonna have a time! (x6)

Call: Singing for a good time
Response: We gonna have a time! (x2)

Call: Shouting for a good time.
Response: We gonna have a time! (x2)

(Clapping begins and the tempo increases)

Call: Good time, a good time
Response: We gonna have a time! (x2)

Call: Talking 'bout a good time.
Response: We gonna have a time!

Call: Good time, a good time.
Response: We gonna have a time! (x2)

This selection is from Smithsonian Folkways 40031.

GOSPEL

Nineteenth-century folk music came from a variety of sources. The themes for the sermons of Baptist preachers draw their inspiration from the Bible and everyday experience, while choirs in AME churches often took their messages from the New Testament of the Bible. By the dawn of the twentieth century a new wellspring, the gospel song, began penetrating and affecting each of these genres. Spirituals arose from the devastating effects of slavery; their message of hope and of flight to a new land captured the attention of black Americans. Around the turn of the century, just as racism reemerged and blues, ragtime, and jazz began emerging, a younger generation of African Americans started composing simple "gospel" songs of praise. Within a decade these songs had attracted the attention of churchgoers and, significantly, sheet music and songbook publishers.

Such compositions drew from the black secular and sacred experience to create something new. While hymns are directed toward God, the message of gospel songs is aimed at humankind. The term **gospel** is subject to a number of definitions. For some it refers to any type of sacred selection, implying that the phrases "gospel music" and "religious music" are interchangeable. Others divide religious music into more specific categories: hymns, spirituals, and jubilees. Hymns are older songs drawn from the published Protestant hymnals of the nineteenth century, also known as Dr. Watts's hymns. They are sometimes lined out or even performed as solos. Spirituals refer to the largely antebellum songs of unknown authorship that passed through oral tradition. Themes of freedom, movement, and unburdening predominate. Their form is usually ab or verse/chorus. **Jubilee** has two distinctive meanings. The initial reference was to songs about freedom or release from slavery and the happiness at being set free. More specifically, they refer to the type of formalized spirituals performed by the Fisk Jubilee Singers (among other groups) that emerged during Reconstruction. In the 1930s the term was reinvented in reference to up-tempo songs performed by black gospel quartets that feature vocal effects, high rhythmic interest, strong lead vocal, and a "pump" bass. The **Golden Gate Quartet** pioneered this style of jubilee gospel singing in the middle 1930s.

The specific meaning of "gospel song" relates to the fact that it can be traced to a specific composer—**Thomas A. Dorsey**, Cleavant Derricks, Rev. C. A.

MUSICAL EXAMPLE

This West Coast–based group had a successful pop music career in the late 1960s and early 1970s. Here they betray their roots in the Baptist church with this version of a spiritual-like song that, despite its title, is not related to Albert Brumley's well-known gospel song. This style of gospel singing was first heard in the early 1950s. It features a "drive section" toward the middle of the song in which the chorus is repeated ("Do you feel like shouting?") while the lead singer improvises. During this section they stay on the tonic chord both to spotlight the lead singer and as a means to heighten the tension and emotion of the song.

Title "Before You Get to Heaven (I'll Fly Away)"
Performers The Chambers Brothers
Instruments drums, guitar, and four voices
Length 3:25

Musical Characteristics
1. A duple 2/4 meter is quickly established by the instruments.
2. Call-and-response style is apparent between the lead singer and the chorus.
3. Crescendo dynamics are featured during the drive section.
4. There is a gently syncopated rhythm.
5. The moderate tempo increases slightly.
6. The shouting lead vocal includes a falsetto singing style.

It's a rough and rocky road, before you get to heaven. (x3)
And I feel like shouting all the time.

You have to cry sometimes, before you get to heaven. (x3)
And I feel like shouting all the time.

You have to pray sometimes, before you get to heaven. (x3)
And I feel like shouting all the time.

You got to love everybody, before you get to heaven. (x3)
And I feel like shouting all the time.

You have to moan sometimes, before you get to heaven. (x3)
And I feel like shouting all the time.

"Drive" section: Do you feel like shouting?
   I feel like shouting!
   and so on.

This selection is from Smithsonian Folkways 31008.

Tindley, **Rev. Herbert W. Brewster**, or Lucie Campbell. These early gospel songs were also the first type of black sacred music to be transmitted first within small groups and then to a large audience by way of the printed mass media. Gospel songs and the more emotional performance techniques are sometimes found among both black and white performers—especially as the genre became more widespread in the 1930s. Moreover, some gospel songs by white composers such as Albert Brumley and Fannie Crosby became part of a shared black and white repertoire.

Early gospel songs incorporated bright imagery and simile to achieve their power and directness. In 1893 W. Henry Sherwood published *The Harp of Zion*, one of the earliest hymnals to use gospel songs. By the 1920s these newly minted gospel songs impinged upon all aspects of black religious music. This appears to be particularly true for the **guitar evangelists**, whose recorded repertoires are peppered with written compositions. **Blind Willie Johnson**, for example, recorded "Sweeter as the Years Go By," written and published by C. H. Morris in 1912. Blind Joe Taggart, Washington Phillips, and others waxed C. A. Tindley's 1916 song, "Leave It There" under the title "Take Your Burden to the Lord." A 1909 composition by Benjamin Franklin Butts, "It's All Right Now," appeared to be a staple of Arizona Drane's repertoire, as her accomplished recording in 1927 implies. Some of these songs had already entered into oral tradition by the 1920s, while others seem to have been learned from printed sources such as *Gospel Pearls*. The full flowering of gospel publishing did not occur until the 1930s and 1940s when these new compositions hit the black religious community with the force of atomic power.

In the 1930s the gospel scene exploded. The works of the earlier gospel composers continued to gain popularity, primarily through their performances in church and the printed medium. Turn-of-the-century composing pioneers, such as Rev. C. A. Tindley, inspired the younger performers. By the early 1930s the commercial companies had expanded their recordings of sermons, vocal quartets, and guitar evangelists to include more of the increasingly popular gospel songs. "Georgia Tom" Dorsey, often referred to as the father of gospel music, emerged as the most influential of the early gospel performers whose work was heralded and greatly advanced by the mass media. Along with sisters Sallie

Roberta Martin and the Roberta Martin Singers: The Legacy and The Music

Roberta Martin, gospel pioneer, was honored by the Smithsonian Institution in the 1980s. Courtesy of Kip Lornell.

Martin, Roberta Martin (no relation), and Willie Mae Ford Smith, this triumvirate soon revamped Chicago into the nodal point for the commercialization of gospel music in the African American community.

Dorsey began his career as a blues performer. His first widespread exposure came with Ma Rainey, for whom he served as pianist and musical director until 1928 when he joined Tampa Red (Hudson Whittaker). This duo proved enormously successful with a series of records with lightly salacious tunes such as "It's Tight Like That," "Somebody's Been Using That Thing," "Billie the Grinder," "Stewin' Your Mess," and "The Stuff You Sell." Along with Big Bill (Broonzy) they were among the front-line purveyors of "hokum blues," featuring snappy guitar or guitar/piano duets, double entendre or humorous lyrics, and clear vocals. This music was strictly uptown, played for fun, but ultimately unsatisfying for Thomas Dorsey. In 1932 Tampa Red and Georgia Tom broke up their partnership. Red remained with blues and hokum music, but Dorsey turned his full attention to gospel composition and performance.

Dorsey's gospel recordings, "How About You?" and "If You See My Savior," recorded in March 1932, debuted nearly a decade after he began writing gospel songs. His debut sold quite poorly, which is not surprising considering the country was hitting the depths of the Depression and 75 cents was too much for even the most uplifting recording. Although Dorsey went on to record a few more religious titles, he quickly proved his worth as a composer. Nearly four hundred songs flowed from his pen, including such American classics as "Take My Hand Precious Lord," "If You See My Savior, Tell Him That You Saw Me," "Little Wooden Church on the Hill," "Peace in the Valley," "When the Gates Swing Wide," "Hide Me in Thy Bosom," and "Search Me Lord." Many of these enduring compositions were published as sheet music, while others appeared in the National Baptist Sunday School hymnal, *Gospel Pearls*, the first edition of which appeared in 1921.

Dorsey also served as one of the principal organizers of the National Gospel Music Association. He and his fellow Chicagoans founded this organization in 1935 and it rapidly expanded to chapters across the United States. By the late 1930s gospel music was being performed in black churches throughout the entire country.

Gospel music clearly benefited from the media's attention. Although gospel recordings were not plentiful until after World War II, they did trickle out slowly. Radio proved more helpful as performers with Sunday programs increased, spreading the word to those who could not or did not attend church services that featured this new music. The printed media became the most critical factor in disseminating gospel music throughout the community. Small publishing houses began printing songbooks containing the words and simple four-part musical notations for these new compositions. These songbooks sold well as gospel fans looked forward to each new edition. Used as a point of departure, songbooks provided groups with an established reference for embellishing the printed arrangements for their own purposes. In its actual performance black gospel music is highly dramatic and personal. No printed score could hope to (or want to) limit the singers' vocal techniques, their reworking of harmonies, or the use of syncopation to heighten their performance.

By the late 1930s Roberta Martin had emerged as one of the most important innovators in gospel music. Her recordings from the 1940s and 1950s suggest that even in the middle of the twentieth century, black gospel music combines West African and western European elements. Her melodies betray an allegiance to black American folk and African traditions in her use of few tones (often pentatonic scales or the mixolydian mode), conjunctive melodies, and a persistant emphasis on one principal tone. Most of the songs adhere to the simple ab song form. Her harmonic language is closer to standard western European usage, with a clear emphasis on the primary chords. She also demonstrates a clear preference for **compound duple meters**, especially 12/8.

Another major innovation spawned by this music, the gospel concert/caravan, began in the late 1930s and signals its movement from the grassroots to the popular realm. Gospel programs brought together performers for special shows outside of the church service itself. Of course this was not distinctly new because out-of-town groups were sometimes invited to sing at special Saturday evening or Sunday afternoon programs. The innovation occurred when singers got together and toured full time. The community had not previously been able to financially support such groups, but gospel's newly minted popularity permitted this. Thomas A. Dorsey's progeny hit the road as part of a package that performed on tours during the week as well as on weekends. Although they were several years ahead of their time, the Soul Stirrers of Houston, Texas, became the first gospel quartet to begin touring, trading their full-time day jobs for full-time touring in 1938.

Black gospel music represents a blend of musical as well as cultural innovation. First, it is music whose harmonic and melodic structure was deliberately similar to popular tunes. Composers like Dorsey felt that one way to reach a mass audience with a spiritual message was to package the songs in familiar musical settings. Second, its message was equally straightforward with themes that appealed to the heartstrings: mother, duty, and home. Third, its simplicity was clearly aimed at an audience that could easily participate and become enveloped in gospel music. Fourth, gospel became the first African American religious music for which direct authorship of songs could be ascribed. Finally, gospel music emerged as the first style to be packaged with the mass media in mind and clearly aimed toward an increasingly sophisticated audience that looked to radio, records, and printed sources for sacred music.

PENTECOSTAL SINGING AND GUITAR EVANGELISTS

Holiness sects came into existence during the last decade of the nineteenth century as people sought to gain a second blessing or sanctification through direct possession or intervention on the part of the Holy Spirit. Holiness services, both black and white, are highly emotional, featuring spirited preaching, equally compelling music, and even more improvisation. Significantly, the performance practices found in Pentecostal churches form the foundation for modern black (and, in some instances, white) popular music during the mid- to late twentieth century.

Spontaneous holy dancing, shouting (ecstatic speech), and glossolalia (speaking in tongues) are three notable aspects of Holiness services that occur as congregation members are possessed by the Spirit. These ritual acts are part of most Pentecostal services, though they are almost never captured on record. One would have to listen to or attend an entire service to taste its true flavor, but several important black Pentecostal performers did record as early as 1926.

By the time of these initial recordings, most of the black Holiness sects were no more than thirty years old. The majority of these Churches of God were founded in the Deep South between 1895 and 1905. Most significant is the **Church of God in Christ**, founded in Lexington, Mississippi, by Charles C. H. Mason in 1895. Shortly after the turn of the century, Mason moved the church headquarters to Memphis, where it remains today. The Church of God in Christ has grown to be the largest African American Pentecostal church. In the early twenty-first century Pentecostal adherents comprise close to 20 percent of all black churchgoers, many of whom belong to urban congregations (temples) with small memberships.

Pentecostalists believe in the baptism of the Holy Spirit, the "second baptism" that people receive because of special calling. This spiritual rebirth or calling is reflected in their fiery music. Holiness singers believe that they are called to praise God with a variety of instruments, as cited in the Book of Psalms. Rev. F. W. McGee, who established a temple in Chicago's South Side in the middle 1920s, and the blind pianist Arizona Dranes were among the outstanding early Holiness recording artists. McGee was a preacher whose sermons were recorded by Victor with the accompaniment of various stringed instruments and horns. Other sanctified preachers, such as Rev. D. C. Rice, preferred to lead small ensembles in performances of popular Holiness songs. Small jug bands accompanied at least a few of the groups associated with Memphis's Holiness groups—Reverend Bryant's Sanctified Singers and the Holy Ghost Singers. Perhaps the most dramatic and musically moving of these performers was Arizona Dranes. Her OKeh recordings of "Bye and Bye We're Going to See the King" and "I'm a Witness" are masterpieces of this genre. Black sanctified music is characterized by dramatic vocals, the use of instruments (stringed and horns) not usually associated with sacred traditions, cooperative vocal ensembles that eschewed close harmony for collective improvisation, and a fierce spontaneity.

Because of the popularity of the guitar—due to its portability, the ability of its strings to bend for flatted tonalities, and its relative low cost—a small group of guitar evangelists became part of rural black music. The truth is that nearly all rural black musicians played sacred music; some specialized in it, and a handful of them were recorded beginning in the 1920s. Rev. Edward Clayborn, whose recordings for Vocalion are characterized by a pronounced duple meter and a strong regular rhythm punctuated by his slide guitar, preferred homiletic pedantic songs: "Everybody Ought to Treat Their Mother Right" and "Men Don't Forget Your Wives for Your Sweethearts." Blind Joe Taggart, thought to be from South Carolina, roamed the southeastern states preaching and singing. He was occasionally accompanied by a fiddle and second guitar on his recordings. Other evangelists from this period—Blind Roger Hayes, Blind Willie Davis, Blind Mamie Forehand, Blind Gussie Nesbit—seemed attracted to the profession by a love for God and music and because of their physical liabilities, too.

MUSICAL EXAMPLE

Pentecostal sects can be found throughout the United States. They are growing rapidly, although not as quickly as other fundamentalist churches. In predominantly black neighborhoods they often hold services in small storefront churches. Many parts of the rural South are dotted with Pentecostal churches, though they tend to be strongest in the Deep South. This recording was done on location at the First Independent Holy Church of God—Unity—Prayer in Marion, Alabama, in 1954. The church was founded and fronted by Elder Effie Hall, who leads her small congregation on this piece.

Title "Don't Let His Name Go Down"
Performers Elder Effie Hall and Congregation
Instruments guitar, percussion, tambourine, and four voices
Length 1:24

Musical Characteristics
1. It has a simple, syncopated rhythm.
2. The mix of voices and instruments produces a rich homophonic texture.
3. The song stays on the dominant chord with some subdominant harmony heard in the singing.
4. The background singers primarily sing in unison.
5. A fervent, improvised feel propels the chorus.

Oh, don't let His name go down! (repeat)

Chorus: I'm goin' to do what I can, hold up His hand

Don't let His name go down!

Well, don't let His name go down! (repeat)

Chorus (substitute "all" for "what")

His name is holy and sanctified! (repeat)

Chorus

(Repeat the first verse)

Glory!

This selection is from Smithsonian Folkways 2658.

Mississippi guitar evangelist Rev. Leon Pinson appeared at the Festival of American Folklife. Courtesy of the Ralph Rinzler Folklife Archives and Collections, Center for Folklife and Cultural Heritage.

(The options for visually handicapped blacks born near the turn of the century were as limited as their educational opportunities.)

Blind Willie Johnson, born about 1902 near Marlin, Texas, was one of the finest rural black musicians to record and arguably the most accomplished guitar evangelist. He spent much of his life as a street singer and came to the attention of Columbia officials in 1927. A virtuoso guitarist and an arresting vocalist with an exceptionally wide range, Johnson sang to the accompaniment of his slide guitar. A female singer named Willie B. Harris participated in several of his sessions, serving as a wonderful foil to his singing, which ranged from a sweet falsetto to an emotive growl. Their repertoire included many of the most familiar gospel songs: "Let Your Light Shine on Me," "John the Revelator," "You'll Need Somebody on Your Bond," and "I Know His Blood Will Make Me Whole." His recorded masterpiece, "Dark was the Night—Cold Was the Ground," however, is a solo piece in which his slide recalls the holy moaning of a Baptist church service. "You'll Need Somebody on Your Bond" is a vocal duet with his wife, Angeline, and is underpinned by his delicate slide guitar:

> Well, you gonna need somebody on your bond,
> You gonna need somebody on your bond,
> Now it's way, at midnight,
> When Death comes slippin' in your room
> You gonna need ah, somebody on your bond.

PREACHERS ON RECORD

Preachers became the first and arguably the most vitally powerful voices to reach the faithful. One of the clearest, most widely recognized voices belongs to **Rev. J. M. Gates** of Atlanta, the spiritual forefather for Martin Luther King. Gates's initial May 1926 Columbia release, "Death's Black Train Is Coming," proved so wildly successful that the company immediately released its session mate, "I'm Gonna Die with the Staff in My Hand." The Gates phenomenon continued, and by year's end he had visited the studios of Pathe, Plaza, OKeh, Victor, Vocalion, and Gennett. Most of these recordings were accomplished in New York City studios, though Reverend Gates did stay at home for his first session and for one in November 1926.

Rev. J. M. Gates's success illustrates the power and influence of the electronic media in promoting traditional music. In the spring of 1926 he was a very popular Baptist preacher with a large and devoted congregation in Atlanta, Georgia. Less than one year later Gates had recorded nearly eighty selections that mixed small group singing with his own preaching. Gates visited New York City on two occasions for marathon sessions, where he recorded many of the same titles/themes—"Baptize Me," "Death's Black Train Is Coming," "Dying Gambler," "I Know I Got Religion"—because they were powerful sermons and popular themes. Many of these selections were marketed by title only; the artist was not always listed. Thus Gates's most striking themes were repeated at least in part because of the pressure of record companies to sell product. These factors all worked to propel a respected local religious leader into the forefront of the nationwide race record industry in a staggeringly short period. Reverend Gates's popularity proved long-lived, too, for he continued to record, albeit sporadically, until 1941.

Rev. J. C. Burnett, a Kansas City preacher, soon followed Gates into the Columbia studios. His sermon on "The Downfall of Nebuchadnezzar" sold exceptionally well; apparently record buyers were moved by his interpretation of Daniel 4:14 and his hoarse emotive preaching. Burnett proved to be popular and stayed with Columbia Records for about three years; he recorded again after the close of World War II. While few of the early preachers enjoyed the long-lasting success that greeted Reverend Gates, nearly seventy of them continued to be documented by record companies throughout the 1920s and into the 1930s. By the close of the prewar record era in 1943 these preachers had recorded some 750 sermons on a wide variety of subjects ranging from biblical passages to moral issues such as drinking, drugs, and fidelity, to topical statements about floods, tornadoes, and the flight of Lindburgh. Reverend Burnett warned his listeners of gambling's dangers in a 1927 sermon, "The Gambler's Doom," that strayed from his usual biblical stories:

> I have seen the gambler standin' with his cards in his hand. And the fifty-two cards in the deck represent the fifty-two weeks in the year. And the 365 spots on the cards, represent the 365 days in the year. And the highest cards, my friends is the Ace; represents God on high over all. And the deuce represents Jesus' law "one of you could seek me and then you would find me." And the trey represents the three Godheads of the Trinity.

One of Gates's most pedantic sermons on a topic of everyday problems urged his listeners to "pay your furniture man"—who collected weekly or monthly for furniture purchased on time-payment plans.

How well did these recorded sermons reflect the experience of attending a church service? Clearly they could not replicate the emotional atmosphere of a live service. Live sermons benefited from the interaction between the preacher and congregation, whose "amens," "yes, Lords," and other responses punctuated the oration. Studio sermons most often included "a congregation" of between two and six voices, but these blanched in comparison to the experience of attending church. Moreover, the sermons were truncated to fit into three-minute packages, all but eliminating certain aspects of a church service and sermon: speaking in tongues, "anointed speech," and the strong extended ritual interaction (verbal and behavioral) could not be captured on disk. There is no replacement for the experience of attending a church service, but sermon records helped to remind the faithful of their worldly obligations and exposed them to different styles of preaching.

GOSPEL QUARTETS

More palatable folk music continued to predominate the mass media as the United States entered World War II. Led by the Golden Gate Quartet, both secular and sacred vocal quartets were beginning their rise to prominence. The Gates (as they were usually referred to) pioneered the jubilee style of quartet singing in Norfolk, Virginia. This modern "neo-jubilee" singing has little to do with Reconstruction jubilee groups; it represents an aesthetic innovation that profoundly affected black American sacred music. Jubilee singing incorporated new lyrical and musical ideas. Their lyrics often told a semilinear story based on Bible parables, such as the Gates's well-known versions of "Job" and "Noah." Unlike blues or the earlier spirituals, which tend to be nonlinear and cohere through emotional connections, jubilee songs are closer to sermons or nodal ballads in their ability to relate a story. Jubilee groups also featured a lead singer, whose dramatic but smooth *cante-fable* style clearly foreshadowed popular Motown singers like Smokey Robinson or Levi Stubbs. The pumping percussive bass helped to create the propulsive polyrhythms and carefully accented

AFRICAN AMERICAN RELIGIOUS FOLK MUSIC

Golden Gate Quartet, circa 1941.
Courtesy of Kip Lornell.

syncopations that characterize jubilee quartet singing. By way of their popular Bluebird and Columbia recordings and their NBC radio network broadcasts, the Golden Gate Quartet disseminated this music from the New York base throughout the entire country. This happened over a three-year period, profoundly affecting the course of black religious music for the next decade.

The radio, however, continued to broadcast comedy programs and news of the war as well as all types of music into people's homes. Of the major strains of black folk music, only religious traditions were part of radio's standard fare. Fifteen-minute or half-hour broadcasts by black vocal gospel groups became the norm in many cities across the United States. Nashville's Fairfield Four broadcast daily over 50,000-watt WLAC, while just to the east in Knoxville the Swan Silvertone Singers began their day with a fifteen-minute program on the less powerful WNOX.

By the war's end there was a pent-up demand for live performances by black gospel quartets, which was fermented by several years of restricted travel and widespread radio broadcasts. Prior to World War II only a handful of gospel quartets braved the difficulties of life on the road to become full-time touring groups. People now wanted to see and hear the groups that they had enjoyed on the radio. Independent record companies helped to fan the flames by issuing records by groups that enjoyed local or regional followings: New York City's Trumpeteers on Score Records, the Harmonizing Four of Richmond (Virginia) on Gotham, and the Spirit of Memphis on King and Peacock. The mass media helped reinforce the interest in gospel quartets by getting this music before the public and moving it into the popular realm. Between 1945 and 1950 this grassroots black music became intensely public as hundreds of quartets toured the country performing in large auditoriums, small churches, and school halls.

A new style, "hard gospel" quartet singing, began competing with and complementing the jubilee groups by the close of the decade. "Hard" refers to the emotionally powerful lead singing epitomized by Ira Tucker of the Dixie Hummingbirds and Julius Cheeks of the Sensational Nightingales. These singers utilized every trick in the repertoire of Afro-American folk singers: falsetto, rasps, growls, moans, highly ornamented phrasing, and so on. Their strongest, most pronounced improvisation came during the drive sections of live performances. The drive section, a repetitious groove during which the same chords or ostinato figure is repeated, encourages the lead singer to heighten emotional or spiritual feelings through improvisation. Hard gospel singing acknowledges the importance and influence of solo performers such as Alex Bradford, Mahalia Jackson, and Rosetta Tharpe.

Many of the black gospel quartets during this period become versatile, featuring singing in both the jubilee and hard gospel style. A cappella singing characterized the styles of many of these groups, but by the early 1950s most groups had added at least one instrument (usually a guitar) to their lineup. Instruments added a solid rhythmic foundation and provided the harmonic underpinning for the singing. Their repertoires were also undergoing changes, as more of the popular gospel songs liked Roberta Martin's "Swing Down, Chariot" or Reverend Brewster's "Move on Up a Little Higher" became integrated into programs. The role of the bass singer was de-emphasized, probably in light of the addition of instruments that often took the bass line. Two new time signatures, 12/8 and 6/8, or compound duple meters, augmented the standard duple meters. These so-called gospel meters became quite popular and were extensively used for certain songs. Another one of Reverend Brewster's gospel compositions from the 1940s, "Surely, God is Able," is regularly performed in 12/8 time.

By the early 1950s black gospel quartets concentrated on their programs as much as they did the religiosity of their musical message. Professional groups regularly performed in matching, often brightly colored, suits and had elaborate stage performances worked out. Certain groups earned reputations as "soul killers" because they put on such dramatic and moving programs. Money became an overriding concern because many of the singers had to support families. On one level black gospel quartet music had moved well beyond its grassroots status, functioning as a manifestation of popular culture. On the other hand, there were many local, community groups singing this music. They would never be stars or even semiprofessional singers, but they sang at local churches and were occasionally in demand for out-of-town programs.

Inevitably the quartet boom ended. Professional groups such as the Soul Stirrers, Pilgrim Travelers, C.B.S. Trumpeteers, and Spirit of Memphis could no longer support themselves as touring and recording artists. Some quartets disbanded; others retreated to semiprofessional status. Many of the grassroots quartets remained true to the music of their youth, and some have celebrated anniversaries of fifty or more years: Royal Harmony Four (Memphis) and the Sterling Jubilees (Birmingham). This process took several years to wind down, but by the late 1950s the era during which quartets were wildly popular was over. Their popularity was further diminished by that of choirs and soloists during the 1960s; nonetheless, modern quartets accompanied by electric guitar, bass, and drums remain in mainstream black churches.

By the twenty-first century popular black gospel music moved into new areas. The soloists, especially Mahalia Jackson but also Cassietta George and Delores Ward, are now old school. Larger vocal ensembles, notably large choruses and choirs like the Mississippi Mass Choir, gradually began to be heard on records and over the radio. Not surprisingly hip-hop has made inroads into gospel, once more reinvigorating gospel and (just as Dorsey sought to bring sacred music into the modern era in the early 1930s) bringing it closer to popular trends.

FINAL THOUGHTS

Religious music maintains its strong roots in black folk culture. Even the most modern gospel has clear links with the past, most often through the vocal styles that still emphasize the moans, growls, and other tricks that have been heard in black churches for decades. The older spirituals are still sometimes performed, but even modern gospel uses older songs. Pentecostal churches retain their conservative values; their updating is more superficial: electric instruments, microphones, and so on. Of all black folk music, the religious traditions continue to be the most vital and lively.

KEY FIGURES AND TERMS

Rev. Herbert W. Brewster
camp meetings
Church of God in Christ
compound duple meter

Thomas A. Dorsey
Rev. J. M. Gates
Golden Gate Quartet
gospel

AFRICAN AMERICAN RELIGIOUS FOLK MUSIC

Great Awakening
guitar evangelists
Blind Willie Johnson
jubilee
Pentecostal beliefs

ring shout
Slave Songs of the United States
spirituals
Dr. Watts's hymns

SUGGESTED LISTENING

John Alexander's Sterling Jubilee Singers. *Jesus Hits Like An Atomic Bomb.* New World 80294. Strong contemporary recordings that illustrates the diverse repertoire of an old-style gospel group that hails from one of the strongholds for quartet singing, Jefferson County, Alabama.

Georgia Sea Island Singers. *Georgia Sea Island Songs.* New World 80278. Half secular and half sacred material, its all spiritual music performed by members of one of the most firmly rooted of all black music communities.

Blind Willie Johnson. *Sweeter as the Years Go By.* Yazoo 1058. Some of Johnson's best and most moving songs are included on this set.

Osceola Mays. *Spirituals and Poems.* Documentary Arts. A low-key but moving collection of (mostly) nineteenth century a cappella spirituals performed solo by this female Texas artist.

Rosetta Tharpe. *Gospel of Blues.* MCA B0000C52FF. A reissue of her best-known work for Decca, recorded mostly in the 1940s.

Wiregrass Sacred Harp Singers. *The Colored Sacred Harp.* New World 80433. Contemporary recordings of African American sacred harp singing from southern Alabama.

Various. *Acapella Gospel Singing.* Folklyric 9045. An excellent survey of male gospel quartet singing from the 1920s to the 1950s, including the Golden Gate Quartet and the Soul Stirrers, among others.

Various. *Been In The Storm Too Long.* Smithsonian Folkways 40031. An anthology of Georgia Sea Island material that includes examples of spirituals, shouts, and prayers recorded in the early 1960s.

Various. *Classic African American Gospel from Smithsonian Folkways.* Smithsonian Folkways SFW 40194. This release samples the broad Asch/Folkways catalogue and includes quartet singing, solo spirituals, and more modern gospel.

AFRICAN AMERICAN RELIGIOUS FOLK MUSIC

Various. *Kings of the Gospel Highway*. Shanachie SHA-CD-6039. Some of the best male quartet performances by the likes of the Sensational Nightingales and the Soul Stirrers can be heard here.

Various. *Wade in the Water, African American Sacred Music Traditions, Box Set*. Smithsonian Folkways 40076-2-4. This four-CD set is a fine survey of contemporary genres. The four compact discs ("African American Spirituals: The Concert Traditions," "African American Congregational Singing: Nineteenth Century Roots," "African American Gospel: The Pioneering Composers," and "African American Community Gospel") are also available separately.

Various. *When Gospel Was Gospel*. Shanachie SHA-CD-6064. A superb anthology of post-WW II that includes classics by Clara Ward, the Swan Silvertones, Mahalia Jackson, and Roberta Martin.

SUGGESTED READING

Ray Allen. *Singing In the Spirit: African-American Sacred Quartets in New York City*. Philadelphia: University of Prennsylvania Press, 1992. An ethnographic study of the (mostly male) gospel quartet community in New York City.

Horace Boyer. *How Sweet The Sound: The Golden Age Of Gospel*. Champaign: University of Illinois Press, 2000. An historical survey of gospel music (with strong photographs) that focuses on the decades of the 1920s through the 1960s.

Candie and Guy Carawan. *Ain't We Got A Right to the Tree of Life?* Athens: University of Georgia Press, 1989. An ethnographic study of black life on the Georgia Sea Islands that emphasizes musical culture.

Bill Darden. *People Get Ready: A New History of Black Gospel Music*. New York: Continuum Books, 2005. Perhaps the best and most balanced history thus far written on this topic.

Jonathan C. David, with photographs by Richard Holloway. *Together Let Us Sweetly Live: The Singing and Praying Bands*. Urbana: University of Illinois Press, 2008. Based on years of field research, David has written a heart-felt book about the Cheasapeake Bay version of ring shouts that persist into the twenty-first century.

Tony Heilbut. *The Gospel Sound: Good News and Bad Times*. New York: Anchor Books, 1975. An overview of commercial gospel music from the Depression through the late 1960s, with sketches about such important figures as Mahalia Jackson, the Soul Stirrers, and Marion Williams.

AFRICAN AMERICAN RELIGIOUS FOLK MUSIC

Kip Lornell. *"Happy in the Service of the Lord": African American Sacred Harmony Quartets in Memphis*, 2nd edition. Knoxville: University of Tennessee Press, 1995. This book serves as an introduction to the black American quartet tradition and then focuses on Memphis over a sixty year period beginning in the 1920s.

Deborah Smith Pollard. *When the Church Becomes Your Party: Contemporary Gospel Music*. Detroit, MI: Wayne State University Press, 2008. Pollard explores the continuing—and often symbiotic—relationship between the sacred and the secular worlds of music into the twenty-first century.

Bernice Johnson Reagon, ed. *We'll Understand It Better By and By—Pioneering African American Gospel Composers*. Washington, D.C.: Smithsonian Institution Press, 1992. A series of essays that discuss the history and importance of composers such as Charles Tindley, Lucie D. Campbell, Thomas Dorsey, and Kenneth Morris.

Art Rosenbaum. *The African American Ring Shout Tradition in Coastal Georgia*. Athens: University of Georgia Press, 1998. A very worthy book that describes this almost extinct religious culutral complex. The text is carefully and lavishly illustrated with photographs by Margo R. Newark.

Robert Stone. *Sacred Steel: Inside an African American Steel Guitar Tradition*. Urbana: University of Illinois Press, 2010. Along with his sound recordings and film, Stone has contributed a solid book about this tradition, which should be far better known.

Gayle Wald. *Shout, Sister, Shout!: The Untold Story of Rock-and-Roll Trailblazer Sister Rosetta Tharpe*. New York: Beacon Press, 2008. Tharpe grew up in the Pentecostal church, but spent much of her fascinating life mediating between the worlds of secular and sacred music.

Willa Ward-Royster and Toni Rose. *"How I Got Over": Clara Ward and the World Famous Ward Singers*. Philadelphia, PA: Temple University Press, 1997. An account of the life and times of one of the most influential gospel soloists of the 1950s and 1960s.

Alan Young. *Woke Me Up This Morning: Black Gospel Singers and the Gospel Life*. Jackson: University Press of Mississippi, 1997. Young examines the music and lives of mostly contemporary, community-based, southern black gospel singers.

Jerry Zolten. *Great God A'Mighty! The Dixie Hummingbirds: Celebrating the Rise of Soul Gospel Music*. New York: Oxford University Press, 2003. Thoroughly researched and nicely written, Zolten explores not only the history of the Dixie Hummingbirds but also their impact on gospel music in the 1940s and 1950s.

AFRICAN AMERICAN RELIGIOUS FOLK MUSIC

SUGGESTED VIEWING

The Gospel According to Al Green. Mug-Shot Production/Magnum Entertainment, Inc. A lengthy portrait of this former soul singer's carrer, including scenes in his Pentecostal church in Memphis.

Various. *Sacred Steel.* Arhoolie Foundation Films. A documentary that examines several of the African American steel guitarists working in various Holiness churches in Florida and New York.

Various. *Say Amen, Somebody.* (Bonus Deluxe) Rykodisc. This stirring ninety-minute documentary covers some of the most important figures in the history of black gospel music, includes extensive notes and a fifteen-track compact disc.

Various. *Singing Stream.* Shanachie/Folkstreams.net. A documentary that provides a fine contextual and musical look at the Landers Family of gospel singers based in Granville County, North Carolina.

Various. *The Performed Word.* Gerald Davis Films/Folkstreams.net. Folklorist Davis explores the improvised African American sermon within the context of the aesthetics of African American expressive culture.

Chapter 7

AFRICAN AMERICAN SECULAR FOLK MUSIC

- Work Songs
- String Bands
- Fife and Drum Bands
- Ragtime and Coon Songs
- Ballads
- Songsters and Rural Music
- Down-home Blues
- Modern Blues
- Final Thoughts

It would be difficult to underestimate the profound impact of nineteenth- and twentieth-century black American folk music upon our culture. In this chapter you will learn about the types of secular black folk music that developed in the United States beginning in the nineteenth century. Because slavery's legacy left so many African Americans in rural southern areas, most of this music originated in the South. These innovations represent a move away from the early Africanized styles of folk music and directly into a uniquely and demonstrably African American hybrid, a process that began slowly but inexorably. The changes only accelerated with the end of legalized slavery, which was justifiably celebrated in songs like "The Year of Jubilee."

The dawn of the twentieth century saw the creation of ragtime, blues, jazz, and other influential forms of vernacular music that also reflect their southern heritage. Some of the instruments, most notably the fifes and drums or quills, are often homemade, partly reflecting the harsh economic conditions under which many blacks lived in the United States. The themes heard in many work songs—separation from loved ones, oppression by one's "Captain," hard work, longing for freedom—further underscore the difficult conditions under which many people lived. The important role played by songsters suggests the importance of all types of music within rural black communities, which were often far removed from the mainstream of American popular culture. Nonetheless, some of this music, especially blues, has now become a universally accepted part of our own vernacular musical vocabulary. The blues has even migrated well beyond our borders to influence popular music in other parts of the world.

Indeed, the music discussed in this section of *Exploring American Folk Music* forms the foundation for much of our contemporary popular music. Virtually all forms of twentieth- century popular music, most notably rock 'n' roll, directly evolved from these southern black roots. Although it might seem like a long distance from Scott Joplin's ragtime to the Gershwin Brothers, Elvis Presley, and the hip-hop nation of the 1990s, the direct links to earlier black folk music are there. (The precise nature of these relationship is more fully discussed in chapter 11.)

WORK SONGS

A **work song** is simply any song performed by workers that assists them in carrying out their task. With the exception of sea shanties and possibly some nineteenth-century cowboy songs (only a handful of which would be of black origin), work songs have been principally the domain of black American laborers. Anglo-American shanties, for example, flourished throughout the nineteenth century, particularly between 1820 and 1860, but faded as sailing ships were supplanted by steam vessels. Sea shanties accompanied all types of nautical work, including raising and lowering sails or hauling in an anchor. The songs themselves derive from a variety of sources: the minstrel stage, English ballads, popular contemporary ditties, even military marching songs. As long as the words and tune were well known, almost any song could be used as a sea shanty.

African American work songs, however, constitute a much richer, longer-lasting tradition. Black workers have utilized songs to accompany everything from shoe shining to poling a riverboat. In the nineteenth century, novels, diaries, and other printed sources describe all types of work songs, but it wasn't until the twentieth century that they began to be properly documented. These songs occasionally utilize harmonization and usually follow a simple, recurrent structure featuring unison singing or some type of call and response. Because so many twentieth-century work songs were collected in prisons, their themes are often related to incarceration. Sometimes even a religious folk song, like "Sign of Judgement," can be transformed into a work song. Most work songs, however, are based on secular themes, often escape or freedom of movement.

Regardless of their origins, work songs fulfilled several basic functions. One was to pass the time while workers carried out monotonous, repetitive jobs

Texas prisoners chopping wood in the 1930s. Courtesy of the Library of Congress.

such as hoeing a row of cotton, chopping or pulling weeds, caulking a boat's hull, or loading a truck. Work songs also provided the singers with a sense of solidarity by participating in a communal act. The singing gave workers a greater measure of control, co-opting that role from their boss or overseer. An even closer tie was forged by those whose task required special pacing or timing, such as spike driving, **track laying**, or hauling in fish nets. Crushed, mangled fingers resulted when the timing of a song leader heading a spike-driving crew wavered or faltered, so understanding the task and an ability to time the work, rather than possessing a marvelously powerful voice, was a prime requirement for a respected song leader. Finally, early work songs relieved tension by allowing blacks to complain about their living conditions and treatment by their employers or overseers.

Though only circumstantial evidence backs this up, work songs tended to be short and repetitive. This permitted almost anyone to join in their singing. A work song might consist of a half-dozen words improvised by the leader and a (usually repetitive) response by fellow workers. The musical phrases were brief, usually no more than four or five measures. But the key to avoiding true repetition was slight melodic and textual variations. The success of a song leader depended on his ability to improvise to make the singing more interesting. This ability, as we shall see, is another key element to high in-group respect accorded to African American musicians.

MUSICAL EXAMPLE

Prison work songs are a part of our musical past, though they could be heard in some sections of the South as recently as the 1970s. Such songs were most widely documented on wire recordings by the Library of Congress in the 1940s and later by other collectors. This selection was recorded in the early 1950s by a group, which included Pete Seeger, who traveled to Texas looking for work songs. They recorded a number of solo "arhoolies" as well as group work songs similar to this well-known hoe chopping song about breaking new ground for planting. Its themes of hard work and separation are common in work songs.

>**Title** "Chopping in the New Ground"
>**Performers** Texas Prisoners
>**Instruments** one lead voice and six voices in response
>**Length** 1:38

Musical Characteristics
1. You hear seven a cappella voices singing in antiphonal style.
2. There is a loose, unison response to the song leader.
3. The lead voice sings in a relatively tense vocal style.
4. A conjunctive pentatonic melody is heard in the response.
5. The piece has a very steady, moderate rhythm.

>Oh, Captain Charlie
>(Good God A'mighty)
>Oh, Captain Charlie
>(Oh, my Lord)
>[These responses alternate throughout the rest of the song]
>I'm chopping in the new ground
>I'm chopping in the new ground
>I'm chopping my way back
>I'm chopping my way back
>My way back home, sir
>My way back home, sir
>Oh, Captain Charlie
>Oh, you remember what I told you
>If you didn't row, sir
>Oh, you would not make it
>Make it back to Rosie

To Rosie and the baby
Oh, Captain Charlie
We're chopping in the new ground.
We're chopping all day long
Chopping all day long, sir
Oh, Captain Charlie
Oh, do you remember
Remember how she looked, sir
We're choppin' in the live oak
Way down in Brazos
Way down in the Brazos
Oh, Captain Charlie
Oh, Captain Charlie

This selection is from Smithsonian Folkways 4475.

Today work songs have all but disappeared due to mechanization and, in some states, relatively recent changes in prison systems. The well-documented conservative atmosphere maintained in the Texas penal system remained until the 1970s when court orders forced it to change. Significantly, the work song tradition continued within this inhuman system well into the final third of the twentieth century. In 1972 Bruce Jackson recorded the same songs that previous generations of prisoners sang. One of these, "Alberta," became a group work song sung in unison as the prisoners weeded and is clearly influenced by the blues.

See Alberta comin' down that road (x3)
Walkin' just like she got a heavy load.

Wo, 'Berta, don't you hear me gal? (x2)

Twenty-one hammers fallin' in a line (x3)
None a them hammers, boys, that ring a like mine.

Ring like silver and it shine like gold (x3)
Price a my hammer, boys, ain't never been told.

Big Leg 'Berta, if you come and be mine (x3)
Have to do nothin' in the summertime. (Jackson 1972, 280)

STRING BANDS

Many rural musicians around the entire United States, and from all racial and national origins, play in informal, small string ensembles. Though poorly documented, we know that black folk musicians performed together in **string bands** across the South. In fact, black string bands were once quite widespread, particularly in the southeastern United States. Some slaves were inevitably exposed to European music in the form of Haydn's Sonatas and other popular eighteenth-century composers, but most no doubt played country dance tunes on fiddles. Individual musicians or small string ensembles also filled the air during less formal occasions: cornhuskings, beer gardens on a Saturday evening, and parties. Occasionally blacks were encouraged to develop their musical skills on pianos, violins, as well as on a variety of brass instruments. Slave owners often fostered musical interests because blacks sometimes provided musical entertainment. African musical practices, particularly drumming, were almost always discouraged.

Slaves also performed dance tunes on fiddles and banjolike instruments. Throughout the South they played for Anglo-American balls and assemblies, but they also played for their own enjoyment and recreation. Many brief accounts of black music exist in the diaries, newspapers, and contemporary written accounts of the period between 1700 and 1800. Unfortunately this music was not notated on staff paper, and since sound-recording equipment was not developed until the 1880s, these fleeting recollections must suffice. As early as 1754 a runaway Maryland slave's most distinctive identifiable trait was as a "banjer" player. So pervasive were the accounts of black banjo playing that by the early 1800s it was described in an offhand manner as though it were part of everyday life.

The fiddle was quite popular among the colonists, who used it in formal parlor performances and to accompany dances of all types. Slaves not only played fiddles, but they also crafted them. One early reference to a runaway slave describes him as "a black Virginia born Negro fellow named Sambo, about 6 ft. high, about 32 years old. He makes fiddles, and can play upon the fiddle, and work at the carpenter's trade" (Southern 1983, 64).

Despite the popularity of the banjo and fiddle, the two are rarely mentioned in the same references. Apparently most blacks played one or the other. Nor were these instruments played in tandem, as they are so often paired today. But during the 1830s such duets had become a staple in early minstrel shows and there are many drawings and paintings of such musicians. By the turn of the century the guitar (and on rare occasions a mandolin) was added to this basic unit, creating a fuller and richer sound. But the fiddle and banjo remained at the core of these string bands.

Joe and Odell Thompson, cousins from Orange County, North Carolina, played together into the 1990s. Courtesy of Kip Lornell.

All-black rural dances almost always included a fiddle or banjo, sometimes augmented by a rhythmic instrument (often bones or a washboard). Rhythms, often polyrhythms, and the use of various percussion instruments are certainly one of the most fundamental contribution by blacks to American music. It could be as simply performed as "patting **juba**"—patting hands together, on thighs or the chest, the antecedent of the hambone games found among black children today. Sticks or the jawbone of a large animal provided two more percussive instruments.

Based on rather sketchy twentieth-century aural evidence the following observations about black string bands appear to be true. The banjo playing itself betrays two basic traits. First, the melody played is simplified to the point that it basically sketches out the melodic line with little improvisation. Second, rhythmic complexities are held in high regard, even to the point of virtuosity. There seem to be some direct links between black banjo playing and early blues guitar playing, particularly those from Mississippi. In Piedmont, North Carolina, several of the black banjo players that I documented in the 1970s transposed their banjo technique to guitar, even to the point of tuning their guitar like a banjo. There are also some striking similarities to black banjo-picking techniques and the open-tuned frailing style of a delta blues man, such as Bukka White.

Similar observations can be made about black fiddle playing. The emphasis is generally upon rhythmic rather than melodic improvisation. Their playing seems to be more forceful and intent upon driving the 2/4 or 4/4 beat home for dancing instead of creating a beautiful melodic line. When the instruments play together it is usually in a simple *ab* tune form.

Lyrics for other forms of black secular music are even simpler. Prior to the emergence of blues about 1900, a large number of short lyric songs constituted a major body of African American music. Some, such as "Old Black Joe," came from the minstrel stage, but the majority were brief ditties that came from dance tunes. Such tunes were performed for solo dancing as well as for square dances, which were integral to the black tradition well into the twentieth century. Many are part of a shared black/white repertoire that reflects late-nineteenth-century rural American life more than it betrays racial origins. Tunes or songs like "Roundtown Gals," "Molly Put the Kettle On," "Soldiers Joy," "Georgia Buck," and **"John Henry"** were favored by rural musicians across much of America. The lyrics of "Georgia Buck" are racially neutral and underscore the simple forms (*ab* in this case) of most banjo tunes:

A: Georgia Buck is dead
  The last word he said
B: "Never let a woman have her way."

A: She'll lead you astray
  Try to have her way
B: "Never let a woman have her way."

FIFE AND DRUM BANDS

Fife and drum band music is perhaps the best example of a regional style of black American folk music undocumented on race series. Once a tradition that existed in several sections of the South, by the race record era fife and drum bands were largely confined to the deep mid-South. This music evolved from the military tradition and became transformed by black musicians after the Civil War into the twentieth century. In central and northern Mississippi fife and drum bands sometimes played for funerals, but they primarily came to provide entertainment for dances and other less-somber community functions. Fife and drum bands in some respects were the Mississippi equivalent of the black fiddle and banjo tradition that flourished and still exists in Virginia and North Carolina.

Napoleon Strickland fife and drum band performing at the Festival or American Folklife in the 1980s. Courtesy of the Ralph Rinzler Folklife Archives and Collections, Center for Folklife and Cultural Heritage, Smithsonian Institution.

The music itself was played on two primary instruments, drums and cane fifes, constituting a small ensemble. Two snare drums and a bass drum constitute the drum section, while the cane fife usually has four or five holes. The cane provides the main melodic interest, though with a very limited range of about an octave. Drums provide this music with its strong rhythmic interest, a marked duple meter (2/4) with an underlying polyrhythmic feeling as at least one of the drums plays an improvisatory line. Alan Lomax of the Library of Congress's Folksong Archive undertook the only prewar recording of this music: the Hemphill Band of northern Mississippi. This Como County band consisted of family and neighbors who played locally for many years. Hemphill also played the ten-hole quill, another wind instrument that is almost never heard in modern America.

Northern Mississippi remains about the only place that fife and drum band music is still performed. The major summer holidays—Memorial Day, Fourth of July, and Labor Day—provide the context for this music, a legacy of its military heritage. Picnics featuring barbecued goat and plenty of liquor begin in the afternoon and run well into the night, while the fife and drum bands play and people march behind or dance to the music. These picnics are male-dominated functions, both musically and socially, though many women attend them. Finally, the level of musical improvisation in fife and drum band music has increased with the passage of time and the integration of blues and other forms into this interesting tradition.

RAGTIME AND COON SONGS

Ragtime is yet another black musical style to emerge in the late nineteenth century. Initially a midwestern innovation, by the turn of the century it was being performed across the country. This music developed among itinerant piano players who made their living performing in rough sporting houses, **juke joints**, and bars where drinking, gambling, and prostitution were commonplace. They started playing highly syncopated tunes (later called *rags*) based on established and popular polkas, marches, and schottisches. Ragtimelike tunes were being published and heard on the minstrel stage by the late 1880s.

Ragtime itself synthesized classical piano technique and distinctly African American folk dance tunes, such as the slave-dance-derived "cakewalk." J. Russell Robinson, **Scott Joplin**, Tom Turpin, and James Scott were among the pioneering pianists whose rags were eventually published in sheet music and issued on piano rolls. The popularity of ragtime dramatically increased during the mid- to late 1890s and the concurrent publication of ragtime on sheet music. The classic rags of the first decade of the twentieth century, many of which were published by John Stark, compared themselves with the best of the contemporary European music. The popular era for ragtime lasted until World War I, when jazz began to establish itself and composers like Zez Confrey began composing popular songs with roots in both idioms.

This dramatic instrumental music was characterized by its use of complex duple meters in the treble, which often contrasted with simpler (often 2/4) meter in the bass. Ragtime's classic form tended toward a march (*ababa*) or a quadrille (*abacd*). Most rags are written in major keys, though some of their strains are in minor keys. The clearest vernacular influence is found in the scales that often feature flattened third- and seventh-scale degrees, similar to its contemporary style—blues. Ragtime's commercialization marked the second time that white America had "discovered" black regional music and brought it to the attention of the entire country. What began as an unwritten folk music informally passed from one piano player to another was quickly embraced by the music publishing business, which reduced ragtime to notation and piano rolls in order to enhance its dissemination.

In addition to the published piano rags, the pens of the Tin Pan Alley songwriters developed the **"coon song"** genre, affording whites another opportunity to lampoon black Americans. Once more white America reveled in its celebration of the musical image of smiling, gap-toothed, chicken pie–eating, and oversexed Negroes. Ernest Hogan's 1896 composition, "All Coons Look Alike to Me," kicked off the coon song era. Another song from this era, Ben Harney's "Mr. Johnson," comes from the same mold:

> A big black coon was lookin' fer chickens
> When a great big bulldog got to raisin' de dickens,
> De coon got higher, de chicken got nigher,
> Just den Johnson opened up fire.
> And now he's playing seben eleben,
> Way up yonder de nigger heaben,
> Oh! Mr. Johnson, made him good.

Such songs inspired a generation of songwriters, including Irving Berlin and George M. Cohan, whose own work greatly influenced twentieth-century American popular song.

BALLADS

Just as in the Anglo-American tradition ballads associated with black American culture also relate a story. By the early twentieth century, ballads had become integrated into the repertoire of African American rural songsters. A singer such as **Lead Belly** (born Huddie Ledbetter) was a repository for ballads, particularly those associated with Texas ("Ella Speed" or "Midnight Special") as well as from African American culture in general ("John Henry"). Lead Belly's versions of these songs remind us that the **African American ballad** tradition is distinguished from its Anglo-American neighbor by a lack of narrative coherence and linear narrative, its subjectivity, and a tendency to glorify events.

Ballads in the black tradition are also often *centonical*—they borrow thematic elements from a variety of sources to build something new. Such songs have generally been called "blues ballads." More recently the term "nodal ballad" has been suggested because they tend to take a theme and use it as a point of departure for casual storytelling.

"John Henry" is doubtless the most well known member of this tradition. Popular among both black and white musicians, "John Henry" was a steel-driving man whose story is believed to have occurred in West Virginia in the 1870s. This song's many versions are archetypal of black ballads for it recounts the story of a strong man competing against a steam-powered drill. In most versions John Henry dies after defeating his mechanical foe and is celebrated as a mighty man. "John Henry" has been collected among blacks across the South from the early 1900s to the present and is sometimes played as a fiddle tune. In the late 1920s Joe Evans and Arthur McClain recorded this rather complete version:

> John Henry he was a li'l baby boy
> Sittin' on his mama's knee,
> Had a nine-pound hammer, holdin' in her arms
> Goin' be the death of me . . . (x4)
> John Henry went to that Big Bend tunnel
> Hammer in his hand,
> John Henry was so small and that rock was so tall
> Laid down his hammer and he cried. (x4)
>
> John Henry asked his shaker,
> "Shaker did you ever pray?
> Cause if I miss that piece of steel
> Tomarrow be your buryin' day." (x4)
>
> "Who's gonna shoe your pretty little feet,
> Who's gonna glove your li'l hand?
> Baby who's gonna kiss your rosy cheeks
> When I'm in a differ'nt land?" (x4)
>
> John Henry took sick and went to bed,
> Sent for the doctor and in he come.
> Turned down the side of John Henry's bed,
> "Sick and can't get well, oh partner,
> Sick and can't get well."

While "John Henry" is ubiquitous, other black ballads have remained regionalized or even more local. The story of "Railroad Bill" relates how an Alabama turpentine worker, Morris Slater, became entangled with the law and eventually fronted a series of bold attacks on trains before being shot to death in 1897. This ballad has primarily circulated in the southeastern states, most widely in Tennessee and Virginia. "The Mystery of Dunbar's Child" exemplifies a ballad with exceptionally limited geographic circulation. This song describes the kidnapping of two children from a 1912 Opelousas, Louisiana, picnic. The only known version of "The Mystery of Dunbar's Child" comes from Richard "Rabbit" Brown, a New Orleans singer/guitarist who recorded it for Victor in

Two of the best songsters—Libba Cotten and John Hurt—at the 1964 Newport Folk Festival. Jim Marshall photo courtesy of the Ralph Rinzler Folklife Archives and Collections, Center for Folklife and Cultural Heritage, Smithsonian Institution.

1928. Because of its strong narrative and chronological sense, this ballad is unusual in black tradition.

The majority of ballads associated with black culture, however, fall in between the popularity of "John Henry" and the almost utter obscurity of Rabbit Brown's song. "Frankie and Albert" tells of a lovers' quarrel that leads to death for Albert, who was shot by Frankie after she spied him with another woman. This song is also known as "Frankie and Johnny," possibly because the sheet music for the song appeared with this title in 1912. The printed publication of ballads helped their circulation, but black singers always took decided liberties in reshaping them to suit their own needs. The publication in 1909 of "Casey Jones" helped to popularize this ballad among both black and white performers. In 1927 Memphis singer Walter "Furry" Lewis recorded this song for Victor. "Casey Jones" has also been part of Anglo-American ballad tradition and even made it into contemporary pop music by way of the Grateful Dead.

It is not surprising that another man of mythic proportions, Stack O' Lee, has rivaled John Henry for the attention of black songsters. Stack O' Lee (also known as Staggerlee, Stagolee, etc.) was a purely bad man, a bully who in some versions of his tale kills Billy Lyons following a gambling game. Another murderous "bad man," Dupree, who in the somewhat confused narrative promises Betty a diamond ring and ends up hanging for the murder of a policeman and

MUSICAL EXAMPLE

Huddie Leadbetter, "Lead Belly," was one of the best-known black folk musicians of the twentieth century. He also helped to popularize the twelve-string guitar, which was one of his trademarks. Lead Belly was a quintessential songster, with a wide repertoire of sacred and secular songs. Following his "discovery" by the Library of Congress in 1933, Lead Belly popularized "Goodnight Irene," "Black Betty," "Midnight Special," and a host of other songs. He recorded extensively for the Library of Congress, the American Record Company, and Folkways before his death in 1949.

Title "Rock Island Line"
Performer Lead Belly
Instruments voice and guitar
Length 2:32

Musical Characteristics
1. This is a *cante-fable*, a performance that is partially sung and partially spoken.
2. Once the singing begins, the tempo of this song increases.
3. At times, Lead Belly's voice and guitar act in tandem creating internal antiphony.
4. After a rubato introduction the song settles down into a gently rocking duple (4/4) meter.

Spoken: This is the Rock Island Line. These boys is cutting with pole axes and the man that cuts right-handed he stands opposite side of the other man; the other one cut left-handed, he stand on the other side. Boys, one thing about that Rock Island Line, which is a might good road to ride. In that road, the man going to talk to the depot agent; when he's going to come out to cut with the Rock Island Line freight train, coming back from New 'leans this away. That man blows his whistle different than men's blow whistles here. 'Cause he's talking to the depot agent, tell him something when that switchboard call over that line, that means for that freight train to go into that hold. The man's going to talk to him.

Sung: I got goats. I got sheep. I got hogs. I got cows. I got horses. I got all livestock. I got all livestock.

Spoken: Depot agent let him get by. He got down, going to tell him.

Sung: I fooled you. I fooled you. I got iron. I got all pig-iron. I got all pig-iron. The old Rock Island Line.

Chorus: Oh, the Rock Island Line is a mighty good road.
   Oh, the Rock Island Line is a road to ride.
   Oh, the Rock Island Line is a mighty good road.
   If you want to ride, you gotta ride it like you find it,
   Get your ticket at the station for the Rock Island Line.

Jesus died to save our sins, Oh great God, we're gonna meet him again.

Chorus

I may be right, I may be wrong, you know you gonna miss me when I'm gone.

Chorus

ABCWXYZ that's how it goes, but it don't take me.

Chorus (repeat)

This selection is from Smithsonian Folkways 40044.

---

a detective, also circulated among black singers in the late 1920s. "Dupree Blues" is derived from a ballad published by Andrew Jenkins, a white composer and recording artist from Atlanta who sang the song as "Frank Dupree." His version is based on a true incident, which resulted in the hanging of Frank Dupree on September 4, 1922.

Bad men, murderers, and men of strength seem to have captured the interest of black songsters because their exploits are more celebrated than those in other ballads. "Stavin' Chain," is an intriguing song that appears to straddle the line between ballad and blues. Stavin' Chain is the nickname for a man who in black culture is bigger than life. In the collected and recorded versions of the songs about him, Stavin' Chain was in Parchman Farm (a notorious Mississippi prison) for killing a man, a train engineer of might, a man with sixteen women but who wanted sixteen more, and a dead man who lives in hell with his Stetson hat on. All of these different Stavin' Chains symbolized a man of extraordinary means, electric energy, and sexual power. He appears to have been a hero with many chameleonlike virtues who triumphed over many situations and conquered many women. There are many balladlike songs about Stavin' Chain, though none can be counted as a true ballad.

Ballads of British origin are not entirely unknown to black performers. Not surprisingly they are rarely encountered in black musical culture and tend to be among the most popular of the broadside or Child ballads. The bawdy ballad of adultery "Our Goodman" (Child 302), known as "Drunkard's Special" or "Cabbage Head" among New World performers, was collected during the early part of the twentieth century and later recorded by Dallas-based singer Coley Jones. The North Carolina performer Blind Boy Fuller's "Cat Man Blues" (while not a ballad) utilized the same theme on his 1936 recording of this song. As recently as 1973 it was recorded by the New Orleans pianist Professor Longhair. The Irish broadside ballad "The Unfortunate Rake," the sad lament of a lad dying of venereal disease, became "St. James Infirmary" or the "Dying Gambler" as sung by blacks. Two Ramsey State Convict Farm (Texas) inmates recorded by John A. Lomax in 1933, "Iron-Head" Baker and Moses "Clear Rock" Platt, also performed several British ballads, "Maid Freed from the Gallows" (Child 256) and "The Farmer's Curst Wife" (Child 276). "Maid Freed from the Gallows" also appealed to Lead Belly, who recorded the song several times during his career.

SONGSTERS AND RURAL MUSIC

The term **songster** implies that the performer not only possesses a fine voice but also knows many songs in a variety of genres. Many of the black rural singers of this century are, in fact, songsters. Record companies and field researchers often billed them as "blues singers"; however, such versatile musicians as Walter "Furry" Lewis (Memphis), Pink Anderson (South Carolina), Jim Jackson (Memphis), Henry "Rufe" Johnson (South Carolina), John Hurt (Mississippi), and Mance Lipscomb (Texas) performed blues, work songs, ballads, religious songs, and so forth.

Songsters participated in church music, too. After a Saturday night in the juke joint, at least some of the patrons would adjourn to church pews for their Sunday worship service. The most "churchified" citizens of Leigh, Texas (where the well-known songster Lead Belly lived early in the twentieth century), no doubt stayed out of these joints, but many people moved back and forth between the secular and sacred sides of life.

Lead Belly's physical movement from Leigh illustrates the most important early means of transmission for regional styles of folk music. Geographers call such movement *relocation diffusion*, referring to the spread of a new idea or innovation through the migration of an individual or a folk group. Between 1906 and 1911 Lead Belly lived in several places in eastern Texas and Louisiana,

AFRICAN AMERICAN SECULAR FOLK MUSIC

Lead Belly in the late 1940s. Courtesy of the Ralph Rinzler Folklife Archives and Collections, Center for Folklife and Cultural Heritage, Smithsonian Institution.

calling Shreveport and nearby Marshall home for short periods. His music traveled with him and he, in turn, picked up new influences and musical ideas.

Wandering black folk musicians were not an uncommon sight early in the twentieth century. Folk music provided entertainment, and small rural towns always welcomed a good musician with new ideas and a fresh sound. Some were itinerant musicians who, like Lead Belly, moved from town to town. Many other black folk singers found steady employment with traveling minstrel or medicine shows or with a circus. Road shows provided steady employment for peripatetic musicians eager to see the world around them. This tradition harkens back to the antebellum minstrel tradition that first flourished in the 1840s, but by the time of Lead Belly's adolescence at the opening of the twentieth century, minstrelsy was beginning its inevitable decline and transformation.

The mobility of certain black musicians, the fact that most of these musicians were musically illiterate (in the sense of reading musical notation), and the orientation of African Americans toward the verbal arts, all helped to promote the aural/oral tradition in black folk music. Beginning in the middle 1920s commercial recordings played a critical role in disseminating musical information. With few exceptions, the odd-printed broadside or sheet music featuring a folk song, this music has not been transmitted through formal musical channels. There are no formal conservatories for black (or white) musicians to attend nor university courses, such as "Advanced Blues Singing Techniques,"

"The Rudiments of Afro-American Accordion Playing," or "Gospel Quartet Ear Training." Early in the twentieth century black singers learned their music by way of family members, like Lead Belly, whose accordion technique came from his uncle, or older members of an immediate musical community.

Music was especially important for many blacks living in the rural South. It provided a source of entertainment and escape from a daily diet of hard work and poor food. Racism, both legal and social, was regaining strength with the passage of "Jim Crow" laws restricting the right to vote, reinforcing segregation, and reapplying the stranglehold of economic subjugation. Many of the gains won during Reconstruction were slowly eroding into a legal and social mire that brought despair to the black community by 1990.

Weekends in the churches and at the rough juke joints provided diversion, offered solace, and brought relief from daily toil. These venues presented the public side of folk music. Within the black community, public musical performances fulfilled several functions—one of which was pure entertainment. A performer such as Lead Belly played for many public events within his own community. As a youth he worked at dances, known as breakdowns or smoky jumps in his section of east Texas. These rowdy dances featured free-flowing liquor, gambling, and mixing of the sexes and often served as the social centerpiece for many rural people. From small Texas towns like Leigh to the Mississippi Delta through the Carolinas, Saturday night functions drew the community together to visit, discuss problems, gossip, and relax from six days of demanding work. Because of their activities, Saturday night dances drew adults only. They began at dusk and usually lasted until well into the night, occasionally until sunup.

The actual music heard at dances varied according to the region of the country. In North Carolina, for example, the music was often provided by small string bands consisting of fiddle, banjo, and guitar. Missouri blacks were more likely entertained by a ragtime piano player when they congregated to forget their troubles. In Texas, Lead Belly or one of his contemporaries performed a mixture of lively duple-meter polkas and two-steps, elegant waltzes, and slower tempo "drags," which gave the dancers a chance to become better acquainted. People called out requests that the musicians could nearly always fulfill, for this was a tightly knit group composed of people who knew one another quite well.

Well into the twentieth century most blacks living in the rural South fit into the patterns associated with a classic folk community: insular/isolated, family oriented, agrarian, conservative, cohesive, homogeneous, and slow changing. This era prior to paved interstate highways, the electronic media, and mass public education helped to reinforce traditional and regional culture. The folk roots of twentieth-century blues and gospel music lie in the antecedents that emerged from such communities.

AFRICAN AMERICAN SECULAR FOLK MUSIC

DOWN-HOME BLUES

Blues first evolved as a distinctive style near the beginning of the twentieth century. The product of multigenesis in the Deep South (east Texas, Mississippi, Louisiana, and Alabama), blues was a synthesis of the traditions that preceded it: dance tunes, minstrel songs, secular ditties, and spirituals. Because of its origins, it is impossible to assign a specific date and geographical location for the first blues performance.

There are several reasons why blues developed at this time. First, the period of Jim Crow racism added misery and hard times to the black community. Ku Klux Klan activity gained momentum during the 1890s, too, with the number of lynchings increasing and the per capita income for blacks stagnating or falling. These factors meant that black American citizens lived in an increasingly segregated society, enduring attacks on their civil and legal rights. Reconstruction promised freedom and opportunities for blacks, but thirty years after the Year of Jubilee the specter of increased racism shadowed the United States.

Second was the more ready availability of mail-order guitars and their greater popularity among folk musicians. Guitars were perfect for black folk musicians because these instruments were portable, their primary chords (I, IV, and V) were easy to play, and their strings easily bent to accommodate the sometimes flatted tonality commonly found in black folk music. Early blues guitarists sometimes tuned their instrument to an open D or E chord and used a knife or the neck of a bottle to increase their ability to produce tonalities outside of their European models. Bottleneck blues guitar (still an important performance practice) also gave guitarists a voice that was more human in its qualities, allowing them to create an interesting foil between their instrument and their voice. Interaction between a guitarist and his voice as well as between the singer and audience have become important ingredients of the blues tradition.

Because the early-twentieth-century black community closely adheres to our model of an idealized folk society, change and innovation is expected to be gradual. In this instance it took the blues tradition at least ten years to diffuse across the South and gain acceptability. Nonetheless, blues provided one of the most important, creative outlets in response to increased repression and a renewal of hard times after the heady days of Reconstruction. Blacks (and a few whites) protested in other ways: newspaper editorials, feeble legislative reforms, and the formation of support organizations. But these did not hit the same type of responsive chord as blues, which became an important rallying point for the frustrations of blacks and one of their most important and lasting musical contributions to American culture.

Early blues probably sounded similar to the "hollers" sung as people worked hard in the fields and to the secular ditties popular during the 1880s and 1890s.

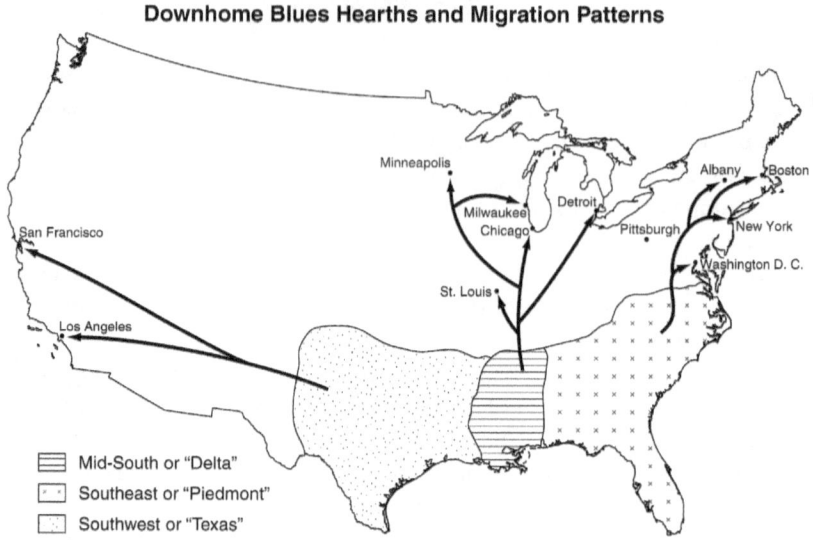

Certainly the subjects would have been similar: mistreatment, money problems, and difficulty between the sexes. **Field hollers** are one of the most immediate precursors for blues, and their free-form structure betrays the relationship to the later innovation. This particular example comes from Virginia in the late teens:

> Ef I had 'bout fo'ty-five dollahs
> All in gol' yas, all in gol'
> I'd be as rich as ol' man Catah.
> I'm gwine back to South Ca'lina;
> Fah away, yas, fah away.
> I'm gwine see my Esmeraldy.
> I can't stay, no, I can't stay.
> (Scarborough 1925, 219)

Blues are built upon a series of rhymed couplets that speak the "truth" about life, one of the principal reasons why this new music appealed to its listeners. As the musician played the "lowdown" music and sang about mutual concerns, blues promoted a dialogue between the musician and audience. Because the early blues were played at house parties and dances rather than formal concert halls, audiences shouted encouragement and sometimes interacted with musicians by joining in the singing. Dancing, another means of releasing energy and frustration as well as creative movement, quickly became another important ingredient in this dialogue.

The first blues songs were almost certainly of variable length, probably between ten and fourteen bars. The standardization of the twelve-bar format appeared in sheet music as early as 1912; however, the twelve-bar blues form did not become codified for at least one decade. Early blues musicians often played cycles of whatever bar length suited them. The length of early blues was probably determined by the words being sung. A song like "Poor Boy" was perfectly suited to this new style of music and was likely to be recast in the emerging blues style. Sociologist Howard Odum described this song, which he collected in Georgia circa 1909. This nascent version was sung to the accompaniment of a guitarist playing with a knife and included lyrics echoed by today's blues persons:

> I'm a po' boy 'long ways from home,
> Oh, I'm a po' boy 'long ways from home.
> I wish a 'scursion train would run,
> Carry me back where I cum frum.
> Come here, babe, an' sit on yo' papa's knee.

Possibly because this version of "Poor Boy" was taken from early fieldwork, this early blues or blueslike song sounds fragmented when compared to later recorded versions. It is likely that the singer himself organized the song this way, punctuating the heartfelt lyrics with ringing slide guitar, and performed the song using an eight-bar format.

Blues singers demonstrated many musical characteristics that are regional in nature. The early down-home blues styles can be assigned to three general regions: Southwest, mid-South, and Southeast. When singers from these areas migrated outside the hearth areas, they carried their music with them. The preceding musical example illustrates the mid-South or Delta style well.

MODERN BLUES

Black popular music began to permutate into new forms. Jazz-influenced singers such as Billy Eckstine, Ella Fitzgerald, Johnny Hartman, and Sarah Vaughn rose to prominence during the middle to late 1940s. Rhythm and blues (R&B, which is more fully discussed in chapter 11) first emerged in the late 1940s: Bull Moose Jackson, Tiny Bradshaw, Johnny Otis, and others were recording for the same independent labels as the gospel singers. Their music was not

MUSICAL EXAMPLE

Big Joe Williams lived as an itinerant blues singer and musician until his death in 1982. Born near the turn of the twentieth century, Williams spent his formative years in the Mississippi Delta as a contemporary of the legendary blues singers Charlie Patton and Son House before moving to Chicago in the middle 1930s. His gruff, intense vocals are reminiscent of the field hollers that rang throughout the South during the early twentieth century. Though he kept a trailer in Crawford, Mississippi, in later years Williams rambled throughout the United States and also played concerts in Europe.

Title "Night Cap Blues"
Performer Big Joe Williams
Instruments guitar and voice
Length 2:56

Musical Characteristics
1. The tonality is major and is played in duple (4/4) meter.
2. Williams sticks to the basic blues form.
3. His voice and guitar are used as a foil to each other, almost like an internal call and response.
4. The tempo of the song increases during the performance.
5. The highly syncopated guitar accompaniment underlies its homophonic texture resulting in a full texture.

> Put on your night cap, woman, I'm gonna buy you an evening gown. (repeat)
> I'm taking you out tomorrow night, baby, and I swear we sure gonna break 'em on down.
>
> I'm gonna pack my bucket, baby, gonna move back to the piney woods.
> I'm gonna get my bucket baby ... move back to the woods.
> I'm gonna leave here, darling, 'cause you don't mean me no good.
>
> I ain't never been to Georgia, boys, but the half ain't never been told. (repeat)
> Tell me them women down there got something sweet, sweet as jelly roll.
>
> (Repeat the first verse.)

When you raise sweet potatoes, boy, raise you a Nancy Hall.
If you want a sweet potato, boy, raise a Nancy Hall.
If you want a good woman, I swear you better marry one long and tall.

Put on your night cap, baby, I'm gonna buy an evening gown.
I'm going out Saturday night and I am sure gonna break 'em on down.

<small>This selection is from Smithsonian Folkways 31004.</small>

---

only popular, but it was based on the blues, which were undergoing another transformation.

Down-home blues continued to be popular in the South and among southerners transplanted to the North. However, the blues that appeared on commercial disks slowly changed during the 1940s as popular music tastes altered. Small ensembles all but supplanted the single artists that so often appeared on records during the 1920s and into the 1930s. The late 1930s recordings by Sonny Boy Williamson (John Lee Williamson), Washboard Sam (Sam Brown), Tampa Red and his Chicago Five, Lonnie Johnson, and others foreshadowed the new trends in commercial blues. The ensembles frequently consisted of a bass, drums (or washboard), guitar, piano, harmonica, or horns. These additional instruments smoothed out many of the harmonic and stylistic idiosyncracies of the **folk blues** performers, routinizing the music into a more predictable pattern. As commercial record companies learned very well, predictability, albeit spiced with a dash of creativity, is what sells records. The wonderfully individual sounds of Mr. Freddie Spruel, Otto Virgial, and George Clarke all but disappeared following the record industry's reactivation in 1945. An even more pronounced ensemble sound emerged on records and, to a far lesser degree, over the radio following the end of World War II. In New York City the music centered around the East Coast musicians who had migrated northward: Brownie and Sticks McGhee, Sonny Terry, Larry Dale, and others. Their sound, on record at least, was distinctly "country," updated somewhat but not truly transformed. In Los Angeles many of the musicians came from Texas in search of work. The R&B sound of Charles Brown and Amos Milburn tended to predominate West Coast commercial blues.

But the true musical and popular revolution in blues was going on in Chicago. The majority of Chicago's migrants, from the turn of the century onward, arrived from the mid-South: Arkansas, Mississippi, and western Tennessee. This influx of residents from an area where the blues were deep and well developed combined with the electrification of guitars to create a vital, vibrant sound. At the forefront of this movement were **Muddy Waters** (McKinley Morganfield),

AFRICAN AMERICAN SECULAR FOLK MUSIC

Henry Miles Jug Band, a Louisville jug band that operated during the 1930s into the 1940s. Courtesy of Kip Lornell.

Howlin' Wolf (Chester Burnett), Elmore James, and Walter Horton. Each of them arrived in Chicago with highly developed musical skills, full of the fire and emotional rawness that characterized the blues that developed along the Mississippi Delta. These men truly created an important new form by transforming the music of masters such as **Charley Patton**, Eddie "Son" House, Willie Brown, Will Shade, and Robert Johnson into the roots of rock 'n' roll.

The transformation began in the middle 1940s, about the same time as another revolution in black music, be-bop, was capturing the other ear of jazz aficionados. The transitional records of Muddy Waters, Big Joe Williams, and Snooky Pryor with Moody Jones came out in the late 1940s and sounded like Mississippi blues in a modern setting. Around 1951 the revolution hit full force in the form of Muddy Waters's classic band that included Little Walter Jacobs (harp), Otis Spann (piano), Big Crawford (bass), Jimmy Rodgers (second guitar), and Freddy Below (drums). Their classic Chess records virtually define **Chicago blues** and document a band at the height of its considerable abilities. The passion and creativity evident on "Forty Days and Forty Nights," "Standing Around Crying," "Hootchie Coochie Man," and "Mannish Boy" are among the landmarks in black American vernacular music. The Chicago style emphasizes the highly dramatic lead voices of amplified guitars and harmonicas supported by the basic rhythm section of bass guitar, piano, and drums. The music was meant to be heard in clubs on the city's predominately black South and West sides, neighborhood bars where locals came to drink and dance. Bars featuring these bands were the northern equivalent of the juke joint and they proved quite popular. This music was popular on records, too. Small labels such as Chess, Cobra, JOB, and others launched (and perhaps ultimately crashed) their businesses based on the marketability of Chicago blues. The popularity of this music continued through the middle 1950s.

Other electric blues musicians—B. B. King, Bobby Blue Bland, Little Milton—groomed their performing and recording skills in Memphis before gaining a national following. Their music is not cut in the classic Chicago mode, but rather is influenced by R&B and the gospel sounds of the 1940s and 1950s. Horn sections predominated and this music profoundly influenced soul music and the "Stax sound" that emanated from Memphis during the middle to late 1960s.

FINAL THOUGHTS

Black American secular folk music has a complicated history. Older styles of music, particularly blues, still persist. Blues, along with the jug bands from Memphis and Louisville and rural black string bands, represent some of the most interesting examples of regional American folk music. In some general ways string band music and balladry overlap with their Anglo-American counterparts, but their distinctive characteristics have been outlined here. These secular traditions, often in tandem with religious music, have also strongly influenced popular music. The (mostly African American) folk roots of contemporary popular music are fully explored in the penultimate chapter.

KEY FIGURES AND TERMS

African American ballad
Chicago blues
coon songs
field holler
fife and drum bands
folk blues
"John Henry"
Scott Joplin
juba

juke joints
Lead Belly
Charlie Patton
ragtime
songster
string bands
track laying
Muddy Waters
work song

AFRICAN AMERICAN SECULAR FOLK MUSIC

SUGGESTED LISTENING

Carolina Chocolate Drops. *Genuine Negro Jig*. Music Maker. This 2010 release is the best work, thus far, by this group of three younger and talented African American string band music makers.

John Cephas and Phil Wiggins. *Guitar Man*. Flying Fish 470. This guitar/harmonica duo explores their Piedmont Virginia roots in songs like "Police Dog Blues" and "Richmond Blues."

Elizabeth Cotten. *Freight Train and Other North Carolina Folk Songs and Tunes*. Smithsonian Folkways 4009. A delightful selection of songs by this most gentle guitar and banjo player.

Lightin' Hopkins. *Lightnin' Hopkins*. Smithsonian Folkways 40019. This nice set captures the Texas blues man in between his period as a recording artist for the black community and the rest of his career as a folk blues performer.

John Jackson. *Blues & Country Dance Tunes From Virginia*. Arhoolie 1025. A highly varied selection of tunes by this northern Virginia songster.

Robert Johnson. *The Complete Recordings*. Columbia C2K 46222. Forty-one selections by this pivotal figure who recorded these influential recordings in the late 1930s.

Lead Belly. *Lead Belly's Last Sessions*. Smithsonian Folkways 40068. This double compact disc set contains Huddie Leadbetter's final studio recordings of songs and stories (by Frederic Ramsey and released by Moses Arch) and is but one of many fine recordings by Huddie "Lead Belly" Leadbetter available on this label.

Mance Lipscomb. *Captain, Captain*. Arhoolie CD465. Recordings from the 1960s by this talented singer/guitarist, who represents the best of the songsters.

Martin, Bogan & The Armstrongs. *Let's Give A Party*. Flying Fish CD003. Contemporary recordings by a black stringband that toured extensively and recorded several discs in the 1970s, after a decades-long hiatus.

Bukka White. *Sky Songs*. Arhoolie CD 323. The Mississippi-born guitarist "pulls" these blues and blues-like songs from the sky, hence the title.

Sonny Boy Williamson. *King Biscuit Time*. Arhoolie CD310. Classic small group downhome blues recordings from the early 1950s.

AFRICAN AMERICAN SECULAR FOLK MUSIC

Various. *Angola Prison Worksongs.* Arhoolie CD 448. An interesting collection of (mostly) a cappella songs by inmates from this most notorious prison, located in southern Louisiana and recorded in the early 1960s.

Various. *Black Banjo Songsters of North Carolina and Virginia.* Smithsonian Folkways 40079. A vital collection that demonstrates the importance of the banjo in African American folk music in the southeastern United States.

Various. *Classic African American Ballads.* Smithsonian Folkways SFW40191. From the expected "John Henry" to the more obscure "Luke and Mullen," compiler Barry Lee Pearson does a nice job in documenting this important subgenre.

Various. *Deep River of Song: Black Appalachia String Bands, Songsters and Hoedowns.* Rounder CD 011661182325. This anthology looks at the range of black rural folk music from the hill country of Mississippi up to the Blue Ridge Mountains of Virginia.

Various. *Deep River of Song: Black Texicans Balladeers and Songsters of the Texas Frontier.* Rounder CD 011661182127. Cowboy songs, American ballads, old-time tunes form the backbone of these recordings, most of which were done in the mid- to late 1930s.

Various. *The Land Where the Blues Began.* Rounder CD 682161186122. Recordings from between 1933 and 1959 that feature fife and drums bands, work songs, and blues.

Various. *Alan Lomax: Blues Songbook.* Rounder CD 682161186627. A retrospective of the field recordings of blues musicians that began with Lead Belly in 1934 and included the first recordings of Muddy Waters and Fred McDowell.

Various. *Non-Blues Secular Black Music in Virginia.* Global Village/BRI-1001. A cross-section of black protest songs, fiddle and banjo tunes, Native American ballads, and country dance instrumentals.

Various. *The Roots of Robert Johnson.* Yazoo 1073. A selection of classic Mississippi Delta blues recordings in the 1920s and 1930s.

Various. *Traveling Through the Jungle.* Hightone/Testament 2223. A collection of fife and drum band and other related selections recorded in the Mississippi Delta between 1941 and the 1970s.

Various. *Virginia Work Songs.* Global Village/BRI 1007. A compilation of work song traditions found across the state, including ship caulking, oyster shucking, track lining, etc.

AFRICAN AMERICAN SECULAR FOLK MUSIC

SUGGESTED READING

Lynn Abbott and Doug Seroff. *Ragged but Right: Black Traveling Shows, Coon Songs, and the Dark Pathway to Blues and Jazz.* Jackson: University Press of Mississippi, 2007. Through the lens of contemporary newspapers and other printed sources, the authors investigate musical comedy productions, sideshow bands, and itinerant tented minstrel shows in the years before blues and jazz emerged.

Edward Berlin. *Ragtime: A Musical and Cultural History.* Berkeley and Los Angeles: University of California Press, 1980. Of the ragtime studies available, this remains the best concise history.

Cecelia Conway. *African Banjo Echoes in the Appalachian: A Study of Folk Traditions.* Knoxville: University of Tennessee Press, 1995. A solid, pioneering look at the role of black American banjo players in North Carolina and Virginia in the nineteenth and twentieth centuries.

Dena Epstein. *Sinful Tunes and Spirituals.* Urbana: University of Illinois Press, 2003. The author surveys primary and secondary written sources for information about black folk music prior to Reconstruction in this paperback edition of the 1977 classic.

David Evans. *Big Road Blues.* New York: Da Capo Press, 1988. An often fascinating, scholarly study of musical creativity and the transmission of blues in central Mississippi.

William Ferris. *Give My Poor Heart Ease: Voices of the Mississippi Blues.* Chapel Hill: University of North Carolina Press, 2009. Based on his fieldwork in Mississippi in the 1960s and 1970s, Ferris helps lend a sympathetic and insightful voice to these local and often amateur musicians whose life stories and oral histories often make compelling reading.

Ted Gioia. *Work Songs.* Durham, NC: Duke University Press, 2006. An eclectic and provocative look at the history and development of work songs, which are largely but not entirely an African American phenomenon in the United States.

Alan Govenar. *Lightnin' Hopkins: His Life and Blues.* Chicago, IL: Chicago Review Press, 2010. Surprisingly, this is the first full-length biography of this important Texas bluesman and it is both very well written and carefully researched.

Bruce Jackson. *Wake Up Dead Man: Afro-American Worksongs From Texas.* Cambridge, MA: Harvard University Press, 1972. This is an ethnography of the Texas prison system and work songs written in the late 1960s.

Gerhard Kubik. *Africa and the Blues*. Jackson: University Press of Mississippi, 1999. A look at the relationship between (West) African music and the African American blues tradition.

Kip Lornell and Charles K. Wolfe. *The Life and Legend Of Leadbelly*. New York: Da Capo Press, 1999. This is a paperback edition of the scholarly biography of perhaps the best-known twentieth-century black folk singer.

Paul Oliver. *Songsters & Saints: Vocal Traditions on Race Records*. Cambridge: Cambridge University Press, 1984. This noted scholar examines the secular and sacred musical traditions found on records prior to World War II.

Barry Lee Pearson and Bill McCulloch. *Robert Johnson, Lost and Found*. Urbana: University of Illinois Press, 2008. As much as one possibly could, this is a biography of the legendary delta blues musician who died in 1938.

Howard L. Sacks and Judith Rose Sacks. *Way Up North in Dixie: A Black Family's Claim to the Confederate Anthem*. Urbana: University of Illinois Press, 2003. Black and white musical interchange, the lives of everyday people, and an iconic song are interwoven in this carefully crafted and sometimes unsettling book.

Elijah Wald. *Escaping the Delta: Robert Johnson and the Invention of the Blues*. New York: Harper Paperbacks, 2004. A combination of a biography of Robert Johnson and a look at the myths surrounding the development of country blues, Mississippi Delta style, Wald manages to be insightful, scholarly, accessible, and deft all at the same time.

SUGGESTED VIEWING

Lightnin' Hopkins: Rare Performances 1960-1979. Vestapol. Taken from three separate and disparate sources, this film captures Hopkins playing on the streets, playing at a Houston bar, and performing for a national television audience on *Austin City Limits*.

Mance Lipscomb. *A Well-Spent Life*. Flower Films. A gentle and loving portrait of a Texas songster who spent his entire life in south-central Texas.

Louie Bluie. Pacific Arts Home Video. A documentary that examines the fascinating life of Howard Armstrong: string band musician, artist, and storyteller.

Alex Moore. *Black on White, White and Black*. Documentary Arts/Folkstreams.net. An intimate and playful overview of the life and career of the veteran blues pianist Alex Moore, a native of Dallas, Texas.

AFRICAN AMERICAN SECULAR FOLK MUSIC

Peg Leg Sam. *Born for Hard Luck*. Davenport Films/Folkstreams.net. Medicine show performer, raconteur, storyteller, and harmonica wizard Arthur Jackson is the focus of this film.

Various. *Blues Up the Country*. Vestapol. Subtitled "The Country Blues Guitar Legacy," this is an anthology that includes Pink Anderson, Furry Lewis, Jesse Fuller, Josh White, among others.

Various. *Deep Blues*. Robert Mugge Films. This interesting documentary looks at blues in the Mississippi Delta and was shot in 1990. Robert Palmer, whose book of the same name, assisted in the film's production.

Various. *Deep Ellum Blues*. Documentary Arts/Folkstreams.net. The Deep Ellum section of Dallas, Texas, served as a nexus for black folk and popular music until a freeway destroyed the area in the middle 1950s.

Various. *Devil Got My Woman: Blues at Newport, 1966*. Vestapol. Utilizing interviews, informal jam sessions, and some concert footage, this is a buoyant and behind-the-scenes look at Howlin' Wolf, Skip James, Son House, and the other musicians who appeared at that year's Newport Folk Festival.

Various. *Gandy Dancers*. Cinema Guild, Inc./Folkstreams.net. Interviews and musical performances by railroad track laborers form the core of this film.

Various. *Give My Poor Heart Ease: Mississippi Delta Bluesmen*. New Jersey Network/Folkstreams.net. The blues experience through the eyes and words and music of B. B. King, Son Thomas, and others.

Various. *Gravel Springs Fife and Drum Bands*. Center for Southern Folklore/Folkstreams.net. A brief (thirteen-minute) film that documents the social context for this music in the mid-South.

Various. *Jazz Parades: Feet Don't Fail Me Now*. Vestapol/Folkstreams.net. One of the excellent "American Patchwork" series that looks at jazz related traditions, such as the new breed of brass bands, black Indians at carnival, and dancing at a funeral.

Various. *The Land Where the Blues Began*. Vestapol. Another of the "American Patchwork" films overseen by Alan Lomax; this one focusing upon the Mississippi Delta and featuring blues, work songs, and a fife and drum band performance.

AFRICAN AMERICAN SECULAR FOLK MUSIC

Various. *Masters of the Country Blues*. Yazoo. This series of videos draws upon a number of sources, most notably the Seattle Folklore Society. The majority of the performances were filmed in studios during the late 1960s through the middle 1970s while these older blues musicians were on tour. Despite the use of the term "Country Blues" in the series title, the musicians perform a wider variety of material, including sacred songs, ragtime instrumentals, and country dance tunes. The specific titles are: Yazoo 500 "Bukka White & Son House," Yazoo 501 "Rev. Gary Davis and Sonny Terry," Yazoo 502 "Lightnin' Hopkins & Mance Lipscomb," Yazoo 503 "Jesse Fuller & Elizabeth Cotten," Yazoo 504 "Big Joe Williams & Mississippi Fred McDowell," Yazoo 513 "Lightnin' Hopkins & Roosevelt Sykes," Yazoo 518 "Roosevelt Sykes & Big Bill Broonzy," Yazoo 519 "John Lee Hooker & Furry Lewis."

Chapter 8

ETHNIC AND NATIVE AMERICAN TRADITIONS

- Jewish American: Klezmer
- Native American
- Hawaiian American
- Franco-American
- Scandinavian American
- Final Thoughts

Prior to the heightening of the Cold War in the early 1950s a great general interest in the diversity of American folk music had developed, at least among some performers and fans. Moses Asch, Folkways's open-minded founder, included a variety of "ethnic" and Native American recordings among his vast catalogue. Asch's own roots as the son of European/Jewish immigrants living in New York heightened his sensitivity and interest in a wide variety of musical genres. The first record that Asch issued in 1939 was by a Jewish group, the Baggelman Sisters. Along with their version of Huddie Leadbetter's "Goodnight Irene," the Weavers scored high on the pop charts in the early 1950s with "Wimoweh," which was based on a song from South Africa. And the early issues of *Sing Out!* and folk music songbooks were dotted with songs originating outside of the United States.

In the early twenty-first century most American folk music enthusiasts think in terms of either "folk troubadours" like Bob Dylan, Iris Dement, Dave Van Ronk, Nanci Griffith, Arlo Guthrie, and Peter, Paul & Mary or of Anglo-American and African American traditions like blues, gospel, and ballads. But the importance of the traditional music of people for whom English was not often their first language is becoming increasingly apparent. And the most noteworthy examples, such as Cajun music, are truly original American art forms, not simply traditional music imported to the United States. (Because the Hispanic community has grown so large, diverse, and important, their musical traditions are treated in a separate chapter.)

ETHNIC AND NATIVE AMERICAN TRADITIONS

An early Asch record label illustrates the diversity of music that appeared on the label. Courtesy of the Ralph Rinzler Folklife Archives and Collections, Center for Folklife and Cultural Heritage, Smithsonian Institution.

Making the distinction between music in America and American music is critical to understanding this chapter. Because the United States remains the destination for so many immigrants seeking a better life, virtually every country, region, and ethnic group on earth is represented within our population. We have already learned that people bring their cultural baggage with them—foodways, marriage customs, language, and music—most of which gradually assimilates with the already established cultures of the United States. A book that tries to cover all of the ethnic traditions found within our borders would be creating a veritable United Nations of music!

Instead, we will sample these aspects of American music by discussing five important folk or folk-based musical communities/genres/ethnic groups that have developed in the United States as a hybrid of Old World and New World traditions. This hybridization (a form of **creolization**) usually requires decades of contact, although popular culture is transmitted more quickly. Some of the recent Southeast Asian refugees, for instance, have been making videos of their American-inspired popular music since the middle 1980s. And some second- and third-generation Asian Americans have embraced popular expressive culture, most notably hip-hop. The tens of thousands of refugees from Afghanistan who have arrived in the United States since the Russian invasion in 1980 or the more recent migrants from the former Yugoslavia have not been here long enough for their music to blend with ours.

Other groups, such as the Hmung (from northern Laos) and Vietnamese, have established large settlements in California, the Northeast, and in the Twin Cities of Minneapolis and St. Paul. Second- and third-generation Hmung Americans look to American popular music, especially rock but increasingly hip-hop, for their musical inspiration; but older song traditions are used to

ETHNIC AND NATIVE AMERICAN TRADITIONS

address new and often problematic situations they have encountered in the United States, such as the tensions between the patriarchal Hmung value system and the feminist leanings of some third-generation Hmung women.

The social and musical patterns displayed by the Hmung in some ways typify the processes undergone by many immigrant groups that have arrived in the United States in the post-Reconstruction period. The first generation wants to preserve the old ways but the second generation tends to look to America for their language (and slang), new musical expressions, foodways, and other aspects of culture. Sometime later—usually in the third or fourth generation—younger members of the groups look back to their roots. This very general model has its exceptions, of course, but its pattern crops up surprisingly often.

The distinction between ethnic and folk is equally vibrant and integral because they are related but not necessarily interchangeable. Folk has already been discussed and defined, while **ethnic** refers to an identity that is created by one's place of origin, language, religion, and common history. Within this identity, one mixes the levels of culture in which we participate—folk, popular, and elite (or academic). To illustrate some of these distinctions, let's look more closely at German Americans, one of the most long-standing European immigrant groups.

In German American musical culture choral societies known as *Liederkranz* or *Mannerchor* have existed since the nineteenth century. They engage in active interregional competition, and in major cities, most notably Cincinnati and Milwaukee, they sometimes function as the basis for the chorus for opera companies. German Americans have also predominated in other spheres of elite music. The study of historical musicology was basically defined by Germans in the 1870s. German Americans have been very well represented in our classical orchestras and in their repertoires. For example, the Chicago Symphony Orchestra was founded by a German-born conductor. Moravian church music has also strongly impacted upon various forms of American sacred music.

Although German Americans have been quite involved in our musical culture, their offerings generally have little to do with folk music. Most, though not all, of their musical contributions are primarily directed toward elite culture. German American folk music consists almost entirely of German traditional music transported to the United States. One notable exception is the nineteenth century singing schools found in the Shenandoah Valley of Virginia, which were discussed earlier. The Bohemian American polka bands of south-central Minnesota, led by concertina players such as **"Whoopie John" Wilfahrt**, represent another twentieth-century manifestation of folk music. The "New Ulm" or "old-time" sound incorporated German dance tunes with an Americanized rhythm section to create an eclectic, distinctly regional sound. Groups like the Jolly Germans, the Six Fat Dutchmen ("dutchmen" is a local term for people of

ETHNIC AND NATIVE AMERICAN TRADITIONS

The zany cover for this album underscores public attitudes toward polka music. Courtesy of the Ralph Rinzler Folklife Archives and Collections, Center for Folklife and Cultural Heritage, Smithsonian Institution.

German descent), and Eddie Wilfahrt's Concertina Band brought this blend of folk-based music to audiences throughout the northern Midwest.

Religious and secular organizations play important roles in providing solidarity within ethnic enclaves. Various groups such as the Czechoslovak Sokol, Scandinavian Associations, German Turnverein, Polish American clubs, and the Norwegian Sons of Norway (parodied by Garrison Keillor's "Sons of Knute" on his "Prairie Home Companion" radio broadcasts from the late 1970s to the present) provide a support network for newly arrived immigrants. Most immigrant groups have used music as one means of maintaining cultural identity. They have imported their native folk and popular music, often performing it for special events such as Christmas or weddings that are also celebrated traditionally. Music becomes one of the critical ties to their former home across the ocean.

Traditions that have been all but lost or forgotten can later be **revitalized**. Several types of grassroots music that are clearly related to the folk music of non–English-speaking Americans have enjoyed a renaissance over the past few decades. Klezmer, for example, has undergone a renaissance in the Jewish community since the middle 1970s in much the same way that Cajun music has once again found favor in southwestern Louisiana.

Native American music also contains examples of **revitalization** and **revival**, which refer to traditions that have been totally lost for several generations.

ETHNIC AND NATIVE AMERICAN TRADITIONS

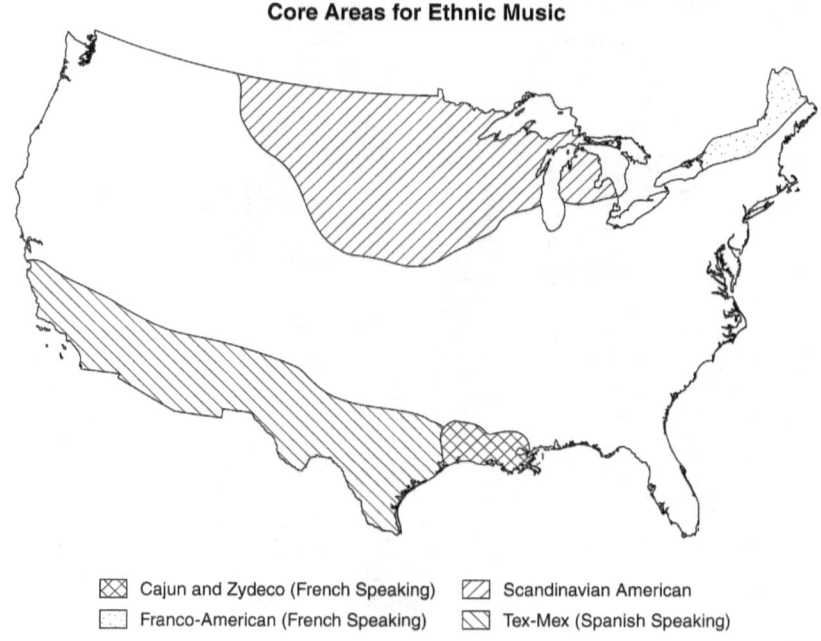

The Pia tribe of central Arizona inhabit the sparsely populated and stark desert country along the Gila River. The majority of the Pia were "Christianized" by strict fundamentalist missionaries. They had lost most of their traditional dances and songs by the dawn of the twentieth century, but in the 1960s and 1970s a select number of traditional songs and dances were reintroduced to younger members of the Pia tribe. Specifically, the round dance songs, which are usually named for birds like swallows, robins, and orioles, were revived. In his work on chicken scratch music, folklorist Jim Griffith has noted that the Pia's musical revival came about as part of a larger effort to shore up their traditional ways of life in light of Western domination. In addition to the music, some of the younger women were introduced to the almost lost art of making traditional dresses and yucca baskets.

Rather than a cursory survey of the entire non–English-speaking world in the United States, this chapter focuses upon five genres of music that have been part of our musical landscape for many decades: Jewish American (klezmer), Native American, Hawaiian, Franco-American (especially Cajun and zydeco), and Scandinavian American folk music of the upper Midwest. These creolized styles have evolved into dynamic, visible traditions. They are among the most influential and widespread types of folk music created by non–English-speaking Americans.

ETHNIC AND NATIVE AMERICAN TRADITIONS

JEWISH AMERICAN: KLEZMER

Brought to the United States by professional musicians from eastern Europe, many of whom migrated here between 1880 and 1920, **klezmer** refers to the instrumental dance music played by small instrumental ensembles. Twentieth-century klezmer, as scholar and performer Henry Sapoznik points out, combines elements of folk and popular music, filtered through the Romanian, Hungarian, Bulgarian, and Russian styles found in eastern Europe, into a delightful, unique blend. The present-day interest in klezmer results from the revitalization of a form of expressive culture that had become all but moribund by the 1960s.

The word *klezmer* is a Yiddish term that contracts the Hebrew words *kley-zmer*, which can be translated as "vessel of melody" or "musician." In Europe, Henry Sapoznik has written, most of these musicians were part of an economic and social underclass that was frowned upon both by rabbis and by the economic elite. They were often itinerate musicians and, therefore, subject to ridicule and scorn because of their lack of money and stability, for they made their living performing for weddings, weekend dances, and other celebrations. In this regard the early blues musicians who played in the rural South during the 1920s and 1930s hold much the same social position as klezmer musicians.

Because klezmer musicians played at so many different types of venues, they soon developed a wide repertoire that favored both dances (waltzes, horas, polkas, and mazurkas) as well as lyrical styles, especially the *doina* (an improvised melody and song rooted in the tradition of Romanian sheep herders). The instrumental music was gradually augmented by a singer, poet, or social commentator who vocalized about the events of the day. These **badkhn**, as they came to be known, served as purveyors of news and information and sometimes satirized members of the audience, public officials, or current events. In this regard badkhns fulfilled an age-old role in musical culture, one that is perhaps best illustrated in the early 2000s by rap musicians.

The Yiddish theater also played an important role in the formation of klezmer. Much of this activity is based in musical theater fashioned from wide and disparate sources, ranging from the musical hall traditions, the dramas of Ben Jonson, and Italian opera to stories from the Bible. And the denizens of musical theater were as peripatetic as their musical counterparts, for they wandered the land in search of an audience. It was only natural that the two entities would find themselves performing at similar venues and eventually some of these theaters employed musicians as part of their companies.

When these musicians reached the shores of America (often via Ellis Island), they continued to practice their craft and versatility continued to be one of their key themes. Many of these musicians played not only klezmer, but they

ETHNIC AND NATIVE AMERICAN TRADITIONS

also performed on the stages of local theaters or sometimes on the circuit that included Boston, New York, Philadelphia, and small towns and cities between. Most of them played any kind of job that came their way, and a few even got the chance to record for one of the major record companies, which were just exploring the possibilities of recording an even wider range of music.

The remarkable and influential musical career of **Dave Tarras** stretched from the early 1920s into the late 1980s. He emerged as the respected and venerated klezmer clarinet player, influencing scores of musicians over the course of his sixty-plus years of playing mostly in and around New York City. Tarras arrived in New York in 1921 and soon became involved in the Jewish/Yiddish/klezmer scene. The diversity of his early musical experience emerged when Tarras recounted the following conversation with Moe Nodiff, Columbia's A & R man for foreign recordings in the middle 1920s:

> Nordiff calls me up and books me to play a record . . . four sides, two recordings. He says, "Mr. Tarras, I'm giving you forty dollars to make a session. And then, if it's all right I'll give you more."
> Forty dollars? I would have done it for nothing. I was making a record!
> "Can you play a Russian session?"
> Yeah.
> "Good, so you'll come down next week and make a Russian session."
> So I went; I make. Two weeks later I make another Jewish session with [not Jewish band leader, Abe] Schwartz; whatever Nodiff give me: Russian, Polish, Greek. (Lornell and Rasmussen, eds., 1997, 59).

Born in the Ukraine in 1897, Tarras brought this music with him when he immigrated to the United States. It wasn't until the 1920s that musicians born in the United States began performing klezmer, and among most of these musicians Tarras was their idol. These musicians included Sam Musiker, Tarras's son-in-law and a featured soloist between 1938 and 1942 with Gene Krupa's very popular swing band, and Howie Leess. Along with American-born musicians, by the 1930s klezmer bands began incorporating pianists into their ensembles. Many of these musicians felt quite at home with jazz and their bands featured improvised solos. Like the swing-influenced jazz, klezmer was also used to accompany dancing.

The music thrived not only in big cities like New York and Chicago but also in the summer Catskill resorts from the teens through the 1950s. Commercial recordings of klezmer bands led by Dave Tarras, Abe Schwartz, and others were popular until its appeal to a younger audience diminished. Klezmer's nadir came during the 1960s and 1970s when the aging of the first and even the second generation of musicians left a void. By the 1980s, however, klezmer

ETHNIC AND NATIVE AMERICAN TRADITIONS

MUSICAL EXAMPLE

"Ot azoy" ("That's the Way") is a highly expressive klezmer performance. Clarinet player Sid Beckerman's father, Shloymke, first recorded the piece for Columbia Records in 1923. The brief vocal refrain (roughly translated "That's just the way it goes") implies a world-weariness that must have been felt by many newly arrived immigrants. Klezmer Plus blends older, veteran players like Beckerman and Howie Less with Sapoznik, Sokolow, and Spielzinger, who became involved with klezmer in the late 1970s. This piece was recorded in front of a live audience as part of the "Folk Masters" series.

Title "Ot azoy"
Performers Klezmer Plus
Instruments Sid Beckerman, clarinet; Howie Less, tenor saxophone; Henry Sapoznik, tenor banjo; Peter Sokolow, keyboard; Michael Spielzinger, drums
Length 3:58

Musical Characteristics
1. The clarinet takes the initial lead and is featured throughout.
2. The simple duple meter is established by Sokolow's accordion and then accented by Spielzinger's cymbal.
3. The piece is taken at a moderate, easy-paced tempo that increases slightly over the course of the performance.
4. The form is *ab* with the group joining in the brief vocal refrain.
5. It is performed in a minor key, which underscores its eastern European roots.

The source for this recording is Smithsonian Folkways 40047.

---

was revitalized by younger musicians like Hank Netsky, Henry Sapoznik, and Andy Statman, who also sparked a renewed interest in this unique aspect of Jewish expressive culture. Sapoznik also helped found Klez-kamp, a midwinter gathering that celebrates the expressive arts in Jewish culture, which recently celebrated its twentieth anniversary.

In the early 1980s there were a handful of bands playing; twenty years later klezmer bands can be found countrywide, their numbers are in the hundreds. Many (but not all) of the musicians who have performed in bands such as the Chicago Klezmer Ensemble, Kapelye, Klezmer Plus, the Klezmatics, and the New Orleans Klezmer All Stars are Jewish.

Scholarly and popular interest in klezmer has also recently coalesced. Not only has Henry Sapoznik produced many widely respected new and reissued recordings of klezmer, but his 1999 book *Klezmer!* also became the first in-depth study of the genre. Mark Slobin, a highly regarded academic ethnomusicologist, followed a year later with *Fiddler on the Move* and in 2001 with an edited volume, *Klezmer: The Evolution of an American Micromusic*. The popular interest in klezmer is underscored by the publication in 2000 of Seth Rogovoy's *The Essential Klezmer: A Music Lover's Guide to Jewish Roots and Soul Music, from the Old World, to the Jazz Age to the Downtown Avante-Garde*.

NATIVE AMERICAN

Long before Europeans and Africans reached our shores, the United States was populated by a wide assortment of distinctive tribes that we now call Native Americans or American Indians. They actually migrated here from Asia by way of Alaska, eventually settling in the United States thousands of years before Christopher Columbus arrived in the New World. Because of their disparate geographical patterns, among other factors, these groups developed at least seven major distinctive cultural areas: Northwest Coast, Southwest, Great Basin, Plateau, Plains, Northeast, and Southeast. Indians within these cultural areas were further divided into about 1,000 smaller units called tribes. Names of some of these tribes are permanently etched into the American past, especially during the European and Anglo-American conquests of the western United States: Sioux, Cheyenne, Cherokee, and Blackfoot. Since the middle of the nineteenth century most have been culturally decimated, greatly reduced in number, and resettled onto reservations.

This tragic cultural transformation has greatly affected the music of Native Americans. We know a great deal about twentieth-century Indian music, but relatively little about earlier periods. Unfortunately, our knowledge of twentieth-century Native American music often does not truly reflect the past. This is due to several critical facts. First, Native Americans did not notate their music. Second, the forced migration of tribes permanently altered their musical traditions. Third, American Indians had very few musical instruments, leaving little for archeologists to discover and reconstruct. Fourth, most ethnomusicologists specializing in this music have concentrated on the period after 1890 when sound recordings provided them with aural documentation. Finally, the impact of European and African American music greatly affected Indian music, most especially in the Northeast and Southwest.

It is safe to say that music has been a very important, perhaps even vital, component of Native American culture so we can make this sweeping observation:

ETHNIC AND NATIVE AMERICAN TRADITIONS

Seminole women cooking, taken during the research conducted by Francis Densmore (circa 1915). Courtesy of the Ralph Rinzler Folklife Archives and Collections, Center for Folklife and Cultural Heritage, Smithsonian Institution.

their music is closely tied to myth and religion, is fundamentally similar across the United States, and in some cases even bears similarities to that found in Central America. For most tribes music was thoroughly integrated with religion as an essential ingredient in worship, rites of passage, and other related ceremonies. Supernatural powers, usually known as spirits, transferred power and specialized knowledge to humans by teaching them songs. These songs cannot be isolated from worship and religious experiences, and the "success" of a song is judged by how well it fulfilled a spiritual need or helped to provide needed food or water.

These observations about the social and spiritual context for music remain largely true, even in the early twenty-first century, despite the inherent regional and tribal differences that inevitably occur as well as the extended interaction with Anglo and African American culture. For example, the influence of Mexican music upon southwestern tribes has permanently altered the nature of Apache music; their contemporary music is now liberally infused with elements, such as the use of violins, that would not have existed until several hundred years ago. Despite these variations contemporary Indian music continues to play a unique role in helping to define Native American identity.

Our understanding of Indian music from the late nineteenth century is traceable to two female researchers who began their work then. Alice Fletcher researched Native American music from the 1880s until her death in 1923. During that time she published many monographs and books, the most notable of which are *A Study of Omaha Indian Music* (1893) and *Indian Story and Song From North America* (1900). Trained as an anthropologist, Fletcher wrote extensively about the relationship between music and religious ceremonies. Many of these ceremonies had truly cosmic significance; others were designed to heal or assign powers of the occult. Fletcher's pioneering work holds important observations that pertain to contemporary Native American music.

Frances Densmore, born some thirty years after Fletcher, came from a varied academic background and was trained to perform and compose music. She became interested in Indian music after hearing live performances at the Chicago World's Columbian Exposition, though she did not actually begin her own fieldwork with the Chippewa until 1905. Densmore initially recorded Chippewa songs in northern Minnesota and Wisconsin for about five years before turning her attention to tribes in the Plains/Pueblo area. All told she gathered healing songs, songs taken from dreams, ceremonial songs, and others for nearly fifty years. Her most comprehensive collection, *Chippewa Music*, was published between 1910 and 1913, and much of her work was undertaken on behalf of the long-defunct Bureau of American Ethnology.

The modern era of our knowledge of Native American music begins about the same time as Fletcher and Densmore were working. This era of research is also linked with Jesse Walter Fewkes's sound recording in March 1890 of the Pasamaquoddy Indians of Maine. These earliest field recordings inspired Willard Rhodes, George Herzog, and others to include sound recordings as part of their research. Sound recordings preserved Native American music in such a way that it could be disseminated and dissected. Tragically, by the 1930s when sound technology had advanced to the point where the equipment was more portable and the results were more palatable, much of Native American music had been radically transformed. Over the past fifty years the music studied by Alan Merriam, Bruno Nettl, David McAllester, and the other significant scholars of middle-to-late twentieth-century Indian music is significantly different from that first heard by Densmore in 1893.

Although such sweeping generalizations are dangerous, much of contemporary Native American music results from the **Pan-Indian movement** that first developed in the 1920s. This movement has tended to greatly homogenize Indian music because of the propensity to gather in large **powwows** that encompass many tribes, sometimes from different parts of the United States, in search of one true identity for all Native Americans, irrespective of tribal or regional affiliations.

Music and Ceremony Today

David McAllester has written most extensively about the ghost dance and **peyote** cult that spread from Mexico to southwestern tribes in the 1940s. Based upon Indian religious practices, the ghost dance also touches upon Native American modes about the power and significance of dreams and their relationship to healing. The interaction between song and ceremony, which occurs after the ingestion of the peyote, is described by McAllester:

> During the ceremony a drum and rattle, both of special design, are passed, with other paraphernalia, clockwise among the circle of participants. When a member receives the rattle he is expected to sing a number of songs, usually four, after which he passes the rattle on to the next man. The rattle goes ahead of the drum so that, immediately after his turn to sing, each man is the drummer for the man on his left. Four times during the course of the ceremony the leader interrupts the procession to sing special songs which are always used at these times. At other times a participant sings whatever songs he chooses from the repertory at his command, or even extemporizes on the spur of the moment. (McAllester, *Peyote Music*, 1949, 89)

For nearly sixty years peyote use remained strongest among Southwestern Indians. Through much of the twentieth century, however, the Winnebago (Ho-Chunk) People of Wisconsin also gained peyote users as its evangelical adherents spread the word to the north and the east. But in the late 1950s its general popularity increased throughout the United States due to greater Pan-Indian activity. Even non–Native Americans began using peyote during the psychedelic days. Nonetheless, the ghost dance and peyote practices remain central to Navajo culture. In 1989 the United States Supreme Court heard a case in which the lawyers for the Native Americans argued for the legalization of small amounts of peyote for use in Navaho religious ceremonies. The Native Americans lost the case.

Nonetheless, the ghost dance and peyote cult underscore that some regional/tribal ties remain in Native American music and link music and ceremony. The relationship between music and all types of social, religious, and even quasi-religious events remains critical. Even in the current Pan-Indian movement, nearly all musical events remain partly dancing, partly religious ceremonies.

Significantly, strong connections remain between the spiritual world and music. People who sing and dance receive this music from the supernatural, as opposed to creating it themselves. These impulses come from dreams or some other induced state that permits the singers to touch either their distant past or ancestors. In the far Southwest Pia Indians believe that songs preexist and that

MUSICAL EXAMPLE

This brief performance is of the initial song heard in the First Song Cycle of the Washo Indians, which occurs during the night-long meeting of the peyote cult. It was recorded by the noted ethnomusicologist Willard Rhodes in the late 1940s as part of a larger project documenting the varieties of Native American music of the Southwest. Rhodes captured the beginning of the ecstatic trance, just as the peyote was being ingested.

Title "Peyote Song"
Performers Washo Indians
Instruments drum, rattle, voice
Length 1:14

Musical Characteristics
1. This performance has a steady rhythm and is taken at a rapid tempo.
2. The vocals are moderately ornamented.
3. Slight syncopation supplied by the rattle can be heard.
4. The somewhat tense voice is in the middle range.

This performance is taken from Smithsonian Folkways 4401.

---

they are "untangled" in dreams. During World War II some American Indians, most notably Navajo males who served as "dream walkers" for their tribe, were unique in their success at decoding encrypted messages sent by the Nazis. They attributed this special ability to crack codes as part of their inherent spiritual realm. Thus, some Native American performers are viewed not as creative artists but as special vessels who are closely in touch with the past and the spirit world. Because of this unique relationship, the ability to recreate a performance is critical, though the need to recreate these songs precisely varies from tribe to tribe.

A minority of tribes, however, do not make these direct connections between spirit and song. They believe that they can compose new songs based on traditional themes and musical motifs. Plains tribes such as Cheyennes routinely borrow songs from other tribes with whom they have contact. Pueblo Indians, in an attempt to keep their culture "pure," zealously guard their music from outside sources, both Native American and Western.

Nor does Native American music adhere to Western thoughts related to notation and theory, which is anathema to its generally ethereal premise. Indians may not refer to scales, but they are able to distinguish among hundreds of songs that sound similar to untrained ears. Most Native American music is performed by nonprofessionals, who tend to learn through traditional means. The majority of these performers are males who also have some connection with religious practices. Though we are slowly learning that women sometimes take leadership positions in Native American musical activity, male domination reflects the larger world in which men generally take a leadership position in religious ceremonies. Younger musicians, and would-be musicians, take part in these ceremonies and generally learn by rote and through their active participation.

Musical Characteristics

It would be fair to observe that Indian music uses less complex harmony than most other forms of American folk music. In fact, the texture of most Native American music is monophonic; if more than one vocalist is present, then they join together in unison or (occasionally) sing in octaves. **Vocables** constitute an unusual aspect of Native American singing that is widespread across the entire United States. These sound like mere nonsense syllables, but actually refer to nonlexical syllables, which serve to fill in or properly space out the lines in a song. They consist of short syllables like "he," "wi," or "yo"—low-sounding vowels that are usually sung in a nasal voice with glides. While these might sound like gibberish to outsiders, vocables serve also as aesthetic communication that not only helps to solidify their sense of social unity but sometimes also communicates the sound of natural phenomena. Vocables impart a special meaning to the singers (some of whom might be in a highly emotional or ecstatic state) that transcends the function they serve. Since vocables are most often heard as a chorus, all of the participants know when these syllables will occur.

Of course Native American music is not monolithic, and regional variations remain important. Among Native Americans, tribal differences are also quite important. Our knowledge about the different styles of Indian music is limited by the research conducted over the past one hundred years—the music of only about 10 percent of the 1,000 Native American tribes has been studied. Furthermore, research undertaken during the 1940s is difficult to compare with research from the turn of the century because of the major cultural changes that have taken place over the intervening time. As a general rule, the musical styles reflect cultural boundaries and the western tribes display greater variations than their eastern counterparts.

Bruno Nettl suggests that the music of Native Americans can be grouped in six broad regional groups, each of which uses some kind of drum and rattle accompaniment:

Plains (Blackfoot, Crow, Dakota, etc., of the upper West and Midwest). Their music is marked by descending melodic lines using pentatonic scales. Rattles

ETHNIC AND NATIVE AMERICAN TRADITIONS

and shakers produce slight variations among the otherwise repetitive rhythmic patterns. The vocal style tends to utilize low, long tones and is very harsh and pulsating. Plains Indians make extensive use of vocables.

East Coast (Iroquois, Mohawk, Penobscot, etc., from New England through the Great Lakes). These singers favor a more relaxed vocal style. Song forms tend to be more complex, often using a series of contrasting forms such as *aa-baba*. These phrases within the songs are fairly predictable, which helps to promote antiphonal singing. This important feature is unusual in Native American music.

Southwest and California (Yuman, Hopi, Apache, etc., from central California through New Mexico). A wide variety of scales are found among these tribes. Their voices tend to be lighter or toward the middle range with a nasal quality. The melodic lines often are broad and sweeping. Flutes are an important instrument and are often played in accompaniment to singing. The songs are set to intricate strophic texts. Native American music in this group is among the most complex in the United States.

Great Basin (Shoshone, Paiute, Navasupsai, etc., from Utah, Nevada, and northern California). Their music generally consists of short songs with very small melodic range and extreme repetition of phrases with little variation. The singing is relaxed and tends to be in the middle register. Great Basin Indians often use pentatonic or tetratonic scales.

Northwest Coast (Nootka, Salish, Tlingit, etc., of western Washington and Oregon). This style is generally complex. It makes use of small intervals and highly ornamented, varied rhythmic accompaniment. The musical forms are complicated and are built from short, repetitive phrases.

North (Eskimo and Inuit in Alaska). Their music is characterized by varied melodies of three or four notes, although pentatonic scales are not unknown. The songs are accompanied by complex percussion patterns, even dotted rhythms. The forms are nonstrophic and the singing is usually guttural and strained.

Instruments

The instruments used by Native Americans are almost all percussive, which helps to underscore the rhythmic drive heard in much of this music. Aside from the flute, nearly all of them are either rattles or drums. Rattles vibrate when they are struck, plucked, or shaken. Nearly all Native American tribes have used some kind of contained rattle that varies in its construction. Gourds, turtle shells, and woven baskets have all been used to contain small rocks or seeds. Small boxes struck by sticks are among the other types of rattles used by Indians to accompany their religious ceremonies.

Single-headed drums, which are held in one hand and struck by the other, are the most common type. They are ubiquitous except in California, where they are curiously absent. Double-headed drums are quite rare and may be a nineteenth-century innovation. Small kettledrums, sometimes filled with water to achieve a unique sound, have also been used by Indians in the East and the Plains.

The bullroarer is an instrument found across the world, but its presence in the United States is unique to Native Americans. Bullroarers are widely found in the West but are almost unknown east of the Mississippi River. They produce a nonmelodic sonority that is controlled by their size and construction. The most common bullroarers are made of a flat piece of bone or wood with a serrated edge that is attached to string or rawhide and whirled through the air.

Native American music today is increasingly Westernized and quite different than it was prior to colonization. Many younger Native American musicians are turning toward commercial country, rock, and hip-hop for their inspiration. Significantly, of the 1,000 tribes that once existed, scores have disappeared and most others have been culturally decimated. The push to Christianize Native Americans has changed many of the traditional modes of worship. Westernization has also radically altered the social and economic structures of Native American tribes, further disrupting the ways in which music has been used

Heartbeat, contemporary Pan-Indian musical ensemble. Pat Ashley, Sr., photo, courtesy of the Ralph Rinzler Folklife Archives and Collections, Center for Folklife and Cultural Heritage, Smithsonian Institution.

among Indians: Music is now used to entertain tourists in addition to the closed, sacred ceremonies. Many Native Americans maintain a balance between tradition and cultural change in a constant mediation between the white man's world and an Indian heritage.

Powwows

Due to increased electronic communication and the enforced movement of different tribes onto reservations, some Native Americans have unified into a Pan-Indian movement that has provided a stronger sense of solidarity. The general concept of such gatherings is not new; American Indians have come together to celebrate such multi-tribal functions as harvesting for centuries. But beginning in the late nineteenth century the idea of a gathering across tribal lines—now called a powwow—began to gain favor and today is the most well known public gathering of Indians in the United States.

Powwows are usually held in the summertime and are most commonly staged in the Plains and Northwest, but now can be found from Maine to California and from Texas through North Dakota. The name for these weekend events derived from an Algonquian term referring to a healing ceremony. In the early twenty-first century, the name has been applied to a gathering involving socializing, foodways, and spiritual enlightenment. Arts and crafts are also sold, partly for cultural reasons but also for tribal fund-raising.

ETHNIC AND NATIVE AMERICAN TRADITIONS

MUSICAL EXAMPLE

This selection was recorded in the early 1970s at an outdoor powwow in a small village at the Leech Lake Reservation in north-central Minnesota. This lovely area of the state remains quite wild and many of the Native Americans continue to spend much of their time hunting and fishing. Unlike many powwows this one drew almost exclusively from members of the Chippewa (also known as Ojibwa), who populate the upper Midwest and south-central Canada. Most of the participants are males between the ages of twenty and forty.

Title "Song from an Outdoor Powwow"
Performers Ojibwa Indians
Instruments drums, rattle, and voices
Length 1:03

Musical Characteristics
1. A deliberate quarter-note rhythm is produced by the drums.
2. The tempo increases slightly during the performance.
3. The voices tend to be in the upper register and are tense.
4. A pentatonic scale is used by the singers.

This selection is from Smithsonian Folkways 4392.

Music and dance are central to powwows, of course. The singing is dominated by males who usually sing in unison to the accompaniment of a single large bass drum. The dancers usually wear ornate and often highly symbolic regalia. Regional and specialized tribal dances are sometimes held in addition to the commonly practiced round dances. Over the past twenty years there has been a movement to increase unique tribal customs, such as the inclusion of games like lacrosse or gambling "hand games," within Pan-Indian powwows because of the clear danger of homogenization. These local or tribal variations might seem minor to the casual observer but they help to make each powwow a bit different. This movement is, I believe, part of a larger trend within the United States to celebrate our distinctive regional and ethnic identities.

Despite such trends, the folk music of Native Americans has been radically altered by the forces of time and the inevitable intrusion of Anglo-American culture. A small but growing number of Indian rock 'n' roll and electrified country music groups play at powwows, augmenting the more traditional music that has been part of these ceremonies. Several American Indian pop groups, including the rock-oriented White Boy and the Wagon Burners, played at the Smithsonian's Festival of American Folklife during the 1990s. A few other groups—most notably Heartbeat: Voices of First Nations Women—have come together to showcase female Indian performers, many of whom look not only to their own heritages but also to other forms of American vernacular music, such as blues and gospel. Not surprisingly commercial country and western music has also been embraced by many Native Americans. Buffy Sainte-Marie, a Native American "folk" singer, first became a popular figure the early 1960s folk revival—recording for Vanguard, among other labels—while Jim Pepper emerged in the late 1960s as one of the few Indians playing modern jazz.

Hawaiian American

Because of its multifaceted heritage and its physical distance from the mainland, Hawaii's folk and grassroots music seems not only exotic but far removed from that found in the rest of the United States. The population consists of people descended from early Polynesian Hawaiians, Asians, Caucasians, Puerto Ricans, and others who have migrated from nearby islands over the past several hundred years. They helped to form a unique enclave in America's rather small empire before the Islands achieved statehood in 1959. A conspicuous revitalization of traditional chant and dance that began in the late 1960s has moved these folk arts into a valued place among contemporary Hawaiians. The statewide movement to recognize local traditions has been called the "Hawaiian Renaissance" and has brought well-deserved recognition to many of the Islands' folk artists.

"Gabby" Pahinui, in particular, has received plenty of attention. He was a slack-key guitarist who almost single-handedly kept the tradition going from the late 1930s until the Renaissance began. Pahinui was not alone, of course, but his determination to keep playing in the older slack-key style typifies the struggle faced by many musicians in his position. Fortunately, Pahinui lived long enough to see a renaissance of this music, which owes its origins to the Hispanic traders who have frequented the Islands over the past 150 years.

Despite the emphasis on instrumental music over the last century, the Islands' traditions have been predominately vocal. Hawaiian singing is closely allied to the concept of *mana* (cosmic energy), a belief in a sacred life force that fostered a reverence for creativity. Several types of vocal music could be heard in Hawaii, but the mele (chant) proved to be the most important. Soloists predominate in traditional Hawaiian chanting; those who could please their listeners with a sustained, unbroken performance were most sought after. Secondarily, a chanter should excel at prolonging and controlling vowel fluctuation and changing tone through manipulation of the chest muscles. Mele are usually narratives commenting upon religion, historical events, or societal issues.

The well-known **hula** actually refers to a dance that interprets a mele. Due both to increasing urbanization and shifting tastes, the older style of hula that interprets animal life has almost disappeared from the Hawaiian repertoire. Hulas can be performed sitting down or standing up. But in either case, the complicated gestures are keyed to words or phrases in the mele. Hula mele are rather formalized into contrasting sections, often *abcbcbcd*, to make them easier to follow. Seated hulas are often accompanied by body percussion or some sort of instrument, while standing hulas are generally augmented by at least one percussionist/chanter. At least two mele, *oli* and *kepakepa*, are strictly chanted traditions that are never interpreted by a hula.

Aside from the guitar, most of Hawaii's folk instruments are percussive and the majority of them are affiliated with hula mele. For example, the *pahu hula* is a wooden drum made from a hollow log and its use is limited to accompany the *hula pahu* (hula dance). Other drums are made from indigenous material such as coconut shells (*puniu*). Rattles made of various indigenous gourds constitute the other important form of Hawaiian percussive instrument. Even beating wooden sticks against one another (*kala'au*) can accompany this dancing.

Western music began to be heard in the Islands almost as soon as Captain Cook landed there in 1778. By the early nineteenth century, the influence of Western secular and sacred music began to be felt. The early missionaries brought hymnals and the French introduced classical music and the necessary instruments to play it. Asian immigrants also brought their own folk and popular music. Ukulelelike instruments made their way to Hawaii in the early 1880s, brought over by Portuguese travelers.

Slack-key guitar (tuned to an open chord) techniques brought over by Mexican and other Hispanic immigrants in the 1830s proved to be the most significant import. By the late 1880s many of the Hawaiian guitarists were tuning their guitars to a major triad, a C-E-G in a C-major chord, and playing a style with a slide that produced a unique sound. **Joseph Kekuku** is alleged to be the man who innovated this style when he slid a comb across the strings of his guitar, which was placed across his knees. As Bob Brozman, Lorene Ruymar, and other scholars of the Hawaiian slide guitar have suggested, the sound of a slide guitar may have appealed to Hawaiians because its sustained tones reflect the elongated vowels sung by mele chanters. As the twentieth century dawned on the shores of Waikiki Beach, slack-key guitar was firmly entrenched as part of Hawaii's vernacular music. And some one hundred years later, slack-key guitar music (along with the hula dance) is now so closely associated with Hawaii that many people have forgotten its origins.

This style became influential on the mainland when a fad for Hawaiian music began in 1915. George E. K. Awai's Royal Hawaiian Quartet, along with other local musicians and dancers, evoked a sensational response at the

ETHNIC AND NATIVE AMERICAN TRADITIONS

MUSICAL EXAMPLE

This mele hula was recorded during a performance on April 8, 1980, at the Bishop Museum in Honolulu. According to the performer, it was initiated by the goddess, Hi'iaka, younger sister of Pele, the volcano goddess. Ko'olau is the lush windward side of the island of O'ahu, which is steep and ripe like a rainforest. The rustling sounds of the shell wreaths that embellish the dancers are the sound you hear in the background.

Title "A Ko'olau Au' Ika I Ka Ua"
Performer Hoakalei Kamau'u and Kawaiokawaawaa Akim (caller)
Instruments drum and voice
Length 1:35

Musical Characteristics
1. There is basically a duple meter feel with some minor rhythmic embellishments.
2. A steady moderate tempo, which increases slightly, is quickly established.
3. The voice is in a fairly high register and has some vibrato.
4. A modified call and response is used.

A Ko'olau au 'ike I ka ua
E kokolo a lepo mai ana e ka ua
E ka'i ku ana [ka'i] mai ana I ka us
A'e nu mai ana I ka ua I ke kuakiwi
E po'i [ho'i] mai ana I ka ua me he nalu
E puka, e puka, mai ana e ka ua
From Ko'olau, I watch the rain
The rain that pours on the earth
The rain passes by in columns
It rumbles as it falls in the mountains
The rain rises like the waves of the sea
Lo, the rain comes, it comes

This selection is from Smithsonian/Folkways 40015.

ETHNIC AND NATIVE AMERICAN TRADITIONS

Panama-Pacific International Exposition in San Francisco. Almost immediately the Victor company moved to exploit the situation. Their 1915 catalogue states: "Victor recently announced a fine list of favorite Hawaiian numbers, rendered by the now famous Hawaiian Quintette, who have made such a success in the 'Bird of Paradise' Company; the gifted Toots Paka Troupe, and the Irene West Royal Hawaiians, who have appeared in vaudeville. Although these fine records were intended mainly for customers in the Hawaiian Islands, they have been largely acquired by those Victor customers who like quaint and fascinating music such as this" (Victor Record Company catalogue, November 1915).

The shockwaves hit Tin Pan Alley with great force and they began churning out pseudo-Hawaiian songs for a mass market. As other Hawaiian musicians toured the United States they brought along other songs, but they also performed the Tin Pan Alley material that their audiences requested. Hulas became caught in this craze, too. Vaudeville stages and circus shows were considered incomplete if they didn't include a cootch or hoochie cootchie dancer, who was almost never Hawaiian and generally quite provocative. By the 1920s many American musicians were singing songs in English with Hawaiian themes, called *hapa haloe*. This craze culminated in 1937 when the hapa haloe "Sweet Leilani" garnered an Oscar for best song.

Anglo and Afro-American folk musicians heard this music and embraced the basic concept of playing an open-tuned guitar with a slide. Some black musicians were already using a similar style, but the Hawaiian fad served to reinforce its popularity. The slurring of the slide upon the strings mirrored the ability of harmonica players to move between the whole and half steps of Western scales. Many of the hillbilly musicians who pioneered the recording of country music were familiar with this style, too. A few musicians, such as the Dixon Brothers, enjoyed extensive recording careers using Hawaiian-style accompaniment. Jimmie Rodgers made several successful records in 1930 using Lani McIntire's Hawaiians to back up his patented blue yodeling and singing. Even Maybelle Carter used the slide technique on a 1929 session, though her influence probably came more directly from African American musicians. Certainly the pedal-steel guitar, which developed in the late 1930s and flourished in country music during the 1940s and 1950s especially in western swing and honky-tonk, owes a great deal to the slack-key and Hawaiian fad. Even a Tennessee hillbilly like Roy Acuff included a "Hawaiian" guitar player in his popular band—the Smokey Mountain Boys—during their heyday on the Grand Ole Opry.

Contemporary Hawaiian folk music involves a synthesis of older traditions and Western influences. It is largely performed for the booming tourist trade, not its informal traditional context. Hulas accompanied by chanting are available to any tourist on a daily basis. The revitalization has continued not only

ETHNIC AND NATIVE AMERICAN TRADITIONS

Hawaiian performers at the Festival of American Folklife. Courtesy of the Ralph Rinzler Folklife Archives and Collections, Center for Folklife and Cultural Heritage, Smithsonian Institution.

because of the recognition of its past, but also because of a vested economic interest in the tourists who wish to see things uniquely Hawaiian.

Into the twenty-first century, Hawaii maintains its status as a syncretic cultural center. Most of the Islands' citizens are minorities, many of whom came from Asia as well as other islands around the world. For most of the twentieth century Puerto Ricans settled in the Islands, bringing their music with them. The resulting synthesis is a unique blend that would almost sound at home as much along the borderland of Mexico and the United States as it does in Muai.

FRANCO-AMERICAN

Cajun Country

Despite the fact that a state line divides Texas and Louisiana, Cajun country constitutes a distinctive cultural region that is clearly distinguished by its language, customs, foodways, and music as well as by its physical geography. This small section of the Deep South is one of the United States's most easily identifiable cultural areas, and its unique characteristics remain largely unknown to most people around the country. Just as the rich sauces and tangy spices of Cajun food have attracted enthusiastic multitudes over the past few decades, the indigenous Cajun and zydeco music also continues to grow in popularity.

ETHNIC AND NATIVE AMERICAN TRADITIONS

Cajun fiddlers Michael Doucet and Dewey Balfa (circa 1990). Courtesy of the Ralph Rinzler Folklife Archives and Collections, Center for Folklife and Cultural Heritage, Smithsonian Institution.

This intriguing part of the country is unique because of its unusual blend of settlers. In the middle 1700s the English deported large numbers of French colonists from Nova Scotia, then known as Acadia. They were dispersed across the world, but many of them moved south, sailing down the eastern coast of North America in search of a fresh start. A few thousand of them eventually resettled in the southeastern part of Louisiana, the physical geography of which in some ways resembled their flat and wet homelands in western France, though a whole lot warmer.

These newcomers eventually intermingled with local residents, resulting in a cultural mixture known as Cajun. Cajuns speak a unique brand of French different from its Parisian counterpart. This is partially because most of the Arcadian people originally came from the maritime Breton and Norman sections of France, far from Paris. Moreover, the Cajun language is actually a creolized blend that mixes French with English and the African languages imported from Africa and filtered through the French West Indies.

This uniquely creolized section of the United States is itself fragmented by region. Along the bayous of south-central Louisiana, many of the residents still live in relative isolation. Boats remain a principal mode of transportation along with a continuing emphasis upon traditional ways of fishing and self-sufficiency. Further west, closer to the Texas border, the land is grassy and prairie-like. In the middle 1800s this was the frontier, something like our present-day conception of life and lifestyles on the wild western frontier. That spirit is found today in the wildcatting oil towns of Lafayette and Big Mamou, where the local economy still rides the waves of boom-or-bust economy. It is a land of unparalleled beauty, and many are drawn to explore the bountiful wildlife found in its obscure bayous. There is no place else like it in the United States.

Musical development

Cajun music evolved with the language and the rest of its culture. The early settlers brought with them their older French songs and dance music played on fiddles. They eventually picked up the keening, high-pitched vocal style of the indigenous Native Americans, which has become a trademark of the music. The African American residents contributed a slightly syncopated rhythmic sense and the concept of improvisational singing. Hispanic settlers introduced the guitar to the Cajuns, while Anglo-Americans provided them with new tunes. By the 1850s, most of the basic elements of this highly creolized music were in place.

In the nineteenth century dances were usually held in homes on weekends with fiddles, sometimes in pairs, providing most of the music. The diatonic accordion, so well known in Cajun music today, was not introduced into the area until after the War Between the States by German settlers who came to Texas in the 1840s and 1850s. The fiddles and accordions were soon joined together because they could be heard over the loud and raucous dances. By early in the twentieth century, small dance bands consisting of an accordion, fiddle, some percussion instrument (spoons, washboard, or triangle), and a guitar were found in dance halls all across Cajun country. They played a mixture of polkas, waltzes, two-steps, and other European-derived dance tunes for appreciative audiences. Cajun dances were often held on weekend nights in small, rural dance halls lined with wooden benches under which their children slept while their parents danced the night away.

During Reconstruction small waves of Anglo-Americans moved into southwestern Louisiana and southeastern Texas. The discovery of oil in the early twentieth century brought them into the region by the thousands. Their arrival, followed by the 1916 ban on speaking creolized French in the schools, signaled an important change for Cajun culture. The modern era of the twentieth century was invading this once remote portion of the United States and began a more rapid alteration of their once isolated corner of the world. This trend was exacerbated by the socialization fostered by World War I, a slowly expanding transportation system, and the explosion of the mass media. Each of these factors helped to force this unique culture into a secondary position as Cajuns quickly moved to become "true Americans." Cajun music fell victim to this general trend. While some of the musicians stubbornly clung to the traditional songs and tunes, many others absorbed the contemporary trends.

Documenting Cajun music

Fortunately a handful of Cajuns made commercial recordings in the late 1920s. Most notable were the fiddle duets of Dennis McGee and Sady Courville, which still sound hauntingly archaic. But the first Cajun records, "Allons a Lafayette" ("Lafayette") and "La Valse Qui Ma Portin De Ma Fose" ("The Waltz That Carried Me to My Grave") were made by Joseph Falcon and his wife, Clemo Breaux. Falcon remembers that the Columbia record executives in the temporary New Orleans studio were dubious about the entire affair:

> They looked at us . . . they were used to recording with orchestras. "That's not enough music to make a record," they said. So George [Burrow, a jewelry store owner from Rayne who wanted to sell Falcon records] had 250 records paid for before I even went to make them. So George started talking: "We got to run it through because that man there . . . is popular in Rayne; the people are crazy about his music and they want his records." But they said, "We don't know if it's going to sell." They then turned around and asked him, "How much would you buy?" He told them he wanted 500 copies as the first order . . . and he made out a check for 500 hundred records. They started looking at each other. "Well," they said, "you go ahead and play us a tune just for us to hear." (Strachwitz and Welding, *American Music Occasional*, vol. 1, 1970, 15)

By the middle 1930s the Hackberry Ramblers had synthesized Cajun music with the pioneering western swing sound and were among the first Cajun musicians to use amplified instruments. Electric steel guitars were soon heard in dance halls across southern Louisiana, as were the current popular tunes by Bob Wills and his Texas Playboys, the Lightcrust Doughboys, and Al Dexter and his Troopers. These songs were now pushed forward by the drums that Cajun groups began using. At the front of this modernization of traditional Cajun music was Harry Choates, whose popularity ensured him jobs as far west as Waco, Texas.

In fact, many Cajuns were leaving home for oil-related jobs in central Texas and Oklahoma. California became home for many transplanted Cajuns during World War II as they left the bayou for the West Coast defense industries. Many of them settled along the coast in the metropolitan San Francisco Bay area and around Los Angeles, both of which have long supported Cajun music (as well as western swing and country music) to a degree that would surprise many people unaware of these migration patterns.

The impact of Cajuns on related forms of music cannot go unnoticed. Cajun singers such as Joe Werner of the Riverside Ramblers influenced Webb Pierce, among others. In the early 1950s Hank Williams was based in Shreveport, Louisiana, home of the "Louisiana Hayride" and his recording of "Jambalaya" (which draws part of its tune from "Grande Texas"). Many of the western swing bands

ETHNIC AND NATIVE AMERICAN TRADITIONS

MUSICAL EXAMPLE

There is no Cajun song better known than this one; in fact, it is often referred to as the Cajun national anthem. You will almost inevitably hear "Jole Blonde" if you attend a Cajun music gathering. It first reached the ears of many people in the late 1940s when Harry Choates's version reached the national charts, which spawned many cover versions and answer songs. Since then it has become a song associated not only with Cajun music but also with southwestern Louisiana and southeastern Texas in general. This version was recorded in the mid-1950s.

Title "Jole Blonde"
Performers Tony and Rufus Allemand
Instruments Tony Allemand, fiddle and vocals; Rufus Allemand, guitar
Length 2:02

Musical Characteristics
1. It is played in a simple triple meter—3/4.
2. You hear a homophonic texture with the fiddle supplying the melody.
3. The tonality is major.
4. Allemand's voice pitches in a relatively high register.
5. He uses a slightly ornamented vocal style that emphasizes the emotional nature of the song.

Ah! ma joli' blond'.
Gar dez don qu'o c'est qu't as fait.
Tu m'as quitte' pou' t'en aller.
Je n'ai pas ma canne en mains, mais toi t'vas l' voir!

Ah! my joli blond'.
Moi j'm'en vais-t-a naviguer.
Tu vas pleurer-Zavant longtemps pou't'attaper;
Tu voudras t'en rev'ni avec ton vieux neg'.

Ah! my beautiful blond.
Look what you've done.
You left me to go away.
I don't have my stick on hand, but you'll get it!

Ah! my beautiful blond.
I am going to sea.

ETHNIC AND NATIVE AMERICAN TRADITIONS

You will cry before long, that'll teach you;
You will want to come back to your old negro.

This selection is taken from Smithsonian Folkways 4438.

---

included popular Cajun songs such as "Jole Blonde," a polka, or a two-step in their repertoire. From the 1940s until the present, Cajun music has left a small but important mark upon commercial country music.

The internal revitalization of Cajun folk music began slowly in the late 1940s. Led by the accordion-playing Iry Lejeune, the older songs once more began popping up at dances and on play lists of the local radio stations. Many of these musicians were born in the 1920s to parents with strong ties to traditional Cajun culture. Musicians such as Joseph Falcon and Nathan Abshire were natives and, therefore, immersed in their indigenous culture, though their language and music were kept more private during the decline of the Cajun culture itself. Spurred on by local record and radio entrepreneurs like Eddie Schuler and George Khoury, who knew they had a limited but faithful commercial audience for Cajun music, the inexorable reinvigorization of grassroots Cajun music had begun.

In retrospect, the decades-long attempt to "officially" obliterate Cajun culture that began just before 1920 was doomed from its outset. Cajuns are exceptionally hardy folk and they tenaciously cling to their traditions. Since the 1930s outside researchers, among them Alan Lomax, have been visiting southwestern Louisiana to document the indigenous music. Interest in Cajun music also increased during the early days of the folk revival. Harry Oster, then an English professor at Louisiana State University, spent considerable energy recording Cajun and other styles of indigenous music in southern Louisiana during the middle to late 1950s. At the suggestion of Ralph Rinzler and Mike Seeger, the 1964 Newport Folk Festival became the first major "event" at which Cajun music was featured outside of its home. Despite the uneasiness of Louisiana's more polished, uppercrust society, state officials were ultimately pleased that the music of Gladius Thibodeaux, Louis Lejune, and **Dewey Balfa** was so well received. Since then Cajun folk music has been heard all across the United States and the world.

Inside Louisiana itself the Council for the Development of French in Louisiana (CODFIL) has been active in promoting the culture through their efforts to promote French and Cajun language in the public schools. The University of Louisiana at Lafayette, located in the heart of Cajun country and whose sports teams are known as the "Ragin' Cajuns," operates a center devoted to the study of Cajun expressive culture and history. These groups have also helped to coordinate several regional festivals featuring local music, most notably the annual Cajun Music Festival in Lafayette. Today younger musicians such as Bruce Daigrepont, Zachary Richard, Michael Doucet, Steve Riley, Marc Savoy, along with an older generation that includes Tony Balfa and Nathan Menard, perform their indigenous music at folk festivals and clubs across America.

During the middle 1950s and into the 1960s, citizens across the United States received a small dose of Louisiana's musical culture in the form of **swamp pop**. This new sound intermixed R&B and contemporary country music with the Cajun and creolized music with which they grew up. Musicians such as Warren Storm, Phil Phillips, Rod Bernard, Johnnie Allan, and Bobby Charles Anglicized their names, eschewed the fiddles and accordions of their forebears, and turned to the popular music. The result was a unique blend that resulted in regional and national hits like "Sea of Love," "Let's Do the Cajun Twist," "Mathilda," and "Runnin' Bear." Only the "British Invasion" of 1964 slowed down the output of swamp-pop artists and assigned the music to the status of regional pop music.

Zydeco

Zydeco is a unique regional music that is closely related to Cajun music and is most simply described as creolized African American Cajun music. Traditional zydeco music and its performance contexts are very similar to its white counterparts. Found primarily in venues that stretch west from Lafayette to Houston, zydeco has developed since Reconstruction. Whether the musicians favor the older Cajun sound or prefer the blues or soul-tinged music, it is all propelled forward by a rhythmic drive and syncopation that betrays its Afro-Caribbean background.

The black Americans of southwestern Louisiana are truly creoles because they are usually a mixture of African, French, and Spanish descent. Although English is becoming the Lingua Franca, many older black Americans in Cajun country still speak a hybrid language that also mixes its heritage into a blend that Cajuns have trouble understanding!

Most blacks and mulattos came to Louisiana as slaves for French planters in the late eighteenth century or as "freed coloreds" following the Haitian revolution that ended in 1803. The music they played became known as zydeco, a creolized form of the French word for snapbeans. Scholars are not certain exactly how the term "zydeco" developed into its present meaning, but among themselves local residents often say that it is derived from an old southwestern Louisiana dance tune known as "Les Haricots Sont Pas Sales" ("The Snapbeans are Not Salted"). This term also shares its origins with the Afro-Caribbean culture that spices up all of this area. The spelling for this lively dance music is not standardized, and the word sometimes appears as *zodico*, *zordico*, or even *zologo*. Zydeco refers not only to music but also to the event where the dancing and music take place. Thus, one can host a zydeco, referring not only to music but food, dancing, and socializing. Especially popular are zydecos held at a *fais-do-do*, an informal house party where the music and dancing last far into the night.

Although zydeco and Cajun music are closely related, distinctions can be made. Zydeco tends to be played at a quicker tempo. Its melodies are generally simplified with more emphasis placed on its syncopated rhythms. In a Cajun two-step the first and third beats are accented, while a zydeco two-step accents the second and fourth beat. The repertoire of zydeco musicians also tends to include more blues and fewer waltzes than do Cajuns. Cajun bands usually feature a triangle, while zydeco bands favor a washboard fastened to a vest and known as a *frottoir*. Prior to the contemporary models, nineteenth-century zydeco musicians favored a scrapped animal jaw or a notched stick to provide the rhythmic drive.

Among older zydeco musicians, the Fontenot and Ardion families are noted for their skill, though for many years they played mostly for neighbors and friends. Local interest in zydeco music has increased over the past 20 years to the point that Alphonse Ardoin observed:

> I have a grandson . . . that I'm trying to teach. He's only three years old, but he's interested already. He doesn't know how to play anything yet, but he takes the accordion and plays with it . . . To be a musician, you have to be committed to music and have it in your family. It has to be in your blood for you to learn easily. (Ancelet 1984, 87)

Without a doubt, **Clifton Chenier** was the best-known zydeco musician. Before passing away from kidney disease in 1984 he toured extensively, bringing his modern zydeco music to large concert halls and small dance halls across the country. Chenier transformed zydeco music by using his larger piano-keyed accordion and incorporating elements of blues and rock 'n' roll. His early recording efforts included some R&B releases for Specialty and Post. But Chenier's breakthrough came in the late 1960s when he began playing at blues festivals and recording his unique music for Arhoolie Records. His band usually included a saxophone and full rhythm section in addition to his brother Cleveland's washboard.

The impact of zydeco has grown to international proportions since the 1990s. The amplified blues-based bands of Nathan & The Zydeco Cha Chas, Terence Semien, Beau Jocque, Queen Ida and the Bon Ton Zydeco Band, and Buckwheat Zydeco have toured Europe as well as the United States. They perform for local dances as well as international blues festivals. The initial 1983 Opelousas Zydeco Festival underscores the fact that this music originated and continues to thrive in Louisiana and was (finally) recognized there before disseminating across the United States and beyond.

ETHNIC AND NATIVE AMERICAN TRADITIONS

Canray Fontenont (fiddle) and "Bois Sec" Ardoin (accordion) belong to two families long involved with old-time zydeco music. Courtesy of the Ralph Rinzler Folklife Archives and Collections, Center for Folklife and Cultural Heritage, Smithsonian Institution.

Since 2000 the unique music and cuisine of southwestern Louisiana has moved into the consciousness of people around the world. In Seattle or Milwaukee one can now find blackened fish or gumbo on restaurant menus and people dancing the two-step in dance halls. Cajun people are not only survivors, but they are also wonderful ambassadors for their way of life and folkways. A group of younger musicians born in the 1950s, such as accordionist Zachary Richard and fiddler Michael Doucet, have found a large audience outside of the area of their birth. Today the recordings of Beausoleil, C. J. Chenier (Clifton's son), and the Balfa Brothers command their own "Cajun" section at major audio outlets as well as Internet sites. Clearly, the trend to "Americanize" Cajuns that peaked in the late 1940s has failed in a grand manner.

In fact, in the second decade of the 2000s, music festivals featuring Cajun and zydeco musicians are commonplace through the United States. The usually staid Filene Center at Wolf Trap Farm Park—located just outside of Washington, D.C., and the summer home to the National Symphony Orchestra as well as a variety of touring popular music acts—has hosted the "Louisiana Swamp Romp" since 1990. The lineup for June 2008 included Geno Delafose & French Rockin' Boogie and Beau Jocque & the Zydeco Hi-Rollers. A zydeco and Cajun music program such as at Wolf Trap would have been simply unthinkable even as recently as the middle 1980s, but the popularity of this music outside of its hearth area is now so widespread that these acts routinely tour in Europe, too. This fact simply underscores the popularity of roots music not only in the United States but among enthusiasts from across the globe as well.

Northeastern States

Though not as well documented nor as widely recognized, the music of French-speaking residents of the northeastern United States belongs in our survey. The population of northernmost New England and New York State includes hundreds of thousands of Franco-Americans, most of whom are Catholic. But there are also substantial Franco-American enclaves as far south as Hartford, Connecticut, and New Bedford, Massachusetts, attracted by the labor needed in the timber mills and factories that dot New England and the opportunities for maritime work along the coast. In 2010 "Francos" (as they often self-identify) accounted for 18 percent of all New Englanders.

Some are descended from the migration of Arcadians in the middle eighteenth century, but the majority are more recent migrants from Canada. Most of these Canadian immigrants have crossed the border from Quebec over the past 150 years, initially into northern New England but by 1900 throughout the region. Initially, their Franco-American music maintained close ties with Quebec and the French-speaking maritime provinces. Some of their folk songs still recollect France or their ancestors' time in Canada and have been sung by generations of Franco-Americans. A substantial body of these songs are associated with the times of the Canadian explorers and of the plight of French-Canadian farmers.

There is also a tradition of drinking and bawdy songs, *gaulois*, that tend to be dominated by male singers. Much of this singing activity takes place in bars and taverns rather than at home. "La Bonnefemme Robert" ("Old Lady Robert") remains one of the most popular obscene, anticlerical songs. Some men of Arcadian descent also continue the tradition of singing a soulful lament, *complainte*, that complains of life's difficulties.

Francos also support an a cappella vocal tradition. When people gather for *soirée*, an evening social gathering, singing is often part of the interaction and includes a *chanson* or solo lyric song, antiphonal songs that underscore the community nature of these events, and a *turlette*, "mouth music" or lilting that is related to the Irish tradition. These vocal traditions are perhaps more pervasive in Quebec, but their importance in New England further suggests the respect felt by Francos for their cultural roots.

The influence of the Catholic church is also felt. For example, well-known Gregorian songs that have been heard in church provide the melody for folk texts. Some of these songs make fun of the church and its activities. There was also a turn-of-the-century movement to transform the vocal traditions into large choral pieces or to incorporate dance tunes into more formal instrumental compositions.

French American dance music continued to be more widespread and common in the late twentieth century. Most noteworthy are the waltzes and two-step quadrilles that are most often played on the harmonica, fiddle, or accordion. These instruments usually provide the basic melody while the harmony is supplied by a piano with the *tapper du pied*, a rhythmic clogging of the feet, or the spoons adding rhythmic interest. Most of the dance tunes, such as "Fisher's Hornpipe" or "Le Reel de Sherbrooke" are well known on both sides of the U.S./Canadian border. In northern Vermont the well-respected Beaudoins and Reindeaux families maintain the older instrumental traditions.

While families are critical in transmitting and maintaining the Franco musical traditions, the performance of Franco-American folk music in New England has evolved into a more eclectic Americanized brew. Most of the artists come from Franco-American families (where the speaking of French is becoming increasingly optional), while others have become bicultural by virtue of marriage, and a few have fallen under its spell because of physical proximity to so many Francos. And if you live close enough to the Quebec border, you can watch French Canadian folk music on television and hear it on Canadian radio!

In other words, the cultural geography of New England—as well as the impact of mass media—has fostered this type of interaction. This blending has resulted in country western music sung in French, the continuation of ballads with clear ties to France, nineteenth-century fiddle tunes being performed for country dances, and topical songs about the timber industry—all part of Franco music. It is a mélange that remains unique but it also illustrates a process that occurs in other cultural groups throughout the United States. The "Scandahoovian" melting pot of the upper Midwest provides another example.

SCANDINAVIAN AMERICAN

Norwegians, Swedes, Finns, and Danes began settling in the United States during the early eighteenth century. The largest wave of Scandinavian immigration took place over a seventy-year period beginning in 1850, when they flooded the upper Midwest from Michigan to North Dakota. Most groups still tend to think of themselves as Danish American, Finnish American, Norwegian American, or Swedish American. There is also a sense of a general Pan-Scandinavian culture, but that is subservient to individual nationalistic identities. And, of course, many people rally around the Lutheran church, still its single most important religious institution. Today Scandinavian Americans live throughout our country, but the highest concentration still resides in the upper Midwest.

ETHNIC AND NATIVE AMERICAN TRADITIONS

Ballads

Early in the twentieth century ballads formed a small but important part of Scandinavian American folk music. New immigrants brought with them a proud tradition of epic, often mythic, storytelling and ballad singing. Eventually these traditions, such as the mythical Finnish Kalevala epics, found a new, distinctly American voice. Ballads were sometimes sung to the tunes of well-known Lutheran hymns. By the late nineteenth century nearly half of all of the Norwegian broadside ballads were being set to such hymns. Most importantly they were transformed into emigrant ballads during the nineteenth century. Transmitted both orally and by way of printed broadsides, emigrant ballads informed the listeners of the tribulations and the joys of life in the New World. This excerpt from such a ballad sends a warning back to potential emigrants:

> Things certainly were fine over there,
> to hear him tell about it.
> They didn't have to work like slaves for a living,
> and instead of hardtack they ate fine white bread.
> No taxes and no foreclosures,
> gold to be had for the digging,
> and crops that grew of themselves.
> That's what they said, and lied like the devil.
> (T. Blegen, *Norwegian Emigrant Songs and Ballads*, New York: Arno Press, 1979, 208–9)

Instrumental Music

Like so many other groups, Scandinavian American instrumental music is linked to dancing. A combination of polkas, waltzes, and other related tunes can be heard in dances throughout the upper Midwest. Even some of the older Swedish polkas can be heard today, most of which come from the musical activity of Edwin Johnson and his descendants. Younger revivalist bands such as Wiscandia and Bob & Becky Wernerehl play some of Johnson's tunes. The revitalization of older styles gained momentum during the late 1970s, resulting in the occasional use of plucked zithers—the Finnish Kantele, for instance, by groups like Minnesota's Koivun Kaiku (Echoes of the Birch). Like their German American counterparts, youthful polka bands such as the Ridgeland Dutchmen, the New Jolly Swiss Boys, and the Mississippi Valley Dutchmen, as well as younger Norwegian Americans such as LeRoy Larson, have stirred a renewed interest in local folk music.

A nationalistic spirit has kept the traditions closely identified with specific countries or regions with the "old" land. As early as 1926 fiddler/vocalist Erik Kivi recorded "Merimiehen Valssi" and "Porin Poika," which were released on

Victor's 78000 series. These were the first commercial recordings of Finnish American folk music recorded in the United States. The record sold only about 1,000 copies, but the market was deemed large enough that more than 800 Finnish American records were eventually issued during the 1920s and 1930s. Columbia thought enough of this market to issue an entire printed catalogue of Finnish American material that appeared on its 3000-F series. Not all of them were folk music, of course, but traditional music was well represented. Many types of Scandinavian American music (dance music, laments, nationalistic songs, and hymns) were documented on commercial recordings, but the industry's interest in the music waned during the 1940s. So did the community support for the music.

Polka and More Polka!

Polka music is played all across the United States but is perhaps most closely identified with the northern European population that settled in the Midwest (specifically, the Upper Peninsula of Michigan, the Twin Cities, and into North Dakota) during the nineteenth century. Until recently polka music has been danced by millions but carefully studied by few. For many midwesterners of Scandinavian, German, Czech, Polish, and Slovenian heritage, this is deep music that holds important cultural meanings. Polka is dance music, to be sure, but it also implies a social complex replete with family histories, foodways, community interactions, and hard work.

With its easily learned 2/4 duple meter, polka music was all the rage in Europe in the 1840s and a far cry from the sedate and serious waltzes and minuets. In Europe the polka was viewed as down home, boisterous, and dangerous to polite society.

Because it has been over one hundred years since many of these northern Europeans have immigrated to the United States, today's polka music and dance is distinctly American. And, despite the ethnic pride displayed in names such as Karl and the Country Dutchmen and Norm Dombrowski's Happy Notes, there has been considerable musical interaction among the musicians.

Nonetheless, enough differences remain to distinguish the bands, their musical repertoire, and their national or regional origins. This is perhaps most easily noted in their choice of instruments. The contemporary Polish American style, which is particularly strong in Chicago and Milwaukee, highlights reed and brass instruments (most often clarinets and trumpets). Their German (Dutchmen) and Czech neighbors favor similar lineups but often add a tuba or sousaphone to the ensemble, giving these bands an even richer sound. Polka musicians of Slovenian heritage favor an accordion over concertina, while Norwegian American polka bands are more likely to feature a fiddle in their lineup.

ETHNIC AND NATIVE AMERICAN TRADITIONS

MUSICAL EXAMPLE

This performance is by a large instrumental ensemble that is more typical of the Dutchmen polka bands of Wisconsin and Minnesota. "Minnesota Polka" is one of the mainstays of German American bands and was recorded and played over the radio in the 1930s by Whoopie John Wilfahrt and later by the Six Fat Dutchmen from New Ulm, Minnesota. The band's leader, Karl Hartwich (born 1961), is one of the few people making a full-time living playing this music. He presently lives near the Mississippi River in southwestern Wisconsin, deep in the heart of polka country.

Title "Minnesota Polka"
Performers Karl and the Country Dutchmen
Instruments Karl Hartwich, concertina; Don Burghardt, trumpet; Myron Meulbauer, trumpet and clarinet; Marty Nachreiner, clarinet; Doug Young, tuba; Jerry Minar, keyboard; Holly Johnson, drums
Length 2:25

Musical Characteristics
1. It is played in a simple, yet lively, 2/4 duple meter.
2. You hear crisp and well-articulated brass and reed lines.
3. The tonality is major.
4. The tuba explores a wide range and adds a slight syncopation to the music.
5. Hartwich's concertina playing is not only very clean, but he also strongly emphasizes jaunty rhythmic accents at the end of his phrases.

This selection is taken from Smithsonian Folkways 40088.

These may appear to be subtle distinctions but they are important not only to the musicians themselves but also in the overall sound of each tradition.

Polka music in the Midwest has also evolved its own media. *Polka News* is the most widely read of the polka publications, though there are also many smaller, regional magazines. And the upper Midwest, from Michigan through North Dakota, is dotted with small (mostly on the AM band) radio stations that devote at least a portion of their broadcast day to polka music. More recently public radio stations, most notably in Wisconsin, have taken up the mantle with weekly programs devoted to the regional styles of polka music. In the 1950s

Norm Dombrowski's Happy Notes, one of Wisconsin's most popular Polish American bands. Courtesy of the Ralph Rinzler Folklife Archives and Collections, Center for Folklife and Cultural Heritage, Smithsonian Institution.

television programs around the United States featured local talent of all types and midwestern stations hosted more than a few polka bands during the 1950s and 1960s. *The Lawrence Welk Show* did more to promote midwestern polka styles than anything else on nationwide television. In his informative notes to "Deep Polka," Richard March writes that in the early years of 2000 "syndicated polka TV shows like Colleen Van Ellis' 'Polka, Polka, Polka' are invading cable, and State Senator Florian Chmielewski of Sturgeon Lake, Minnesota, claims to have the longest running program in TV history. 'Chmielewski Fun Time,' has been on Duluth's KDAL ever since 1955, over 2,000 programs" (Leary and March 1996, 7).

Norwegian American Folk Music

The first Norwegians came to the United States in 1825. They soon migrated westward from New York into the Midwest, reaching Wisconsin within fifteen years. By the 1850s they had moved as far west as southeastern Minnesota, and within twenty years the Red River Valley had become the region with Minnesota's highest percentage of Norwegians. Like many recent immigrants these newly minted Norwegian Americans stuck together, often settling in the same county and township. Wisconsin in the 1840s was a land of hardy pioneers, so "sticking together" could mean a few miles to the nearest neighbor.

A rural lifestyle helped to promote a sense of community within Norwegian American enclaves. Summertime work exchanges helped to raise barns and establish local quilting circles. During the winter, which lasts from November to April, these same families gathered weekly. Except for the small pious Haugean sect, which discouraged dancing, fiddle music, and other related activities, they met for weekly dance parties. Each week a different family hosted the dance, clearing out the parlor and opening the house to all of the neighbors. Neighbors provided the music and some of the food. The dancing often lasted until well into the night.

But by the turn of the twentieth century Norwegian immigrants rarely sailed across the Atlantic Ocean as familial units. Males typically came first, worked on farms, and later sent for their family. Farmwork often exposed them to other cultures, thus contributing to the mixing of ethnic music traditions. They also came from different regions in Norway, resulting in a more heterogeneous population. The formation of **bygdelags**, social and cultural societies consisting of people from the same region of Norway, was the response to this fragmentation as well as the physical isolation of rural farm life. Bygdelags helped to perpetuate not only the language but also regional dialects, customs, and music. Norwegian food such as *lefse*, an unleavened bread, and sweet krumkakes were found on the tables at the close of formal meetings. They brought people together to celebrate Norwegian Constitution Day on May 17 (Syttende Mai). By the 1920s there were scores of bygdelags throughout Minnesota and Wisconsin.

Julebukker is an old Norwegian custom that occurred in some communities. It can be translated as "Christmas fooling" or "Christmas ghosting." In twentieth-century Wisconsin it evolved into a masquerading event featuring cross-dressing and other masking devices. The disguised visitors would enter a neighbor's house, and the occupants would try to guess the true identities. The teasing usually ended in a dance with fiddles, accordions, and guitars providing the music for waltzes, polkas, and "Yankee dances" (a square dance).

The **Hardanger fiddle** emerged in the late 1800s and early 1900s as a unique type of violin used to accompany the regional dances brought over by Norwegians. This occurred in part through the bygdelags and in part through the localized concentration of immigrants from western and southern Norway. Named for the rural section of Norway from which it originated, these distinctive fiddles are ornately decorated. A Hardanger fiddle is also a little bit shorter and narrower than other fiddles and features a fingerboard that is virtually flat. The layout of the fingerboard encourages the musician to play more than one string at a time. Strung underneath the fingerboard and attached to the bridge are four or five strings, which sound sympathetically. This gives the Hardanger a fuller sound and an unusual timbre. Hardanger fiddles were important enough to spawn the Hardanger Violinist Association of America in the early twentieth century. Further evidence of revitalization is the contemporary revival of this organization in Wisconsin and Minnesota.

The distinctive, localized styles of rural dance and music imported from the old country inevitably evolved into Norwegian American styles. The older couple dances—springer, pols, and springleik—gave way to the more generalized European forms of polkas and waltzes. Although the use of the Hardanger fiddle declined during the twentieth century, conventional fiddles remained the lead melodic instrument. They were slowly augmented by both button and piano accordions. Greater contact with other Scandinavian Americans, particularly Swedes, and "Americans" led to a broader repertoire. A study of Norwegian American instrumental music conducted by ethnomusicologist LeRoy Larson in the early 1970s concluded that approximately 10 percent were of Norwegian origin and another 10 percent were from Sweden. Even Norwegian Americans were not immune to the process of regional adaptation, which accounts for the ability of musicians to perform music for specific ethnic groups or a more general Scandinavian American audience.

Norwegian swing

Early in the twentieth century Norwegian American folk music was still heard in informal public events, such as a barn-raising, or homes but dance halls slowly emerged as the location of choice for this music, and a semiprofessional circuit of musicians and "barn dance" halls developed during the 1920s. Thorstein Skarning and his Norwegian Hillbillies were among the bands that played for dances in barns that no longer held cattle but were specifically engaged for such events. They worked the same circuit as other Scandinavian American bands such as the Viking Accordion Band and Ted Johnson and His Scandinavian Orchestra. These small ensembles of between five and ten pieces often included not only fiddle and accordions but also a variety of reed and brass instruments that performed arrangements of older folk dance tunes.

By the late 1930s such "ethnic" bands had paralleled a trend in American country music by groups like the Hoosier Hotshots to professionalize. Both styles moved to increase the size of their ensembles by adding reed and brass players to augment the basic ensemble of stringed instruments. In this respect they became more similar to the small swing bands of Benny Goodman or Glen Miller. Their core repertoire of old-time instrumentals did not change, but it was augmented by popular dance tunes and novelty songs to appeal to a wider audience. Informal attire was replaced by either matching suits or "hayseed" rural costumes consisting of overalls, plaid shirts, and straw hats, which helped to solidify their rural, down-home image.

These tactics worked for a while; they transformed Norwegian American folk music into a format that was more palatable for a larger audience until the close of World War II, when this music faced a sharp decline and most of the bands retired. A cadre of musicians playing more traditional styles of Norwegian American music remained, though they rarely performed in public. Such musicians have become more apparent during the revitalization of old-time music that began in the middle 1970s.

Contemporary Norwegian American folk music

Twenty-first-century Norwegian American folk music, which is largely instrumental, can be heard at monthly dances held at community centers or in the homes of older musicians. It is also one of the drawing cards for the annual Norwegian festivals held in Detroit Lakes, Fergus Falls, and other small communities in central Minnesota. The Nordic Fest at Decorah, Iowa, hosts an annual three-day old-time music program, while in Mount Horeb, Wisconsin, there is a smaller Scandinavian musical festival. Perhaps the largest such event is the fiddle contest at Yankton, South Dakota. Because the crowds can sometimes grow quite large, it is not uncommon for these bands to use amplifiers or amplified instruments. The music is presented as an important manifestation of Norwegian culture and people often ask for the old tunes, waltzes, polkas, and reinlanders (a Norwegian variant of the schottische) that they heard fifty or sixty years ago.

Accordions and fiddles have moved back to the front of the band and they are often backed up by guitars, pianos, or a bass guitar. The musicians themselves tend to be in their sixties and seventies with a sprinkling of younger folks learning the repertoire. The repertoire tends to be eclectic, mixing some older Norwegian American tunes such as "Tutlut's Waltz" with pieces learned from contemporary visiting Norwegian musicians or from tapes of Norwegian folk music. Distinctly Bohemian, Irish, and Swedish American tunes learned from other Minnesota, North Dakota, and Wisconsin residents form another part of the repertoire. The music tends to be played in simple or compound duple or triple meter with contrasting *ab* sections. The texture is not very dense and the dynamic range falls into the middle and is rather narrow. The overall feeling is one of very clearly articulated and melodic playing underpinned by a steady rhythm meant for dancing, yet there is enough subtle rhythmic interest to keep even the most demanding listeners tapping their toes in anticipation of the next variation.

FINAL THOUGHTS

The study of ethnic (folk) music in the United States in not nearly as advanced as our analysis and writings about Anglo-American and African American traditions. This is partially because the work of folklorists, anthropologists, and

ETHNIC AND NATIVE AMERICAN TRADITIONS

ethnomusicologists has only recently concerned itself with the musical worlds found inside the political boundaries of the United States. The music itself is as varied as the ethnic and racial groups, but for Americans who live outside of these ethnic traditions, this music sounds fresh and new.

Ethnic music in the twenty-first century is infused by popular culture more quickly and readily than by folk culture. This results in music, such as contemporary urban manifestations like Puerto Rican salsa or South African high life, that lies on the edge of our scope. Revitalization movements that began in the late 1960s and early 1970s (which were further inspired by *Roots*) not only reinvigorated indigenous musical traditions, they also helped to place the spotlight on several of the ethnic groups described in this chapter. Finally, the popular and scholarly interest in "world music" has further highlighted interest in once all-but-invisible ethnic musical communities that proliferate across the United States.

KEY FIGURES AND TERMS

badkhn
Dewey Balfa
bygdelags
Cajun
Clifton Chenier
creolization
Frances Densmore
ethnic
Hardanger fiddle
hula
Joseph Kekuku
klezmer

Pan-Indian movement
peyote
powwow
revitalization
revival
slack-key guitar
swamp pop
Dave Tarras
vocables
Whoopie John Wilfahrt
zydeco

SUGGESTED LISTENING

Clifton Chenier. *Live at St. Mark's*. Arhoolie 313. There are many fine Chenier albums on Arhoolie, but this live performance is particularly compelling.

Flaco Jimenez. *Flaco's First*. Arhoolie 370. The early commercial recordings (1956–58) by this giant of conjunto accordion can be found here.

Kapelye. *Future and Present*. Rounder 249. A set of traditional and more forward-looking klezmer by one of the premier groups of the revival.

ETHNIC AND NATIVE AMERICAN TRADITIONS

Klezmer Plus. *Featuring Sid Beckerman and Howie Leess.* Flying Fish 70488. A well-integrated mix of younger and veteran musicians and an interesting repertoire make this a valuable release.

Dennis McGee. *The Complete Early Recordings.* Yazoo 2012. The title sums it up nicely: twenty-six by one of the acknowledged masters of Cajun fiddling with accompaniment by Ernest Fruge and Sady Courville.

Andy Statman. *The Andy Statman Klezmer Orchestra.* Shanachie 21004. An early (1983) set by one of the pioneering groups in the new wave of klezmer music. It features a rather unusual lineup of bass, guitar, french horn (doubling on trumpet), and clarinet (with a mandolin double).

Jimmy Sturr. *Come Share the Wine!* Rounder 6116. Born (and still living) a mere sixty-six miles north of New York City in Florida, New York, this 2007 release underscores why Sturr (a multi-Grammy-winning Irishman) remains the king of our polka nation.

Dave Tarras. *Yiddish-American Klezmer Music 1925–1956.* Yazoo 7001. The definitive survey of this most influential of the genre's clarinet players.

Donald Thibodeaux. *Fred's Hot Steps.* Arhoolie 9006. A fun recording by this old-style Cajun accordionist.

Various. *Borderlands: From Conjunto to Chicken Scratch.* Smithsonian Folkways 40418. A collection that covers conjunto from the lower Rio Grande valley up through the older style of music performed by the Yaqui Indians in southern Arizona.

Various. *Cajun Fais Do-Do.* Arhoolie 416. An anthology of older style Cajun music by Nathan Abshire, Adam Landrenear, and others recorded in the 1970s.

Various. *Cajun Social Music.* Smithsonian Folkways 40006. This collection of recordings from the 1970s includes performances by Nathan Abshire, Hector Duhon, and Marc Savoy.

Various. *Chicken Scratch.* Canyon 6093. An anthology of Southwestern styles featuring Elvin Kelly, Los Reyes, and the Molinas.

Various. *Conjunto! Texas-Mexican Border Music,* 3 vols. Rounder 6023/24/30. A well-annotated, three-volume sampler featuring some of the recent masters of the genre—Flaco Jimenez, Santiago Jimenez, etc.

ETHNIC AND NATIVE AMERICAN TRADITIONS

Various. *Corridos y Tragedias de la Frontera, 1928–37* ["Tragic Corrdios of the Frontier"]. Folklyric 7019/20. A two-CD set of classic border ballads that comes with a 168-page book!

Various. *Creation's Journey: Native American Music.* Smithsonian Folkways 40410. Taken from 1992 and 1993 recordings, this collection includes powwow music, Christian songs sung in Cherokee by Native Americans living in the United States, Canada, Mexico, and Bolivia.

Various. *Deep Polka: Dance Music from the Midwest.* Smithsonian Folkways 40088. Twenty-six contemporary recordings by polka bands that reflect the German, Danish, Finnish, Czech, Croatian, and Norwegian heritage of the upper Midwest.

Various. *Deeper Polka: More Dance Music from the Midwest.* Smithsonian Folkways SFW40140. A follow-up to *Deep Polka* that is well documented and delightful and that covers seven different midwestern polka traditions.

Various. *Fifteen Early Tejano Classics.* Arhoolie 109. A reissued sampler including a variety of styles including rancheras, polkas, and boleros that were originally recorded in the 1940s and 1950s.

Various. *Hawaiian Drum Dance Chants: Sounds of Power in Time.* Smithsonian Folkways 40015. A sweeping anthology of isolo chants and chants accompanied by dancers, drums, and percussion recorded between 1923 and 1989.

Various. *Honor the Earth Powwow.* Rykodisc 10199. Performances by Minnesota and Wisconsin Ojibewa as well as Menominee and Winnebago singers are heard on this recording made in the 1991 event of the same name.

Various. *Jakie, Jazz 'Em Up—Old Time Klezmer Music 1912–26.* Global Village C-101. A lively collection of vintage klezmer recordings by Abe Schwartz, Art Shryer's Modern Jewish Orchestra, and others.

Various. *Klezmer Pioneers: 1905–1952.* Rounder 1089. A collection that includes some of the best recordings of Abe Schwartz and other early greats.

Various. *La Musique Creole.* Arhoolie 591. A sampler of creolized African American/French music from Louisiana spotlighting Canray Fontenot and Alphonse "Bois Sec" Ardoin.

ETHNIC AND NATIVE AMERICAN TRADITIONS

Various. *Louisiana Cajun and Creole Music: The Newport Field Recordings.* Rounder CD 011661612129. These down-home recordings from 1964 to 1967 mark the first time that some of these folks recorded and most of them performed outside of their communities.

Various. *Mademoiselle, Voulez-vous Danser?* Smithsonian Folkways 40116. This set, subtitled "Franco-American Music from the New England Borderlands," contains country dance tunes, call-and-response *soiree* songs, fiddle tunes, and a cappella lyric songs recorded throughout New England during the late 1990s. A helpful booklet makes this the best volume of its kind.

Various. *Music of New Mexico: Hispanic Traditions.* Smithsonian Folkways 40409. Ballads, lyric folk songs, and sacred selections are among the genres represented on the twenty-six-track anthology that was recorded in the early 1990s.

Various. *Music of New Mexico: Native American Traditions.* Smithsonian Folkways 40408. Music by Pueblo, Navajo, and Mescalero Apache are included in this set, which nicely complements the *Hispanic Traditions* compilation.

Various. *Navajo Songs.* Smithsonian Folkways 40403. This collection of songs recorded in the 1930s and 1940s surveys the rich variety of Navajo vocal music.

Various. *Powwow Songs: Music of the Plains Indians.* New World 80343. Performed mostly by Sioux Indians, this is a well-annotated set of functional songs used to accompany various contemporary powwow contests, war dances, and round dances.

Various. *Songs and Dances of the Eastern Indians From Medicine Spring & Allegheny.* New World 80337. This music is provided by two geographically disparate tribes (Oklahoma and New York) that share similar musical styles.

Various. *Songs of Love, Luck, Animals and Magic.* New World 80297. Native American music by two northwest tribes—the Yurok and Tolowa—that includes ceremonial and love songs as well as ceremonial music.

Various. *Texas-Czech, Bohemian-Moravian Bands.* Arhoolie CD 7026. An engaging and lively sampling of recordings made between 1929 and 1959.

Various. *Vintage Hawaiian Music: Steel Guitar Masters 1928–34.* Rounder 1052. *Vintage Hawaiian Music: The Great Singers 1928–34.* Rounder 1053. These two packages provide a nice sampling of commercial recordings of folk and folk-based Hawaiian music.

ETHNIC AND NATIVE AMERICAN TRADITIONS

Various. *Voices Across the Canyon: Volume One & Volume Two*. Canyon 7051/2. These two compact discs offer the listener a sampling of Canyon's extensive catalogue of Native American recordings of over four hundred albums, which they have been building since 1951.

Various. *Wood That Sings: Indian Fiddle Music of the Americans*. Smithsonian Folkways 40472. This is the first anthology that provides the listener with a cross-section of contemporary and traditional American fiddle music.

SUGGESTED READING

Barry Ancelet. *The Makers of Cajun Music*. Austin: University of Texas Press, 1984. A nice overview that features wonderful photographs, plenty of primary data, and interviews.

Shane Bernard. *Swamp Pop: Cajun and Creole Rhythm and Blues*. Jackson: University Press of Mississippi, 1996. The definitive history of this unique style of regional pop music that emerged in the 1950s.

Ryan André Brasseaux. *Cajun Breakdown: The Emergence of an American-Made Music*. New York: Oxford University Press, 2009. A thorough history of Cajun music, with a particular emphasis on the gradual expansion of this music from southwest Louisiana that began shortly after World War II.

Tara Browner. *Heartbeat of the People: Music and Dance of the Northern Pow-wow*. Urbana: University of Illinois Press, 2004. This brief, utterly accessible ethnographic study explores contemporary intertribal powwows.

Tara Browner. *Music of the First Nations: Tradition and Innovation in Native North America*. Urbana: University of Illinois Press, 2009. Browner has edited an excellent and broad anthology that touches on issues as diverse as powwows and Inuit drum dance songs.

Mark DeWitt. *Cajun and Zydeco Dance Music in Northern California*. Jackson: University Press of Mississippi, 2008. Through both migration and the folk revival, DeWitt links the music and culture of southeastern Louisiana with the San Francisco Bay.

Bertha Little Coyote and Virginia Giglio. *The Songs and Memories of a Cheyenne Woman*. Norman: University of Oklahoma Press, 1997. An interesting collaboration that reveals the life story and music of a Cheyenne woman, which was written while Ms. Coyote was in her eighty-fourth year. The book is accompanied by a compact disc with stories and music.

ETHNIC AND NATIVE AMERICAN TRADITIONS

Victor Greene. *A Passion for Polka*. Berkeley and Los Angeles: University of California Press, 1992. Historian Greene uses polka as a springboard for a larger study of the history and development of ethnic musics in the United States.

James H. Howard and Victoria Lindsay Levine. *Choctaw Music and Dance*. Norman: University of Oklahoma Press, 1997. When most of the Choctaw were forced from Mississippi to Oklahoma in the nineteenth century, they brought their songs and dance with them. This handy book focuses on the social organization of today's dance troupes, their costumes, choreography, and music.

Charles Keil, Angeliki Keil, and Dick Blau. *Polka Happiness*. Philadelphia, PA: Temple University Press, 1992. These authors have crafted a series of essays about polka music that examine not only musical culture but also the importance of ethnic identity in establishing that culture.

Ellen Koskoff. *Music in Lubavitcher Life*. Urbana: University of Illinois Press, 2001. A close examination of the musical culture of this ultra-orthodox group, which is highly concentrated in the Crown Heights section of Brooklyn, New York.

Mirjana Lausevic. *Balkan Fascination: Creating an Alternative Music Culture in America*. New York: Oxford University Press, 2006. This book examines how Balkan music and culture has been transformed into a Balkan-American tradition since the 1950s.

James Leary. *Polkabilly: How the Goose Island Ramblers Redefined American Folk Music*. New York: Oxford University Press, 2006. An important study that suggests a reexamination of how highly regional forms of folk music can be viewed in the twenty-first century.

Ben Sandmel (with Rick Olivier—photographer). *Zydeco!* Jackson: University Press of Mississippi, 1999. An extended narrative about this form of creolized African American music, which is richly illustrated by Oliver's photographs.

Henry Sapoznik. *Klezmer: Jewish Music from Old World to Our World*. New York: Schirmer Books, 1999. Sapoznik does an outstanding job of not only profiling some of the genres most interesting and outstanding musicians (such as Dave Tarras), he also provides a historical overview of the genre.

Ann Savoy. *Cajun Music: A Reflection of a People,* Vol. 1. Gretna, LA: Bluebird Press, 1984. Although this is primarily a songbook, it is interspersed with interviews, background information, and photographs.

ETHNIC AND NATIVE AMERICAN TRADITIONS

Mark Slobin. *Fiddler on the Move: Exploring the Klezmer World.* New York: Oxford University Press, 2000. The author takes a careful and close look at klezmer as an American musical phenomenon. It's neither a history nor a survey of the field, rather Slobin looks at this music from a variety of perspectives and approaches.

Mark Slobin, ed. *Klezmer: The Evolution of an American Micromusic.* Berkeley and Los Angeles: University of California Press, 2001. This edited volume features essays that focus on klezmer from musical, cultural, and historical perspectives.

Willie Smyth, ed. *Spirit of the First People: Native American Music Traditions of Washington State.* Seattle: University of Washington Press, 1999. This book consists of essays that explore not only the history, but the variety of Native American musics found in Washington and adjoining states and provinces.

Michael Tisserand. *The Kingdom of Zydeco.* New York: Arcade Press, 1998. Based on oral histories and interviews, this book relates the history and development of this form of African American music in southwestern Louisiana.

Judith Vander. *Songprints: The Music Experiences of Five Shoshone Women.* Urbana: University of Illinois Press, 1988. A scholarly and accesible study of the lives and music of contemporary Shoshone women.

Judith Vander. *Shoshone Ghost Dance Religion: Poetry Songs In A Great Basin Context.* Urbana: University of Illinois Press, 1997. Don't be put off by the unwieldy title; this is an important book that follows up on Vander's earlier, more highly focused look at Shoshone women's music.

Sean Williams and Lillis O. Laoire. *Bright Star of the West: Joe Heaney, Irish Song Man.* New York: Oxford University Press, 2011. Born in 1919 and a New York City resident from 1965 until his death in 1982, Heaney brought his older style of Irish singing to new audiences across the United States for nearly twenty years before his death in 1984.

SUGGESTED VIEWING

Balfa Brothers. Various. *Les Blues de Balfa.* Aginsky Productions/Folkstreams.net. The Balfa brothers (Dewey, Rodney, and Will) are the focus of this film about family, music, and Cajun culture.

Clifton Chenier. *Hot Pepper: The Life and Music of Clifton Chenier.* Flower Films. A portrait of the late, undisputed "King of Zyedco."

ETHNIC AND NATIVE AMERICAN TRADITIONS

Popovich Brothers. *The Popovich Brothers of South Chicago*. Facets Multimedia/Folkstreams.net. A portrait of a family of musicians—who play tamburitza music—who are at the heart of the Serbian-American community of south Chicago.

Various. *A Jumpin' Night at the Garden of Eden*. Michael Goldman/Folkstreams.net A substantial documentary about the history of Klezmer from the teens through its 1970s revitalization and into the 1980s.

Various. *Del Mero Corazon* ("Straight from their Heart"): *Love Songs of the Southwest*. Flower Films. Norteno music and culture is the focus of this documentary.

Various. *Cajun Country: Don't Drop the Potato*. Vetapol 13077/Folkstreams.net. Denis McGee, Wade Fruge, the Hackberry Ramblers, and Bois Sec Ardoin are among the featured performers in this Alan Lomax conceived project about horse racing, bar-room dancing, cattle drives, and music, which is part of the "American Patchwork" series.

Various. *Every Island has its Own Songs: The Tsimouris Family of Tarpon Springs*. Florida Department of State/Folkstreams.net. Food, family, and Greek bagpipe music can be found here.

Various. *From Shore to Shore*. Cherry Lane Productions/Folkstreams.net This film explores Irish/Irish American music in the twentieth century.

Various. *In Heaven There Is No Beer*. Flower Films. A light-hearted but thoroughly ethnographic look at polka music in our nation's heartland, featuring legendary performers like Jimmy Sturr, Walt Solek, and Eddie Blazonzyck.

Various. *J'ai Ete Au Bal* ("I Went to the Dance"). Flower Films. A wonderful documentary about Cajun and zydeco music featuring such masterful musicians as the Balfa Brothers, Queen Ida, and Dennis McGhee.

Various. *Keep Your Heart Strong: Life Along the Pow-Wow Trail*. Intermedia Arts Minnesota. This film explores the phenomenon of contemporary Native American powwows.

Various. *Kuma Hula: Keepers of a Culture*. Rhapsody Films. A detailed study of hula music and dancers, which was shot in the late 1980s by Robert Mugge.

Various. *Medicine Fiddle*. Up North Film/Folkstreams.net. A brief film about the Menoninee and Ojibwe fiddlers and step dancers whose creolized traditions are linked to the fur trade and lumber camps.

ETHNIC AND NATIVE AMERICAN TRADITIONS

Various. *Polka from Cuca*. Ootek Productions. This documentary combines interviews, performances, and dance footage of a 1994 gathering of Norwegian, Polish, Slovenian, and other local bands that recorded for the Cuca label in Sauk City, Wisconsin, in the 1960s.

Various. *Spend It All*. Flower Films. This is a lusty look at Cajun culture, which highlights the music of Marc Savoy, Nathan Abshire, and others.

Various. *That's Slack Key Guitar*. Vestapol 13039. Each of the seven slack-key Hawaiian guitar masters tells their own story in words and music. The players include Raymond Kane, Ledward Kaapana, and Dinan Aki.

Various. *The Last of the Klezmer*. Yale Strong Films. A documentary about some of the klezmer pioneers, such as Dave Tarras and Naftule Brandwein, during the twilight of their careers.

Various. *Wisconsin Powwow and Naamikaaged: Dancer for the People*. Smithsonian Folkways 48004. A two-video documentary about the importance of powwows for contemporary Native Americans. The first video provides an overview, while the second focuses upon a young Ojibwe dancer, Richard La Fernier, as he prepares for a powwow. The videos are accompanied by an excellent booklet that describes an Ojibwa powwow in great detail.

Various. *Ziveli! Medicine for the Heart*. Flower Films. Les Blank's warm look at Serbian-American expressive culture, foodways, and music in northern California and Chicago.

Chapter 9

THE HISPANIC AMERICAN DIASPORA

- The Southwest
- Florida
- New York City
- Final Thoughts

In this chapter we will explore the immensely important, diverse, and burgeoning Hispanic musical presence in the United States, focusing on the Southwest, south Florida, and New York City. These sections of the country have long welcomed immigrants from Mexico, Cuba, and Puerto Rico. These waves of immigration have resulted in a mixture of folk and popular styles with strong and lasting ties to home that help to bring the world closer. Despite the fact that there are many examples of Hispanic American musical communities and traditions throughout the United States, this chapter will concentrate on the Mexican American (and tangentially to Native American) traditions heard along the Texas, Arizona, and California borderlands, Cuban American and Nicaraguan music from south Florida, and Puerto Rican styles in New York City.

Hispanic American folk and folk-based music is very closely related to styles brought from their native countries. Most groups have been here long enough to begin the process of acculturation and fusion to create truly Americanized forms, such as conjunto or chicken scratch. This chapter will also discuss styles of folk and folk-based (sometimes called "folklorico") music that are heard throughout the United States and that have enriched the music brought to us by Spanish-speaking musicians. Such interaction is perhaps best illustrated by mariachi music, which draws upon folk and popular elements and also largely ignores the political borders that divide Mexico from California or Texas.

This mixture of folk and popular elements in mariachi as well as Mexican and Mexican American elements points out the complex nature inherent in any discussion of folk music found among such a broad and diverse group of peoples. Mariachi, for example, is included in this chapter precisely because of this blend in addition to the fact that many Mexican Americans view it as authentic music that reflects their heritage and "Mexican-ness." The Hispanic and Hispanic American folk music that you will be reading about here reflects the vitality, energy, and interactive nature of these musical forms and the communities from which they spring.

Perhaps more than in any other part of this book, the fluid nature of music—its ability to cross culturally constructed lines, such as "elite," "classical," and "race," we use to demarcate boundaries—is clearly evident. Most of the Hispanic American genres discussed in this chapter have their roots in folk music, but the intersections with popular idioms in particular are conspicuous throughout this chapter. In many of its aspects, this chapter complements chapter 11, which discusses the impact that Afro- and Anglo-American folk genres have had on popular music in the United States, and chapter 8, which looks at other styles that add to the diversity of American music. The present chapter further underscores the dynamics of musical culture change, the complex nature of ethnic identity as expressed through music, and the increasing impact that Hispanic culture (not only in music but also in foodways and literature) is having upon the United States in general.

The impact of Hispanic culture in the United States is only going to increase. During the late twentieth century, Americans of Hispanic descent—both newly arrived immigrants and people whose ancestry can be traced back to the eighteenth century—have been the most rapidly growing minority in the United States. The most recent waves of immigrants include hundreds of thousands of political, social, and economic refugees who have fled war-torn Central American countries, such as Guatemala, over the past twenty-five years. The Washington, D.C., metropolitan region, for example, is home to the second-largest Salvadorian enclave outside of El Salvador (Los Angeles is home to the largest number of displaced Salvadorians). Countless Puerto Ricans, Cubans, and Colombians call New York City and northern New Jersey home. This trend began early in the twentieth century, although Cuban immigration substantially increased at the end of the 1950s when Castro came to power. The musical traditions that arrived with the immigrants have remained largely isolated within their own communities. Occasionally, though, some form of Latin popular music will exert its impact on the Anglo-American mainstream. Beginning with the tango, which first hit the United States in 1913 by way of a popular Broadway show, dance-related forms such as rumba, samba, mambo, bossa nova, and salsa reach out of their own neighborhoods and into our living rooms in (approximately) fifteen-year cycles.

These waves exemplify the trendy and hip nature of our popular culture and underscore both its ephemeral nature and its insatiable thirst for the exotic and the new. One only has to look at the resurgence of popular interest in both

1930s swing and 1950s "lounge" music during the early 2000s to find another set of examples of this phenomenon. Most of these dance-oriented forms are, for better or worse, largely removed from the folk culture that produced them. If a dance remains popular within its community, the dance tends to remain more closely tied to its origins. "Bomba" (a Puerto Rican folk dance) is still closely linked to the drums that are so integral to its performance; one syncretic form of religious folk songs, "coritos," praise songs utilized by some Hispanic Pentecostalists, bears the unmistakable stamp of black American music, and ultimately of West Africa, in its use of a strophic form and antiphony. Furthermore, the Puerto Ricans' use of electric guitars, reed instruments, and drums reflects contemporary black American Pentecostal performance practices.

Despite the frequent ghettoization of this musical culture, the Hispanic influence remains quite profound and the presence of Latinos along our southern borders is a fact of life and has been for decades. Citizens of Del Rio, Texas, or Tucson, Arizona, think nothing of hearing Spanish spoken on the streets, and the contentious issues surrounding bilingual education (should English be our "official language?") became a major political issue in California in the early 1990s and continues today. But for most people living in Maine or North Dakota, for instance, Mexico and Cuba and Costa Rica seem to be a world apart— especially in February. Nonetheless, the impact of Spanish language, foodways, and music is being increasingly felt across the entire United States. Nowhere is the impact of Hispanic culture more profound than across the Southwest.

THE SOUTHWEST

Much of what is now called the Southwest (that vast expanse between Texas and California) was initially explored and claimed as Spanish territory by the late sixteenth century. This is an extremely dry and warm portion of the United States and consists of several unique cultural and physical regions with their own distinctive characteristics. The "four corners" (the intersection of Arizona, Colorado, New Mexico, and Utah) is both rugged, rural, and home to Pueblo and Navajo people. This thinly populated section of the Southwest stands in strong contrast to the urban maze of Los Angeles that is home to so many Mexican Americans and others who immigrated from El Salvador as well as dozens of other countries. So, while the southwestern states share a few characteristics, the cultures within them are as distinctive as the people who populate this land.

It is impossible to understand the cultural history of the Southwest without a brief discussion of the role of Catholic missionaries who arrived in the New World from across the entirety of Europe. Missionaries brought not only their own religious convictions but also previously unknown crops, animals,

A sign from 1999, proclaims the Seventh Annual Conjunto Music Festival held in San Benito, Texas. Courtesy of the Ralph Rinzler Folklife Archives and Collections, Center for Folklife and Cultural Heritage, Smithsonian Institution.

and—most unfortunately—diseases. They also brought their ways of dress, architecture, and music. And many of the missionaries were Franciscans, who held music in high esteem and included vocal and instrumental instruction as part of their objective. In New Mexico, for example, by the time of the Indian rebellion, which lasted from 1680 until almost 1700, they had established some two dozen missions. The Franciscans established themselves later in present-day California and by the 1820s the order had founded some twenty-one missions, many of them along the coast between San Diego and San Francisco. At these missions the friars sang Gregorian chants, performed religious drama that included songs, and a few of the missions even installed organs. So much of the Hispanic music, especially along the Mexican/American border, is touched by this cross-fertilization of Spanish and European tradition, which began several decades ago yet continues to reverberate today.

Mexico, which touches nearly 1,000 miles of the border along Texas, New Mexico, Arizona, and California, has provided the United States with more citizens than any other country in Central or South America. Until the late twentieth century our southern border was rather casual, with the Rio Grande River providing the dividing point along the vast stretches between Texas and Mexico. For so much of its length, however, one can literally step over or wade through the river—a fact that invites border crossings, increases the commerce between the two countries, and generally enhances the cultural interaction between Mexico and the United States. In many fundamental ways that reflect basic cultural values, the differences between border towns in the United States and their Mexican counterparts such as Calexico, California, and Mexicali, Mexico; El Paso, Texas, and Ciudad Juarez, Mexico; or Nogales (a name shared both by Arizona and Mexico) are often difficult to discern.

Fortunately, several scholars with a special interest in Mexican American folk music have published important studies since the middle 1970s. The eldest, Americo Paredes, for many years taught courses in folklore and English at the University of Texas. His special interest in the folk songs and ballads about life and strife along the border culminated in a highly respected study, *A Texas-Mexican Cancionero: Folksongs of the Lower Border*. More recently ethnomusicologist Manuel Pena published *The Texas-Mexican Conjunto: History of a Working-Class Music*, a book that surveys the history and development of the best-known and most widespread genre of Hispanic American folk music. Finally, anthropologist Jose Limon's work on the expressive culture along the border, including music, is most widely available in his book, *Dancing with the Devil*.

Tex-Mex Music

Mexico is clearly the wellspring for most of the Hispanic folk music performed in the southwestern United States. Mexican Americans are primarily concentrated along the border states and into Colorado; however, they represent an increasing presence in the Midwest. The Chicago metropolitan area has a large Hispanic population, primarily of Mexican heritage. A similar growth in the Hispanic population holds true for smaller cities, such as Omaha and Des Moines. Along the Mexican/American border many of the older citizens refer to themselves as "Tejanos," especially those with decades-long ties to the United States. Many younger people refer to themselves as Chicanos in recognition of the raised consciousness brought about by the civil rights movement of the late 1950s and early 1960s. Though largely a black American political and social movement, the spirit of civil rights served to awaken many Mexican Americans to the injustices they, too, endured. Labor organizer Cesar Chavez, Dolores Huerta (co-founder of the National Farm Workers Association), singers Linda Ronstadt and Selena, along with politician Henry Cisneros are among the better-known Chicanos and Chicanas to emerge on the political, entertainment, and social scene since the 1960s.

Not surprisingly the music of most Chicanos is most closely tied with Mexico's *norteno* styles that come from its northernmost states and that developed at the close of the nineteenth century. In the United States these regional forms of music are usually grouped under the name **Tex-Mex**, perhaps chauvinistically, because so much of the music and its culture is concentrated along the lengthy border of Texas and Mexico. *Musica Tejanos* is another, slightly older term that describes much the same musical culture, one that occasionally reflects not only its Anglo and Mexican background but also the occasional influence of Caribbean, French, and African American music. The French introduced or solidified the popularity of dances such as polkas, waltzes, and mazurkas, and it was

MUSICAL EXAMPLE

This dance song is performed by a member of one of San Antonio's strongest musical families. His older brother (Flaco), his father (Santiago Jimenez), and grandfather (Patricio) all played accordion and Jimenez, Sr.'s recording career began in the late 1930s. Santiago Jimenez, Jr., continues to perform for crowds of Chicanos and Chicanas who dance to waltzes, polkas, huapangos, and shottisches at small clubs and bars in and around his hometown. "I'm Going to Leave You in San Antonio" tells of a man whose two-timing girlfriend is about to run off with another man.

> **Title** "Ay ti dejo en San Antonio"
> **Performer** Santiago Jimenez, Jr.
> **Instruments** Santiago Jimenez, Jr., lead vocals and accordion; Tobby Torres, vocal and bass; Jessie Castillo, bajo sexto; Cookie Martinez, drums
> **Length** 3:10

Musical Characteristics
1. The song is in a major tonality.
2. The tempo is both steady and moderate.
3. Its rhythm is jaunty and straightforward with just a hint of syncopation.
4. Jimenez's lead vocal is supplemented by the harmony of Tobby Torres.

> Say ranchero, jugador y navegante
> Ya me voy para nunca mas volver
> Me dejastes sen dinero y sin rolante
> por el mundo te me echastes a corror.

> I'm a rancher, a gambler, and a rambler.
> I'm leaving and never coming back.
> You left me without money and without wheels.
> You threw me off to run around the world.

This selection comes from Smithsonian Folkways 40047.

German immigrants, many of whom began settling in central Texas in the middle nineteenth century, who helped to reinforce the presence of the accordion. During Reconstruction Tejano bands consisting of guitars, violins, and a small variety of wind instruments were regaling dancers across all of southern Texas.

Conjunto musicians Ben Tavena King and Frank Corrales (circa 1975). Courtesy of the Ralph Rinzler Folklife Archives and Collections, Center for Folklife and Cultural Heritage, Smithsonian Institution.

Conjunto is almost certainly the best-known form of Tex-Mex music. This music is also known as "musica norteno" (music of the north), which reflects its origins in northern Mexico. By the late 1930s this style of music had established itself as the most prominent form of folk music along the border and is one of the most familiar outside of its hearth areas. These small ensembles feature a small diatonic **button accordion**, acoustic bass, and an oversized twelve-string guitar called a bajo sexto. Its inclusion of the German diatonic button accordion, which is also an integral part of older Cajun and zydeco music, underscores the impact of German culture in Texas. But it is also possible that this influence was reinforced from the south in the form of German immigrants from Monterrey, Mexico, who introduced "acordeons" to northwestern Mexicans in the 1880s. The fact that the accordion has become so closely associated with this music suggests the wider creolization of European culture in Mexico and Central America that occurred in the late nineteenth century.

Early in the twentieth century Mexican Americans residing in southern Texas often hired conjunto musicians to play for fandangos, which were often disparagingly referred to by local Anglos as lower-class entertainment. And surely this was working-class music and it was performed at venues disdained by the upper classes and by Latino blue-collar workers. In short, conjunto represented much of what the ruling class found disreputable and of which they strongly disapproved; nonetheless, conjunto thrived in Texas and just to the south of the border as well.

Norteno accordion playing probably began as a solitary pursuit with the other instruments being added, perhaps as the demand for conjunto music for dancing increased. As its popularity increased, conjunto musicians gradually replaced the wind instruments and violins with the now ubiquitous bajo sexto. During the 1920s through the 1940s the two-row button accordion was favored by the majority of musicians, most notably Santiago Jimenez of San Antonio and Narciso Martinez, who lived in the lower Rio Grande Valley. They were the first stars of conjunto and the equivalents of fiddler Gid Tanner in north Georgia or Blind Boy Fuller, the North Carolina blues man. Each was a folk artist whose pioneering recordings and, in some cases, radio broadcasts had a wide and lasting impact within their discrete geographical, cultural, and racial communities. By the 1940s Jimenez, Martinez, and their peers had largely usurped the prominence previously reserved for the *guitarreros* (ballad-singing guitar players) when they added vocalists—usually the accordion or bajo sexto player—to their ensembles.

One of the many changes that followed the close of World War II was the musician's shift to the two-row button accordions. This more versatile instrument worked well as a lead instrument as the bajo sexto and bass took over conjunto's rhythmic and harmonic functions. The drums were also added to many conjunto ensembles at about this time, resulting in the four-piece band that is so familiar today. The rhythmic drive of conjunto also altered the way in which many of the younger accordion players approached their instruments. Instead of the relatively smooth style favored by men who came of age in the 1930s, these younger proponents favored a more staccato attack.

Conjunto bands also began to amplify their instruments in the late 1940s and virtuosos such as Flaco Jimenez (Santiago's son) and Tony de la Rosa (who received a 1998 National Heritage Fellowship awarded by the National Endowment for the Arts) began touring more extensively, reaching a wider audience. By the 1960s both men along with a handful of others were playing for fellow Chicanos who had migrated north and east in search of better and more opportunities. Though still concentrated along the border, conjunto can now be heard wherever Mexican Americans live.

Corridos

Like all ballads, **corridos** tell a story. They are often about dramatic events, and the greatest and lengthiest cycle of corridos are set along the border of Texas and Mexico over an eighty-year period between about 1850 and 1930. Many of these recount the long-standing struggle for civil rights and social justice and are clear precursors for the Chicano movement. Fulfilling the role provided by spirituals during the black American civil rights movement, corridos served the Chicano movement during its emerging years. For example, corridos were composed for Cesar Chavez to celebrate his heroic efforts to help organize farmworkers in California and to boycott grapes during the late 1960s and into the 1970s.

"Gregorio Cortez" is a fine and well-known example of a border ballad. According to Americo Paredes, the song is based on a true event that occurred on June 12, 1901. It relates the tragic story of Texas sheriff Morris's death at the hand of Gregorio Cortez, who himself was avenging the death of his brother, whom Morris had recently killed. The song itself focuses on the hero's escape and ultimate capture and underscores the type of events that so many Mexican Americans faced in their daily lives. This, and other border ballads, suggest the importance of group solidarity in the face of oppression.

After 1930 the number and importance of border ballads diminished and their topics expanded. During World War II, for example, corridos about war heroes and conflicts emerged. Following the assassination of John F. Kennedy in 1963, corridos about President Kennedy flooded the marketplace. John F. Kennedy, with his progressive politics and his Catholic upbringing, was a particular favorite among Mexican Americans. These verses from the corrido "In Honor of Kennedy," which was written by Gatton Once Castellans, are typical of the genre:

> I'm going to sing for you, ladies and gentlemen,
> Only in this way can I express
> This grief of affliction
> My great sorrow and heavy heart
>
> The year of sixty-three
> On the twenty-second of November,
> In the City of Dallas
> They killed the President.
>
> Three very well-aimed bullets
> The assassin fired,
> Two hit the President,
> The other hit the Governor.
>
> And it was almost noon
> When this happened,
> When the great President's
> Life was taken.

May God have him in His glory
As an example of reason,
And counsel his family
To have much faith and resignation.

Here I end my song, good people,
The tragedy that I wrote,
With the grief of affliction,
In honor of Kennedy.

And, not surprisingly, the authors of corridos have kept up with current events. As narcotics trafficking has increased along the border, there have been a rash of corridos about drug dealers. The ballads about Pablo Acosta, a benevolent drug lord whose trade straddled the border around Ojinaga and Chihuahua, Mexico, and Presidio, Texas, provide a fine example of this phenomenon. Likewise the increasing traffic in smuggling immigrants across the border into the United States has resulted in corridos about "mules" (the men and women who, for a fee, guide people across the border and past the border patrol) and the number of people who die in the attempt to cross over. Another cycle of songs about the political and social conflicts related to the struggle for the rights of Indians surfaced in the southern Mexican state of Chiapas during the middle 1990s.

The role of women in writing and disseminating corridos (and associated musics) remains limited. **Lydia Mendoza** provides the exception to this generalization. Mendoza was a pioneer and a hero to many older residents of the Mexican American community from Texas through California. Her recording career began in 1928 as a twelve-year-old girl singing with her family in an impromptu San Antonio hotel room recording studio and has continued into the 1990s. She emerged as the first Spanish-speaking female folk performer to gain a wide audience through her recordings and performances in the Americas. During her long and distinguished career, Lydia Mendoza has performed at countless venues: for her peers in small taverns and road houses in south Texas, for President Jimmy Carter at the John F. Kennedy Center in Washington, D.C., in 1978, and for adoring crowds in South America.

Mendoza's gender makes her unusual for a guitarrero and singer of corridos, but her early background is hardly unique. Her family as far back as her grandmother played music and she had relatives on both sides of the Texas/Mexican border. Born in 1916, Mendoza came into a family that eventually grew to eight brothers and sisters. In a long interview Lydia Mendoza recalls the circumstances of her youth:

> I believe I've had a vocation for music almost from the time I was born. I remember clearly that I began to feel drawn towards music when I was four. You must realize that my mother played guitar, and at home after dinner, after she and my dad had rested up, she would pick up the guitar and begin to play and sing ... I liked music so much that even then I wanted to play guitar, and I told my mother that I wanted to play like her, and she told me that when my hands got big enough she'd teach me—and that's the way it happened ... When I was about eight or nine, I could play perfectly well.
>
> I was the prime mover of music in the household. I liked it, so I wanted my brothers and sisters to play, too ... And I guess they liked it, because they all learned to play instruments, and we got a group together. Mother played the guitar, I played violin, one of my sisters the mandolin, a brother played the triangle, and father played tambourine. So we got up a musical group, and then we dedicated our lives to music on a full-time basis. We started off all over the lower Rio Grande Valley, and later on we got as far as Detroit, Michigan, always with our music. We lived one year in the Lower Rio Grande Valley—McAllen, Weslaco, Edinburg, and Kingsville. We would stay a while in one little town ... (and) play in restaurants and barbershops. Dad would go in and ask permission to play—mostly on Saturdays, when there would be lots of people—and then if folks were there we'd sit down and sing, and people would give us tips. (Lydia Mendoza, *Ethnic Recordings*, 1982, 119–20)

Mendoza later settled in San Antonio, Texas, where she married and specialized in guitar playing. She became popular through her radio appearances and her early recordings for the Bluebird Record Company (1934–1940). She later recorded a variety of material for RCA Victor, Peerless, Colonial, Imperial, and other smaller labels, but is best known for her corridos. Whatever form it takes, her brand of music has always held special appeal for working-class residents not only along the Texas/Mexico border but wherever Mexican Americans have settled in the United States.

The music of corridos has always been fairly simple. In the middle nineteenth century these songs were often performed a cappella but by late in the century guitars were often used to provide accompaniment. Today they are usually performed in triple meter (typically 3/4 or 6/8) with conjunto band-style accompaniment—guitar, accordion, and bajo sexto—and are most often focused on the three primary chords (I, IV, and V).

Mariachi

Daniel Sheehy (an ethnomusiciogist who curates the Smithsonian Folkways collection) writes that **mariachi** "may mean a single musician, a kind of musical group, or a style of music. In addition to the music itself, three dimensions of mariachi musical life—cultural, musical, and social—are key to understanding it fully. Since the 1930's, the mariachi ensemble and its music have been an

Malachi musicians at the 1975 Festival of American Folklife. Courtesy of the Ralph Rinzler Folklife Archives and Collections, Center for Folklife and Cultural Heritage, Smithsonian Institution.

emblem of Mexican identity, a cultural icon to anchor a Mexican culture in transition" (Lornell and Rassmusen, eds., 1997, 132).

Although it is popular throughout Mexico, mariachi is also quite fashionable among Mexican Americans residing in southern Texas, New Mexico, Arizona, Colorado, and California. Not surprisingly, mariachi can be heard in other parts of the country with large Chicano populations. This music can also be heard in places, such as restaurants, movies, and Disneyland, where Mexican culture is represented to a larger mainstream. Mariachi can be found south of Mexico as well. I heard many mariachi (and a few conjunto) orchestras as well as several musica ranchera (country music) ensembles at a half dozen of the local restaurants during a 1994 weeklong stay in San José, Costa Rica. In these instances mariachi serves as a symbol of Mexican culture and represents the intersection of popular and folk traditions.

In its more down-home settings—both in Mexico and the United States—this music is heard in many contexts, most of which revolve around family or community events such as birthdays, cookouts, wedding anniversaries, and neighborhood festivals. Because so many of them are performers for hire, mariachi musicians also perform for audiences at cafés and restaurants or occasionally on street corners—for anyone who will meet their fees. Some mariachi ensembles hold long-standing gigs (often at restaurants and sometimes for many years on a weekly or even a nightly basis) but many of them perform on an ad hoc basis.

Mariachi music is quite distinctive and stands in strong contrast to other forms of folk music found in the Mexican American community. Mariachi is folk-based music, and in the past the term has had three separate but related meanings: an individual performer, a musical ensemble, or a style of music. Today mariachi almost always refers to an ensemble of between five and ten players that combines fiddles, trumpets, and guitars with two stringed instruments, the vihuela and guitarron, which are less familiar to most citizens of the United States. The violins and trumpets serve as the lead instruments, providing the melody and taking the occasional solo, while the rhythm is driven by the guitar and vihuela and the guitarron takes the role of the bass instrument. The instrumentalists typically also sing and most of the songs are performed in Spanish.

Contemporary mariachi music has its roots in Mexico in the 1930s, making it roughly the same age as bluegrass. Much of the pre-nineteenth-century Mexican folk music was generically referred to as **mestizo** (a Spanish term for creolized styles) that was usually played on violin, some form of guitar, and harp with vocal accompaniment. Nonetheless, its roots go back to at least the middle of the nineteenth century in the northwestern state of Jalisco, when the first references to mariachi appeared. The earliest uses of this word suggest not only music but also the blue-collar musical culture associated with it. The early development of mariachi, which occurred close to the Mexican border near California, was not well known outside of this section of the country.

Mariachi remained a regional style of music until the first decade of the twentieth century. At this point the guitarron and trumpet had all but replaced the harp and began to be widely used by most mariachi ensembles. This is also when mariachi began to move from its hearth area and diffuse, first to the center of political and economic power (Mexico City) and slowly to the rest of the country and into the borderlands of the United States. This diffusion was propelled less by the mass media (the first recordings of mariachi appeared on cylinders around 1908) but by the Mexican Revolution that lasted from 1910 to 1917. The revolution shifted the official cultural bias from Europe to the Mexican vernacular, including not only mestizo culture but also the accomplishments of its native inhabitants (a group, like their northern counterparts, that for many years had been largely ostracized from official Mexican culture). This form of nationalism helped to launch the popularity of this music throughout the country and, more slowly, into the United States. Mariachi was used to promote political events during the 1920s and 1930s and its popularity was underscored by the in-migration of so many rural residents (many of them from the northwestern states) to Mexico City.

The mass media finally caught on to the mariachi revolution in the early 1930s when these ensembles appeared in films produced by the fledgling Mexican-based motion picture industry and began regular broadcasts on XEW. This clear-channel Mexico City radio station featured many forms of Mexican folk music to an audience throughout the country as well as into northern South America and the United States. This trend continued throughout the decade and was further amplified by the indigenous "cowboy" films that were so popular in Mexico and had their counterparts in the Republic "B" films that featured Tex Ritter, Gene Autry, Roy Rogers, and other silver screen cowboys. Some of them featured mariachi music, thus bringing this music to audiences throughout the country and, increasingly, to an audience that had relatives in the United States. By the outbreak of World War II, mariachi had become the type of music most closely identified with Mexico's musical culture, and the trumpet had been established as the most prominent lead instrument in these ensembles.

These interactions of the popular media, nationalism, and its folk roots helped to reinforce the "folkness" of mariachi. For many Americans mariachi has gradually emerged as *the* quintessential form of Mexican music and, by extension, Mexican American music. Its folkness in the eyes of people in the United States who consume mariachi has been reinforced by three factors. First, the songs are sung in a foreign language and, therefore, seem more exotic. Second, the music is performed on instruments (the guitarron and vihuela) that resemble members of the guitar family but are ultimately unfamiliar to most of the people eating at a Mexican restaurant in Duluth, Minnesota, or Altoona, Pennsylvania, that may have hired a mariachi to entertain their patrons. And finally, the outfits worn by the musicians probably strike many people as "native."

Such commoditization has helped to sell mariachi to a wider audience than, for example, that of conjunto music. This and other forms of Mexican American styles may be more closely allied with their folk roots, but none of them has been as widely disseminated as mariachi. While the grassroots support and interest in mariachi has been strong within the Chicano community, its association with things more urban, commercial, well ordered, and familiar has helped to move the interest in this music to a far broader geographical and ethnic series of communities. According to Sheehy, **Silvestre Vargas** epitomizes the ability of a musician to market mariachi and has led one of the best-known bands, Mariachi Vargas de Telcalitlan, since the 1950s. It is Vargas who can be heard on dozens of recordings, on soundtracks, and on live shows both in Mexico and the United States.

The culture of mariachi in the United States has altered greatly over the past several decades. By the middle 1970s this music was being taught in San

Antonio, Texas, and soon thereafter in other Texas schools and in Arizona and California. These efforts were quickly followed by festivals that combined performance with master classes. Now mariachi is being taught in formal academic settings, from high school through the college level, and there are more than a dozen major festivals in the southwestern United States. Mariachi was recognized by colleges and universities a bit earlier (at UCLA in the middle 1960s) in programs in ethnomusicology.

Secondarily, mariachi has moved upscale in some other arenas. It has been the province of males and has most often been heard in *cantinas* (drinking establishments that largely cater to males of all ages), small restaurants, and other similar establishments. The movement occurred when larger restaurants highlighted mariachi ensembles on a stage to provide its patrons with a more formal show. It seems to have begun in Los Angeles and within a decade has moved to larger cities, such as Denver, Houston, and Tucson, with a major Hispanic presence.

In the minds of some of the musicians these two changes altered the musicians' station, moving them to a higher social—and often economic—status. These changes in status and performance situations have opened mariachi to a somewhat more diverse audience and have also diversified its racial and gender makeup. A handful of European-Americans, including Mark Fogelquist and Daniel Sheehey, have moved from the academic ranks to become noted mariachi performers. Likewise women, most notably Rebecca Gonzales (a Chicana violin player), are now a small but growing part of the contemporary mariachi scene.

Native American Influences

It would be inaccurate and misleading to suggest that all styles of Mexican American music that are found near the border are the result of an Anglo-American and Mexican mix. Native Americans were part of the cultural landscape of the Southwest long before either Spanish or Anglo settlers arrived. Given the historical development and cross-fertilization that has characterized the region for several centuries, such creolization should not be surprising. These musical/cultural interactions represent a complex series of interactions with roots, in the music that accompanies matachines dances, back to medieval Spain.

Ethnomusicologist Brenda Romero notes that "the longest continuously Latino populated areas in the United States are Northern New Mexico and Southern Colorado, where music has always been an integral part of the daily life of the Hispanic population who traditionally describe themselves as Mejicanos" (Lornell and Rassmusen, eds., 1997, 156). The Native American population—mostly Pueblo—of this region has been living on this dry and rugged land for tens of thousands of years. This rich cultural mix has become even more complicated over the past 150 years, when most of the Anglos arrived in the Southwest, and has resulted in uniquely American genres, two of which—**matachines** and **waila**—are discussed here.

The fiddle tunes that accompany matachines dances provide one of the most interesting forms of Hispanic Indian musical forms. This style is associated with the Pueblo and *Mejicanos* citizens of northern New Mexico and has been part of the local expressive culture for centuries. The term "Mejicanos" is preferred by older Hispanic Americans (the younger ones usually prefer Chicano) living just north of the urbane small city of Santa Fe as well as farther south near Albuquerque. In these rural areas the Pueblo and Mejicanos have lived in close proximity for some three hundred years, often in stunning poverty, and the matachines performances are one result of this blend.

The matachines is more than music, for it combines music, dance, and ceremony that, ironically, evolved in Mexico as a way to proselytize Indians, though today it is associated with either saints or the Christ Child. The matachines has survived through scores of years and reflects the importance of renewal and faith through its preservation. American Indians frequently adopt ceremonies from other sources (mostly other tribes), especially those that are perceived to be powerful or effective. In this instance, however, this ritualized form was adopted from their Spanish neighbors and is largely performed as a pantomime while wearing masks and with musical accompaniment. It is a family and community event that is essentially closed to non-Pueblos and is most closely allied with New Year's or Christmas when we are looking forward to the renewal offered by the new year.

Over the passage of many decades, the relationship between the Mejicanos and the Indians evolved. The Pueblos felt that it was critical to include the fiddles and the tunes played by their Hispanic neighbors as part of this ceremony, which celebrates a king's spiritual victory. According to Romero the term *matachines* might be taken from an anachronistic word for a masked dance or with an Italian term referring to a jester or roving performer. The ceremony is accompanied by a guitarist and fiddler, who play one special melody with each of its discrete sections. The *danza* (the matachines complex itself, not a specific dance) spotlights four characters and between eight and twelve dancers.

In this part of the world among Pueblos "music is always sung and almost always paired with dance, an essential component of communal ceremonies. Dance helps to demonstrate the interdependence of man, nature, and the spiritual world" (Lornell and Rassmusen, eds., 1997, 160). The songs utilize both vocables and words and are typically sung in unison, which underscores the cooperative or community-oriented nature of Pueblo life. The old-style instrumental music, which is becoming increasingly rare, is usually provided by a fiddle/guitar duet with strong roots in melodies found as long ago as the fourteenth century in Spain.

The twentieth-century matachines, then, is a blend of the Mejicanos and Pueblos of New Mexico. Despite this syncronicity that led to so much intertwining, the Mejicanos matachines and Pueblos matachines remain related but separate affairs. Though they live in close proximity and celebrate the matachines in similar ways, the Pueblo in particular zealously guard this ceremony. Because the matachines has implications beyond its religious (remember that the ceremony is held near Christmas) connotation, it has become integrated into their social structure. The San Juan Pueblos (who live near Albuquerque), the dance, and all of its parts are organized by the tribal authority, so that the whole complex of events has become the Indians' social structure throughout the year.

Nonetheless, some Mejicanos—almost all of them musicians—participate in the Pueblo matachines. Few Pueblos today play the older guitar-accompanied fiddle tunes that are integral to their matachines danza. Much of the rest of the ceremony is more blended. The choreographed movement, for example, can be traced to Spanish sources, yet the costuming is unambiguously Indian. Even with all of this cross-cultural movement, Pueblo's believe that this ceremony is authentic. Romero writes that "time and circumstances, as well as its ritual practice, have authenticated the ceremony. Most Pueblos are aware that the ceremony was brought by the Spanish-Mexicans but believe it is theirs now, incorporating into it various general ceremonial practices common to the more traditional Pueblo dance and adapting Spanish-Mexican practices in unique ways" (Lornell and Rassmusen, eds., 1997, 179). They are comfortable with the matachines and the ways in which the religious meanings are transmitted to other members of the community. Although someone from outside of the community can dissect the ceremony and point out the diverse elements that go into contemporary matachines, it serves its purpose as long as the Pueblo believe that it is a legitimate cultural expression.

Another syncretic form of Hispanic-Anglo-Native American folk music in the Southwest is generally known by the colorful name **chicken scratch**. Much contemporary chicken scratch, with its use of saxophone, accordion, and guitars, can be described as a highly regional and idiosyncratic version of country/western music crossed with a polka band. The fact is that this music has strong roots in the Southwest's mix of Mexicans, Indians, and Anglos.

Although I'd heard of it, my initial encounter with chicken scratch occurred at the 1993 Festival of American Folklife—the annual event held on the Mall that is framed by the Smithsonian Institution, the Lincoln Memorial, and our nation's Capitol. That summer's annual event featured the "United States–Mexican Borderlands" and included foodways, crafts, and storytellers as well as music. I expected conjunto and mariachi but I thought that I'd wandered into the wrong festival when I heard what initially sounded (at a distance) like a Dutchmen polka band from central Minnesota! As I walked closer my error became clear—the rhythmic drive and instrumentation weren't quite right. When I turned the corner, saw the band members, and heard the band switch from a polka to a rancherolike song sung in Spanish, then I realized what I'd stumbled upon. At last . . . live chicken scratch music.

Chicken scratch (or waila, as it is also often referred to) is most often performed by members of the Tohono O'odham Tribe, whose nation is situated in southern Arizona just to the west of Tucson. Like so much of the history of the Southwest, the Tohono O'odham were touched by the Jesuit and Franciscan missionaries who worked with so many American Indians long before this area of the country was part of the United States. The Tohono O'odham were taught not only about the Catholic faith but were sometimes also instructed how to play violins, guitars, and other related stringed instruments. This facility to perform held ramifications for music in church and was translated to the secular realm, where Tohono O'odham musicians soon learned tunes that were utilized to accompany such European dances as the waltz, schottische, and (of course) polka. Small ensembles of Tohono O'odham musicians—most often playing guitar and fiddle—played for small events and local festivals as far away as Tucson and as early as the mid-1800s.

The instrumentation used to provide waila music changed very little until the late 1940s, when the influence of conjunto music altered this lineup. The guitars and fiddles were gradually augmented and often replaced by the standard norteno instrumentation of guitar, string bass, drums, button accordion, and, oftentimes, alto saxophone. The change reflects not only the influence of Mexican Americans on Indians but also the acculturation that is one of the hallmarks of the Southwest. Furthermore, the prominence of saxophones in today's waila can be at least partially attributed to the boarding schools attended by so many Tohono O'odham youngsters beginning in the 1920s. Folklorist Jim Griffith observed that "during the 1960s most reservation villages had electricity, and electric instruments became practical. As a result, most [modern] waila bands used electric guitars and bass guitars, and accordion and saxophone players play into microphones" (Lornell and Rassmusen, eds., 1997, 193).

The context for contemporary waila, which is ultimately derived from a Spanish term, *baile*, meaning "social dance," varies. It is heard at the wildly popular dances mostly held on the nation, and at weddings and birthday parties. But the most important context is the village feasts, which everyone from the youngest to the most elderly attend. "These feasts occur on the assigned day that a particular saint is venerated in the village. If possible, the priest will come by and say the mass in the morning. . . . After the mass and procession are

THE HISPANIC AMERICAN DIASPORA

MUSICAL EXAMPLE

Chicken scratch is a highly regionalized and creolized musical genre. It's also very chameleonlike because it sometimes sounds like a midwestern polka band or, at other times, similar to older styles of fiddle music from northern Mexico. Southern Scratch falls into the former category, and it's one of the most popular and active groups in southern Arizona. The group mostly performs for local community events, though they are occasionally asked to play for folk music festivals elsewhere in the United States. According to Jim Griffith, this schottische remains the most popular rhythm among Tohono O'odham dancers and "Madre Mia Chote" is one of the genre's most popular tunes.

Title "Madre Mia Chote"
Performers Southern Scratch
Instruments Ron Joaquin, bass; Ben Jose, guitar; Rupert Vagaes, accordion; Fernando Joaquin, saxophone; Jose Velasco, Jr., drums
Length 3:20

Musical Characteristics
1. The song is in a major tonality.
2. The moderate tempo is perfect for dancing.
3. Its meter is duple with a rhythm similar to a polka.
4. The form is a simple *ab* with a *c* section inserted in the middle.

This selection is taken from Smithsonian Folkways 40418.

---

over the feasting starts. . . . Traditional feast foods include shredded beef stew with red chile, beef and beef bones cooked with corn, squash, and other vegetables, pinto beans, potato salad, locally made flour tortillas and wheat bread that has been baked in a communal, outdoor oven, and Kool-aid, coffee, and cake" (Lornell and Rassmusen, eds., 1997, 197). Village feasts are important not only for their meaning to the Catholic population but also for the socialization that occurs on a nation that encompasses three million acres in which many of the people live in very small enclaves.

The polka still dominates when waila is played. Lately the *cumbia* (a style that migrated from Columbia through the Caribbean) has augmented the waltz and mazurkas in breaking up the steady diet of polkas. The accordion and saxophone are the predominate lead instruments, and they often state the melody in unison while playing an eclectic set that might include an old-time fiddle tune followed by "Beer Barrel Polka" and the "Waltz You Saved for Me." Despite the length of songs heard during a dance, waila musicians rarely take solos. The musicians usually restate the melody time and again until the dance is completed. In this respect it is much like the old-time dance music played by fiddle bands in the southeastern United States.

FLORIDA

The southern borderland between the United States and the Hispanic world does not end at the juncture where the Rio Bravo spills into the Gulf of Mexico. Florida, especially its southern third, bears the imprint of many years of Hispanic American culture. In the late fall of 1983 I was employed by the Florida Folklife Program and a fieldwork assignment took me to Ammockolee, Florida. A small town located between Tampa and Miami, Ammockolee's economy is dominated by vegetable crops, such as lettuce and tomatoes, that end up on tables across the country during the winter. And the community contains a large number of Hispanic American (oftentimes of Mexican extraction) and some Haitian workers who live in enclaves in which Spanish is the predominate language, bodaga is the preferred name for the corner grocery store, and where the smell of fried corn tortillas fills the air. Although I have visited Indian reservations in the Southwest and logging towns in the northeastern corner of Maine where French is commonly spoken and few of the roads are paved, this rural and astonishingly impoverished section of Florida caused me to stop and reconfirm that I was in the United States. I wondered if I had not been magically conveyed to one of the nearby, small Hispanic Caribbean islands.

In a sense I *had* been transported to another part of the world. The cultural and economic connections between south Florida and the Caribbean, in particular, are quite strong and long-standing. But since the late 1950s the "face" of southern Florida has radically changed due largely to in-migration by several hundred thousand Cubans, Nicaraguans, Haitians, and smaller numbers of people from South America. In 2010 the greater Miami/Dade area was approximately 15 percent black American, 25 percent Anglo-American, and 60 percent Hispanic. What was once viewed as a winter resort town for snowbirds has been recast as a multicultural, sophisticated, sprawling metropolitan region that serves as one of the most efficacious cities in the United States. And the music, as well as other cultural attributes, of these recent transplants has arrived with them. Most of them have arrived recently enough that their musical language has had little chance to blend with the longer-standing Anglo- and African American traditions, but this process is inevitable and will only accelerate in the future.

These cultural ties are particularly well illustrated by the links between Cuba and the Miami/Dade County metro area and are long-standing, of course, having been established by the late nineteenth century. A steady stream of Cuban immigrants has enriched the Cuban American population in Miami/Dade County over the past one hundred years but the volume increased dramatically when Castro took over control of the country in 1958. In the four years following the Communist overthrow of Batista, nearly 300,000 Cubans (many of them well established and white with a fairly high level of education) arrived in the United States and most of them flocked to southeastern Florida. A second, similarly sized—though more heterogeneous—surge occurred between 1965 and 1973, as flights arrived weekly from Havana. The third major influx happened in 1980 as the "Mariel boatlift" brought approximately 125,000 Cubans. This was the most diverse group yet and helped to ensure that a cross-section of the Cuban population was part of the local Cuban American community. Of the approximately 1.2 million Cubans and Cuban Americans residing in the United States, over 80 percent live in southeast Florida. In Miami the ties to Cuba are so strong that the city is often called the "Second Havana."

Naturally, the Cuban American community brought their cultural matrix with them and so many of the immigrants are recent enough that there is much interest in cultural retentions. Many of these exiles have sought to resurrect their old ways from Cuba, from their playful nicknames for Miami ("Little Havana" and a section of the city known as "the heart of Little Havana") to a specific business strip locally called Calle Ocho (Eighth Street). And it is not only nomenclature that looks back to Cuba for its roots. The hand-manufacturing of cigars was (and to a lesser degree still is) of importance, particularly along the southwest coast in Tampa. Roasted pigs, white rice, black beans, boiled yuca, and fresh figs are staples in the diets of many old-line Cuban Americans. Of course, Spanish is the language that is heard on the streets at least as much as English—another indicator of not only national and cultural associations but also of ethnic (Spanish) identity.

Although the majority of Cuban Americans are at least nominally Catholic, Santeria—a blending of Yoruba and Catholic religious practices—is growing in importance. Santeria is administered by a complicated hierarchy of priests who regularly consult the saints and teach the tenants of the religion, which contends that our world exists on two levels—the earthly one and the spiritual one occupied by the saints (*orishas*). Music is one of the most important elements of Santeria.

Religious gatherings (known as *bembes*) honor specific orishas, and this is where the elements of traditional music and dance enter the scene on a regular basis. Percussion is at the heart of these celebrations, and they are paired in three distinctive ensembles. *Guiro* ensembles consist of dried gourds, a hoe blade that is struck by a metal object, a conga drum, and a vocalist singing in Yoruba. Three congas, the hoe blade, and a singer form a *bembe* group, while the *bata* ensemble includes a trio of drummers playing larger double-headed instruments and a singer. The bata groups are considered the most sacred because their drums are consecrated and they "speak" directly to the saints.

In its use of percussion and complex rhythms, Santeria illustrates the type of syncretism that is so representative of folk and popular Cuban American music. With its strong and contemporary links to Cuba and its more distant but undeniable ties to West Africa, most Cuban American folk music is rooted in small percussion ensembles. Such ensembles are also found in jazz and first rose to prominence in the late 1940s when be-bop musician **Dizzy Gillespie** began incorporating them into his music, thus entering the canons of jazz history textbooks as the pioneer of "Afro-Cuban jazz."

Since the late 1960s, *salsa*—which often utilizes a small horn section—has become the most widespread form of popular music among Cuban Americans. Salsa is based on son, the most popular (and folk-based) form of music that developed in Cuba in the early twentieth century. Much of the folk-based African Cuban music in south Florida also utilizes the antiphonal format that is found in salsa, son, and Santeria. In this respect a black American Pentecostal church service bears some resemblance to a Santeria ceremony.

Santeria is becoming more widespread and accepted as a religious practice in south Florida. It also includes other elements of the local folk culture. For example, special clothing patterned after Afro-Cuban and West African styles—known as *ropa de santo*—is worn for specific ceremonies. Religious goods stores, known as a *botanica*, sell a variety of homemade and mass-manufactured artifacts such as herbs, necklaces, candles, ropa de santo, and oils that are used in these ceremonies.

Not all Cuban American folk-based music is tied with this sacred tradition or with jazz. Some styles are increasingly tied to more popular trends, such as son and guaracha, and are always in the process of reinterpreting and reinventing their musical past into new forms. These reinventions not only pay homage to their roots but also express a look toward their future in the United States—a future that encompasses many of the current popular music forms, including hip-hop, techno-pop, and rock. Since the late 1970s, this melding of folk and pop, American and Cuban, old and new, has been known locally as the "Miami Sound," which gained national prominence in the middle 1980s when the Miami Sound Machine won a Grammy. In 2000 NARAS (National Academy of Recording Arts and Sciences) recognized the increasing importance of Hispanic American popular music by creating the Latin Grammy Awards.

Because so many Cuban American residents of south Florida have arrived since the early 1960s or were born in or around Miami/Dade County, there is a strong trend toward blending the older Cuban and Cuban American folk-based music with the contemporary music they hear all around them. Salsa, which grew up in New York City's Latin clubs before catching on with much of our country's Spanish-speaking population, is a good example of this syncretization. While the process of musical assimilation is to be expected, it is not applauded by all Cuban Americans.

Homereo Gutierrez, for one, laments the loss of the roots, of Cuban folk music and all that it has contributed to Hispanic American music. Gutierrez, formerly president of Fundacion Artistica Cubano-American (Cuban American Artistic Foundation), reflects upon this trend in an interview conducted in the middle 1990s: "Well, it's not the music specifically. It's practically everything. There is no interest in maintaining our roots: musica campesina, Afro-Cuban music, and other genres . . ." Gutierrez clearly mourns the community's failure to maintain cultural continuity—musical and otherwise—as more of his fellow country persons strive to become more "American" and less "Cuban," particularly those born in the United States whose ties with Cuba become more tenuous with the passing years.

Nicaraguans are the second-largest, though most rapidly growing, segment of the local Hispanic population. Approximately 200,000 people of Nicaraguan descent now live in Miami/Dade. Their numbers swelled in the early 1980s when many people fled the 1979 Sandinista Revolution and during the middle 1980s difficult economic conditions compelled a slower but notable influx. The Nicaraguans themselves represent a multicultural mix of mestizo, who are Hispanic and who constitute the majority of Nicaraguans in the southeast corner of the state. About 10 percent of the population consists of creoles from the Atlantic Coast who are usually of Jamaican background, and the trilingual (Miskito, English, and Spanish) Miskitos from rural areas across the country.

Most Nicaraguans have arrived recently enough that their music reflects their Central American roots with little synthesis of styles that they have encountered in the United States. Most of the folk music consists of sons—plaintive vocals accompanied by solo guitarists, but the music played by marimba-based ensembles represents the most distinctive style. The marimba, called the *marimba del arco*, is of African ancestry. It is ubiquitous in Central America, but in Nicaragua the small, twenty-two-slat instrument is played with two or three mallets and accompanied by one or two guitar players. Many of the marimba players are of Indian background, though this is changing. But as the Nicaraguan-derived population grows and establishes itself in Miami/Dade, more interaction is occurring between them, Cuban Americans, and other Spanish-speaking groups. As this process continues, new syncretic forms will no doubt emerge, nearly all of them in the popular realm, though they will always been informed by their folk roots.

NEW YORK CITY

Considering its place as a point of entry for so many immigrants—many of them from Spanish-speaking countries—it is logical that New York City, much like Miami, is host to many types of musical cultures. Unlike the Southwest, with its long history of Hispanic influence, many of these groups are relative newcomers to the greater New York area. Hispanics from throughout Central and South America have moved to New York City, of course, but only a handful, most notably Puerto Ricans, have developed new and syncretic forms since arriving in the United States.

Unlike the recent, explosive immigration into southeastern Florida, Puerto Ricans have been a part of New York's vibrant music scene since the 1920s. Nearly 45 percent of the people of Puerto Rican descent do not reside on the island and most of them live in the continental United States. The majority of them have settled in or near New York City with an increasing number shifting to nearby rural areas in search of migrant farmwork. The number of Puerto Ricans immigrating to the mainland has increased since World War II, joining the growing *Newyorican* (a polyglot term for Spanish-speaking residents of New York City) population, many of whom have moved from Central America. In 2010 there were approximately 3 million citizens of Puerto Rican ancestry living on the mainland with another 3.8 million staying on the island.

The majority of Puerto Ricans living in New York City live—or have ties with—East Harlem, which is perhaps better known as Spanish Harlem. These migrants essentially built a new kind of *barrio* (neighborhood) modeled on their Puerto Rican roots. Spanish Harlem is still home to many social clubs, which are often based on older island ties, and some of them still meet in the informally erected clubhouses that dot the neighborhoods. Gamecock fighting is part of the cultural landscape, and the smell of seafood wafts out of restaurants throughout the barrios. There are also shops that sell the dry goods and clothes typical on the island.

Although they transplanted much of their material and oral culture, Puerto Ricans understand that they are not in San Juan any longer. Puerto Ricans come in many hues (black, white, and mulatto) and, in New York City especially, rapid assimilation has been one of the goals to which they have aspired because of the racial and ethnic prejudice they face. Just as the school authorities in Louisiana for many decades banned speaking French in the classrooms of their southwestern parishes, Puerto Rican (and other Newyoricans) were not permitted to speak Spanish in school. They soon discovered that speaking Spanish in the barrio was fine, but if they wanted to move in the world at large, they would have to learn English, too. This is one of the important steps in the transition from being Puerto Rican to "AmeRican."

THE HISPANIC AMERICAN DIASPORA

Puerto Rican musicians performing at the 1989 Festival of American Folklife. Courtesy of the Ralph Rinzler Folklife Archives and Collections, Center for Folklife and Cultural Heritage, Smithsonian Institution.

Music serves as an integral and significant part of the Puerto Rican experience in the United States and it has been that way for over five decades. In the 1930s Puerto Ricans enriched New York's already vibrant music scene with performances of **jibaro** (campesino) and **plenos**, throughout the barrios. Jibaro refers to music that flourished in the rugged, hilly sections of the Puerto Rican mountains and features guitar, cuatro, maracas, guiro, and voice. The texts of jibaros are emphasized over instrumental virtuosity, and when Puerto Ricans migrated to the United States they transported this tradition with them and wrote new texts about their (often harsh) immigrant experiences. New York plenas, on the other hand, are based on the Puerto Rican street music. This genre is lyrically similar to Trinidadian calypso (which emphasizes social and political commentary) and is accompanied by handheld frame drums, guitars, and sometimes the harmonica and accordion. Both jibaro and plenas have become Americanized not only in their shift of lyrics but also in their increasing use of electric instruments.

New York City emerged as the cultural nexus for Newyoricans (and Puerto Ricans in particular) by the beginning of the Cold War and music was one of the obvious expressions that helped to define the Puerto Rican community. Its large population is one of the reasons why New York City became a center for Puerto Rican music, but the mass media is the other—especially the recording studios, adventurous record companies, and radio outlets. In most respects, New York City had eclipsed Puerto Rico itself as the core of Puerto Rican music in the United States. New York City is also home to Juan Gutiérrez, a Puerto

Rican plena musician who was awarded a National Endowment for the Arts/National Heritage Fellowship Award in 1996.

Despite the distancing from the island, the musical ties between New York City and San Juan remain strong. Many of the song lyrics are nostalgic, particularly when singers look back to the south and east, over the Atlantic Ocean. But as early as the 1920s AmeRicans were reflecting upon their difficult experiences as recent immigrants, often of a different color than those who occupy most of the positions of power, who for the first time were coping not only with prejudice but also with bitterly cold weather and a huge multinational city. In 1927 Rafael Hernandez wrote one of the most poignant examples of this genre:

> I came to New York hoping to get ahead,
> but if it was bad back home, here it's worse.
> Sometimes it's hot, and other times freezing cold,
> sometimes I look like a bundle sliding around on the snow.
> I don't like this, I'm going back to my hut.

FINAL THOUGHTS

United by a common language, the music and musical cultures described in this chapter demonstrate the wealth of Hispanic American folk and folk-based music. This chapter further underscores the geographical diversity of the Spanish-speaking citizens of the United States, who come from countries as different as Cuba and Mexico. Some Hispanic Americans, particularly in the Southwest, have lived here for several hundred years, while others—Cubans fleeing Fidel Castro—have arrived over the past fifty-odd years. Their living arrangements are equally varied and include Mexican Americans who live (often in great poverty) along the southern borderlands as well as Dominicans residing in barrios in New York City, and Haitians who have found refuge in Dade County, Florida. Their musical cultures have occasionally fused with popular styles (to create salsa, for example) or with Pima Indians in Arizona who play walia, but as our Hispanic American population grows there will no doubt be greater cultural interaction and new musical forms will emerge. Like the rest of American musicians, they will look to their roots for inspiration.

THE HISPANIC AMERICAN DIASPORA

KEY FIGURES AND TERMS

button accordion
chicken scratch
conjunto
corridos
Dizzy Gillespie
jibaro
mariachi

matachines
Lydia Mendoza
mestizo
plenos
Tex-Mex
Silvestre Vargas
waila

SUGGESTED LISTENING

Paulino Bernal. *Conjunto Bernal—16 Early Hits.* Arhoolie CD 9010. Sixteen selections recorded between 1954 and 1960 by this forward-sounding conjunto musician/accordion artist from Corpus Christi, Texas.

Nati Cano's Mariachi Los Camperos. *Llegaron Los Camperos.* Smithsonian Folkways SFW 40517. Solid recordings (well documented, too) by one of the strongest and longest running mariachi groups based in Los Angeles.

Rumel Fuentes. *Corridos of the Chicano Movement.* Arhoolie CD 507. Heartfelt and personal songs written and performed in the early 1970s by this singer/activist based in Eagle Pass, Texas.

Las Hermanas Segovia. *Punaladas De Amor.* Arhoolie CD 9028. The Segovia Sisters sing norteno music with a pop twist on these recordings, originally issued by Ideal and Falcon between 1950 and 1956.

Los Alegres De Teran. *Original Recordings 1952–1954.* Arhoolie CD 9048. These are fifteen seminal recordings by the group led by Eugenio Abrego and Tomas Ortiz, widely acknowledged as the founders of Musica Nortena.

Los Pleneros de la 21. *Para Todos Ustedes.* Smithsonian Folkways SFW 40519. Formed in the early 1980s, this New York City-based group explores the intersections of traditional Puerto Rican music with music from the United States.

Lydia Mendoza. *Mal Hombre.* Arhoolie/Folklyric CD 7002. This compact disc surveys Mendoza's lengthy career, focusing on her recordings from before World War II.

Various. *Ballads and Corridos, 1949–1975.* Arhoolie CD 367. The social and political topics covered in this anthology include the assassination of President Kennedy, civil rights struggles, and horse races.

THE HISPANIC AMERICAN DIASPORA

Various. *Borderlands: From Conjunto to Chicken Scratch*. Smithsonian Folkways 40418. The title nicely sums up this collection, which covers vernacular Hispanic music along the Rio Grande Valley from Texas to Arizona.

Various. *Caliente=Hot: Puerto Rican and Cuban Musical Expression in New York*. New World Records CD 244-2. This 1976 release gives an overview of several popular and folk-based styles of music. The cd includes an excellent booklet.

Various. *Conjunto! Texas-Mexican Border Music*, 3 vols. Rounder 6023/24/30. A well-annotated, three-volume sampler featuring some of the recent masters of the genre—Flaco Jimenez, Santiago Jimenez, etc.

Various. *Corridos y Tragedias de la Frontera, 1928–37*. [Tragic Corridos of the Frontier]. Folklyric 7019/20. A two-CD set of classic border ballads that comes with a 168-page book!

Various. *Cuban Counterpoint: The History of the Son Montuno*. Rounder CD 1078. A compilation of popular and folk-based style of music that has also been imported to the United States.

Various. *Music of New Mexico: Hispanic Traditions*. Smithsonian/Folkways 40409. A well-rounded and nicely annotated contemporary anthology that includes a wide array of secular as well as sacred music.

Various. *The Roots of the Narco-Corrido*. Arhoolie CD 7053. This exemplary reissue of material from (mostly) the 1920s and 1930s underscores that the confluence of drugs, violence, and the Mexican-American border is not a twenty-first-century issue.

Various. *The Roots of Tejano and Conjunto Music*. Arhoolie CD 341. An anthology of representative recordings over the period between 1946 and 1969 from the vaults of Ideal Records, the first significant Tejano-owned and -operated record company.

Various. *Taquachito Nights: Conjunto Music From South Texas*. Smithsonian Folkways 40477. Live and lively performances by mostly local groups such as Amadeo Flores, Freddy Gonzalez and Los Super Unidos, Conjunto Aztlan, and others captured on digital tape during the Conjunto Festival of the Narcisco Martinez Cultural Arts Center in San Beninto, Texas.

Various. *Tejano Roots: The Women (1946–1970)*. Arhoolie CD 343. Another anthology of tejano music during a period its modern forms began to emerge with the older styles.

THE HISPANIC AMERICAN DIASPORA

SUGGESTED READING

Ray Allen and Lois Wilcken. *Island Sounds in the Global City: Carribean Popular Music and Identity in New York*. Urbana: University of Illinois Press, 2001. The topics addressed by these essays include calypso and steel pan ensembles as well as Dominican "Merenege" in particular and Puerto Rican music in general.

Paul Austerlitz. *Merengue: Dominican Music and Dominican Identity*. Philadelphia, PA: Temple University Press, 1997. The author looks not only at merengue and its importance in the Dominican Republic but also at its impact on the musical culture of New York City.

Yolanda Broyles-Gonzalez. *Lydia Mendoza: Norteno, Tejano Legacies*. New York: Oxford University Press, 2001. This is a bilingual edition: the first is the English translation, then the original Spanish. The author discusses Mendoza's career and includes an extended essay on the significance of her career as well as her place in tejana music and chicana studies.

Ruth Glasser. *My Music is My Flag: Puerto Rican Musicians and their New York Communities, 1917–1940*. Berkeley and Los Angeles: University of California Press, 1995. A historical study that looks at a wide range of Puerto Rican musics in New York City.

Jose Limon. *Dancing with the Devil*. Madison: University of Wisconsin Press, 1994. A series of thoughtful essays about the history, folklife, and expressive culture of Mexican Americans living along the borderlands.

Anthony Macias. *Mexican American Mojo: Popular Music, Dance, and Urban Culture in Los Angeles, 1935–1968*. Durham, NC: Duke University Press, 2008. Macias focuses on the pre-rock era and Los Angeles in this wide-ranging, interdisciplinary book.

Peter Manuel (with Kenneth Bilby and Michael Largey). *Caribbean Currents: Caribbean Music from Rumba to Reggae*. Philadelphia, PA: Temple University Press, 1995. Manuel and his colleagues survey a great variety of twentieth-century musical styles in the Caribbean (including Cuban and Puerto Rican) and, secondarily, address their importance in the United States.

Manuel Pena. *The Texas-Mexican Conjunto: History of a Working-Class Music*. Austin: University of Texas Press, 1985. A fine book that takes both a musical and historical view of this accordion-based music.

Americo Peredes. *A Texas-Mexican Cancionero: Folksongs of the Lower Border*. Chicago: University of Illinois Press, 1976. This is a classic study devoted to this long-standing tradition of ballad singing.

THE HISPANIC AMERICAN DIASPORA

David Reyes and Tom Waldman. *Land of a Thousand Dances: Chicano Rock 'n' Roll from Southern California*, rev. edition. Albuquerque: University of New Mexico Press, 2008. A fascinating look at the intersection of rock, pop, and Latino culture from the late 1950s to the present.

John Robb. *Hispanic Folk Music of New Mexico and the Southwest: A Self-Portrait of a People*. Norman: University of Oklahoma Press, 1980. An important summary of Robb's many years of collecting and studying this music.

Guadalupe San Miguel Jr. *Tejano Proud: Tex-Mex Music in the Twentieth Century.* College Station: Texas A&M Press, 2002. This history professor has written a brief, chronological survey of Musica Tejana that uses the recording industry as its primary underpinning.

Chris Strachwitz (with James Nicolopus). *Lydia Mendoza: A Family Biography.* Houston, TX: Arte Publico Press, 1993. The life story of this pioneering Tejano music star is told through her own words.

SUGGESTED VIEWING

Various. *The Buena Vista Social Club*. Lion's Gate. The eclectic and interesting American guitarist Ry Cooder gathered together some of the best Cuban and Cuban-American pop and folk-based musicians for a reunion of sorts in this documentary film that gained national theaterical acclaim during the summer of 1999.

Various. *Chulas Fronteras*. Flower Films. The lives and music of both Flaco Jimenez and Lydia Mendoza are highlighted on this documentary about music along the Rio Grande Valley.

Various. *Del Mero Corazon (Straight from their Heart): Love Songs of the Southwest*. Flower Films. Norteno music and culture is the focus of this documentary.

Various. *La Junta De Los Rios*. Documentary Arts of Dallas. A documentary film about the history, music, and culture of the border region around Ojinaga, Chihuahua, Mexico, and Presido, Texas.

Various. *Songs of the Homeland*. Galan Productions. A survey of music and musicians in the United States who maintain strong ties with their Mexican roots.

Various. *Tex-Mex: The Music of the Texas-Mexico Borderlands*. Shanachie. A tour of the cantinas, clubs, festivals, and even prisons where Flaco Jimenez, Lydia Mendoza, and others perform.

Chapter 10

THE FOLK REVIVALS

- Red Roots
- The Mass Media and Popular Culture
- Field Research
- The 1960s Folk Revival
- A British Invasion
- The Blues Boom
- Back to the Mountains
- New Entrepreneurs and Frontiers
- Final Thoughts

A folk **revival** refers to the interest of singers and musicians from outside of a regional, racial, or ethnic group in perpetuating its traditional music. These singers and musicians are often young and just beginning their explorations of grassroots music. Their attention, however, can also stimulate a renewed commercial and popular interest, such as the attention focused on Woody Guthrie and his musical era by Billy Bragg, Wilco, and many others, including Bruce Springsteen. There have been successive waves of folk revivals in virtually each generation as at least some members discover and reinterpret the past. These twenty- to thirty-year cycles vary in size, intensity, and focus. During strong revivals—in the late 1950s through the middle 1960s, for example—our population of acoustic guitar pickers and banjo players with ties to traditional music increases. Since the early 1960s pioneering southern string bands, Appalachian folk songs, and blues have been the object of this curiosity on the part of the general public.

In some instances such attention has served to renew interest in this music within its hearth area. Such renewal (along with the decades-long success of the annual Galax, Virginia, fiddlers' convention) has helped to strengthen the local appreciation of old-time and early bluegrass music in Carroll and Grayson counties. Likewise the interest of some younger polka adherents in the upper

THE FOLK REVIVALS

Blues men Bukka White and Houston Stackhouse leaving the stage of the 1970 Festival of American Folklife in Washington, D.C. Bill Pierce photo, courtesy of the Ralph Rinzler Folklife Archives and Collections, Center for Folklife and Cultural Heritage, Smithsonian Institution.

Midwest has helped (in some small ways) to renew the "ethnic" bands found throughout Wisconsin, Minnesota, and adjoining states. Such renewals or revivals also tend to spark more scholarly interest in these traditions.

Music revivals in the United States are not limited to folk music, of course. Rockabilly, for instance, has been resurrected on more than one occasion—most recently in the middle 1980s when groups such as the Stray Cats traded upon the tough boy, cool, outsider's image associated with the rockabilly pioneers such as Billy C. Riley (whose accompanying group was called the Little Green Men!) and Jerry Lee Lewis. In the late 1990s and early 2000s rhythm and blues (R&B; cum big band jazz) made a strong comeback in large measure because of the "swing revival," which could be more accurately characterized as a renaissance of interest in R&B. Groups such as Big Voodoo Daddy, which provided a portion of the musical interlude during half-time at the 1999 Super Bowl, look back to Louis Prima, Roy Brown, and, especially, Louis Jordan for their musical inspiration. (For more information on R&B, please refer to chapter 11.) A few other contemporary artists, such as the Old 97s, Sun Volt, or Wilco (both with and without Billy Bragg), have amassed a substantial following by marketing the roots aspect of their music and through their reinterpretations of the various genres of American folk music.

THE FOLK REVIVALS

Joan Baez at the 1964 Newport Folk Festival. Ralph Rinzler photo, courtesy of the Ralph Rinzler Folklife Archives and Collections, Center for Folklife and Cultural Heritage, Smithsonian Institution.

In the early twenty-first century, however, the term *folk revival* generally has a more concrete meaning for many people born shortly before or during the baby boom. For them the folk revival began slowly in the late 1950s and peaked with the 1964 **Newport Folk Festival** when Bob Dylan first appeared in public with an electric guitar. This specific revival evokes a certain nostalgia for aging baby boomers: simpler times before the Vietnam War fully exploded, their own misspent youth, civil rights struggles, sing-alongs at hootenannies, and "Puff the Magic Dragon." Much of this chapter focuses on the folk revival that held forth from the late 1950s through the middle 1960s, certainly the largest and most widespread of these revivals of the twentieth century.

The musicians associated with this folk revival essentially belong to two related, but separate, groups. Let's look at them to help reinforce the earlier distinctions between folk music and folk-based music. In one group are rural, southern folk musicians such as Reverend Gary Davis (gospel), Mississippi John Hurt (blues), and Bill Monroe (bluegrass). Their music was bred in the bones. These influential musicians grew up within the musical culture, not to mention the racial and regional communities, that spawned gospel, blues, and bluegrass.

The other group of musicians consists of those who rework, revise, draw inspiration from, or interpret folk music. Eric Von Schmidt, for instance, generally performs blues. He was born and raised in Westport, Connecticut, and studied art on a Fulbright scholarship in Florence, Italy, in the early 1950s. During the late 1950s and early 1960s Von Schmidt played blues around New England, particularly in the greater Boston area. Despite his love and respect for Sleepy John Estes and Lead Belly, Eric Von Schmidt grew up within the white middle class, far from the direct ties to African American culture and music. Moreover, the vast majority of his patrons and fans were white and many were northerners. Von Schmidt later consciously chose to step outside of his own background and identify with the very expressive language of black American blues. Traditional music also inspired Bob Dylan, Joan Baez, and Tom Rush, who began their careers by singing their own interpretations of folk songs but who have evolved into highly respected singers/songwriters. Such musicians play folk music or folk-based music, rather than being folk musicians themselves, which is an important distinction.

RED ROOTS

Many of the musicians who cut their teeth during this folk revival were inspired not only by traditional music but also by an older generation of traditional or folk-based musicians. The early 1960s folk revival was simply another retrospective—one of the periodic, popular excursions into our unique American roots. This was not the first twentieth-century reevaluation that resulted in commercial viability. During the late teens, Henry Ford tried to revitalize American folk dance (and reinforce traditional American values) in the Midwest with the assistance of his self-described "old-time bands" that featured hammered dulcimers.

Traditional music cast in a more politicized form crept into the American consciousness beginning in the middle 1930s, spurred on by the Depression and left-wing activists who viewed it as the "voice of the people." The veterans of this movement—**Woody Guthrie**, Lead Belly, Cisco Houston, for example—largely served as role models for the early 1960s folk revival.

Not all of the folk-based music from this period was overtly political. Another group viewed folk music as a bucolic escape from the pressures of the modern world and a return to traditional American values. Some, such as Richard Chase, spent much of their energy collecting folk tales and songs, performing only occasionally. Others, like Richard Dyer-Bennett and John Jacob Niles, used it as an apolitical springboard to further both their interest in the music and themselves. Trained as an opera singer, Niles parlayed his Kentucky heritage into a new career. He also displayed a modest ability to play his own unique homemade instrument that he called a dulcimer, but which is only distantly related to the standard plucked Appalachian dulcimer. Niles brought his singular interpretations of this music, an uneasy mix of formal Old World sensibilities with southern American folk, to audiences across the country and made some commercially successful recordings for Victor as well as his own label.

Meanwhile **Pete Seeger**, the **Almanac Singers**, **Moses Asch**, Woody Guthrie, the Weavers, **Alan Lomax**, and Lead Belly established themselves as integral parts of the politicized folk song movement. Dr. Charles Seeger, an eminent academic musicologist and patriarch of the famed musical family, served as a de facto cultural commissar of this movement. The "folk camps" (Pineville, Kentucky), craft schools (Penland, North Carolina) and experimental colleges (Black Mountain College, North Carolina) began in the 1930s to explore the possibilities music holds as an agent for social change and to reexamine America's identity.

Union organizing and workers' rights were also major issues, as was the role of the Communist Party in helping to reshape the United States. The Communist newspaper, the *People's World*, once described this music as *"the songs of people, of farmers, of workers, of laborers, and they come from the directed contact with their work, whatever it is"* (Denisoff 1971, 59).

Early in 2000 that exploration and reexamination of cultural roots and music continue in other similar ways. Now camps that specialize in teaching folk music and folk dance dot the American landscape. Their intent is generally less political than musical but their emphasis remains with the American vernacular and passing along the traditions. In the late 1980s Henry Sapoznik started a highly successful "KlezKamp," among other projects. This annual event, held on the East Coast (in or near New York City), attracts several hundred people interested in Jewish culture, klezmer music, and traditional dance.

The 1930s and 1940s marked a period when protest songs decried social and economic conditions of many Americans. The capitalist system was carefully scrutinized and criticized by singers, many of whom belonged to or sympathized with the American Communist Party. Struggles for the recognition of unions, especially in the Appalachian coal fields, were one central theme. Several of the New York City–based activists, notably Seeger and Lomax, helped to bring recognition for the battles fought by their Kentucky brothers and sisters. During the late 1930s Aunt Molly Jackson, Sarah Ogan, and Jim Garland often sang at Union rallies held in the Northeast to raise money for Kentucky union members. They sang the decidedly pro-union "Which Side Are You On?" which opens like an old British broadside:

Come all of you good workers
Good news to you I'll tell
Of how the good old union
Has come in here to dwell.

MUSICAL EXAMPLE

Woody Guthrie contributed many great songs to our contemporary musical culture: "Vigilante Man," "Pastures of Plenty," "This Land is Our Land," and many others. "Do Re Me" is a fine example of the socialist protest songs that he began performing in the late 1930s. A committed popularist and socialist, Guthrie lived through the Depression and felt a great deal of animosity toward the capitalist system that seemed to offer much but deliver little. Guthrie lost a long battle to Huntington's chorea (a slowly debilitating neurological disease) in 1967 that began affecting him some fifteen years before.

Title "Do Re Me"
Performer Woody Guthrie
Instruments guitar and vocals
Length 2:28

Musical Characteristics
1. It is performed in a major tonality.
2. The simple finger-picked guitar accompaniment to his laconic vocal forms a homophonic texture.
3. The song is structured in an *ab* form.
4. The melody is relatively conjunctive and uncomplicated.
5. Guthrie's nasal relaxed vocal falls into the middle register.

> Lots of folks back east they say,
> Leavin' home every day,
> Beatin' a hot old dusty way to the California line.
> 'Cross the desert sands they roll
> Gettin' out of that old dust bowl.
> Think they're a comin' to a sugar bowl,
> But here's what they find:
> Oh, the police at the port of entry say,
> "You're number 14,000 for today!" Oh!
>
> **Chorus:**
> If you ain't got that do, re, me, folks
> If you ain't got that do, re, me,
> Why you'd better go back to beautiful Texas,
> Oklahoma, Kansas, Georgia, Tennessee;
> California's a garden of Eden,

A paradise to live in or see;
But, believe it or not,
You won't find it so hot.
If you ain't got the do, re, me!

If you want to buy a home or farm,
That can't do nobody harm,
Or take your vacation by the mountains or sea,
Don't swap your old cow for a car,
You'd better stay right where you are,
You'd better take this little tip from me.
'Cause I look through the want ad's every day,
But the headlines in the paper always say.

Chorus

This selection is from Smithsonian Folkways 40001.

For these protest singers, whose fervor was rekindled during the era of the McCarthy trials and again throughout the Vietnam War, folk music was the people's music and it served a political end. The period at the beginning of World War II marked a renaissance, a focus on the music and culture that emphasized our underrepresented working class. Folk music came into vogue and could be heard in a variety of informal contexts. These musicians, most of them white and formally educated, performed at informal parties, Communist Party fund-raisers, and pro-union rallies. In New York City the Almanac Singers, who were formed in 1941 and originally consisted of Pete Seeger, Lee Hayes, Millard Lampbell, and John Peter Hawes, stood at the core of this movement. Shortly thereafter Woody Guthrie joined the group, which was dedicated to writing and singing topical "folk" songs favoring the progressive left wing. Their ranks also included black blues singer Josh White, who had moved to New York City from South Carolina in 1935 in search of a new audience. For this collective of performers, the terms "worker," "folk," and "people" meant much the same thing. They lived together in a communal house in Greenwich Village and everyone contributed to the expenses. The Almanac Singers represent the quintessence of the left-wing urban folk song movement of the late 1930s and early 1940s.

The outbreak of World War II slowed down their activity as both Pete Seeger and Woody Guthrie served their country overseas. But the message rang back clearly following first Germany's and then Japan's surrender in 1945. Most of these folks remained active into the 1950s, making the occasional commercial foray into mainstream America. This segment of American culture stood poised and ready to gain their greatest commercial viability when the Kingston Trio, Peter, Paul & Mary, and Bob Dylan began to hit the big time.

THE MASS MEDIA AND POPULAR CULTURE

One obvious question is what caused this particular revival? As traditional music became more widely exposed through the mass electronic media, their base of commercial support moved far beyond the communities that spawned them. Music lovers eventually consumed greater amounts of music by way of their radios and phonograph records and, eventually, television. Urban in- migration, modernization, and the development of suburban tract homes placed more Americans even further from their rural roots.

By the 1950s more people lived in suburban and urban centers than remained on farms in rural areas. Although major record companies never stopped selling traditional music, their interest in it stumbled three separate times: following the Depression's wake when the record industry was all but devastated, in the middle 1950s as rock 'n' roll was suddenly catapulted into the commercial spotlight, and in 1964 and 1965 when the **British Invasion** groups as disparate as Herman's Hermits and the Beatles arrived in the U.S. marketplace. Such changes do not occur overnight, of course, but the banishment of blues, gospel, and of types of folk music from the powerful mass media that touches hundreds of millions of American citizens was swift and undeniable.

The radio was one of the media that reacted most quickly to the changing forces in American popular and folk culture. Outside of urban centers the early-morning farm reports and live fifteen-minute country music shows continued hand-in-hand well into the 1950s. In upstate New York, for example, the vestiges of this era remained for many years. The last early-morning farm market report that I recall hearing on Schenectady's 50,000-watt clear channel giant WGY occurred around 1966. In a few smaller markets, such as in Roanoke, Virginia, WDBJ-TV continued with local early-morning and weekend country and gospel music programming well into the 1960s; however, by the late 1960s most television stations around the United States had adopted the programming formats dictated by the networks. Except for local news and a handful of public affairs programs, local television programming was all but passé by 1970. The style and content of programming in both radio and television are, with only a handful of exceptions, very similar no matter where you travel in the United States.

Record companies followed a similar path. The eclectic, local, traditional performers that were documented prior to 1930, including such delights as Luke

THE FOLK REVIVALS

Highnight, Six Cylinder Smith, Carter Brothers & Sons, and Emery Glenn, were now considered anachronistic and noncommercial. As the demand to shore up the corporate bottom line increased, major companies stuck with proven sellers, most of whom were not folk musicians. A handful of small companies, such as Timely and Asch (in New York City), emerged in the late 1930s. They stepped in to help fulfill this need, but they only issued a handful of records before World War II virtually ground their business to a halt. And they were plagued by limited distribution and little media exposure.

Hundreds of small, short-lived companies sprang up across the United States following World War II: Macys in Houston; Mutual in Bassett, Virginia; J.V.B. in Detroit; or RPM in Los Angeles. The majority of them suffered from undercapitalization and went bankrupt because of the cash-flow drain; however, they were more willing to gamble on untried talent of all descriptions and they fundamentally replaced the major companies in marketing folk music and records with regional appeal, including polka music, blues, and white gospel music.

As the interest of large, corporate entities in American roots traditions declined, there was a concurrent rise in the number and popularity of interpreters of vernacular music. Doris Day, Patti Page, and Tennessee Ernie Ford moved out of their usual pop music territory during the 1950s to provide record companies with their own versions of traditional material. Groups like the Weavers, which helped propel Pete Seeger's performing career to a wider audience, proved immensely successful in the early 1950s. Between 1950 and 1952 this group sold over four million copies of records for Decca with their interpretations of Lead Belly's "Goodnight Irene"; Woody Guthrie's "So Long, It's Been Good to Know You"; two African-inspired tunes, "Tzena, Tzena" and "Wimoweh"; as well as "Kisses Sweeter Than Wine." The lush orchestrations of noted arranger Gordon Jenkins adorned most of the Weavers' records, a far cry from the music's roots but symptomatic of its blanching. Such an aesthetic compromise appeared to be necessary to make the music palatable to the widest possible audience. For better or for worse, Pete Seeger had become a viable commercial entity and he found it problematic to negotiate this exceptionally treacherous path.

The early 1950s can now be seen as a dark, ominous period in American politics that affected our entire society. Joseph McCarthy led the Communist witch-hunt, resulting in a muted creative period in all of the arts. The blacklisting of television and radio writers because of their (perceived or real) left-wing sympathies resonated with the "red-taint" of the late 1930s and disrupted the careers of many authors and actors. As recently as 1999 the Academy Awards were mired in a controversy related to Mr. McCarthy. The debate centered on a proposed Lifetime Achievement Award for Elia Kazan, who cooperated with McCarthy in ways that left many of his fellow screenwriters, directors, and actors uneasy.

THE FOLK REVIVALS

Moses Asch, the founder and director of Folkways Records (1960). Courtesy of the Ralph Rinzler Folklife Archives and Collections, Center for Folklife and Cultural Heritage, Smithsonian Institution.

In terms of the folk music scene one bright light, the *Anthology of American Folk Music*, blazed forth in 1952. Edited by the eccentric and brilliant Harry Smith, this six-record set was one of the cornerstones of the folk revival that was in full blossom a decade later. Dave Van Ronk told me it was like his bible of folk music and Roger McGuinn (a founding member of the Byrds) remarked that it opened up a whole new world for him. The set was divided into three volumes, "Ballads," "Social Songs," and "Songs," containing performances originally recorded for commercial record companies in the 1920s and 1930s.

The anthology was released by Moses Asch on Folkways Records and helped to introduce such regional folk performers as Blind Willie Johnson, Uncle Dave Macon, Hoyt Ming and his Pep Steppers, Columbus Fruge, Ramblin' Thomas, and the Memphis Jug Band to an audience that was all but unaware of their contributions to American music. This set was largely responsible for keeping songs such as "White House Blues" (originally recorded by Charlie Poole and his North Carolina Ramblers), "Fishing Blues" (from Henry Thomas's canon), and "Minglewood Blues" (by way of Cannon's Jug Stompers) in the repertoire of singers across the United States. In 1997 the anthology reemerged in the form of a remastered multi-CD set (including an interactive compact disc devoted to the eccentric Harry Smith), an expanded booklet, great critical acclaim, and surprising popular appeal. NARAS (The National Academy of Recording Arts Science) awarded the set three Grammys, further adding to its mystique and popularity.

In early 1956 Elvis Presley burst into American popular culture, helping to dispel some of the gloom with his brazen, timeless message of teenage angst, love, and sensual lust. Elvis and his Sun Record cohorts—Jerry Lee Lewis, Carl Perkins, Johnny Cash, and Roy Orbison—played rockabilly and pioneered rock 'n' roll. Their raucous and controversial stylings helped to move this grassroots-based music further away from its wellspring and into a more commercial and international realm.

FIELD RESEARCH

Of course the scholarly interest in vernacular music never totally dissipated. A few dedicated researchers continued scouting the countryside, particularly in the South, for undiscovered talent. Harold Courlander, for instance, spent a considerable amount of time away from Washington, D.C., and in Alabama recording black folk musicians during the early to mid- 1950s. He stayed in one central Alabama community for an extended period of time, concentrating on every expression of folk music that he could locate within a limited geographic boundary. The Guggenheim Foundation sponsored Courlander's field research, resulting in a well-respected book, *Negro Folk Music U.S.A.*, and several long-playing phonograph records on Folkways that serve as an important and influential model for the presentation of field research.

Alan Lomax returned from his self-imposed European exile in 1956 and soon resumed his American fieldwork. In 1958 and 1959 Lomax reprised his Library of Congress approach that began on the trips with his father in 1933. These sweeping trips carried Lomax across the entire South, resulting in the "Southern Folk Heritage" series on Atlantic and Prestige's "Southern Journey" set of records. These recordings (now back in print courtesy of Rounder Records—refer to chapter 1) brought important singers like Mississippi blues man Fred McDowell to the attention of the general public just as the folk revival was beginning.

Motivated by an interest in early New Orleans jazz, **Samuel Charters** moved to New Orleans in 1950 and slowly involved himself in researching blues music. One of the pioneers in the field, Charters recalls these heady days as a young white man in the South looking for the lost blues legends that had appeared on race records some thirty years before:

> It is impossible to imagine how much that seemed like a lost world—it was like Atlantis! We had no idea what this world was like, what it represented, and if we would find people from it. When I suddenly began finding that these men were relatively young and that many of them were still alive, I was stunned. The first book that I wrote, *The Country Blues* [1959], I wrote in a very exaggerated, purposefully over-romanticized style. I did it on purpose to emphasize the romance of finding old blues singers. At that point in the '50s I had the South

to myself. Nobody else was doing this. I didn't have any money. I didn't have any university affiliation. I was simply on the road in battered old cars that I borrowed. (Personal interview, Storrs, CT, December 29, 1988)

These men simply reconfirmed what is now abundantly clear: regional folk music had not expired, it merely (all but) disappeared from the commercial marketplace. Contra-dances in Vermont never stopped, not all of Montana's cowboy singers had ridden into their final sunset, nor had the all-day African American shape note singings in the Deep South entirely ceased. Although they have been staples of regional American culture, many years would pass before Tex-Mex cuisine, blackened fish, and Cajun two-step dancing eventually became chic in New York City. Such traditions are submerged from the view of most Americans, who remain largely ignorant of the regional traditions across the United States outside of their immediate view or own experience.

THE 1960S FOLK REVIVAL

The corporate interest in the folk revival really began in 1958 when the Kingston Trio recorded "Tom Dooley," a murder ballad that Frank Warner had collected in western North Carolina from banjo player and singer Frank Profitt. Their version sold a million copies and its success motivated others to reexamine folk music in a more commercial light. Such trends led to an upswing in folk music gatherings and the development of groups such as the Brothers Four, the Limelighters, and other neofolkies. By the early 1960s the revival was in full swing and the more enterprising people once more began marketing this music to a mass audience. This also occurred on college campuses as it gradually became fashionable to listen to this music and once again study the printed legacy of James Francis Child and John Lomax's early work with cowboy singers.

Traditional music suddenly found itself back in demand among the general public. Younger people, in particular, exposed to this music for the first time picked up a guitar or banjo and learned their rudiments in order to become a "folk singer." The music was called "folk" because of its southern background, its roots in traditional forms, the fact that it was largely played on acoustic instruments, and for lack of any other convenient term. To be a folk singer was in vogue and trendy, even sexy.

Subscriptions to magazines such as *Sing Out!* (founded in 1952) increased dramatically. *Broadside*, which featured topical and left-wing protest songs, premiered in 1962. Simultaneously the more clean-cut and pop-oriented *Hootenanny* became a new addition to newsstands across the United States. Not all of the performers caught up in this movement were white-bread, clean-cut college students singing and playing in their local coffeehouses. In addition to the authentic folk musicians, other singers fit into the mold of *Hard Hitting Songs for Hard Hit People*, a collection of American protest songs from the 1930s to the 1950s. This was the new generation of protest singers in the tradition of Woody Guthrie, Cisco Houston, and Pete Seeger, who looked at music as a vehicle for social change.

The civil rights movement and the slowly expanding Vietnam War provided the perfect fodder for *Broadside* readers as well as topical performers such as Mark Spoelstra, Peter La Farge, Buffy Saint-Marie, Bob Dylan, Joan Baez, Phil Ochs, and Tom Paxton. Suddenly musicians with acoustical instruments and songs with difficult themes attracted record contracts, some with major companies like Columbia. While the large companies wanted a slice of the folk music pie, they remained skeptical of the movement's political implications. The McCarthy era had begun less than one decade before and major American corporations are inherently conservative. In the late 1950s **independent record companies**, such as Electra, Broadside, and Folkways, moved in to fill this void.

Folkways Record Company actually began in 1939 when Moses Asch, a Polish-born immigrant who arrived in the United States at the end of World War I, started the Asch Record Company. It all but shut down in 1941 due to the shellac shortage caused by World War II. When the war abated Asch countered first with the Disc Record Company of America and then with Folkways in 1947. His purpose was to record all types of oral material including jazz, poetry, ethnic traditions, the sounds of insects, and grassroots music. Asch himself muses about his work:

> To do a record is to create art, content, and package. I had to do something that would work visually. I issued folk music, which was the bastardized pop of the day, to an audience who would appreciate it even though the guy who sang it was an old black country musician. I had to show this had value and content.
>
> Woody Guthrie came to New York City. He came to me and said, "This is my home and I want to express myself here." We understood each other. Woody was a true hippie, illustrative of Walt Whitman . . . He had a frame and he used the music of American folk song as the base for his words. Woody would fit it into what he wanted to say. (Tracey Shwartz, interview with Moses Asch, 1971)

By the height of the revival (circa 1963) Moses Asch had already issued over a score of records by Pete Seeger, Woody Guthrie, and the New Lost City Ramblers. His stable also included several multirecord sets that surveyed American folk music and history in songs. Albums by blues performers such as Brownie McGhee and Lead Belly and country music pioneer Ernest Stoneman dotted the growing catalogue. Asch himself estimated that Pete Seeger's Folkways

MUSICAL EXAMPLE

When the Harvesters (Ethel Raim, Joyce Gluck, Walter Raim, and Ronnie Gluck) recorded this selection in 1959, they had just arrived in Hollywood after a long drive from New York City. They were a prototype folk group; Ethel Raim worked for *Sing Out!* and taught at the Neighborhood Music School, while Walter had been an assistant conductor of the (Harry) Belafonte Folksingers. The Glucks worked at other full-time jobs and played music on the side. The Jewish Young Folksingers Chorus served as an important, common bond and one of their aims was to perform songs from around the world in Yiddish, Spanish, and Hebrew. This selection, however, is one of Woody Guthrie's best-known songs and speaks of his dream for a truly United States of America.

Title "This Land is Our Land"
Performers The Harvesters
Instruments banjo, bass, guitar, four voices
Length 2:16

Musical Characteristics
1. It is performed in major tonality.
2. Loose harmony singing can be heard on the chorus.
3. The voices fit into middle registers.
4. A simple duple (2/4) meter is heard throughout.
5. It uses a verse/chorus form.
6. A pleasantly rich homophonic texture is established by the mixture of the voices and instruments.
7. The lead singers alternate throughout the song.

Chorus
This land is your land, this land is my land,
From California to the New York island;
From the Redwood Forest to the Gulfstream waters,
This land is made for you and me.

As I went walking that ribbon of highway,
I saw above me that endless skyway,
I saw below me that golden valley,
This land is made for you and me.

Chorus

THE FOLK REVIVALS

I roamed and rambled, and I followed my footsteps,
To the sparkling sands of her diamond deserts,
And all around me, a voice was sounding,
This land was made for you and me.

Chorus

When the sun came shining, then I was strolling,
And the wheat fields waving, and the dust clouds rolling,
This land was made for you and me.

Chorus

This selection is from Smithsonian Folkways 2406.

---

records annually sold between 30,000 and 40,000 copies during the early 1960s. Seeger performed regularly at hootenannies, clubs, and churches. His peripatetic lifestyle brought him across the entire country and much of the world.

Indeed, the folk boom affected musical tastes across the United States. Folk clubs (most of them located in cities) presented music in small venues from Boston to Seattle. Smaller towns dominated by large college campuses—Ann Arbor and Madison, for example—supported folk music venues. Nonetheless, New York remained at the commercial and artistic vortex of this revival movement. In New York City Moe Asch also gave voice to newer and younger folk-based singers like singer/guitarist **Dave Van Ronk**, who resided at the center of the revival.

Dave Van Ronk, too, was attracted to American vernacular music, but early jazz emerged as his first love. He recalls:

What molded me musically, were the "moldy-fig" wars of the late 1940s . . . the traditionalists, who I call the Platonists, felt there was an original form that was pure. They felt the original form had degenerated, so here we have Preservation Hall [New Orleans's famous jazz club] as Plato's Cave. The modernists were aesthetic Darwinists and I think they were every bit as stupid. What is newer and more "developed" is not necessarily better. You can't apply either yardstick to aesthetics . . . Being an adolescent at the time, I was an absolutist and I had to jump one way or the other. As soon as I was aware that this titanic tempest-in-a-teapot was going down . . . I stopped listening to my Dizzy Gillespie records for about seven years. I got over it. I'm happy that I have a huge collection of Gillespie and Parker! (Personal interview, January 21, 1991)

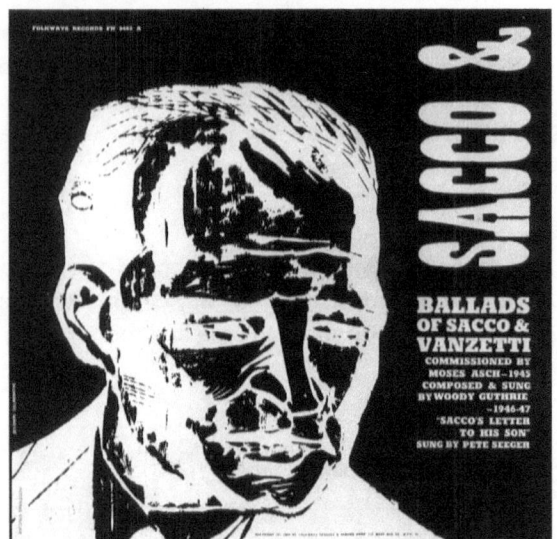

Sacco and Vanzetti cover. Courtesy of the Ralph Rinzler Folklife Archives and Collections, Center for Folklife and Cultural Heritage, Smithsonian Institution.

For about five or six years, Van Ronk stuck with traditional jazz. A high school dropout, he was determined to make his living through musical performance, so he moved to Manhattan and promptly lost forty pounds that first year away from home. Van Ronk not only played guitar but also usually took over the vocal chores because he didn't mind and could sing loudly. By the middle 1950s, however, the "steam had just totally gone out of the traditional jazz revival" to the point that he'd often "play for Union scale and have to slip them back something under the table. You were lucky to get two gigs in a week, more often you'd get one gig in two weeks" (Personal interview, January 21, 1991).

Although Van Ronk loved this music, his future as a performer of traditional jazz seemed bleak. Van Ronk, along with others interested in old 78 rpm records from the 1920s and 1930s, used to haunt the Jazz Record Center on 47th Street where the blues and jazz records were often mixed together. This is where he got a taste for southern blues singers such as King Solomon Hill, Blind Lemon Jefferson, Mississippi John Hurt, and Furry Lewis. He gradually gained a greater taste and appreciation for folk music, especially blues, and decided to make a switch from jazz to folk. After all, he already had both the basic guitar technique and a powerful, gruff voice.

Van Ronk views this move as "technically retrogressive and partly lateral." It was also a sound, and not surprising, aesthetic decision because of his ongoing interest in the grassroots of twentieth-century American music. Just as the Russians were becoming the first to get into the Space Age by launching *Sputnik*, Dave Van Ronk was making the more earthly transition to folk music. It was not that difficult because he moved into a compatible circle of neo-ethnics.

THE FOLK REVIVALS

In New York City these folks tended to congregate in Washington Square. This gathering point not far from New York University at the edge of Greenwich Village became the weekly meeting and training grounds for folk music. People came to swap songs, look over banjos and guitars, talk about upcoming gigs, and see their friends. Barry Kornfeld, a thoughtful veteran of the scene, wrote in a 1959 issue of *Caravan magazine* (No. 18, August/September):

> At 2 pm every Sunday, from the first balmy days of April to the last of the fair October weather, large numbers of instrumentalists and singers gather, from whose ranks there will emerge some fine professionals and some equally fine, or at least equally intense, amateurs who will follow in the footsteps of their predecessors. [We] presupposed the existence of Washington Square gatherings as we had presupposed the existence of grass, trees, and, of course, park departments.

The Washington Square scene really began in the middle 1940s, about the time that World War II drew to a close. Musicians such as George Magolin, who today is as obscure to most folk music lovers as the Seven Foot Dilly, would play his guitar in the afternoons. More famous folkies also made their way to Washington Square during the immediate postwar years. Fiddler Alan Block, Tom Paley (later of the New Lost City Ramblers), Harry Belafonte, progressive banjo wizard Roger Sprung, and Pete Seeger could be heard there on a good day. This assembly point was a true institution by the time that Dave Van Ronk himself became a regular there in the middle 1950s.

These Washington Square hootenannies were rather informal affairs, mostly for fun. Van Ronk often performed by himself but for a while he teamed with Roy Berkeley and they played as the Traveling Trotskyite Troubadours. Perhaps as an antidote to Bobby Darrin, Frank Sinatra, and other contemporary popular singers, it was also a multiethnic group eager for new musical experiences. Live music and musical interaction were the key. Van Ronk recalls:

> The people that I was hanging around with were into all kinds of stuff; everything from bluegrass to African cabaret music. All across the boards. I was a sponge . . . picked up everything that I heard. Everything was going into the same meat-grinder. All of us were sort of like that. People specialized in old-time music would all of a sudden launch into a country blues. It was much more eclectic. (Personal interview, January 21, 1991)

It became more serious, too, as people decided to try to make a living by playing folk music. The Folk Singers Guild was one response to this new interest in traditional music. Though not an all-encompassing organization, the Folk Singers Guild nonetheless affected the New York City folk scene. The hundred or so members were mostly, but not all, musicians. Washington Square served as the primary venue for most Guild members; however, it also organized a few small concerts in local halls. Van Ronk recalls:

> We used to go over to the Sullivan Street Playhouse . . . in the days before the "Fantasticks" moved in. It was on Sunday nights when they were "dark." We would have three, four, or five people doing maybe twenty minutes or a half hour. That was really the only playing experience that most of us got. There wasn't anything else; there were not clubs . . . Gerdes [Folk City] didn't start until about '61. (Personal interview, January 21, 1991)

Paul Clayton, one of the most active New York folk singers in the late 1950s, refused to join the Folk Singers Guild. He used to attend meetings but would never join because he considered himself to be a professional, who made his living singing and recording. By 1960 Clayton had made at least a dozen albums and had served as Van Ronk's principal mentor. Black guitarist Rev. Gary Davis became another of his heroes and he learned much from the older man's highly influential finger-picking style. Van Ronk views Davis as a peer, albeit "older, more experienced . . . and more talented." They worked many of the same clubs, and Van Ronk became most intimately acquainted with Reverend Davis shortly after these recordings were made. In 1961 Van Ronk was booking acts for one of the coffeehouses on McDougal and remembers:

> I had Gary there every possible time I could. Unless it was an absolute full house, then I would be sitting in front of the stage watching those fingers. That's the only way you can really learn. I'd ask him, "How do you do this?" He'd be only too happy to show me [and] then he'd cackle when I got it wrong, which was usually. It was that kind of thing that Gary and I had in common. (Personal interview, January 21, 1991)

McDougal Street was home to Van Ronk at the time of this recording. Izzy Young's Folklore Center, which served as the informal headquarters for New York City's folk singers, sat just a few doors down from Van Ronk's apartment. This long, narrow store was crammed full of books, records, and posters announcing folk and jazz events. A friendly, rambling establishment, the Folklore Center became the crossroads and heartbeat for local folk singers as well as visitors. Young presented some of the first concerts by the New Lost City Ramblers and Peggy Seeger and Ewan MacColl. He later served as the booker for Gerde's Folk City when it was still called the Fifth Fret.

Some folk-based singers, including Van Ronk, all but lived at the Folklore Center. Folk singers, instrument makers, entrepreneurs, and budding academic folklorists could be found there. College programs in folklore were new, and several Washington Square/Folklore Center regulars were attracted to the scholarly life. But in the late 1950s Roger Abrahams, Ellen Steckert, and Kenny

Goldstein, each of whom eventually earned a graduate degree in folklore and taught in universities, hung out there. Abrahams and Steckert went on to record for Folkways, while Goldstein eventually produced scores of folk music records for a variety of labels, most notably Prestige.

Goldstein, in fact, recorded and initially notated Van Ronk's Folkways recordings. Intent on getting a recording out to the public to promote his career, Van Ronk bothered everyone he could think of in the business. He finally got both Electra and Lyrichord interested in recording him, but in 1959 he convinced Moe Asch that he was ready to record. Kenny Goldstein served as the A&R (artist and repertoire) man and the basic link between Van Ronk and Moe Asch.

The selections that Van Ronk recorded for Folkways and other smaller companies draw largely from African American music. They reflect a clear, longstanding interest in his heroes; among them are Bessie Smith, Jelly Roll Morton, Jimmy Yancey, and Louis Armstrong. Van Ronk always admired keyboard players and approached the guitar pianistically, which is one reason why he never played with a slide or bottleneck. Within a few years after making these recordings, Van Ronk's repertoire and approach to music had radically changed. He still loved the early recordings by Scrapper Blackwell, Blind Boy Fuller, and Snooks Eaglin, but his own persona began to emerge: "I was developing an approach and a style that was really quite different from that of my models. A few years down the line, I simply had no interest at all in [merely] emulating my models" (Personal interview, January 21, 1991).

The movement away from mere emulation to the performance of original material described by Van Ronk typifies the experiences of many people in the folk revival. Traditional music first caught the attention of **Judy Collins** and **Bob Dylan**, but after several years they moved on to perform more original material. First they began writing their own songs; albums and live performances mixed folk songs with self-penned verses. Slowly they moved into the popular mainstream by adding electric instruments and even lush string orchestrations.

This process was repeated many times, spawning the "singer/songwriter" movement that touched American popular music in the mid- to late 1960s. Once again we see the symbiotic interchange among corporate America, popular culture, and our own grassroots. Professional performers including Buffy Saint-Marie, Pete Seeger, Tom Paxton, and Joan Baez inarguably helped to ignite a minor musical revolution based on the earlier blues, gospel, and country artists they so admired; however, their careers also intertwined with the cultural upheaval of the 1960s and they soon moved exclusively into folk-based music.

Another independent company, Vanguard Records, began as a classical label in the early 1950s, but quickly signed Eric Anderson, Buffy Saint-Marie, Joan

MUSICAL EXAMPLE

A longtime resident of the northeast, Sandy Ives has for many years taught English and folklore at the University of Maine. In 1959 Ives included this song on a collection that he recorded for Moses Asch. Most of the songs were collected directly from older singers in Maine, often from men working at lumbering camps or fishermen, and they often sang about their life and work. This one he learned from Charles Sibley of Argyle, Maine, and its title refers to the small log buildings in which the lumbermen lived. Notice that it starts with the formulaic greeting so common in Native American ballads.

Title "The Shanty Boys"
Performer Edward "Sandy" Ives
Instruments guitar and vocals
Length 2:24

Musical Characteristics
1. The song is set in a major tonality.
2. Ives sings in the middle register with a very relaxed voice.
3. You hear a spare, homophonic texture.
4. Its musical form is strophic.

> Come all ye good jolly fellows, come listen to my song.
> It's about the shanty boys and how they get along.
> We're all good jolly fellows as you will ever find.
> To wear away the winter months a whaling down the pine.
>
> The chopper and the sawyer, they lay the timber low.
> The swamper and the teamster, they haul it to and fro.
> You'd ought to hear our foreman soon after the break of day.
> "Load up your team two thousand feet—to the river you'll steer away."
>
> Crack! Snap! goes my whip, I whistle and I sing.
> I sit upon my timber load as happy as a king.
> My horses they are ready and I am never sad.
> There's no-one now so happy as the jolly shanty lad.
>
> Noon will soon be over, to us the foreman will say,
> "Put down you saws and ax, my boys, for here's your pork and beans."
> Arriving at the shanty, 'tis then the fun begins.
> A'dippelin' in the water pail and dinglin' of the tin.

THE FOLK REVIVALS

And then to us the cook will say "Come fella, come fly, come Joe.
Come pass around the water pail as far as the water goes."
As soon as lunch is over, to us the foreman will say,
"Put on your coat and cap, my boys, to the woods we'll bear away."

We all go out with a cheerful heart and a well-contented mind,
The days don't seem so long among the way pine;
You ought to hear our foreman, soon after the sun goes down,
"Put down your saws and ax, my boys, to the shanty we are bound."

Arriving at the shanty with wet and damp cold feet.
We all put off our larragians, our suppers for to eat.
We all play cards till nine o'clock, then into our bunks we climb.
To wear away the winter months a-whaling down the pine.

This selection is taken from Smithsonian Folkways 5323.

Baez, and other folk-based artists when their commercial stock rose. These artists did so well that by mid-decade Vanguard's roster expanded to include southern performers like Doc Watson, Mississippi John Hurt, and Skip James. Nearly all of the blues sessions were produced by Samuel Charters, who obtained carte blanche to build Vanguard's blues roster. Charters also explored the Chicago blues scene, producing an influential three-record set, *The Chicago Blues Today!* The Lawrence Welk Group presently owns the Vanguard catalogue and Sam Charters has repackaged much of his own material into a new CD—the only "Mid-Line" series designed to reach a new generation of listeners in the early 2000s. The label has also delved into its vaults to issue a series of compact discs (mostly thematic anthologies) devoted to performers who appeared at the Newport Folk Festivals.

Most of the sharp commercial interest focused on younger, city-bred performers, and Bob Dylan emerged as the one performer who the major companies could not ignore. After shifting his home from Hibbing, Minnesota, to New York City in 1959, Dylan's personality and music gradually impacted upon this burgeoning scene. *Broadside* magazine published his songs "Masters of War," "Blowin' in the Wind," and "It's All Right," and he appeared on the cover of *Sing Out!* in October 1962. Dylan himself was dismissed as a performer early in his career. "Can't sing, can't play . . . nothing special" was the rap against him. However, he not only caught the attention of commercial folk-based music enthusiasts but also the ear of Columbia Record executive John Hammond, who had previously committed Count Basie and Billie Holiday to contracts. In late 1963

THE FOLK REVIVALS

Pete Seeger at the 1964 Newport Folk Festival, Diane Davies photo, courtesy of the Ralph Rinzler Folklife Archives and Collections, Center for Folklife and Cultural Heritage, Smithsonian Institution.

Bob Dylan became a Columbia Record artist. One decade later Hammond's aural facilities for spotting talent once again proved correct when he signed Bruce Springsteen to Columbia Records.

Bob Dylan has profoundly affected American popular music and culture. Except for his early recording (on harmonica) with Mississippi blues man Big Joe Williams, Dylan's music had few direct connections with regional or racial genres of American folk music. He was genuinely inspired by Woody Guthrie, Pete Seeger, and others and continues to acknowledge his debt to the genre. The blues also struck Dylan as powerful music, particularly the message of a song such as Skip James's evocative and poetic "Hard Time Killin' Floor Blues," which he initially recorded in 1931:

> Hard time here, everywhere you go.
> Times is harder, than ever been before.
> Well the people are drifting from door to door.
> Can't find no heaven, I don't care where you go.

But his most significant contribution lies with topical songs and more personal messages aimed at a general audience. Dylan provides the quintessential example of folk-based music reaching a mainstream, popular audience. The importance of this distinction becomes clearer in light of Dylan's audiences in 1963 and thereafter.

The famous August 28, 1963, march on Washington, D.C., during which Martin Luther King, Jr., delivered his renowned "I Have a Dream" speech was attended by Joan Baez, Bob Dylan, and many other "city-billy" commercial folk singers. Dylan lent his heartfelt support to the voting rights and civil rights movement in an event that drew international attention, and he was not the only one to sing out about social injustice and problems. The course had been charted many years before by the Almanac Singers and the Weavers, among others. Tom Paxton, Peter Krug, Phil Ochs, and countless others felt it their duty to comment upon topical issues of the day, but they also wrote songs based on their own personal discontent, malaise, and social injustice. This trait set them apart from their earlier models and established clear precedents for the careers of popular singers/songwriters such as Joni Mitchell, Tom Rush, Cat Stevens, and Neil Young. These folks, in turn, influenced younger European-born pop performers like Sting, the Edge, and Bono, both of whom have demonstrated a social conscience in their songwriting while reaching massive audiences. Performers caught up in the folk boom often included their own interpretations of traditional material in their repertoires before gaining fame for their own writing.

Although television shows like ABC's *Hootenanny* were broadcast to audiences nationwide, the apex of this revival came with the 1963 Newport Folk Festival. This gathering of protest singers, topical songwriters, commercial folk groups, and traditional musicians such as Doc Watson, Frank Profitt, and Clarence Ashley drew an unprecedented, huge crowd of 37,000 people and made a major media splash. Music festivals were nothing new—fiddle contests had been held in the South for decades and Newport itself had been home to jazz festivals since the mid-1950s. The 1963 Newport Folk Festival stood as the largest such conclave and a raving success, both from the popular press and within the folk community's own publications. Its $70,000 profit also underscored the commercial viability of this music.

The folk revival was not confined to New York City and New England. Coffeehouses and small clubs offered folk entertainment in cities and college campuses across the entire country. In Minneapolis, the white blues trio of Kerner, Glover, and Ray played in churches that turned over their meeting space of a coffeehouse, for friends, and eventually at larger folk clubs like the "Extraordinaire." Paul Nelson began a small folk music magazine, The *Little Sandy Review*, in 1959. The North Beach of San Francisco was home to many clubs featuring both jazz and folk music. In Los Angeles, the Ash Grove was for many years the home to folk concerts and the informal home for traveling musicians. Lou

THE FOLK REVIVALS

Curtiss started selling instruments and hosting concerts in San Diego in the early 1960s and is still going in the 2000s.

A few musicians caught up in this movement branched out in a new direction. Erik Darling, Roger Sprung, Bela Fleck, and Billy Faier all began their careers by learning to play old-time or bluegrass. But within a few years they began bringing elements of jazz and influences from nonwestern music into their playing. These experimenters from the 1960s found only a small audience for their hybrids and were about forty years ahead of their time—by the early 2000s they seemed to be much closer to the mainstream.

The year 1965 marked a dramatic change in commercial folk music. After a halcyon half a decade of success, commercial exposure, and a wave of recordings, two major events rocked the relatively small world of American folk music. The summer brought the next Newport Folk Festival with Bob Dylan as one of its principal attractions. Dylan now possessed a public persona that had begun to conflict with the event's self-perception. His motorcycle jacket and electric guitar brought Dylan immediate disfavor. He violated a well-established perception that folk music can't be played on anything that needs to be plugged in—never mind that many country blues players had been using electric guitars for more than a decade. Moreover, his repertoire reflected the undercurrents that flavored his recent Columbia issue, *Another Side of Bob Dylan*.

Dylan had transcended his role as a folk singer, but was not entirely clear about being an American spokesperson. The moralizing tone of his previous songs was tempered by uncertainty and the feeling that he might not have all of the answers. This new persona, so quickly and unexpectedly revealed at Newport, had serious repercussions within the community of commercial folk singers. Over cups of coffee and in the folk press the debate raged over this turn of events: had Dylan sold out, where was folk music headed, have we lost our focus, is folk music becoming too commercial? This angst only fueled the winds of change blown in by the new records from England.

During the folk revival rock 'n' roll and black R&B had entered a near moribund phase. Elvis had joined the army, Chuck Berry was in jail, Jerry Lee Lewis became persona non grata after marrying his thirteen-year-old cousin, and then Buddy Holly died in a plane crash. Furthermore, no new cult heroes emerged in the popular music scene. Black pop music remained equally quiet, though the Motown sound was about to emerge from Barry Gordy's Detroit studio. In fact, there was precious little new to prick the ears and libidos of white and black teenagers. Folk songs offered adults a brief respite from the nasty, African American inspired music of rockabilly and rock 'n' roll. This bucolic era lasted until the British Invasion of 1964 brought the equally subversive sounds of the Beatles, the Rolling Stones, the Dave Clark Five, and others into homes across

THE FOLK REVIVALS

Doc Watson performing in the middle 1960s. Diane Davies photo, courtesy of the Ralph Rinzler Folklife Archives and Collections, Center for Folklife and Cultural Heritage, Smithsonian Institution.

the United States. By 1965 the British had arrived and American pop musicians were reeling.

From a purely commercial perspective the folk revival (albeit diminished) lasted into the late 1960s. It helped to create some hybrids, such as the **folk/rock** of the Byrds and the Flying Burrito Brothers, who reached across the United States with their blend brewed at clubs like the Ash Grove in Los Angeles. Post-1965 Bob Dylan can also be considered a folk/rocker. His records with The Band are particularly fine examples of folk-based rock music. The careers of Simon and Garfunkel, Tim Hardin, and Leonard Cohen also benefited from this movement. On the West Coast, folk/rock was smoothed out yet more and popularized by the Mamas and the Papas as well as Sonny and Cher. The peak of commercial success for folk-inspired rock and pop music was 1965 and 1966.

Inevitably, the rise of Haight-Ashbury and "Sergeant Pepper's Lonely Hearts Club Band" heralded another shift in American popular culture, one that expanded people's minds away from folk music into other realms. By 1970 Americans had lived through acid rock, the 1968 Democratic Convention, massive music festivals at Woodstock and Monterey, Richard Nixon's election, the "Summer of Love," as well as the deaths of Janis Joplin, Jimi Hendrix, and the folk revival. Meanwhile the Vietnam War staggered on into the 1970s.

But this grassroots movement continues today, and the interest in folk culture remains very eclectic though much more highly organized. Individual coffeehouses can be found across the United States, but now folk music associations abound from Norfolk, Virginia, to Seattle, Washington. The Washington, D.C., and Baltimore metropolitan area alone contains the Middle Maryland Folklore Association, the Folklore Society of Greater Washington, The Western Maryland Folklore Society, The Baltimore Folklore Society, and several other smaller organizations. These groups are supported by thousands of members, and each one publishes a monthly newsletter that lists not only musical events at local clubs, informal shape note sings, and workshops for learning to write folk songs but they also include schedules for English morris dancing, swing dance events, New England contra-dancing, square dances, Swedish couple dancing, and other events related to ethnic and folk dancing. One look at the Web sites maintained by these organizations underscores the fact that folk-related activities are alive and thriving both within and just outside of the Beltway.

A BRITISH INVASION

Shortly after Dylan's Newport appearance, the number of records by British musicians became a full-fledged onslaught. Their music began to appear on the American charts, supplanting Motown artists, pop vocalists, and the commercial folk balladeers. The Beatles, Herman's Hermits, the Kinks, Rolling Stones, Dave Clark Five, and the Animals became fixtures on American Top Forty radio. By late 1964 these groups, and others, had begun to tour the United States. The early appearances by the Beatles represented a phenomenon in American popular culture that surpassed the mania displayed for Elvis Presley when his career was launched a decade before.

Significantly, most of these British groups displayed a strong propensity toward American vernacular culture and music. Led by the Beatles, the Rolling Stones, and the Who, British groups assaulted our popular culture with their unique hybrid of electric guitars, working-class English sensibilities, and a distinctive love for black American music. Many of these musicians had been attracted to this music beginning in the skiffle-band (a British version of folk music mixed with rockabilly) era of the middle- to late 1950s. This led many British youth to discover the imported recordings of Howlin' Wolf, Chuck Berry, Robert Johnson, Muddy Waters, Memphis Minnie, and Lead Belly. The middle 1960s saw "cover" versions of American blues music by English rock groups appearing on radios and records in homes across the United States. American youth raved over the Rolling Stones's version of Howlin' Wolf's "Little

THE FOLK REVIVALS

Red Rooster," Cream's cover of "Outside Woman Blues" (Blind Willie Reynolds), Sonny Boy Williamson's "Eyesight to the Blind" by the Who, and Led Zeppelin's rendition of "You Shook Me" (penned by Willie Dixon). No doubt only the most hip American listeners understood the arcane British allusions to blues culture, such as the fact that the Moody Blues are named for a song performed by Louisiana harp blower Slim Harpo in 1963.

American blues musicians such as Big Bill and Muddy Waters (who shocked his British audience with his electric guitar—they were expecting a folk musician!) began touring England and Europe in the middle 1950s. By 1963 packaged "folk blues" tours became annual overseas events that lasted for several years, and the Yardbirds (featuring Jimmy Page and Eric Clapton) began recording with touring stars like Sonny Boy Williamson and Memphis Slim. The combination of touring American blues heroes and the easy availability of early and current blues records only helped to reinforce the popularity of blues in England. So did its lyrics about fun, sexuality, and alienation, tripart themes that appealed to aspiring adolescent musicians.

Some of the early blues reissue records also had profound impact upon future rock megastars. Eric Clapton liked the urban-styled electric blues, but the country blues was his first true passion. Mississippi Delta blues singer Robert Johnson was his hero:

> I was around fifteen or sixteen, and it came as something of a shock to me that there could be anything that powerful . . . if you didn't know who Robert Johnson was I wouldn't talk to you. It was as if I had been prepared to receive Robert Johnson, almost like a religious experience [and] his music remains the most powerful cry that I think that you can find in the human voice, really. (Larry Cohn and Stephen LaVere, *Robert Johnson: The Complete Recordings*, 1991, 22–23, Columbia C2K 46222)

THE BLUES BOOM

This lionization of the African American blues tradition by Europeans not only led to increased record sales and tours overseas, but a renewed interest in this country. The swift change in popular tastes and the general interest in blues truly surprised Sam Charters, who recalls:

> I wrote *The Country Blues* and it come out in 1959, and I went to Europe for one year . . . I had gone simply to get myself away from what I had been doing steadily for ten years. I wanted to get on with my own creative work, I'd always thought of myself as a writer, not as a researcher. I came back in 1961 and the whole world was searching for their local blues singer. They had a copy of *The Country Blues* in one pocket and a tape recorder in hand! To go

with the book I did the first RBF album, which sold and sold and sold. Virtually every song on it was picked up, like "Statesboro Blues" and "Walk Right In," of course. I think that record did as much as anything to introduce the blues. It was the first time that anyone had really heard this. RBF [a reissue record company owned by Folkway's Moe Asch] was set-up to be my window to the world. I did twenty-four or twenty-five of them rather quickly. At about the same time I did the Lightnin' Hopkins recording, which caused an enormous stir. So suddenly it was obvious that there was something out there. (Personal interview, Storrs, CT, December 29, 1988)

Significantly, the consciousness-raising occurred primarily among young whites. Worn copies of race records began appearing on tapes that circulated within a small circle of dedicated fans, and in 1964 OJL (Origin Jazz Library) became the first record company devoted to reissuing this music on long-playing records. The interest on the part of younger whites also resulted in the rediscovery of older blues musicians who had recorded in the 1920s and 1930s. Using clues gleaned from race records, Tom Hoskins, Nick Perls, John Fahey, and others traveled across the Deep South locating Robert Wilkins, Skip James, Mississippi John Hurt, and Bukka White. These men launched new, albeit brief, musical careers complete with concert tours and recordings. Due to declining health or shifts in interests other surviving musicians from this era—Gus Cannon, Memphis Minnie, Peg-Leg Howell, or Kokomo Arnold, for example—only marginally benefited from the revival.

The impulse to relocate black blues singers was not unique to the middle 1960s. Alan Lomax was scouring northern Mississippi for the late Robert Johnson when he located Muddy Waters on Stovall's Plantation in 1941. Samuel Charters traveled to Memphis as early as 1954 to speak with Furry Lewis, Will Shade, Milton Robie, and other veterans. The primary differences were the development of a younger (nearly entirely white) audience for blues, making concert tours and the sales of albums possible. Their way was paved by the folk revival of the early 1960s, followed by the "blues boom" of the middle 1960s.

From a cultural point of view, these shifts also underscore important changes in the consumption of this vital form of American folk music. The blues boom existed through the support of white audiences, not under the aegis of black listeners. Folk blues singers in the 1960s often played in coffeehouses and concert halls, though in the rural South musicians such as R. L. Burnside continued to labor in the juke joints and rough clubs of northwestern Mississippi. While the blues revival affirmed that not all of the older blues singers had died with the advent of rock 'n' roll and soul music, it also reaffirmed that this tenacious music still enjoyed some grassroots support. Not only was R. L. Burnside still playing blues in Mississippi, but other "unknowns" such as Baby Tate, Mance Lipscomb, Bill Williams, Elizabeth Cotten, Elester Anderson, and Jack

THE FOLK REVIVALS

Alan Lomax and his sister, Bess Lomax Hawes. Courtesy of the Ralph Rinzler Folklife Archives and Collections, Center for Folklife and Cultural Heritage, Smithsonian Institution.

Owens also had kept the tradition going. Today, however, this grassroots support from the black community is all but gone—the down-home blues has been commodified to such a degree that its base of support is virtually all white.

BACK TO THE MOUNTAINS

Not surprisingly parallel activity was occurring in white folk music as younger scholars and collectors returned once more to the source. Mike Seeger, the talented multi-instrumentalist of the Seeger family that included Pete, Charles (an eminent musicologist), Ruth (a composer), Peggy (another musician), and Tony (an ethnomusicologist), became interested in bluegrass and old-time music in the early 1950s. By the late 1950s he and two other city-billy musicians, John Cohen and Tom Paley, formed the **New Lost City Ramblers**, the first of the truly conscious revival string bands to explore the many avenues of their roots. The New Lost City Ramblers performed various types of American folk music, though most of it emanated from the South. Many younger people were first exposed to string band music through the ensemble work of the Ramblers. They learned their music directly from folk musicians, older records, and field recordings.

THE FOLK REVIVALS

New Lost City Ramblers Tracey Schwarz, Mike Seeger, and John Cohen (1996). Courtesy of the Ralph Rinzler Folklife Archives and Collections, Center for Folklife and Cultural Heritage, Smithsonian Institution.

A keen field collector with an inquisitive mind, Mike Seeger was also interested in learning the fate of the older musicians that he had heard on Harry Smith's pioneering *Anthology of American Folk Music*. Seeger, Bob Pinson, Joe Bussard, Malcolm Blackard, Donald Lee Nelson, Dave Freeman, and others scoured the South, particularly the southeastern mountains, locating both original 78 rpm records as well as the early recording artists: Dock Boggs in Wise County, Virginia; the daughters of Fiddlin' Powers in neighboring Coeburn; Clarence Ashley of Mountain City, Tennessee; and Dorsey Dixon in Rockingham, South Carolina.

Not only did they rediscover the first generation of recording artists, but these new collectors also found a thriving group of musicians who had never left the South and who had not been preserved on records. Important "new" traditional singers such as Roscoe Holcomb in eastern Kentucky and ballad singer Dillard Chandler, who lived near Asheville, North Carolina, made field recordings that were eventually released on Folkways. Cohen also introduced a new medium to the folk revival, the ethnographic documentary film, that resulted in short films devoted to Holcomb and Chandler. He has continued to produce films and his most important statement on the subject at hand is *Musical Holdouts*, a mid-1970s film that addresses regional genres of American music. Once more technology impacts upon folk music in the United States, this time in a conscious effort to visually preserve and interpret.

THE FOLK REVIVALS

The renewed interest in American folk music inevitably resulted in a new generation of interpreters, whose backgrounds were usually antithetical to the roots and upbringing of the musicians whom they idolized. Many of the revivalists were younger northern musicians attracted to the wide variety of roots music they heard on Folkways or Vanguard Records or saw at folk festivals from Berkeley to Philadelphia. Unlike groups such as the Limelighters or the Kingston Trio, most of these musicians tended to learn this music directly from the masters and faithfully reproduce it. They viewed themselves as carriers of the torch passed from one generation to the other, often fearing that younger members of the community had passed over this music in favor of more contemporary forms: bluegrass, soul, Nashville country, or R&B.

Mac Benford of the Highwoods String Band recalls his own musical experiences that began in the early 1960s:

> The dominant role models for the whole scene were the New Lost City Ramblers, who combined expertise as musicians and folklorists. Their performance style was based on their extensive knowledge for old-time music recorded in the '20s & '30s. In addition to their own performances, the concerts, films, and records that they produced of older musicians still stand as shining examples . . . Many amateur folklorists now began enrolling in academic programs to earn credentials for what they had already been doing for love. As the folk boom of the '60s gathered momentum, the campuses of colleges and universities across the country became meeting grounds for the academic world and old-time musicians. This was the situation when my most notable musical venture . . . first got rolling. The timing couldn't have been better . . . The support we received was so active that in just three years after Highwoods had teamed up to try our luck at the southern fiddlers' conventions in the summer of 1972, we had been chosen to become part of the Smithsonian's Touring Performance Service; we were picked to represent old-time music on a U.S. State Department tour of Latin America; and we had become a favorite group at most of the major folk festivals. (M. Benford, *Old Time Herald*, 1989, 23)

This trend resulted in new performance venues and avenues for both traditional musicians and those who have revived and interpreted earlier styles. A circuit of festivals, coffeehouses, and small concerts halls catering to folk music devotees developed across the country. This circuit supported musical programs by a wide range of artists, ranging from a semiretired blues performer like Sleepy John Estes to an ensemble that has revived the contra-dance music they heard at a town hall in southern New Hampshire or a string band that learned at the feet of Wade Ward in Galax, Virginia.

In the early 1970s Rounder Records emerged at the vanguard of recording and disseminating American grassroots music. Rounder began as an antiprofit collective but thirty years later it has become a minor conglomerate, having

MUSICAL EXAMPLE

One of the most talented and long lasting of these eclectic string bands is the Red Clay Ramblers, who are based in and around Chapel Hill, North Carolina. Founded originally in the early 1970s as an informal group, within a few years the band members had quit their teaching, library, and other day jobs to devote themselves to music. Since then they have toured throughout the United States and parts of Europe, recording numerous times for independent labels and working with several off-Broadway shows. "Tell It to Me" was derived from a 1920s recording by the Tenneva (a diminutive for Tennessee and Virginia) Ramblers. In addition to the old-time tunes, the Ramblers now feature a refreshing mixture of original material, sacred songs, and Irish instrumental tunes.

Title "Tell It to Me"
Performers The Red Clay Ramblers
Instruments Tommy Thompson, banjo and vocals; Bill Hicks, fiddle; Mike Craver, guitar; Laurel Urton, washtub bass; Al McCandless, fiddle; Jim Watson, mandolin and vocals
Length 2:26

Musical Characteristics
1. A rich and varied homophonic texture is heard.
2. There is harmony singing in the lead vocals and on the chorus.
3. It is performed in duple (2/4) meter at a rapid tempo.
4. There are several instrumental leads by the fiddle and banjo.
5. The song maintains a steady, high dynamic level.

> Going up Cripple Creek, coming down Main
> Trying to make a living for to buy cocaine
> Cocaine's gonna kill my honey dear.
>
> *Chorus*
> Tell it to me, tell it to me
> Drink corn liquor, let the cocaine be
> Cocaine gonna kill my honey dear
>
> Sniff cocaine, blow it at night
> Sniff cocaine if it takes my life
> Cocaine's gonna kill my honey dear.

Chorus

Sniff cocaine, sniff it in the wind
Doctor said it'll kill but wouldn't say when
Cocaine gonna kill my honey dear.

Chorus

All you rounders think you're tough
Feed your women on brandy and snuff
Cocaine gonna kill my honey dear.

Chorus (repeat)

This selection is from Smithsonian Folkways 31039.

---

assimilated Flying Fish and several other small labels. The hundreds of issues of old-time, bluegrass, blues, Cajun, and other forms of grassroots and ethnic music are the largest in the United States and appear on such subsidiary labels as Bullseye Blues. They have also led the way in reissuing important material overlooked by major companies, such as releasing the complete (RCA Victor) works of the Carter Family and Jimmie Rodgers on compact discs as well as a six-CD sampler of Huddie Ledbetter's recordings for the Library of Congress. And, of course, Rounder is carefully revisiting the career of Alan Lomax with the release of approximately 120 compact discs of his material over a ten-year period! Today, however, Rounder Records is owned by the Welk Group, a music conglomerate with roots in Lawrence Welk's successful empire that began in the 1920s.

Hundreds of thousands of music fans have been exposed to a wide range of music by these means and to performers with increasingly eclectic repertoires. They hear groups with tongue-in-cheek names such as "The Mighty Possums," "Mice in the Attic," and "Moose Chowder." Many of these bands unblinkingly mix Irish tunes, western swing, British ballads, rockabilly, and southern fiddle tunes. Revival bands of all descriptions became the staple ensemble for many young white instrumentalists interested in alternatives to popular music groups.

As the years go by, this diversity becomes more pronounced and institutionalized. For example, at the 1991 "Dance Augusta" workshops in the hills of West Virginia, the first session was "Cajun week." This workshop attracted enthusiastic dancers primarily from the Middle Atlantic States who came for instruction

THE FOLK REVIVALS

The Highwoods String Band at the Festival of American Folklife in the middle 1970s. Courtesy of the Ralph Rinzler Folklife Archives and Collections, Center for Folklife and Cultural Heritage, Smithsonian Institution.

in "couples dance styles of southwest Louisiana ... in the two-step, jitterbug, waltz, Cajun blues dancing and zydeco." The flyer also advertized that attendees would experience "Cajun culture, dance parties, snacks, and more." The musicians included not only southwest Louisiana natives Dewey Balfa, Bois Sec Ardoin, and Canray Fontenot, but also Tracy Schwarz (one of the New Lost City Rambler's founders), Matt Honey, and Bob Smakula.

NEW ENTREPRENEURS AND FRONTIERS

A new breed of entrepreneurs also entered the record business. Moe Asch started Folkways back in the 1940s, but virtually no one else came into the business during the 1950s because of a perceived audience shortage. This changed, of course, beginning with the folk song revival, and any number of small record companies moved in to fill the void. Chris Strachwitz, for example, founded **Arhoolie Records** in 1960 and continues to operate this label today. The label celebrated its fortieth birthday in 2000 with a deluxe box set, *The Journey of Chris Strachwitz*, that takes a chronological look at Arhoolie's development. Strachwitz had taught school in northern California but was deeply interested in records and regional folk music, and the first Arhoolie issue was by the Texas songster, Mance Lipscomb. His shoestring operation has followed its founder's muse and good taste. Arhoolie continues to be Strachwitz's window to the world, and his catalogue of over 200 releases includes some of the best recordings by Lightnin' Hopkins, Lydia Mendoza, Clifton Chenier, and a host of other artists whose work is discussed in this book. Most other companies—Red House, Folk Legacy, Shanachie—have sprung forth from similar roots and have issued a similarly eclectic mixture of regional, revivalists, folk-based, and older traditional music.

Another aspect of the folk music revival is a renewed interest in ethnic traditions. Earlier in this book I briefly discussed the interaction between commercial record companies and ethnic musicians during the teens and 1920s. Ethnic traditions always existed in their communities; like blues and hillbilly music, they never "died." Unlike the other two genres, ethnic traditions never really moved beyond their grassroots audiences to become part of popular culture. This is partly the result of language differences, making the words sung in Yiddish, Swedish, Ukrainian, or Spanish unintelligible to those whose native tongue is English.

The ghettoization of ethnic music is also related to the relative inaccessibility of the mass media, particularly radio and record companies. Except for those serving a major urban center or smaller community dominated by a members of a certain cultural/language group, most radio stations do not serve the musical needs of ethnic groups. Similarly, record companies generally do not sell enough disks to warrant paying much attention to foreign language records. In this case there simply is not the demand to make such ventures profitable enough to make them attractive. Moreover, the longer the period of time that ethnic groups reside in this country, the more acculturated they generally become. This also creates a weaker demand for the tangible products of their musical culture.

The 1970s and 1980s witnessed the beginning of a strong movement toward multicultural perspectives in the arts, education, and the humanities; there is a reawakened awareness that the United States is not a monolithic society. One minor result of this new assessment is the understanding that ethnic music plays some part in our cultural fabric. Since 1970 we have witnessed revitalization movements in klezmer, native American, Hawaiian, and Norwegian American music among others. This music was merely submerged by the commercial forces that shape our daily consciousness, bubbling along within the confines of its community.

The Folklife Center of the Library of Congress sponsored a conference and a book about ethnic traditional music in the United States. Both Pekka Gronaw and Richard K. Spottswood have undertaken the most basic and extensive related discographical work. Spottswood's seven-volume discography, *Ethnic Music on Records*, is the standard reference on ethnic recordings up to 1943. Despite the increased emphasis on ethnicity, the focus of the most recent folk revival has been upon American folk music as opposed to traditions imported to this country.

Smithsonian Folkways has always included ethnic-American releases in its catalogue, while Arhoolie's Chris Strachwitz's fondness for Spanish American and the creolized forms from Louisiana and east Texas assured their places in his company. The bulk of the recording of ethnic music, however, was undertaken by small companies dedicated to meeting the needs of their narrow-targeted audiences. As they usually do in our capitalist society, commercial companies sprang up to fill the void left by major companies. In New York City, for example, the influx of Caribbean immigrants has created a thriving business for entrepreneurs hustling concerts and dances in addition to records and tapes. Canyon Records in New Mexico has been serving the native American communities, albeit mostly Southwestern tribes, since the early 1960s. The documentation and marketing of popular and folk music of ethnic enclaves remains, even today, largely unknown outside of the communities themselves.

Calypso, reggae, and styles from Haiti, Cuba, and other countries along the Caribbean Rim have influenced music in the United States for many years. This occurred several times during the twentieth century alone, especially with jazz. From its roots in the Deep South, and New Orleans in particular, Cuban polyrhythms affected jazz. Jelly Roll Morton noted the "Spanish tinge" in his own music, perhaps as the result of his own partially Hispanic background. In the late 1940s the craze for instruments such as bongos and conga drums swept through jazz, resulting in tunes such as "Cubana-Be-Cubana-Bop" and "Manteca." (These genres were touched upon in chapters 8 and 9.)

Yet the folk revival has left permanent marks upon our musical awareness. During the 1990s some very popular singers/songwriters, most notably Suzanne Vega, Ani De Franco, Michelle Shocked, Tracy Chapman, Indigo Girls, and R.E.M., all clearly bear the heritage of American folk music in their own work. The popular press continues to trace and help create new musical trends: the 1970s and 1980s brought alternative journals and magazines devoted to American vernacular music. Folk music publications such as *Living Blues, The Old Time Herald*, and other more ephemeral magazines have chronicled the history and development of vernacular music. Today, much information about these musics can be found on the thousands of Web sites (not all of them based in the United States) devoted to American vernacular music from Cajun to surf to Tejano. Most of the noncommercial college and national public radio stations devote some of their weekly programming to folk music, and the attention paid to the revised *Anthology of American Folk Music* underscores the

THE FOLK REVIVALS

Fiddler Dewey Balfa (*center*) and his friends conduct a workshop and performance at Louisiana State University at Lafayette. Courtesy of the Ralph Rinzler Folklife Archives and Collections, Center for Folklife and Cultural Heritage, Smithsonian Institution.

vitality of this music. These examples illustrate that a small, persistent, and formidable network of resources devoted to the preservation and dissemination of folk music exists, much of it now available on-line.

Europeans also retain a strong hand in documenting our musical heritage. All of the major discographies of blues, gospel, and early country music have been compiled by Englishmen and were first published overseas. This ironic situation remains as true today as it did in the late 1930s when Hughes Panaisse wrote a pioneering scholarly book on jazz and assembled its first discography. If only American scholarly interest had been so strong fifty years ago! Several of the major collections of race and hillbilly records are in the hands of European collectors, while record companies such as Interstate (England) and Document (Scotland) issue more records of black blues than any American company. The European-based *Old-Time Music*, *Blues & Rhythm*, and *Soul Bag*, among others, have printed hundreds of issues devoted to American folk music.

Early in 2001 the Coen Brothers' film *O Brother, Where Art Thou?* sparked the latest revival of interest in folk and folk-based film. A critical success, the movie's soundtrack has received almost as much attention as the film. Most of the songs on *O Brother* are quiet, acoustic performances that draw upon American folk music: "Hard Time Killing Floor Blues" (based on the 1931 performance by Skip James) and "O Death" are among its musical highlights. Although the songs were mostly rotated into the mix on noncommercial "public" radio stations, there is at least one potential radio hit on the album: "I Am a Man of Constant Sorrow." This traditional song has been recorded by singers as diverse as bluegrass pioneer Ralph Stanley, English rock singer Rod Stewart, and (Blind Faith and Cream) drummer Ginger Baker. In *O Brother* the song is played (in bluegrass style) by the Soggy Bottom Boys and its video received good play on Country Music Television, the commercial country music industry's equivalent of MTV. Will the circle (once again) be unbroken?

FINAL THOUGHTS

All of this attention, American or otherwise, simply highlights the fact that our grassroots culture continues to fascinate and reinvigorate our music. Even after more than seventy years of intervention, technology remains a strong force in shaping folk music. The most remote sections of America are dotted with satellite dishes, just as the same houses contained primitive radios in the late 1920s.

Despite all of these advances, the VFW in Fairview, Virginia, still holds its bimonthly square dances with old-time string band music mixed with bluegrass. KPLK in New Ulm, Minnesota, is no longer the "Polka Station of the Nation," but they continue to play an hour's worth each day at noon. Just because Bob Wills is dead, western swing and two-step dancing has not disappeared from Texas dance halls—they were alive and well during George W. Bush's White House years. In southwestern Louisiana dance halls Buckwheat Zydeco and Queen Ida continue to meet the zydeco and creolized Cajun music demand. Regional folk music in the United States is not dead, it remains lurking just below the consciousness of popular culture always at the ready to be discovered and revived yet again.

KEY FIGURES AND TERMS

Almanac Singers
Arhoolie Records
Moses Asch
British Invasion
Samuel Charters
Judy Collins
Bob Dylan
Folkways Record Company
folk/rock

Woody Guthrie
independent record companies
Alan Lomax
New Lost City Ramblers
Newport Folk Festival
revival
Pete Seeger
Dave Van Ronk

THE FOLK REVIVALS

SUGGESTED LISTENING

Grateful Dead. *Ladies and Gentleman . . . The Grateful Dead: Fillmore East April 1971.* Arista 14075. A typical "Dead" set from the period that features such folk revival favorites as "Dark Holler," "Going Down the Road Feeling Bad," "New Minglewood Blues," and "Casey Jones."

Bob Dylan. *Nashville Skyline/New Morning/John Wesley Harding.* Columbia/Sony 65373. Original material that portrays Dylan's folk roots as well as his progressive political vision on three separate "folk-rock" albums now packaged together as a set.

Woody Guthrie. *Dust Bowl Ballads.* Rounder 1040. These topical songs and ballads from the late 1930s are arguably Guthrie's best recordings; many other fine records are available on Smithsonian Folkways.

Bruce Molsky. *Contented Must Be.* Rounder 682161053424. The longer that he plays, the clearer it becomes that this D.C.-based fiddler, guitarist, and banjo player is one of the most accomplished musicians to explore old-time music.

New Lost City Ramblers. *The Early Years: 1958–1962.* Smithsonian Folkways 40036. A multivolume repackaging of their best work for Moses Asch.

Mike Seeger. *True Vine.* Smithsonian Folkways 40136. Mike's fine interpretations of a wide variety of songs and instrumentals mostly from the Upland South, from the familiar ("Freight Train") to the sublime ("When Sorrows Encompass Me Round").

Pete Seeger. *If I Had A Hammer.* Smithsonian Folkways 40096. An overview of Seeger's topical material recorded between the 1940s and 1998.

Various. *The Best of Broadside 1962–1988: Anthems of the American Underground From The Pages of Broadside Magazine.* Smithsonian Folkways 40130. A boxed set of five compact discs and an excellent booklet that covers the "protest" music of the folk revival and beyond.

Various. *Close to Home, Old Time Music from Mike Seeger's Collection, 1952–1967.* Smithsonian Folkways 40097. These informal recordings include such important artists as Dock Boggs, Tom Ashley, Elizabeth Cotten, and Snuffy Jenkins.

Various. *Don't Mourn—Organize! Songs of Labor Songwriter Joe Hill.* Smithsonian Folkways 40026. Renditions of Hill's powerful songs by Earl Robinson, Billy Bragg, Hazel Dicks, and others.

THE FOLK REVIVALS

Various. *The Harry Smith Connection: A Live Tribute to the Anthology of American Folk Music*. Smithsonian Folkways 40085. This 1997 recording showcases performances by artists such as Geoff Muldar, Jeff Tweedy, and the Fugs interpreting songs associated with the Harry Smith Anthology.

Various. *O Brother, Where Art Thou*. Polygram 170069. This soundtrack to the Coen Brother's film includes strong and interesting performances by Norman Black, Allison Krause, Ralph Stanley, the Fairfield Four, and a host of other talented (though not necessarily well-known) artists.

Various. *Old Town School of Folk Music Songbook 1*. Old Town School 001. The first of a series of four compact discs that sample the work of students and graduates of this Chicago community music school whose alumni include members of Wilco and the Mekons.

Various. *That's Why We're Marching: World War II and the American Folk Song Movement*. Smithsonian Folkways 40021. Twenty-five selections by the Almanac Singers, Tom Glazer, Josh White, and others that reflect the nation's mood during this troubled period.

Weavers. *Reunion at Carnegie Hall, 1963*. Vanguard 15/16. A triumphant reprise of the group some thirteen years after they first made headlines with "Irene, Goodnight."

SUGGESTED READING

Ray Allen. *Gone to the Country: The New Lost City Ramblers and the Folk Music Revival*. Urbana: University of Illinois Press, 2010. Allen's firmly balanced book looks carefully at this pivotal group and its place in shaping the taste of folk music fans from the late 1950s into the early twenty-first century.

John Bealle. *Old-Time Music and Dance: Community and Folk Revival*. Bloomington: Indiana University Press, 2005. Sharply focused on founding in 1972 and the subsequent development of the Bloomington Old-Time Music and Dance Group, Bealle explores larger questions about countercultures, identity, and authenticity.

Robert Cantwell. *When We Were Good: The Folk Revival*. Cambridge, MA: Harvard University Press, 1996. A scholarly historical examination of the "folk movement" and revivals following World War II.

Ron Cohen, ed. *"Wasn't That A Time": First Hand Accounts of the Folk Revival*. Lanham, MD: Scarecrow Press, 1995. A fine and varied compilation of essays about the folk revival, concentrating on the 1950s and 1960s.

THE FOLK REVIVALS

Bob Coltman. *Paul Clayton and the Folksong Revival.* Lanham, MD: Scarecrow Press, 2008. Though not well known to the general public, Clayton played an important—though often behind the scenes—role as a performer, song collector, and enthusiast.

David Dunaway and Holly Beer. *Singing Out: An Oral History of America's Folk Music Revivals.* New York: Oxford University Press, 2010. In-depth interviews with subjects as diverse as Arlo Guthrie, Bernice Johnson Reagon, Holly Near, and Bob Dylan.

Serge Denisoff. *Great Day Coming.* Urbana: University of Illinois Press, 1971. A pioneering discussion of the relationship between left-wing political and grassroots music.

Peter D. Goldsmith. *Making People's Music: Moe Asch and Folkways Records.* Washington, D.C.: Smithsonian Institution Press, 1998. A biography of Folkway's founder Asch, intertwined with his relationship with the record industry and the folk music scene of the 1940s through the middle 1980s.

Thomas Gruning. *Millennium Folk: American Folk Music Since the Sixties.* Athens: University of Georgia Press, 2006. Unlike most books on this topic, Gruning focuses on the last two decades of the twentieth century and foregrounds issues of gender, ethnicity, race, and authenticity.

Ronnie Lieberman. *My Song Is My Weapon.* Urbana: University of Illinois Press, 1989. A personalized view of the folk revivals and left-wing politics.

Jim Longhi. *Woody, Cisco, and Me: Seaman Three in the Merchant Marines.* Urbana: University of Illinois Press, 1998. A firsthand account of the author's experiences with Woody Guthrie and Cisco Houston during their service together during the early 1940s.

Shelly Romulis. *Pistol Packin' Mama: Aunt Molly Jackson and the Politics of Folksong.* Urbana: University of Illinois Press, 1998 An intriguing book about the role played by this Kentucky-based protest singer and her place in America's progressive political movement in the late 1930s into the 1950s.

Neil V. Rosenberg, ed. *Transforming Tradition: Folk Music Revivals Examined.* Urbana: University of Illinois Press, 1993. This book of essays, several of which are based on firsthand and very personal experience, concentrates on the folk revival since World War II.

Michael Scully. *The Never-Ending Revival: Rounder Records and the Folk Alliance.* Urbana: University of Illinois Press, 2008. Scully details how Boston-based Rounder Records and the umbrella organization known as the Folk Alliance helped shape the commodification of folk music, particularly the period from 1970 until the early 2000s.

William Roy. *Reds, Whites, and Blues: Social Movements, Folk Music, and Race in the United States*. Princeton, NJ: Princeton University Press, 2010. Sociologist Roy provides a different take on the folk revival and focuses on the period between 1930 and 1960.

Eric Von Schmidt and Jim Rooney. *"Baby Let Me Follow You Down": The Illustrated History of the Cambridge Folk Years*. New York: Anchor Books, 1977. This is an entertaining, insider's view of the folk revival in Boston.

SUGGESTED VIEWING

Don't Look Back. Acclaimed documentary filmmaker D. A. Pennebaker's black-and-white feature about Bob Dylan's controversial 1965 tour, which highlighted the schism between the folk and rock elements of popular music.

John Cohen. *Remembering The High Lonesome*. Davenport Films/Folkstreams.net. Not only a recollection of Cohen's film, *The High Lonesome Sound*, it is also a portrait of this longtime member of the New Lost City Ramblers.

Holy Modal Rounders. *Bound to Lose*. Carnivalesque. A documentary about the craziest "folk-inspired" group that has been together on and off since 1963.

New Lost City Ramblers. *Always Been A Rambler*. Arhoolie DVD 204. An hour-long documentary celebrating fifty years of this seminal group that includes lots of historical footage, interviews, and performances by artists ranging from Bela Fleck to the Carolina Chocolate Drops.

Steven Wade. *Catching the Music*. Greater Washington Educational Telecommunications Association, Inc./Folkstreams.net. This film, autered by Wade, explores how musicians as disparate Hobart Smith, Uncle Dave Macon, Virgil Anderson, and Wade himself united in their love of the music made on the five-string banjo,

Various. *Folk City 25th Anniversary Concert*. Rhino-VHS 1977. A celebration of Gerde's club in New York City, with Arlo Guthrie, Tom Paxton, Joan Baez, and others.

Various. *Musical Holdouts*. A fascinating view of traditional and regional folk-based music shot mostly in the early 1970s by John Cohen.

Chapter 11

THE FOLK ROOTS OF CONTEMPORARY POPULAR MUSIC

- Black Codes from the Underground
- Improvisation in Black Musical Culture
- Rhythm and Blues
- Rockabilly
- Early Rock 'n' Roll and Rock
- Motown and Soul
- Hip-Hop and Rap
- Country Music Today
- Final Thoughts

The majority of significant forms of American popular music that have emerged since World War II have strong roots in the recent past. Our focus in this chapter is on the swiftly changing, ephemeral popular music scene that spawned rockabilly, classic rock, hip-hop, and other related forms since the middle 1950s. Each of these genres owes an immense debt to traditional music, in particular the vernacular musical culture of black Americans. Although records by Frank Sinatra, Dinah Shore, or Tony Bennett have sold millions of copies since the 1940s, these very talented vocalists are more closely related to jazz—especially of the swing and "cool" eras—as well as displaying a fondness for such important American popular songcrafters as Cole Porter, the Gershwin brothers (George and Ira), and Jimmy Van Huesen. Songs from the musical theater since World War II, *South Pacific*, *Oklahoma*, *West Side Story*, or *A Chorus Line*, remain immensely popular and are established fare for community and professional theater groups throughout the United States. They, too, come from a similar music aesthetic that is far removed from rock and its close relatives. Disaffected white youths—the single most important group in promoting American popular culture—tend to look toward other individual (often black) rebels or musical outsiders such as Robert Johnson, Little Richard, Aretha Franklin, or Tupac Shakur for inspiration and change in their musical culture. It is the rock-based, black-influenced popular music of the past half century that we will address in this chapter.

BLACK CODES FROM THE UNDERGROUND

Popular black music, with its strong roots in traditional forms, the church, and in the streets, has witnessed the emergence and spread of rhythm and blues (R&B), Motown and soul, funk, and rap since the close of World War II. These styles materialized in periods of approximately ten years. **R&B**, for example, was an important form of music by the late 1940s with **Louis Jordan** and his Tympani Five leading the way. In the early 1960s Barry Gordy's Motown label brought artists such as the Temptations, the Marvelettes, and the Supremes (led by Diana Ross) into homes and dance halls across the United States and, ultimately, to many other parts of the world. Following in the footsteps of the civil rights movement, **Motown** became the first style of black popular music to fully cross over and be unconditionally accepted by American popular culture. Within ten years, funkmeisters Ohio Players, Parliament/Funkadelic, and Larry Graham were being heard on radios and record players across the United States. By the middle of the 1980s the hip-hop nation (most notably rap) emerged as an important, and sometimes controversial, element of black and white youth culture.

The early twenty-first century represents a new era in African American music. By way of records, tapes, compact discs, live performances, radio, television, Internet broadcasts,` and downloads dynamic black American music has influenced music across the world, most notably in Africa and Europe. During the late Reconstruction era jubilee religious singing groups visited countries as far away as South Africa and Australia; one hundred years later James Brown drew hundreds of thousands of almost worshipful listeners to his Ghana concerts. The popular "Highlife" sound of southern Africa that first developed during the 1930s remains highly charged with American jazz and was later informed by R&B. By the mid-1980s respected electric blues performer Johnny Copeland had recorded an album in Africa accompanied by native musicians, following the lead of jazz artists Ornette Coleman and Yusef Lateef, both of whom had previously explored North African/African American collaborations. The twentieth-century products of this African American creative spirit (blues, gospel, and jazz) doubtless rank among our most vital and important contributions to the musical world. Black American music lends clear voices to a culture that cherishes improvisation in its everyday life and whose spirit has deeply influenced musicians not only in our own country but across the entire globe, also.

Aside from the popular forms that have gained widespread exposure through the mass media, the diversity of vernacular music largely remains a series of black codes from the underground. People across the world are familiar with black popular music, especially since it began to cross over with R&B in the late 1940s. They consume the Motown "soul" music of the Four Tops and the Jackson Five that gained popularity in the early 1960s or (a generation later) rap sounds of Public Enemy, Ton-Loc, and Salt-N-Pepa. Far fewer people, however, listen to, or are even aware of, early-twentieth-century blues and gospel artists. Most of us remain blissfully ignorant of the roots of our own contemporary popular music. These folk singers—some of whom were discussed in previous chapters—have descended from a rich, varied legacy buried in the obscurity of everyday life or more often have been simply forgotten. Because their music is rarely studied in our secondary schools and colleges, and all but shunned from today's commercial marketplace, the names, lives, and music of most older black musicians largely remain unknown to the general public. Nonetheless, these musicians have made important contributions to our music history and have clearly shaped the popular music that we so voraciously consume and have made available to millions of interested consumers throughout the rest of the world.

IMPROVISATION IN BLACK MUSICAL CULTURE

More than most musicians, Afro-American folk performers are always trying to create their own sound or utilize vocal techniques or instrumental devices that facilitate this process. I recall many conversations over the past thirty years with blues and gospel musicians who told me they prided themselves on being able to mimic Blind Boy Fuller or Mahalia Jackson as well as their ability to communicate in their own voice. I found, for example, that black gospel quartet singers in Memphis enjoyed being able to sound like Ira Tucker of the Philadelphia-based Dixie Hummingbirds but they were even more interested in working on the vocal qualities that distinguished them from other singers.

Improvisation in black folk music is a valued skill and takes many forms. Instrumental and vocal improvisations represent the basic ways musicians seek individuality in a performance. Most black folk singers view their ability to replicate musical styles as a gift. Inherent aptitude is undeniably part of this process, but many folk musicians (black and white) also go through an apprenticeship with a master musician. This learning process is one aspect of folk music

THE FOLK ROOTS OF CONTEMPORARY POPULAR MUSIC

Houston Stackhouse at the 1970 Festival of American Folklife. Bill Pierce photo, courtesy of the Ralph Rinzler Folklife Archives and Collections, Center for Folklife and Cultural Heritage, Smithsonian Institution.

that bears closer scrutiny, but it clearly involves a long period if the younger musician is striving for mastery. The nuances of performance (vocal inflections interplaying between the voice and instrument, tuning of the instrument, even posturing and facial expressions) are part of learning music.

Showmanship or **clowning** is part of black folk performance practice, too. Older blues singers speak in awe of the tricks that musicians such as Charlie Patton and Tommy Johnson performed in the 1920s: playing the guitar while holding it above their head, behind their backs, or picking it with their teeth! I have seen the late South Carolina medicine show performer, Peg-Leg Sam, perform spellbinding visual tricks with his harmonica, a legacy of his years on the road.

Sacred musicians are not beyond pulling a trick or two. Gospel performers sometimes work a crowd by walking among them or by leaping onto church pews while singing with microphone in hand. The concept is simple—to communicate with the audience—and all of these practices are important in engaging the audience, grabbing their attention, keeping them focused on the performance, and drawing them into the event. It is a means of integration between audience and performer that African American performers have used since at least the days of "Jump Jim Crow."

James Brown, a more contemporary popular singer, uses some of these same performance techniques. Brown is certainly one of the most dynamic performers in twentieth-century music and one of our most influential live performers. His sliding dance steps and general athleticism might harken back to the "buzzard lope" of the mid-nineteenth-century minstrel stage but it also presages Michael Jackson's moon walk and the gymnastic moves of the later hip-hoppers. To see James Brown performing "Cold Sweat" or "Papa's Got a Brand New Bag" in the middle 1960s was like watching Muhammad Ali at the height of his abilities, when Ali's statement that he could "float like a butterfly and sting like a bee" sounded not only like poetry but also the truth. The emotional and highly charged performance practices might be shunned as mere antics by many audiences, but in front of an understanding black crowd they are quite acceptable, often anticipated and even expected. And you can take it as gospel that musicians or musical groups as diverse as Mick Jagger, the B-52s, KISS, and every Anglo-American adherent to hip-hop (from Vanilla Ice to Eminem) would not be as animated on stage had black American performers not shown them the way.

Clothing provides musicians with another chance to improvise and insinuate change. Fashion trends, in fact, are sometimes set by musicians. Since the late 1980s a **"B-Boy"** fashion sense, characterized by hi-top, multicolored, untied sneakers, sweat suits, bright hats, baggy britches, and long key chains swept across the nation from its hearth area in hard-core urban areas. These fashions now cut across racial and ethnic lines, informing other African Americans as well as Asian Americans and white folks in the heartland of North Dakota. What began as a community-based, folk expression perpetuated by younger urban black males was soon adopted (and adapted) by popular culture trendsetters and quickly transported throughout the United States. The widespread dissemination of hip-hop music (most notably rap) followed a similar pattern, helping to reinforce a "homeboy" attitude.

The voice itself is quite a versatile tool and black singers often use a variety of techniques, such as growls and slurs, to create an original sound. Mississippi blues singers like Howlin' Wolf or Robert Johnson often employed a falsetto and a vocal leap of an octave for dramatic effect. Wolf preferred an eerily cast guttural howl (hence his name), while Johnson's thinner wordless moans have influenced a new generation of singers as the repackaging of his 1937 and 1938 recordings have sold over a million copies! Bobby McFerrin, who emerged as a solo and jazz singer in the early 1980s, calls upon an arsenal of similar vocal effects that reflects his African American heritage. Improvisation forms the core of McFerrin's performances (when he's not conducting) and he freely draws upon "false" voices (falsetto and bass ranges), whoops, vocal trills, and other techniques in his performances. Looking back to the Reconstruction era (if not earlier), another essentially solo artist, the lone worker in the field, sang freely improvised arhoolies. These singers frequently utilized not only free meter but

THE FOLK ROOTS OF CONTEMPORARY POPULAR MUSIC

MUSICAL EXAMPLE

Sonny Terry was born just after the turn of the century in the Piedmont of North Carolina. Totally blind since childhood, Terry earned his livelihood by way of music. The harmonica was his chosen instrument and he became a virtuoso instrumentalist by the time that he was in his twenties. His early repertoire included country dance tunes, religious songs, and blues. Terry also learned to play many of the standard novelty pieces, such as "Lost John" and "Fox Chase." This exceptional train imitation was recorded in the middle 1950s.

Title "Locomotive Blues"
Performer Sonny Terry
Instruments harmonica and voice
Length 3:22

Musical Characteristics
1. Terry cleverly mixes his instrument and vocal effects into a seamless whole.
2. There are numerous changes in tempo that reflect the story line.
3. Note the many effects—slurring, whooping, etc.—that Terry obtains from his small instrument.
4. The performance mixes singing with speech.

Spoken: Well ladies and gentlemen, this that old local train leaving out from Washington, D.C., heading south. The old fireman got up and rung his bell; he rung it like this, you know. Woosh!

Well, you know that old fireman sat down and the old engineer got on up and blowed his whistle, blowed so lonesome; sorta like this.
Then the old engineer sat down, said "Oh, well, leaving here." Just reached down and grabbed the starter, pulled it off and started off easy; like this.

They got way on down the curve ... When that old fireman rung the bell, something like this again. Ssshh!

And then old fireman sat down and the engineer said "Blow your whistle 'cause we're going a little fast here. Maybe a cow be on the rail and we can slow up on it." Blow his whistle lonesome, you know.

> They got on down, pulling that little grade, you know, the train got to slowing down, got to doing like this.
> Got over that grade, balling the jack, way on down the road. Getting on close down towards Richmond, Virginia.
> He's blowing for Richmond, Virginia, now.
> Pulling up in the yard now, fixing to stop. Woosh!

Smithsonian Folkways 32035.

---

also vocal techniques such as octave-based yodels and half-tone slides or slurs to regain the proper pitch.

Gospel quartet singers like Wilmer Broadnax ("Little Axe") of the Spirit of Memphis or Claude Jeter of the Sawn Silvertones are highly regarded for their battery of vocal tricks. In fact, the church has been the training ground for many secular singers. Sam Cooke, Aretha Franklin, "Little Johnny" Taylor, Dinah Washington, Lou Rawls, and Dionne Warwick are just six of the scores of performers who came up through the gospel ranks to reach stardom in the 1960s or later. And the church—often Baptist but sometimes Pentecostal—is where many of them learned to reiterate words or phrases for dramatic effect ("Lord, Lord, Lord"), toss out words or phrases in a call and response with their audience ("Let me hear an Amen!"), or employ a wordless moan for emotional emphasis. In one guise or another, most live performances of black popular music in the new millennium contain many of these same elements that help to underscore the symbiotic—and to some degree, seamless—relationship between the secular and sacred in African American musical culture.

The career and musical contributions of the Golden Gate Quartet illustrate this process: the mix of the secular and sacred as well as the crossover from a mostly black to a racially mixed audience. It is also important to understand that this gospel group made such a transition about twenty-five years before Barry Gordy found a wider mainstream audience for his Motown artists beginning in the early 1960s. While their career was briefly discussed in chapter 6, it is worth reemphasizing three critical points. First, they integrated secular with sacred material in their performances as early as 1937. Second, Willie Johnson's innovative approach to vocalizing combined singing with speaking, just as do many hip-hop artists. Third, their music found a wide audience not only among churchgoers but also among fans of popular music, and they easily crossed over from a black world to reach the ears of white listeners by way of their recordings and nationwide radio broadcasts. The Gates, as they were known to their fans, inspired an entire generation of quartets, including the Dixie Hummingbirds, Pilgrim Travelers, and the CBS Trumpeteers.

THE FOLK ROOTS OF CONTEMPORARY POPULAR MUSIC

The CBS Trumpeteers were one of the most popular gospel quartets in the early 1950s. Courtesy of Kip Lornell.

To capture a more distinctive sound black folk performers sometimes imitate sounds heard in nature or in the real world. The Golden Gate Quartet, for instance, rose to national prominence in the late 1930s partly on the strength of their uncanny train imitation, "Gospel Train," an early, striking example of the jubilee quartet sound. Daniel Womack, a musician from rural Virginia, highly prized his vocal ability to imitate animals ranging from birds to dogs. In both black and white tradition the harmonica is used to imitate a fox chase or a train chugging down the track. Fiddlers (mostly white) have been heard to simulate birds on "Listen to the Mockingbird," which remains a standard tune at fiddle contests, and many rural guitarists, such as Delta blues artist Bukka White or West Virginian Frank Hutchison, used a slide or bottleneck to simulate the sound of a freight train speeding down the track.

On a recording such as "Rock Lobster" by the B-52s, the female vocalists Cindy Wilson and Kate Pierson pay unconscious hommage to musicians like Daniel Womack with their wacky imitations of birds, fish, and other animals. These rockers from Athens, Georgia, also owe a small debt of gratitude to funksters such as George Clinton for their onstage garb as well as their retro hairstyles and advanced fashion sense, in particular. In "Love Shack" the B-52s look at a funky backwoods music and pleasure establishment, which is their own late-twentieth-century equivalent to the African American juke joint that could be found throughout the South into the 1950s. Such varied influences might not always be consciously acknowledged, but the fact that the B-52s are a pop group from the South with a strong sense of twentieth-century American popular musical styles underscores the sense that these musical/cultural connections might not be directly understood but their existence is undeniable.

Lyrical improvisation is another way in which black musicians make their own songs. This is most often accomplished through the use of oral formulas involving the substitution of phrases or words to create a new work. It is often found in strophic forms of black folk music: blues, work songs, and spirituals that utilize a verse-and-refrain format. Formulas can help to extend the length of a song. The camp meeting song, which probably began life as a spiritual, "Our Meeting Is Over," extends its length as well as its emotional meaning through simple word substitution:

Father, now our meeting is over, father we must part.
If I never see you anymore, I have loved you from the start.
Mother, now our meeting is over, mother we must part.
If I never see you anymore, I have loved you from the start.
Brother, now our meeting is over, brother we must part.
If I never see you anymore, I have loved you from the start.

Blues singers often make even greater use of more complex oral formulas based on the memorization of specific lines, verses, and songs. More importantly, this memorization helps the singer to perform verses that appear to be created spontaneously but are largely built upon patterns. Using this format as a building block, blues singers can sustain long, intricate performances. Some blues musicians are more inventive than others, of course, and make better and more extensive use of these oral building blocks. Others rarely vary their performances from one instance to another, almost as though a song is complete—a finished product—once it is composed and sung. Most singers rely upon these formulas to some degree, jauntily creating a new image by substitutes: "My jet black gal won't give me but one thin dime" becomes "That women of mine keeps all my spending change." By the same token "House lady, house lady, what in the world is wrong with you?" uses a few key substitutions to become "Good gal, good gal, how come you do me like you do?"

Scholars have observed that the blues is an example of improvisation in everyday life; blues singers like Sleepy John Estes, Robert Pete Williams, and Big Joe Williams are among the most interesting and powerful poets in the field. Their language was both colorful and inventive and they draw upon their own experiences. In this regard they followed the advice given to many budding authors of fiction: write (or, in this case, sing) what you know about! The peripatetic Big Joe Williams often utilized the theme of wanderlust and physical movement in his songs. In the case of a blues singer like Estes, the best of his compositions from the late 1930s dealt with people, incidents, and places in or near his hometown of Brownsville, Tennessee, in songs such as "Floating Bridge," "Railroad Police Blues," or "Brownsville Blues."

The images found in blues by these artists are often both powerful and arresting. A longtime resident of Angola Prison in Louisiana, Robert Pete Williams often mused about his life and its relationship with the penal system. In thinking about how his life had been changed by the system, Williams (seemingly) tossed off the telling line "I've grown so ugly, I don't even know myself" in one of his songs. Blues lyrics sometimes transcend the everyday world into the surreal. The stanza from a blues song by Bo-Weevil Jackson (also known as William Harris): *"Heard a mighty rumbling deep down in the ground" (repeat) / "Was the boll-weevil and the Devil stealing somebody's brown"* suggests an unlikely and unearthly relationship between a pesky insect that wrought destruction upon cotton plants in the South during the decade of the 1910s and Satan. This is quite a concept, one that not only expands but also radically transcends the usual themes found in rural down-home blues.

Visual and physical showmanship, an array of vocal techniques, and lyrical improvisation practiced by many black American performers contrast with the general aesthetics of Anglo-American musical culture. Grassroots black performers strive first to learn or even master the idiom, of course, but the next step is to make it their own, to place a unique imprimatur or stamp onto it. This is where the creative aspects of black culture come into greatest relief. These creative aspects of African American folk culture have most fully informed both black and white popular music since Reconstruction but especially over the last four decades of the twentieth century.

RHYTHM AND BLUES

African American popular music in the postmodern era has not escaped it roots. Nor has it tried to here in the twenty-first century. The "new negro" of the 1950s was striving to affect changes through social, economic, and cultural advances, which come under the category of progress through the civil rights movement. However, the historical facts of slavery, disenfranchisement, and segregation proved to be a powerful legacy, serving to remind black and white Americans of a racist past. Similarly, the folk roots of black music have been confirmed time and again, appearing and reappearing in various guises, into the present day.

THE FOLK ROOTS OF CONTEMPORARY POPULAR MUSIC

Rhythm and blues, a term coined in 1949, emerged as the first "new" black popular music following the close of World War II. Like so many forms of modern popular music, R&B grew out of jazz (most directly swing and be-bop) and the blues. The down-home blues had for many years been moving to the urban North as blacks spearheaded the Great Migration. Unlike rural blues, R&B is not the province of a solo artist, but is performed by a small ensemble. It first gained national prominence in New York City and Los Angeles. R&B owes a strong debt to swing bands, piano boogie woogie, and the Louis Jordan style of "jump bands." Saxophones and, to a lesser degree, trumpets became an important voice—more prominently as a soloist—in these ensembles. These ensembles also often utilized guitars and, as electric guitars became more commonplace in the early 1950s, they took a more prominent role as a solo voice. The use of a full rhythm section of piano, bass, and drums also helped to promote the popularity of this music. All of these musical factors, as well as the country's social climate, helped to set the scene for early rock 'n' roll. R&B from the late 1940s quite frequently used the blues form and a simple duple meter or a quadruple meter.

The traditional heritage of R&B is perhaps most evident in the vocals. "Shouters" like Roy Milton, Big Mama Thorton, Joe Liggins, Ruth Brown, and Amos Milburn used some of the moans and guttural vocal techniques of the earlier powerfully rich rural blues singers and gospel stylists. Many R&B performers also engaged in the call-and-response patterns so commonly found in black folk music. Sometimes it was a vocal chorus responding to the lead singer; in other instances the saxophone section engaged in a dialogue with the vocalists. Either way, the effect remained the same—a dialogue among the participants of the performance.

In this regard, an R&B show from the early 1950s would have reminded one of a down-home Baptist church service with its interaction among the ensembles on stage and the audience helping to blur the established lines that usually demarcate the two components of the performance. The ongoing (and expected) antiphony that characterized live performances of this music underscores the familiarity of the participants with its well-established conventions and rules. It is significant that R&B flourished during segregation when black participants knew what to expect and how to interact, which also established some of the ground rules or expectations for the adoring audiences who came to worship at the feet of Elvis Presley later in the 1950s.

By the middle 1950s R&B vocal groups like the Platters, Drifters, Larks, Nutmegs, Orioles, and Coasters, which owed a great deal to their sacred counterparts, began gaining national attention. These vocal ensembles adopted song forms other than twelve-bar blues, using eight- and sixteen-bar songs that reflect the influence of gospel and even Tin Pan Alley composers. Such ensembles soon spawned a host of white groups, many of them from greater New York City and Philadelphia, that emulated their vocal styles, stage mannerisms, and repertoire. By the late 1950s groups such as the Capris, Danny and the Juniors, and Dion and the Belmonts had become better known than their black counterparts.

Within a few years these vocal ensembles were joined by solo male singers such as Brook Benton and Jackie Wilson, many of whom began their careers with vocal harmony groups or in church singing groups. R&B gradually blended with other forms of black popular music. By the middle 1960s the style that Ray Charles, Sam Cooke, and Aretha Franklin represented so well in the late 1950s and early 1960s became known as **soul**.

The popular R&B of the early 1950s had a profound influence on early rock 'n' roll as it evolved a few years later. The earliest R&B practitioners mainly appealed to the black community but by 1953 it was slowly gaining a younger, white audience who were discovering (sometimes via the radio, occasionally through records) Piano Red, Amos Milburn, Big Mama Thorton, Buddy Johnson, Big Joe Turner, and other performers who were already well known in the black community. **Little Richard**, an outrageous performer whose piano antics, forceful shouting, and commanding stage presence won him a large multiracial audience, enthralled and captured their imaginations. Not only was Little Richard moving salaciously on stage—shaking his entire body, jumping on top of the piano, playing the keyboard while sitting on the ground—but he also wore makeup! Little Richard was exactly the kind of African American blues performer that caused parents a great deal of worry and anxiety. But teenagers like Jerry Lee Lewis and Elvis Presley appreciated not only his music but also his unpredictable and rebellious spirit. These are the very performance practices that can be traced back to such disparate earlier sources as rural down-home blues singers, minstrel shows, and Pentecostal churches.

ROCKABILLY

Rockabilly, a dynamic biracial musical hybrid, began in **Memphis** with **Sam Phillips** and **Elvis Presley** as its primary entrepreneurial and musical progenitors. While recording musicians for out-of-town companies (mostly the Chess Brothers in Chicago and the Bahari Brothers in Los Angeles), Phillips decided to strike out on his own. He launched **Sun Records** in 1951 with a roster of artists from Memphis or the mid-South: "Dr." (Isaiah) Ross ("The Harmonica Boss"), Rufus Thomas, the Ripley Cotton Choppers, and Hot Shot Love. His roster included many black musicians because Phillips not only understood there was a void in the marketplace but he had also been recording blues and gospel artists as an independent producer. The fact that he loved their fierce, hot, energetic music was of great importance because his quest was driven not only by a commercial but also by a personal interest. A southern upbringing also helped Phillips to understand that he needed a white interpreter of African American music to sell lots and lots of records—a goal he could reach only by breaking free from the straightjacket of race. But who could span this gulf, which in the South in the early 1950s must have seemed immense?

Elvis Presley literally walked into his studio in July 1954, and although he was raw, Presley possessed all of the fundamental musical ingredients for which Phillips was searching. Growing up in Tupelo, Mississippi, and then migrating to Memphis before he was a teenager, Presley admired hillbilly music, particularly the talents of Roy Acuff, Ernest Tubb, and Hank Williams. His family was also immersed in the emotionally expressive Pentecostal Assembly of God. Presley and his backup duo had infused these influences with a 4/4 shuffle beat and the syncopated feeling of race music. Phillips quickly understood the importance of these facts as soon as he heard Presley dig into his version of Arthur "Big Boy" Crudup's "That's Alright, Mama," which had been a hit among African Americans several years beforehand.

Despite the fact that he was white and living in an overtly racist society, the spirit of black music was at Presley's core: a slightly accented backbeat, the vocal shading and slides, an energetic defiance, extensive use of the twelve-bar blues form, guitar licks that echoed B. B. King and Lonnie Johnson, and the repertoire. Like his friends, Presley had been exposed to blues through phonograph records and, more importantly, by what he heard over the black-orientated WDIA. The young Presley was also a regular listener to a radio show on WHBQ, which featured one of the first "shock jocks." Dewey Phillips (no relation to Sam) and his "Red, Hot, and Blue" program were wildly unpredictable and very popular; his show was characterized by zany antics and the fact that he would play records by black artists.

The music that Presley performed wasn't quite country and it wasn't really "black." Sam Phillips was struck by this synthesis, but who would consume this music? Radio was still basically segregated and most record companies continued to maintain separate race and country series. Still, there had to be a marketplace for this music somewhere. Figuring that somebody would purchase this music, Phillips released Presley's initial effort as Sun 209, "That's All Right," and "Blue Moon of Kentucky" (a Bill Monroe number) by "Elvis Presley—Scotty and Bill." The other musicians referred to were Scotty Moore (guitar) and Bill Black (bass) who made up the rest of Presley's spare trio. The revolution began quietly in Memphis in 1954 but by 1956 Elvis (along with early rock 'n' roll) was everywhere!

THE FOLK ROOTS OF CONTEMPORARY POPULAR MUSIC

Jerry Lee Lewis Sun label. Courtesy of Kip Lornell.

Rockabilly is, and remains, aggressive and uncomplicated. Classic rockabilly is performed by a small ensemble (usually a trio or quartet) using an insistent duple meter to accompany an often frenzied vocal. The structure of rockabilly is most often built upon the blues form, propelled by an upright string bass at a moderate to fast tempo. Nearly all of its pioneers came from a rural, southern background. The entire sound is frequently characterized by an echo created in the studio and through the use of inexpensive amplifiers. In some respects rockabilly complements the sound achieved by Chicago blues artists such as Muddy Waters and Howlin' Wolf.

Rockabilly's secular black folk roots are augmented by a strong dose of religion. Presley openly admired African American gospel singers and sometimes went to hear the Spirit of Memphis quartet perform in local churches in the middle 1950s. His vocal techniques, especially the strained growls, would seem to come from equal doses of church and state.

Within a year of Presley's initial release, Memphis (and the Sun Studio in particular) became a mecca for aspiring rockabilly and other artists whose music was on the edge of commercial viability. They came from throughout the mid-South and were as steeped in black music as their hero. Billy Lee Riley drove across the Mississippi River from northern Arkansas, while Carl Perkins dropped down almost due south one hundred miles from Tipton, Tennessee. They were soon followed by Jerry Lee Lewis of Ferriday, Louisiana, who helped to popularize the boogie woogie and honky-tonk style of piano. Lewis picked up his wild piano style from listening to local blacks and from his experiences in the Pentecostal church. From Memphis itself Johnny Burnette, his brother Dorsey, and Paul Burlison stepped forward to form the Rock 'n' Roll Trio. Their classic 1956 recordings for the New York City–based Coral label mark the diffusion of this music from its birthplace to a distribution network outside of the mid-South.

These early rockabilly artists were wild-acting, often eccentric, characters. They not only sang and played like black men, but they sometimes adopted the Afro-American aesthetic of clowning. Like their black counterparts in contemporary rhythm and blues, singers such as Roy Brown and Wynonie Harris, they put on a good show. Jerry Lee Lewis, for example, played the piano with his feet. Red suits, a red Cadillac, and matching dyed red hair became Sonny Burgess's trademark. Billy Lee Riley and His Little Green Men were famous for "Flyin' Saucer Rock & Roll," a rockabilly song about Mars and music. These young men liked to take chances and Sam Phillips gave them the room to create. Fast cars and alcohol were two facts of life for most of the rockabilly pioneers. They also liked bawdy songs by black artists. In addition to Presley's borrowings, the early covers by white artists included Malcolm Yelvington and the Star Rhythm Boys' "Drinkin' Wine Spodee-O-Dee" (Sun 211) and several other songs inspired by Roy Brown's "Good Rockin' Tonight."

Inevitably, the message, spirit, and influence of rockabilly spread beyond the mid-South. By 1955 Gene Vincent, Wanda Jackson, and Eddie Cochran were boppin' in the Midwest and on the West Coast. The music slowly became safer and more generic as Buddy Holly, Ricky Nelson, and the Everly Brothers instilled pop sensibility into their music and lifestyle. Rockabilly became more smooth, less raw, and gained acceptance across the country. By 1960 it had been virtually subsumed by more mainstream rock 'n' roll. Despite this subsumation, rockabilly remains a subset of rock and popular music, one that undergoes occasional revivals. Most recently rockabilly has been rediscovered by punk rockers in the late 1970s and, to a lesser degree, by the neoswing devotees of the late 1990s.

EARLY ROCK 'N' ROLL AND ROCK

Ten months after Elvis Presley first stepped into the Sun studio, *Billboard* certified "Rock Around the Clock" as a hit. Bill Haley and the Comets (earlier known as the Saddle Men, in deference to their background in country music) appealed mostly to white teenagers, providing an alternative to the even more rebellious image of rockabilly. Both genres shared many of the same musical characteristics: heavily accented backbeats on the second and fourth beat, a solo lead singer who was occasionally joined by a vocal chorus, the vocal alternating with an instrumental chorus, and the extensive use of electric guitar as a lead instrument. Unlike in rockabilly, it was not uncommon for rock 'n' roll musicians to employ a small horn section, usually featuring an alto or tenor saxophone.

Even Elvis Presley was moving toward rock 'n' roll as a safer alternative to rockabilly or, one might argue, as the next evolutionary step. Late in 1955 he became an RCA Victor artist and within a year was reaching an increasingly large and interracial audience. Records such as "Hound Dog," "Don't Be Cruel," and "Jailhouse Rock" sold well and he was emerging as a megastar. Once again at the heart of his music was the blues in a rapidly paced, energetic style. Presley was selling records to black, white, and Hispanic audiences in every corner of the United States within two years of singing with this major label.

This crossover appeal helped to open the door for Little Richard and Chuck Berry. Their style of highly charged rock 'n' roll with lyrics aimed at a teenage audience brought them to the attention of white listeners. Even New Orleans's **Fats Domino** was able to sell his souped-up rhythm and blues to a white audience. **New Orleans** R&B proved to be particularly appealing to white audiences toward the close of legal segregation. This music usually employed the same instruments as rock 'n' roll, but it was saturated with polyrhythms derived from its Afro-Caribbean background. Electric guitars were less prominent and the music was often played at a more leisurely tempo. New Orleans R&B had plenty of energy, but it lacked rockabilly's frenetic edge.

Domino was a leading exponent of this music and led the way to commercial success with hits such as "Blueberry Hill" and "I'm Walking (to New Orleans)." He was joined by lesser-known New Orleans–based artists such as Lloyd Price and Huey "Piano" Smith. They were best known in the African American community but each of them enjoyed a bit of success in rock 'n' roll circles. Price, for example, is perhaps best known for his version of "Stagger Lee," while Smith is usually identified with the "Rockin' Pneumonia and Boogie Woogie Flu." It is worth noting that Price's hit can be traced back to a song from the 1890s, and the theme of Smith's song (illness) was used by earlier black artists such as Blind Willie Johnson and Memphis Minnie.

There was a cultural backlash and parental outcry (mostly among white parents) against rock 'n' roll, which was disparaged as antimusic, destructive, antisocial, and crude. It was further argued that rock 'n' roll championed promiscuity, juvenile delinquence, a rebellious nature, and racial unrest. A film such as *Black Board Jungle*, which featured "Rock Around the Clock," became one of the pioneering cinematic promoters of rock 'n' roll.

The infusion of African American musical culture into white music not only underlined the entire debate, it was a core (though often unspoken and implied) issue. Atlantic Records was at the vanguard of this movement; it was one of the important commercial forces in selling black American culture to white youths beginning with its jazz series in the late 1940s and then through its popular R&B recordings of the early to middle 1950s. Such small, independent companies as DeLuxe and King helped to promote similar musical tastes

THE FOLK ROOTS OF CONTEMPORARY POPULAR MUSIC

among black and white youths, who bought many of the same records and who wanted to attend integrated concerts! These social changes proved to be very problematic for a legally segregated society and helped to promote a social climate that made the civil rights movement possible.

Fortunately for America's parents and our cultural stability, the impact of rock 'n' roll diminished within a few years. Just as the folk revival was gaining steam in the late 1950s, rock 'n' roll began taking a more innocuous stance. Electric guitars, emotional vocals, energy, and the defiance characterized by rockabilly in particular was slowly giving way to slicker musicians. The blues and its musical compatriots were moving aside (at least temporarily) to accommodate the Tin Pan Alley school of songwriting. Bobby Darrin, Paul Anka, and Pat Boone made romantic love hip again, once again looking back toward the era of the quintessential bobby-soxer, Frank Sinatra. Meanwhile, the Crew-Cuts' and other white doo-wop groups' sentimentalized and overproduced versions of the black vocal group style sold in large numbers. They were followed in short order by the California surf music of the Beach Boys, Jan and Dean, the Ventures, and others. By the early 1960s rock 'n' roll had ceased to be a viable vehicle for rebellious expression.

This is not to say that the white popular music—mostly rock—moved entirely away from these blues-orientated roots. At the height of the interest in fun in the California sun, late in 1963, the British "invaded" our shores. The invasion was led by the Beatles, who led the way for the Rolling Stones, the Who, Cream, and others. By 1965 it was chic to be an English popular musician and the cliché is that record companies were signing anyone with a British accent.

Ironically, these British artists helped to reintroduce blues back into American popular music. Assisted by the folk revival, which clearly recognized the importance of blues, the blues-influenced British rockers infused our airwaves and their own long-play records with their versions of songs by Howlin' Wolf, Sonny Boy Williamson, Slim Harpo, Robert Johnson, and many others. These blues-inspired recordings, along with groups like the Big Brother and the Holding Company, Grateful Dead, the Jefferson Airplane, and the Lovin' Spoonful, which had strong roots in the folk revival, reinstilled the blues form and repertoire into rock music. At the 1965 Newport Folk Festival the Chicago-based (and racially integrated) Paul Butterfield Blues Band conspired with Bob Dylan to go electric and quickly became an important force in the blues revival.

Even such acid-inspired groups as Country Joe and the Fish, the Jimi Hendrix Experience, and the Thirteenth Floor Elevator included extended "blues jams" as part of their live performances. It was not unusual for a venue as hip as the Fillmore West to have a double bill with, for example, the Quicksilver Messenger Service and the Muddy Waters Blues Band. So, the rock music of the mid- to late 1960s had come to embrace not only the blues form but also to publicly acknowledge their tremendous influence on their music both in interviews and on stage.

Though its influence has ebbed and flowed, the impact of blues on rock music remains to the present day. Create this scene in the mind's eye and ear: It is a hot sultry night with beer flowing and sweaty bodies (men and women) pumping and grinding as they dance together while mosquitoes seem to emulate their two-legged counterparts. The guitarist retunes his guitar to an open chord, slips a metal slide on the small finger of his left hand, and launches into a strident, repetitive figure high on the neck of his old blond stratocaster. The rhythm guitarist echoes the walkin' boogie line of the bass guitar and the drummer sets up a quick shuffle beat. The singer's wavering, grave, though high-pitched, voice begins a song about the Highway 61 that parallels the Mississippi River down through the Delta, familial violence, and the power of the Lord. The sonic qualities of this particular performance, especially the sound of the instruments blending and blurring together into a single voice, reminded me of the Bihari Brothers' powerful live recordings of Elmore James in a Canton, Mississippi, juke joint in 1953, which were issued on their Flair label and are now considered classic sides.

But this was not an African American blues band entertaining patrons in some backwater club. The performer was pop music icon Bob Dylan (on tour with Paul Simon in July 1999) once more revisiting his own roots. His set also included some folk/rock material, such as "Its All Over Baby Blues," accompanied by pedal steel guitar and an all-acoustical version of "Like a Rolling Stone." He and Simon performed three songs together—one Dylan tune and Simon's "Sounds of Silence"—but the only song that worked well was an ebullient "That'll Be the Day." Ironically, this was another look back to the late 1950s when Buddy Holly was the king of pop-a-billy and both Dylan and Simon were cutting their teeth on folk-based and popular music.

Major popular music stars are not the only ones who look toward their roots. Many punk rockers, for instance, maintain some of the defiant, snarling, and intense stage posturings of a blues musician like Howlin' Wolf, or Bob Dylan for that matter. Aerosmith played many blues-based songs but made a great impact with their cover of Bull Moose Jackson's salacious "Big Ten Inch," which had initially tittilated black audiences in the early 1950s. In the early 2000s, blues (and soul) rockers Robert Cray and Kenny Wayne Shepard caught the ear of young white audiences. Simultaneously, the "swing revival" that peaked in 1999 is less a rebirth of swing artists Benny Goodman or Tommy Dorsey than a rekindling of interest in the R&B of Louis Jordan and Big Joe Turner by groups such as Big Voodoo Daddy, Swing Six, or Brian Setzer's Orchestra. As we have seen so often in this chapter, what goes around, comes around or, to state this aphorism another way, what's old becomes new again . . . if you live long enough.

THE FOLK ROOTS OF CONTEMPORARY POPULAR MUSIC

MOTOWN AND SOUL

Soul emerged as the next wave of urban popular black music, and Motown Records in Detroit served as its northern headquarters. Founded in 1960 by Barry Gordy, Jr., Motown (and its allied Tamala label) preceded the soul revolution by several years. However, by the end of the decade Motown had grown into one of the largest corporations owned and operated by blacks in the United States as well as a powerful force in popular music. Mary Wells, Diana Ross and the Supremes, the Four Tops, Stevie Wonder, and the Jackson Five were among its top acts. Motown specialized in pop/soul and their music emphasized sophisticated, sometimes innovative, string arrangements played by studio orchestras. Motown records tended to have strong appeal throughout the black community with crossover appeal to a white audience, too. In fact, it used the color-blind slogan "the sound of young America" in an effort to reach white listeners. Their attempt largely succeeded.

Elsewhere, especially in the Stax studio in Memphis and Atlantic Record's Muscle Shoals, Alabama, studio, a different brand of soul music was being documented. This was the "deep" southern soul of Betty Wright, O. V. Wright, Wilson Pickett, Aretha Franklin, and **Otis Redding**, which was much closer to its black musical heritage than its Detroit counterpart. With more direct links to blues and gospel, southern soul tugged at the heart and emotions of its listeners. These often occurred in "soul ballads," slow tempo songs with heart-wrenching lyrics about the problems between men and women.

Otis Redding stepped forth as the quintessence of male southern soul singing. Following a career that included stints as a vocalist with various R&B bands, a frustrating career singing imitations of Little Richard, and washing cars, Redding hit it big in 1962. Like Elvis Presley nearly ten years before him, he got his break in a Memphis recording studio. But Redding was in the Stax studio, his second home until an airplane crash took his life on December 10, 1967. During this five-year period Redding recorded hit after hit in the soul idiom. Several of his recordings, "Respect," "Try a Little Tenderness," "Sitting on the Dock of the Bay," and "I've Been Loving You Too Long," became identified with Redding. Interestingly, others originated from some unlikely sources: the Rolling Stones' "Satisfaction" and Bing Crosby's "Try a Little Tenderness."

Redding's singing is instantly recognizable, unmistakable, and springs directly from his southern black ancestry. All soul singers owe debts to blues singers like Bessie Smith, Peetie Wheatstraw, and B. B. King, but Otis Redding was particularly close to the gospel tradition. Like the great gospel soloists, he had great control over the dynamics in his voice and enjoyed playing with subtle rhythmic shifts to vary his message. Redding had also mastered other techniques—mellismas, rasping, chanted interpolations—heard every Sunday in

African American churches and familiar to black Americans across the United States.

As mainstream popular black music, soul lasted about eight years longer than Otis Redding. Other Stax artists such as Sam and Dave and Carla Thomas had major hits on both the soul (black) and pop (white) *Billboard* charts. Curtis Mayfield, who was involved in the gospel and civil rights movement, emerged as one of the important socially aware black music voices during the late 1960s. In the early 1970s the Gamble and Huff soft-soul sound of the O'Jays, Spinners, and Herald Melvin and the Blue Notes shifted the focus to Philadelphia but by mid-decade funk and disco had supplanted soul music as the predominate form of black pop.

HIP-HOP AND RAP

Hip-hop refers to contemporary black music and culture. It emerged from the urban, black, and largely male-dominated culture—from the streets of New York, Detroit, and Los Angeles. Hip-hop began as a purely "black thing" and remained that way for several years before the mass media and mainstream white culture discovered it. Rap, the most tangible product of hip-hop, caught most people's attention and caused the greatest controversy.

Rap music itself results from the hybridization of folk and popular trends. It materialized nationwide in the early 1980s and has made extensive use of the technological aspects (twelve-inch singles, scratching, electronic sounds, and dance remixes) that place it solidly within the popular realm. The funk style gained popularity in the early and middle 1970s, but rap slowly moved in to supplant soul as the next major force in black popular music.

This music was first heard in black clubs and discotheques in New York City in the middle 1970s when DJs began talking and chanting over highly syncopated instrumental tracks by Funkadelic, Chic, Parliament, and other funk artists. Think of a song like "One Nation Under a Groove" by Funkadelic or George Clinton's "Do Fries Go with That Shake" and you have quintessential cosmic funk as it was heard across the country in the middle 1970s. Its most immediate musical precedent, however, is the "toasting" style pioneered by Jamaican disc jockeys in the 1960s who recited simple rhymes, political poems, and plain doggerel over a prerecorded track. American blacks were exposed to toasting in the Caribbean clubs of Brooklyn and the South Bronx. By the late 1970s the Sugar Hill Gang, Grandmaster Flash and the Furious Five, and Soul Sonic Force were selling their ten-inch "dance mix" singles in black and gay clubs throughout New York City. Within a few years major record companies had stepped in and even white pop artists such as Blondie got into the act.

THE FOLK ROOTS OF CONTEMPORARY POPULAR MUSIC

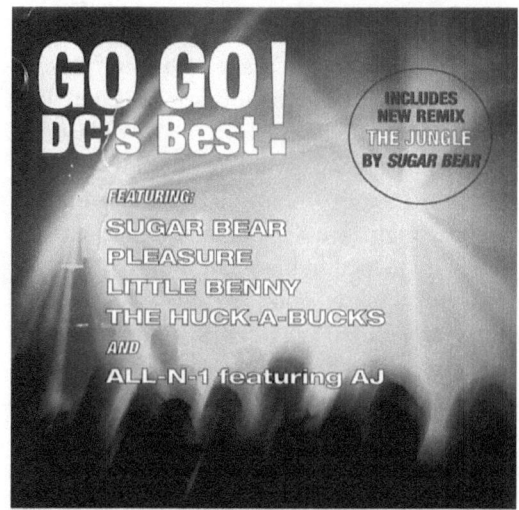

Go-Go record promotional flyer. Courtesy of Kip Lornell.

Rap quickly moved into America's cultural mainstream. Break dancing became popular among black and white kids throughout the United States. The year 1984 saw the release of two films, *Breakdance* and *Beat Street*, evolving around this urban musical culture.

Local permutations, such as **go-go**, a mixture of funk and rap, remain popular in Washington, D.C. Go-go artists like Chuck Brown, Trouble Funk, Little Benny, The Huck-A-Bucks, and Experience Unlimited engage their audience in antiphonal style, much like a Pentecostal church service: "Do you want to get down?" "Let's get down, let's get down!"

Part of the controversy regarding rap revolves around the political and sexual nature of the lyrics, which are often seen as volatile, lewd, and misogynistic. These are traits that tie rap directly to black folk culture. Black protest songs are a long-standing part of black oral tradition that goes back to the time of slavery and continues into the work songs of the twentieth century. They tend to be sung or spoken rather than written about within the black community. Rap is simply the latest voice of protest that has been heard in Mississippi fields and the streets of Harlem for over two hundred years. The obscene lyrics are another part of black tradition that can be heard on blues records from the 1920s and in the toasts that most black males know. The same bragging and proud aesthetic of playing **the dozens**, an insult game heard throughout black America, though predominately among the young, has been transferred to rap.

Rap's preoccupation with strongly syncopated accents and body percussion also has a strong, long-standing link to folk culture. Throughout the nineteenth and twentieth centuries most styles of black music held rhythmic interest in high esteem. Earlier manifestations include the fife and drum bands, washboards that are used to accompany blues singers and in zydeco bands, and the jaw bones that provided an accompaniment to black accordion players. Body percussion is tied to this aesthetic and is still seen today in children who play a game of hambone, during which they use both hands to slap their body in a pronounced, sometimes syncopated, duple meter and recite short rhymes. A standard opening line is "Hambone, hambone, where you been? Around the world and back again." This verbal format also emphasizes that call (question) and response (answer) remains vitally important in black culture.

The technological aspects of rap, particularly **sampling**, provides another example of an earlier African American aesthetic at work. Sampling involves selecting a short piece of music, running it through a computer or synthesizer, and then inserting it into your own rap. Sometimes it is a distinctive phrase or a loop that plays over and over again. Contemporary artists usually sample older styles of black music (James Brown is a particular favorite), thus using an oral means of infusing older styles with rap. Part of rap's creativity stems from a synthesis that is based upon the black American musical legacy.

Rap gained its greatest controversy through its association with street life and violence. Notorious B.I.G., Tupac, NWA, and other rappers came up from the streets and their background is clearly delineated in their music, which is identified with guns, drugs, and other less savory aspects of urban black life. Obscenity is another related issue. Aside from the famous trial of Luther Campbell for his use of obscenities in Florida, there is the issue of censorship by record companies. These major companies, all of which are ultimately owned by three multinational corporations, routinely issue expurgated compact discs for general consumption and for radio air play, while simultaneously putting the uncensored version in the marketplace. Record companies use the euphemistic terms "clean version" and "explicit lyrics" in the *Grammy Awards Guide* monthly catalogue of new releases, but it is a long-standing battle in the record industry that goes back to the era of race records. The more things change, the more things stay the same.

COUNTRY MUSIC TODAY

Perhaps as a backlash to what is perceived as the continuing commercialization of contemporary country music (Nashville style), there has been a movement back to its earlier days. Today's commercial country music stations may have carved out their own niche, with a play list that is distinctive from their rock counterparts, but the music is far more akin than it once was. An artist such as Jewel receives a great deal of attention from the pop music pundits and the general press and occasionally a country artist will cross over into the world of rock.

An "alternative country" scene, with feet and ears firmly planted in all types of music—mostly rootsy regional country styles such as western swing, string band music, and honky-tonk—exists on the commercial fringes. In the mid-1990s groups like Uncle Tupelo, the Bad Livers, and the Old 97s explored the earlier byways of country music, creating a movement that sounded simultaneously neo and progressive. The little edge of commercial country music is sometimes called "No Depression" in honor of Uncle Tupelo's influential recording of "No Depression in Heaven." Some of the more rock-oriented members of these bands spun off into more pop groups like Son Volt and Wilco, both of which enjoyed success outside of the country music axis.

Nonetheless, country music is clearly aware of its roots, though it pays more lip service than actual hommage to its creators. The country music business establishment acknowledges the importance of Jimmie Rodgers, the Carter Family, Bob Wills, and a handful of other pioneers in shaping its sound. Today's country music stars—Garth Brooks, Shania Twain, the Dixie Chicks, or George Strait—have a strong sense of things past, though it seems directed toward the heroes of honky-tonk like George Jones. The next tier down in popularity, artists like Ricky Scaggs and Marty Stuart, have an even stronger and more direct sense of the earlier days. Both men clearly love genres like bluegrass and western swing and Stuart, in particular, is a respected collector of instruments, records, and other artifacts of country music history back to the 1920s. Dolly Parton fits into this category as well. Her first release in 2001 was a bluegrass album, released on the Sugar Hill label. Despite this respect, the future of contemporary country music appears to be orientated toward popular mass culture, rather than its idealized rural heritage.

FINAL THOUGHTS

Although we live in a postmodern world and new millennium marked by rapid musical and cultural change, our roots are never entirely obscured. The trends in popular music have become increasingly fleeting, ephemeral, but also more diverse as we become a more global society via the Internet and other means of wireless communication. Nonetheless, the latest musical revolution is always informed by whatever proceeded it, and two dynamic, energetic, and emotional forms of black folk music that emerged in the twentieth century—blues and gospel—continue to have a strong impact on popular music. Some of the musical and stylistic traits they developed, most importantly the blues form itself,

THE FOLK ROOTS OF CONTEMPORARY POPULAR MUSIC

their reliance upon syncopated rhythms, and certain vocal techniques, have become so inculcated in late-twentieth-century pop music that we tend to forget from where they come. At one time, they were truly bred in the bone; now they are passed along through other, equally important, means.

KEY FIGURES AND TERMS

B-Boy	New Orleans
clowning	Sam Phillips
Fats Domino	Elvis Presley
the dozens	R&B
go-go	Otis Redding
hip-hop	Little Richard
improvisation	rockabilly
Louis Jordan	sampling
Memphis	soul
Motown	Sun Records

SUGGESTED LISTENING

B-52s. *Time Capsule*. Reprise 46920. A retrospective of the group's lengthy career that includes some of their most fun selections–"Rock Lobster," "Love Shack," and "Party Out Of Bounds."

Billy Bragg & Wilco. *Mermaid Avenue*. WEA/Elektra Entertainment. A fascinating collaboration in which these men take unpublished Woody Guthrie lyrics and put them in a contemporary (though thoroughly roots-oriented) musical context.

James Brown. *Star Time*. Polydor 849 108-4. Five hours of classic R&B/soul from the late 1960s and 1970s by the "hardest working man in show business."

Freddy Fender. *Interpreta El Rock*. Arhoolie CD 9039. Originally released (circa 1962) as an album on the small Ideal label, these wild recordings meld rock 'n' roll with musics from the Mexican border into what might be called Tex-Mex Garage Rock.

Son Volt. *VH-1 Crossroads*. WEA/Atlantic. This enhanced compact disc includes a wide range of original material and "guest artists," such as K.D. Lang and Blues Traveler.

Wilco. *Summer Teeth*. WEA/Warner Brothers. A pop-oriented effort (somewhat in the vein of Big Star and Alex Chilton) by perhaps the strongest of the roots rockers.

THE FOLK ROOTS OF CONTEMPORARY POPULAR MUSIC

Lucinda Williams. *Ramblin'*. Smithsonian Folkways 40092. The earliest (and most folk-based) recordings by this popular artist, which was initially released on Folkways in 1979.

Various. *The Complete Stax/Volt Singles 1959–1968*. Rhino 21801. A multi-CD boxed set that samples the mid-South soul sound of the mid- to late 1960s.

Various. *Four Decades of Folk Rock*. Time Life Records. From the 1960s into the 2000s, this nicely illustrated set of four compact discs does a good job of surveying the field from Bob Dylan to Son Volt.

Various. *Get Hot or Go Home: Vintage RCA Rockabilly 1956–59*. Country Music Foundation 014. A double set that covers the genre quite nicely and comes with an illustrated eight-page booklet.

Various. *The R & B Box: 30 Years of Rhythm & Blues*. Rhino 71806. Six carefully selected compact discs that cut across labels make this the best overview of R&B from 1943 till 1973.

Various. *Sun Rockabilly—The Classic Recordings*. Rounder SS-37. A set that, in fact, contains the classic Sun rockabilly performances by Billy Lee Riley, Warren Smith, Malcolm Yellvington, and other mid-South musicians.

SUGGESTED READING

Michael T. Bertrand. *Race, Rock, and Elvis*. Urbana: University of Illinois Press, 2005. Bertrand explores the complicated intersections of the mid-South in the 1950s that touches upon the civil rights movement, independent record companies, and youth culture.

Nelson George. *The Death of Rhythm & Blues*. New York: Pantheon Press, 1988. Although it focuses on the 1960s through the 1980s, this book reviews the changes in black popular music since the 1930s in light of the white-dominated music industry.

Robert Gordon. *It Came From Memphis*. New York: Faber & Faber, 1995. An idiosyncratic, insiders look at the transformation of regional and folk music in the mid-South and Memphis into contemporary popular music by way of rockabilly.

Peter Guralnick. *Last Train to Memphis: The Rise of Elvis Presley*. New York: Little, Brown, 1994. A masterful examination of Presley's life and times through 1958, the author also

THE FOLK ROOTS OF CONTEMPORARY POPULAR MUSIC

looks at the roots (blues and country, in particular) of the King's musical style. This is the first of a two-volume biography.

Peter Guralnick. *Lost Highways: Journeys & Arrivals of American Musicians*. Boston: David R. Grodine, 1979. A series of thoughtful essays covering blues, country, and rock performers from the 1940s through the 1960s.

Greil Marcus. *Mystery Train: Images of America in Rock 'n' Roll Music*, 5th edition. New York: Plume, 2008. Marcus writes provocatively and insightfully about the role of Robert Johnson, The Band, and Elvis Presley in American grassroots and popular culture.

Craig Morrison. *Go Cat Go! Rockabilly Music and Its Makers*. Urbana: University of Illinois Press, 1996. The definitive scholarly history of rockabilly music from its Memphis origins through its various revivals.

Gerry Naylor. *The Rockabilly Legends: They Called It Rockabilly Long Before It Was Called Rock 'n' Roll*. Milwaukee, WI: Hal Leonard Books, 2007. Certainly not the final word, but a useful recounting of the genre, which mostly focuses on 1954–59 and familiar names such as Presley, Cash, and Orbison.

Nick Tosches. *Unsung Heroes of Rock 'n' Roll*. New York: Scribner's, 1984. Poignant and humorous views of some of the less known and sometimes outrageous pioneers of the idiom.

SUGGESTED VIEWING

Chuck Berry: Hail! Hail! Rock 'N' Roll. MCA. This is a detailed, popularized documentary about the grassroots rock 'n' roller, which features wonderful concert footage and lots of Eric Clapton, Keith Richards, and other blues-influenced musicians.

James Brown Live in America. Rhino. Basically a concert performance, this is a vintage and exciting program by one of the most influential R&B/soul singers.

Various. *The American Folk Blues Festival 1962–1966*, Vol. 1 (1962). Regional Music & Music Distribution 75009. The first in an extensive series of DVD issues covering groups of touring American blues and folk musicians that included Muddy Waters, Otis Rush, and John Lee Hooker, who directly influenced British rock artists such as Eric Clapton and Mick Jagger.

Various. *Blue Suede Shoes: A Rockabilly Session*. MCA. Dave Edmunds, Eric Clapton, and others help to recreate the rockabilly music that influenced them in this informal film.

THE FOLK ROOTS OF CONTEMPORARY POPULAR MUSIC

Various. *The History of Rock 'n' Roll*. Time Life. This ten-volume set encompasses the music's historical development, though the first two volumes—"Rock 'n' Roll Explodes" and "Good Rockin' Tonight"—are the most relevant to this chapter.

Various. *Let the World Listen Right*. DarSan Productions/Folkstreams.net. The musical intersections (hip-hop, blues, and gospel, in particular) found in Mississippi in the early twenty-first century are the subjects of this modest film.

Various. *Style Wars*. Public Arts Films/Folkstreams.net. This 1983 film looks at the roots of hip-hop culture, including its many traditional, improvised arts.

Various. *The Music District*. California Newsreel/Folkstreams.net. Local filmmaker Susan Levitas documents three genres of black music in Washington, D.C., gospel quartet singing, go-go, and the stirring sounds of the brass bands emanating from the United House of Prayer for All People.

Chapter 12

URBAN FOLK MUSIC

- Introduction
- Blues and Gospel in Chicago
- San Antonio's Country and Conjunto Traditions
- Washington, D.C.
- Final Thoughts

INTRODUCTION

Most people very closely associate folk music with rural areas of the United States and with music performed on acoustic instruments. In the twenty-first century the contra-dance tradition in Nelson, New Hampshire, which has been ongoing since the early nineteenth century, certainly qualifies as a local community event featuring folk music. Likewise southwest Louisiana and southeast Texas has served as the hearth area for Cajun and zydeco music since the late nineteenth century, decades before touring musicians and sound recordings brought the music to eager listeners across the country. Even contemporary cowboy poets and singers—such as Joel Nelson (Alpine, Texas) and Ernie Sites (Wendell, Idaho)—still roam the vast ranches that dot the plains and hills from Texas through California, rarely plying their trade in locations that we would consider to be urban.

Traditional music and folk-based music, however, is played throughout the United States. To paraphrase Woody Guthrie's "This Land Is Your Land," folk music can be heard from California's redwood forests to New York's Staten Island. "The Folk Revivals" chapter, in particular, notes the importance of folk music in large urban areas with New York City functioning as the urban folk music epicenter. Beginning in the 1930s the city has been home to record companies such as Folkways (and, later, Elektra), which documented artists like Dave Van Ronk and Lead Belly, while Gerde's Folk City hosted early concerts

URBAN FOLK MUSIC

by such important musicians as Bob Dylan and Judy Collins in the early 1960s. Since the mid-1940s a considerable Cajun music community has thrived in the San Francisco Bay area of California due to the migration of residents of southeastern Louisiana seeking steady employment—most notably—in the regions's huge shipyards.

"Ethnic and Native American Traditions" (chapter 8) underscores the fact that a variety of traditions, from klezmer music in New York City to native Hawaiian hulas in Honolulu, are integral to the sounds of our cities. A reel or jig heard accompanying an Irish American step-dance competition held in south Boston and the strains of accordion-laced norteno wafting from houses in some sections of Phoenix illustrate traditional music in urban areas. African Americans brought blues from the Piedmont of Virginia and North Carolina to cities from Richmond, Virginia, to Albany, New York. Chapter 9, —"The Hispanic American Diaspora," features an entire section on New York City with Puerto Rico at its core.

Folk music is not, and has never been an entirely rural phenomenon, and this chapter accentuates the decades-long importance of traditional music in our urban (and its nearby suburban) areas. Sometimes it involves the interest in a rural vocal or instrumental tradition from which the participants are culturally and geographically far removed. For example, singing from the "Sacred Harp" books—a mid-nineteenth-century musical/cultural phenomenon described in chapter 5—has found venues in many urban areas throughout the United States. You can find smaller monthly and sometimes larger annual sings in Ann Arbor, Michigan, New Haven, Connecticut, Boston, Massachusetts, Denver, Colorado, and San Diego, California. In the Twin Cities of Minneapolis and St. Paul, Minnesota, a local group (currently found at http://www.freude.com/mnfasola/) has been singing monthly at local churches and at the University of Minnesota since 1985.

These cities, and all other urban areas throughout the country, also support a network of folk music clubs. Since the 1960s, when the popularization and commodification of grassroots music became more common, such clubs have presented a wide range of talent representing an even greater range of genres. Folk music clubs come in many sizes and intents. The planned community of Reston, Virginia, lies some ten miles outside of the Beltway that surrounds Washington, D.C. Since 1985 The Folk Club of Reston-Herndon ("Preserving the Traditions of Folk Music, Folk Lore, and Gentle Folk Ways") has featured music programs. In addition to a large annual event, they have long held monthly concerts at the Tortilla Factory, a local Tex-Mex eatery. These concerts generally feature a nationally or regionally known folk act (2009 found Gordon Bok, Bill Staines, Garnet Rogers, and Bryan Bowers on the roster) in addition to local artists appearing in a "Showcase."

On the other hand are the (hopefully) for-profit clubs that operate in smaller and larger cities and often draw upon a similar range of artistic talent to the monthly concerts put on by The Folk Club of Reston-Herndon. Many of these singer-songwriter/folk-based performers work a circuit of geographically and ideologically similar clubs. A group might perform at Eddie's Attic (Atlanta, Georgia) one night, move north to Asheville, North Carolina's The Grey Eagle, and then drive west over the Smokey Mountains to play at the Bluebird Café in Nashville, Tennessee.

The Folk Alliance—founded in 1989—operates largely in the urban realm in the twenty-first century and maintains close philosophical ties among the folk clubs, societies, and the performers who appear at them. According to their Mission Statement: "Folk Alliance International exists to foster and promote traditional, contemporary, and multicultural folk music and dance and related performing arts. The Folk Alliance seeks to strengthen and advance organizational and individual initiatives in folk music and dance through education, networking, advocacy, and professional and field development." This umbrella organization also holds an annual conference that moves among large cities in the United States. Memphis, Tennessee, hosted their annual conference on February 11–16, 2011.

This nationwide organization largely grew out of The California Traditional Music Society (CTMS), founded in 1978, which is, according to their Web site, "dedicated to the preservation and dissemination of the traditional Folk Music, dance, and related folk arts of America's diverse cultural heritage. Our goals are to broaden public involvement with Folk Music, celebrate ethnic traditions, and promote cross-cultural understanding." Based in Encinitas, California, CTMS largely serves those living in the greater Los Angeles area through a series of concerts, a community music school, and jam sessions featuring bluegrass, Celtic music, blues, and Cajun music.

Among other topics, this chapter discusses the African American **blues** and **gospel** traditions in Chicago and San Antonio's Hispanic and country music history. Both cities have their post-revival clubs and associations. The Old Town School of Folk Music, according to its Web site, "opened in December of 1957 with its first home at 333 North Avenue. The first five years of the School's history mirrored the boom in folk music at that time. Enrollment grew and programs expanded. Over 150 students attended guitar and banjo classes on a weekly basis. Folk dancing, and family sing-alongs rounded out the programming. The School also offered concerts by nationally renowned artists. Pete Seeger, Mahalia Jackson, Jimmy Driftwood, Big Bill Broonzy, and Josh White were just some of the many folk music artists who performed at the Old Town School in its early years. The School continued to grow, contributing to and benefitting from the **folk revival** movement of the 1960s. It developed a special atmosphere of community and camaraderie, and helped to launch some of the brightest artists on the folk music scene: Roger McGuinn of the Byrds, Bob Gibson, John Prine, Bonnie Koloc, and the late Steve Goodman all studied at the Old Town School."

In addition to this nationally recognized school, Chicagoland boasts several other small clubs or bars that regularly feature folk music. Several restaurants, most notably Abbey Pub and Irish Mill, spotlight Irish music. At least one other venue—the relatively upscale Uncommon Ground—hosts local and regionally recognized acoustic folk artists.

San Antonio, Texas, has nothing quite like the Old Town School of Folk Music, nor does the city support as many venues featuring singer-songwriters. Each June, however, it hosts the annual Texas Folklife Festival, which features music and dance reflecting the diversity of vernacular cultures from across the state. Long overshadowed as a "music city" by nearby Austin, San Antonio is much closer to the Mexico border than the state's capital and has the largest Hispanic population of any major city in the United States. This proximity to Mexico, as we shall see, gives San Antonio's grassroots music a particular background and sound.

But the development of country and **bluegrass** music in Washington, D.C., stands as the main focus for this chapter. In addition to the impact of country and bluegrass music in D.C., dozens of local clubs featuring all flavors of grassroots music, from Salvadorian to blues, and the various folk music societies, the Smithsonian Institution began its folklife festival in 1967. Begun by Ralph Rinzler (Bill Monroe's one-time manager and a member of the Greenbrier Boys) as the Festival of American Folklife, this annual multi-day festival transforms the Mall into a smorgasbord of crafts, foodways, storytellers, and music. Now called The Smithsonian Folklife Festival, in 2011 this free event featured a major component devoted to Rhythm & Blues, an area focused on "The Nature of Columbian Culture," and a fortieth anniversary celebration of the Peace Corps. Highlights of recent festivals include vernacular music found in regions (the Mississippi Delta, Appalachia, and the Mid-Atlantic Maritime) and states such as Virginia, Wisconsin, and Iowa.

BLUES AND GOSPEL IN CHICAGO

The vernacular cultures of a city are largely defined by the people who live there, many of whom migrated to the city in search of better employment or a new life. Even though several generations may have passed, strong ties with

Junior Wells, ca. 1960, played harp with such Chicago blues stalwarts as Buddy Guy and Muddy Waters. Courtesy of Jay Bruder.

their "home" often remain. Citizens of St. Louis or Kansas City, for instance, often continue to visit their relatives in southern Missouri who decided not to move to a nearby major urban center.

As discussed in the "Cultural Geography and Traditions" section of chapter 1, these migrants bring their music, foodways, speech patterns, and other traditions with them. Well into the twenty-first century Chicago's Southside remains largely populated by black Americans with roots in Mississippi, Alabama, Louisiana (or a "transitional" midsize city such as Memphis) even though their ancestors may be moved North as part of the Great Migration, from the teens through the 1940s. The movement of hundreds of thousands of black Americans brought the Mississippi Delta blues tradition from its rural home to a new urban environment, transforming the music from its acoustic and often solo format to a small electrified ensemble featuring a powerful lead guitar and the distinctive sound of an amplified harmonica—sometimes referred to by blues fans as a "Mississippi Saxophone."

URBAN FOLK MUSIC

Muddy Waters provides the quintessential example of this movement. Born in Rolling Fork, Mississippi, in 1913, as McKinley Morganfield, he began playing guitar while in his late teens. He came under the sway of Delta blues guitar legends such as Robert Johnson and Eddie "Son" House. Armed with his guitar, Waters visited Chicago in 1940 but soon moved back to central Mississippi. Library of Congress researcher Alan Lomax, in collaboration with Fisk University scholar John Work, recorded Waters on his acoustic guitar in 1941 as part of a project documenting black folk music in Coahoma County, Mississippi. Lomax returned a year later and recorded Waters at Stovall Plantation about ten months before the aspiring musician relocated permanently to Chicago.

In Chicago Waters met many other musicians who'd also moved up from the mid-South. By the late 1940s he and harpman Little Walter (Louisiana), along with pianist Otis Spann (Mississippi), had formed a band that transformed the gritty, eclectic, sometimes highly idiosyncratic Delta blues into a powerful musical juggernaut that could easily be heard above the din of a local bar and that more often conformed to the predictable twelve-bar blues form. Waters provided the leadership, stepping in front of the band, brandishing his slashing lead guitar, almost always played using a slide on his finger, and shouting and growling the words to original songs such as "Mannish Boy," "Still a Fool," "Long Distance Call," and "Hootchie Cootchie Man." Even a rather casual listener can discern the roots of Chicago blues heard in the Delta blues recordings of the 1920s and 1930s eventually transformed into the electrified blues band that informed rock 'n' roll when it emerged in the middle 1950s. For more about blues in general, please refer to the "African American Secular Folk Music" chapter.

Gospel music also holds an important place in Chicago and was similarly fueled by the Great Migration. **Rev. Thomas A. Dorsey**, a former blues man who worked and recorded with guitarist Tampa Red in the late 1920s, is often hailed as the "Father" of modern gospel music. Dorsey helped to transform gospel music (see "African American Religious Folk Music" for further information), through his work as a composer and songbook publisher, as the person who helped to promote the choir movement and assisted in organizing black gospel groups not only in Chicago but across the country.

As critical as Dorsey was in altering and promoting gospel music in Chicago, he did not stand alone. Kenneth Morris, an organist and significant composer, worked for many years at the First Church of Deliverance as a musician and choir director. Morris introduced the electric organ to gospel music while church member Sallie Martin formed the self-named Sallie Martin Singers in the late 1930s, which at one time included the well-known R&B singer Dinah Washington, then called Ruth Jones.

In 1927 sixteen-year-old Mahalia Jackson moved to Chicago from her native New Orleans. She soon joined the Greater Salem Baptist Church and began touring the city's churches and surrounding areas with the Johnson Gospel Singers, one of the earliest professional gospel groups. Two years later Jackson met Thomas A. Dorsey and by the mid-1930s they began a fourteen-year association of extensive touring, with Jackson singing Dorsey's songs in church programs and at conventions. His heartfelt "Take My Hand, Precious Lord" became her signature song, which helped to promote both this song (and others) as well as the songbooks that he sold in person and through the mail.

Born in Helena, Arkansas, in 1907, Roberta Martin moved to Chicago at the age of ten and began taking piano lessons. She thought about a career as a concert pianist until she took a job accompanying the Young People's Choir at Ebenezer Baptist Church, where she soon met the charismatic Dorsey. With his encouragement she and Theodore Frye organized the Martin-Frye Quartet, a mixed-gender youth group consisting of Eugene Smith, Norsalus McKissick, Robert Anderson, James Lawrence, Willie Webb, and Romance Watson, in 1933. Martin renamed the group the Roberta Martin Singers in 1936 and added Bessie Folk and Deloris Barrett Campbell to the group in the 1940s. Most of the songs composed by Martin, most notably "Only A Look" and "Try Jesus, He Satisfies," were published by Roberta Martin Studio of Music (incorporated in Chicago in 1939), which would eventually publish works by significant gospel artists ranging from Professor Alex Bradford to James Cleveland. In addition to her work as a performer, composer, and songbook publisher, Martin also served as the choir director of the Pisgah Baptist Church in Chicago for nearly twenty years.

The importance of gospel and blues music in Chicago suggests several trends that help to inform urban folk music across the country. The first relates to the transformation of rural traditions into more modern forms, particularly the evolution of acoustic delta blues into amplified Chicago blues. Second is the commodification of music from a community and racially based form with strong regional ties into one that commanded a place in the commercial marketplace including sound recordings, and live performances not only in Chicago but also around the world. Furthermore, some of these musicians—most notably Waters and Dorsey—now occupy iconic status as "founding fathers," "pioneers," and "innovators" whose works continue to directly inform the sound and direction of blues and gospel music and influence popular music trends, such as neo-soul.

Muddy Waters, in particular, and blues, in general, remain the face of folk-based African American music in Chicago for many people. Once the domain of working-class black Americans who flocked to hear this music on Chicago's Southside from the late 1930s into the 1960s, blues now draws mostly white patrons from across the world in search of an "authentic blues experience." They flock to clubs such as Buddy Guy's Legends, Kingston Mines Chicago Blues, or

Blue Chicago, most often to hear the house band belt out blues standards like "Sweet Home, Chicago."

SAN ANTONIO'S COUNTRY AND CONJUNTO TRADITIONS

San Antonio (the second-largest city in Texas) boasts a folk and vernacular music that bears the strong flavor of immigrants moving north in search of a better life. In a city where country music of various flavors has long held sway, immigrants from south of the United States Mexican border have indelibly stamped the music found in San Antonio. Most notable are Latino musicians such as Tejano accordionist Flaco Jimenez, whose work draws from his fellow **conjunto** and norteno musicians, but who also boldly ventured into the rock and pop arenas. More about Hispanic vernacular music can be found in chapter 9.

For decades San Antonio has been a destination city for south Texans as well as citizens of northern Mexico and became a majority Hispanic (or Latino) in the 1980s. Nonetheless, country music, often associated with western swing, has impacted the local music scene since the genre emerged in the 1930s. Adolph Hofner–born in 1916 in nearby Lavaca County, Texas, into a family of Czech-German origin—grew up listening and playing to Czech and Hawaiian music. His family moved to San Antonio around 1926 and within a few years Adolph, his younger brother Emil, together with Simon Garcia, formed the "Hawaiian Serenaders." Inspired by the extremely popular Fort Worth–based Milton Brown and His Brownies, Hofner decided to set aside his Czech-German musical roots and joined Jimmie Revard's Oklahoma Playboys. By 1938 he formed Adolph Hofner and His Texans, and continued to front bands in the western swing tradition until a 1993 stroke derailed his career. More about western swing can be found in the "Anglo-American Secular Folk Music" chapter.

Adolph Hofner's Czech-German heritage underscores the ethnic diversity that has long impacted the culture of south Texas. The Texas hill country (located between San Antonio and Austin) is not only geographically unique, it's significant for the fusion of Spanish and Central European (German, Swiss, Austrian, Alsatian, and Czech) influences in food, beer, architecture, and music. In fact, the hill country forms a distinctively multicultural "Texan" culture separate from the state's better known southern and southwestern influences.

In terms of local music, the accordion gained popularity in Tejano music by the nineteenth century due to the German settlers, many of whom migrated to the hill country in the mid- to late nineteenth century. Eventually more of these central Europeans moved from small towns and farms to nearby cities: San Antonio to the southwest and Austin to the east. By the 1940s creative musicians like Adolph Hofner and his Hispanic counterpart, Santiago Jimenez, Sr., helped to give folk music in San Antonio its specific characteristics.

Legendary conjunto accordionist and songwriter Santiago Jimenez, Sr., was born in 1913, in San Antonio, where he mainly lived until his death seventy-one years later. His father, Patricio Jimenez, also played the accordion and moved to San Antonio from Eagle Pass, Texas, some 150 miles southwest of the city and a suburb of Piedras Negras, Mexico. An accordion player by the age of eight, Santiago began playing music on live, local radio broadcasts as early as 1933. In 1936 Jimenez released his first record, "Dices Pescao" and "Dispensa el Arrempujon," on Decca, which marked a long recording career that lasted into the 1980s. Jimenez soon became known for his creative use of the tololoche, a Tejano contrabass that became a staple in conjunto music beginning in the mid-1940s. Always the traditionalist, he had a lifelong association with the traditional two-row button accordion. In the late 1960, Jimenez moved to Dallas for ten years, working as a school janitor, before returning to San Antonio in 1977, where he rekindled his music career. He made some final recordings with his son, Flaco, in 1980 for Arhoolie Records.

To this day conjunto music and the Jimenez family remain firmly linked through the work of Flaco Jimenez, Santiago Jimenez, Sr.'s son born in 1939. He began performing with his father in 1945 and recording in 1954 as a member of the norteno band Los Caporales. Flaco became a fixture in the San Antonio norteno scene into the 1960s when he began performing with Douglas Sahm in the 1960s. Sahm, perhaps best known as the founding member of the Sir Douglas Quintet, helped to broaden Flaco's musical horizons. Over the next twenty years Flaco often traveled outside of south Texas, working with an eclectic mix of musicians from former Bill Monroe sideman Peter Rowan to Bob Dylan to grassroots music guru Ry Cooder.

In 1986 Jimenez won a Grammy Award for "Ay Te Dejo En San Antonio," a song he learned from his father. For many years, most notably in the 1990s Jimenez joined the supergroup Texas Tornados, with Augie Meyers, Doug Sahm, and Freddy Fender, that earned a Grammy Award in 1990. Flaco Jimenez won another Grammy in 1996 for the Best Mexican-American Performance followed by a third Grammy in 1999 for the Best Tejano Performance. Although these collaborations led to a greater awareness and appreciation of his music outside of the norteno community, Jimenez remains closely tied to both San Antonio, his extended family, and his musical roots.

While conjunto in San Antonio never impacted popular music in the same ways that Chicago's blues and gospel music did, it nonetheless has touched the music world outside of south Texas. The success and recognition gained by Flaco Jimenez since the 1970s perhaps illustrates this most dramatically. His Grammy Awards and his work with a pop icon like Bob Dylan mean that even casual music consumers will pay attention to him and more people outside of his San Antonio home know about Flaco Jimenez's life and work.

The importance of conjunto music from San Antonio was underscored on August 13, 2010, with the passing of Estaben "Steve" Jordan at the age of seventy-one. Always innovative and experimenting with traditional forms and styles, Jordan (born in rural Elsa, Texas) moved north to San Antonio as a child. Following a peripatetic path for much of his early adult life, Jordan returned to San Antonio on a permanent basis in the early 1970s. Not only an accordion player, he also played harmonica and various keyboards. Jordan's bravado, deviance, innovation, and showmanship often drew comparisons with Jimi Hendrix. That his passing earned attention from the national digital and print press, including full-length obituaries in the *Washington Post*, suggests a more serious interest in Hispanic music.

WASHINGTON, D.C.

Country Music

With the advent of air conditioning, increasingly sophisticated urbanization, and a great increase in population following the close of World War II, Washington, D.C., quickly evolved from a medium-sized city straddling the North and the South, where foreign diplomats received extra compensation because the District was built upon a swamp, to a major metropolitan area. But a March 11, 1974, *Washington Post* headline correctly trumpeted "D.C. Is Also Nation's Bluegrass Capital." Country music was nothing new in a city with so many immigrants from the states immediately to the south and west. Bluegrass, however, had only emerged some twenty years previously. The rest of this chapter is devoted to country music and bluegrass in our nation's capital, which is usually better known for its home-grown go-go music and as the birthplace of Duke Ellington, up to the early 1960s when the folk revival changed the local musical landscape.

Country music has, in fact, been integral to the District of Columbia's soundscape since the term emerged as a means to promote the rural, old-time music that was gradually appearing on commercial recordings. In April 1923 WRC (named in honor of its original owner—the Radio Corporation of America) signed on the air and occasionally featured country music. Several years later, low-power and short-lived WTFF broadcast a weekly radio program by pioneering artist, Jimmie Rodgers, who was quickly establishing himself as the first male start of country music.

"**The Hill Billies**" appeared on WRC in 1926 and became among the first country music artists to develop a following in the District of Columbia. Led by brothers Al and Joe Hopkins, Tony Alderman, and John Rector (all of whom were originally from in or near Galax, Virginia), their ties to the city were actually deeper and longer than it might appear. As early as 1910 Al Hopkins launched his professional music career when he (and his younger brothers Joe, Elmer, and John) formed a vocal group called the Old Mohawk Quartet, which sang regularly at Washington's Majestic Theater, a venue favored by many traveling vaudevillians.

About 1912 the family moved to 63 Kennedy Street in a rapidly urbanized section of northwest Washington, D.C. After living in the city for many years, the Hopkins family returned to Carroll County, Virginia, to visit relatives in the spring of 1924. Joe and Al met barber and fiddler Tony Alderman at his Galax barbershop and they soon formed a trio. Within several months John Rector, who ran a local general store and played the five-string banjo, joined the group. The recordings of Henry Whittier (who lived in nearby Fries, Virginia) inspired these musicians to take the train to New York City in search of work as well as an opportunity to record.

This quartet began working the vaudeville circuit in 1925 when they spoke with A & R man Ralph Peer about recording. After an initial 1924 trial recording session for Victor, which was listed as by the Southwestern Virginia String Orchestra, the group eventually recorded for OKeh (1925) and then for an extended period of time for Vocalion beginning in 1926. Peer suggested that they needed to find a shorter and more descriptive name for their group, and they decided upon the "Hill Billy" moniker, thus becoming the first recording artists to use this descriptor.

Around the same time they first recorded for Vocalion in the spring of 1926, the group settled in Washington, D.C., both because WRC was such a powerful station that it reached audiences up and down the Atlantic seaboard and because the city provided a gateway to cities to the northeast as well as back home to rural southwestern Virginia. Their weekly Saturday evening broadcasts over WRC quickly became popular among the relatively small number of local residents who owned radios and also reached a larger audience that stretched from Philadelphia to Richmond and from Pittsburgh to the Maryland beaches. These broadcasts brought in letters inviting the group to play at local venues within WRC's extensive coverage area--a healthy supplement to the ties that they had already established by way of vaudeville. A photograph in the March 1926 issue of *Radio Digest* was labeled "Hill Billies Capture WRC: Boys from Blue Ridge Mountains Take Washington with Guitars, Fiddles, and Banjos; Open New Line of American Airs."

The Hill Billies, led by the shrewd and resourceful Al Hopkins, symbolized country music for Washington, D.C. Because these young men from southwestern Virginia reminded them of themselves—their past and their own roots—this group represented an important, modern example of music and **citybilly** culture. In these respects the Hill Billies foreshadowed both the emergence of bluegrass and the folk revival that began in the late 1950s.

But the Hill Billies were important for several other reasons. They were among the first country musicians to trade on their roots by exploiting the country attire (later "western") often associated with men who work outdoors for a living. The Hill Billies were also one of the first groups to include a piano—an instrument often found in rural parlors—on their Vocalion recordings. When Calvin Coolidge asked them to play for him, they became the first country group to appear at the White House. The Hill Billies also appeared in an early talking film, "The Original Hill Billies," with Al Hopkins, a 1929 fifteen-minute Vitaphone film meant to be shown at commercial movie theaters in conjunction with full-length features.

Jimmie Rodgers also spent time broadcasting in Washington, D.C., beginning in December 1927, near the start of his illustrious recording career. Rodgers reached a small number of local country music lovers by way of his weekly broadcasts over WTFF, the radio station of the Fellowship Forum, which signed on the air for three evening hours, four days a week. Like so many early country music recording artists, Rodgers easily mixed folk, blues-based material, with pop songs from the past thirty years, including "There's Going to be A Hot Time in the Old Town Tonight," as well as songs that worked well on the vaudeville circuit. Rodgers's recording career proved so successful that by the summer of 1928 he moved on, leaving the District for New York City and then for life on the road before his untimely death due to TB in May 1933.

An unexpected connection exists between Jimmie Rodgers and bluegrass in D.C. During his career, Rogers recorded with ten different steel guitar players as well as more than a score of other sidemen performing on various instruments. While broadcasting over WTFF in Washington, D.C., Rodgers meet songwriter and instrumentalist Ellsworth Thomas Cozzens, who became the first of the steel players with whom he recorded. Cozzens played locally with the Georgetown-based Blue and Gray Troubadours, who also broadcast over WMAL around the time that Rodgers came to town.

In mid-February 1928 Ellsworth fellow Blue and Gray Troubadour guitarist Julian R. Ninde accompanied Rodgers to Camden, New Jersey, in order to record four selections for RCA Victor. This was the first session to feature more than Rodgers' guitar accompaniment and included two selections, "Dear Old Sunny South" and "Treasures Untold." This trio recorded only once and Ellsworth and Ninde never saw Rodgers after he left the District some four months later.

The connection between Rodgers and local bluegrass comes in the form of Mike Auldridge, the dobro player with the seminal local bluegrass band, the

MUSICAL EXAMPLE

Mr. Stoneman and his musical family recorded dozens of tracks for commercial record companies beginning in the mid-1920s. Folkorist and musician Mike Seeger made this field in 1957, possibly at Sunset Park, Chester County, Pennsylvania. "The Wreck of the Old 97" has been widely recorded by country artists, mostly from the southeastern states, beginning in the middle 1920s. This popular disaster song focuses on a 1902 train wreck that occurred on the tracks just north of Danville, Virginia, when engineer Steve Brodie took over a train that was running one hour late and tried to make up the time before losing control several hours into his shift.

Title "The Wreck of the Old 97"
Performer The Stoneman Family
Instruments vocals and guitar, fiddle, rhythm guitar, banjo, string bass
Length: 2:51

Musical Characteristics
1. The banjo played by family friend Gene Cox is finger-picked in bluegrass fashion.
2. The lead vocal by "Pop" Stoneman is very unadorned and somewhat detached.
3. Though not characterized as such, the instrumentation and the musicians' approach to playing owes much to the emerging bluegrass style.
4. The tempo is moderate, steady, and deliberate.
5. The rhythm guitar not only underpins the song's harmony, it also provides additional syncopation.

> Oh, They gave him his orders in Monroe, Virginia,
> Saying "Steve, You're way behind time."
> This is not the Thirty-Eight but the Old Ninety-Seven
> You must put her in Spencer on time.
>
> It's a mighty rough road from Lynchburg to Danville,
> In a line of a three mile grade.
> And its on this grade that he lost his average,
> And you see what a jump he's made.
>
> They were going down the grade, making ninety miles an hour,
> When the whistle began to scream;

He was found in the wreck with his hand on the throttle,
And he was scolded to death by steam.

And a telegram came to Washington City
and this is what it said,
"A brave engineer that run old Ninety-Seven,
Is a-lying in Danville, dead."

Oh, its come all you fair ladies, you must take warning
From this time, now and on.
Never speak harsh words to a true loving husband;
He may leave you and never return.

This selection is from Smithsonian Folkways 40192.

Country Gentlemen and, more recently, with the Seldom Scene. Couzzens was Mike Auldridge's maternal uncle. Moreover, Auldridge recalls Couzzens talking about his brief period working with Rodgers and playing both "Dear Old Sunny South" and "Treasures Untold" at family gatherings in the early 1950s.

During the Depression thousands of black and white residents of West Virginia, Virginia, and North Carolina moved north, helping bolster the population of the District. Many of them were attracted by the prospect of steady work provided by the federal government, though relatively few found such jobs during this difficult period. Citizens with a strong interest in the music provided by the musicians with background similar to theirs continued to migrate to our nation's capital and while no D.C.-based country music group active during the 1930s had the same impact nor was as groundbreaking as The Hill Billies, what is now called "country music" continued to increase its firm hold on local music lovers.

Local radio stations such as WRC, WMAL, and WJSV continued expanding their diet of live country music broadcasts. These fifteen-minute or half-hour programs occasionally featured nationally recognized acts, such as the Delmore Brothers, but more often focused on locally based groups. The Capital Barn Dance (promoted via a live weekly radio broadcast) emanated from Portner's Arena, which sat near the banks of the Potomac River just south of Georgetown and was long ago torn down and eventually replaced by the John F. Kennedy Center.

Because **Ernest Stoneman** is so well known and central to the development of bluegrass in Washington, D.C., a biographical sketch illustrates how Stoneman brought country music to the city. Born on May 25, 1893, near Galax

(Carroll County) in southwestern Virginia, an area steeped in folk songs, which now hosts one of country's longest-running and best-known fiddle contests, Ernest Stoneman was the oldest of three brothers born to Elisha and Rebecca, who died during childbirth in 1896. Principally a farmer, the stern Elisha also worked as a Baptist preacher who traveled the region giving sermons. When Ernest wasn't attending his one-room school, he was busy hunting rabbits or fishing down at the creek.

He was ten years old when his grandmother taught him "Molly Hare" on the autoharp. He next picked up the banjo, first learning "Cripple Creek" and eventually played a little Jew's harp, harmonica, fiddle, and guitar. Vocal leads proved to be Stoneman's strong suit, usually accompanied by his own guitar or autoharp. He learned many popular songs from the 1890s as well as the ballads from the Blue Ridge, and his repertoire is more fully explored in the "Anglo-American Secular Folk Music" chapter.

When Stoneman was twenty, he met his future wife, Hattie Frost—the daughter of Bill Frost, a fine fiddler and banjo player. Hattie, only twelve at the time, was courted by Ernest until she turned eighteen, and they married in 1918. Because Hattie sang, read music, and played the organ, banjo, and fiddle, she became Ernest's musical partner as well. Her younger sister Irma Lee Frost, primarily a church organist, participated as a mandolinist, while her banjo-playing twin brother, Bolin, also joined the Stoneman family group. Many of the hymns the Stonemans recorded came from Irma Frost's collection of shape note hymnals.

While working as a carpenter in Bluefield, Virginia Stoneman went into a furniture store and heard a record of local musician Henry Whitter on a phonograph. Ernest, who had played with Whitter on occasion at country dances, was inspired to try and make commercial recordings as well. He wrote two phonograph companies—Columbia and OKeh–for which Whitter had done his recordings and received an invitation to audition. Stoneman made a harmonica rack and thought strumming his autoharp would make a different accompaniment for his singing. He took a job in nearby West Virginia to earn extra money and saved $47 for his trip. Arriving in New York City, he first auditioned for Columbia on September 1, 1924, but ultimately reached a deal with OKeh. For five years he made dozens of sides for Okeh, Edison, Gennett, and RCA Victor.

These relatively good times changed when the Great Depression hit in late 1929. Record sales, which were an important part of the Stonemans' income, plummeted from their high in 1928. Before long Ernest Stoneman couldn't interest a record company in his music, and both his live, local musical performances and his work as a carpenter all but dried up.

The Stonemans would have twenty-three children (only eleven of whom survived into adulthood) and most of them also played music, often in various family ensembles. By the early 1930s he was broke and saddled with rising debt, which apparently peaked at around $500, as well as a large family to provide for. Creditors eventually put a lien on their house, sold the house from underneath them and repossessed the furniture. When the sheriff came for their car in December 1932, the family drove north to Alexandria, Virginia, just across the Potomac River from Washington, D.C.

Because Ernest could find only occasional work as a substitute postal carrier, the family resided in an abandoned old house and lived in abject poverty. He and his son Eddie recorded several sessions for ARC in January 1934, but none of the six sides that were released sold very well. After Ernest lost his part-time job with the Railway Mail Service Hattie and nine of the children moved back to Galax for nearly a year, living in an old log cabin her grandfather owned. In the spring of 1935 Ernest finally located a house in nearby Washington, D.C., and the family moved back from Galax.

Ernest, Hattie, and their son Eddie occasionally played on Alexandria-based WJSV, which became WTOP in 1943, but music work remained scarce. The family's peripatetic lifestyle continued for several years because they often couldn't afford to pay the rent and moved around the Washington area. The Stonemans, now with eleven children, eventually settled in Carmody Hills, Maryland, barely one mile from the Washington, D.C., line in Prince Georges County.

Following the close of World War II, the older Stoneman children gradually found employment, got married, and moved from home. Ernest Stoneman continued working odd jobs until he finally found a more permanent position at the U.S. Naval Gun Factory. With Stoneman's diminishing family and steadier employment, his financial distress eased somewhat. Moreover, by the early 1950s, the Stoneman Family (as they were now known) began getting more gigs playing a mix of old-time country and the newly emerging bluegrass.

The influx of southern-born servicemen during World War II and thereafter helped to cement the District of Columbia's place in the field of country music. They brought their musical interests with them, most of which were satisfied by way of live performances on stage and on the radio. At the close of World War II, just as the world was beginning its slow return to normalcy, the local interest in country music increased dramatically—a change due largely to Connie B. Gay.

Connie B. Gay, born in Lizard Lick, North Carolina, in 1914, helped to change the shape of commercial country music during the period after World War II. Gay became one of the founders of the Nashville-based Country Music Association in 1958 and served as its first president (1959–60). He was elected into the Country Music Association's Hall of Fame in 1980 and what was initially called the CMA\Founding Presidents Award became the Connie B. Gay Award in 1988 and is widely considered to be the organization's most prestigious award.

URBAN FOLK MUSIC

Pictured here are the Howington Brothers, Dub and Roy in front with the Tennessee Haymakers: Herbie Jones, George Saslaw, and Jimmy Dean about 1949. Dean would go on to become a nationally recognized television personality by the mid 1950s. Courtesy of Bruce Bastin.

Despite his longtime ties with the Nashville-based Country Music Association, Gay remained closely associated with Washington, D.C., for most of his adult life. Roy Clark, Jimmy Dean, and Patsy Cline were among the artists with strong D.C. ties that he helped to make household names across the United States. But, perhaps most important, Gay helped to shape the sound and the appeal of country music during the ten-year period after the end of World War II when it was veering toward popular music and when the sound of bluegrass (along with honky-tonk) was developing as a distinctive genre under the wider "country music" umbrella.

The televison version of "Town and Country Time" began airing over WMAL-TV on a late Saturday night—from 10:00 PM TO 1:00 am. The premier show on the final Saturday of September 1955 included a wide cross-section of country music talent from across the United States. Among the highlights was the D.C. premier of western swing pioneer Bob Wills and the Texas Playboys, who opened the show. Country music star and nascent rockabilly artist Marvin Rainwater (then a regular on Red Foley's "Ozark Jubilee") along with Autry Inman, who was in the middle of an extended "Grand Ole Opry" engagement, and steel guitar wizard Jerry Bryd rounded out the imported talent. Jimmy

In 1948 Jim[my] Dean made his recording debut with the Howington Brother on the locally operated DC label. Courtesy of Jay Bruder.

Dean and the Texas Wildcats (who included Joe Wheeler, Miss Dale Turner, Luke Gordon, Dub Howington, Jimmy Case, and the delightfully misnamed "Tiny" Jenkins) represented the local contingent and became the regular local "stars." Some 3,000 enthusiastic fans attended the first television broadcast. While bluegrass was absent from the initial *Town and Country* television show, and local talent was not fore-grounded, the "Town and Country Time" radio broadcasts sounded very different.

When Connie B. Gay persuaded the station manager of Arlington, Virginia's WARL-AM that the newly launched station needed to capitalize on the interest in local country music talent, "Town and Country Time" was born on November 7, 1946. At first it aired for one-half hour, beginning at noon, but eventually proved to be so successful that it became a three-hour afternoon broadcast that stretched until 3:00. According to an article in the December 5, 1989, *Washington Post*, Gay "began broadcasts from the basement of his home in Arlington through a telephone hookup to the station's transmitter," where he "relayed country news and country views."

Within one year, this energetic entrepreneur decided that country music on radio was not enough. By the spring of 1947 he expanded his local music empire into promoting live music programs. Building upon local radio listeners who tuned in each noon for Gay's "Radio Ranch" he began a series of programs at Turner's Arena under the "Gay Time" rubric. These proved successful and the November 7, 1948, *Washington Post* included this brief news piece under the "Gay Time Show Returning Here": "Connie B. Gay has announced that Turner's Arena will be the new home of Gay Time, the hillbilly show, which returns to

Washington next Friday. Gay says he has signed Bill Monroe of "Grand Ole Opry" fame, for opening night. In addition to Monroe, there will be Clyde Moody, Pete Cassell (the blind minstrel), Chubby Wise and Grandpa Jones and Ramona. There will be the Radio Ranchmen and some added attractions. One of them will be Linnie Ayleshire of Springfield, Mo., who makes his music out of saws, balloons and bureau drawers."

Gay took a major chance in the fall of 1947 when he rented venerable Constitution Hall in order to promote a show featuring Eddy Arnold. Much to the surprise of the local music establishment, it sold out. This unexpected success inspired Gay to increase his efforts to promote country music in D.C. at a major venue, and in 1948 his music shows in Constitution Hall sold out for twenty-six straight weeks.

Gay followed this coupe with a series of country music cruises on the Potomac. He began promoting them in 1950, following the formula that made his local radio show so successful: mixing local and national talent. On July 3, 1950, he promoted the "Grand Old Opry Cruise," which included Cowboy Copas, Sugarfoot Garland & his Oklahoma Cowboys in addition to two local bands: Don Patton's Swing Boys and Ralph Case and his Square Dancers.

At first Connie B. Gay's WARL program reflected the trends in commercial country music across the United States. His radio shows, which ran from 1946 through 1955, often emphasized the "western" in the term "country and western," with local groups such as Jimmy Dean's Texas Wildcats. Likewise another group with a strong local following, Dub Howington and the Tennessee Haymakers, embraced the newly emerging rockabilly sound. Record companies and radio stations alike were still trying to figure out how to label and market country music, so during the late 1940s terms like hillbilly, country, or country and western were often used somewhat interchangeably. In D.C., Gay traded on both the term "hillbilly" and the "western" connection, as witnessed by his "Radio Ranch" and the "Radio Ranchmen." Dean had his first hit, "Bummin' Around," in 1953 on the 4 Star label, but had no other hits for the rest of the decade. He signed with Columbia Records in 1957.

In 1954, Dean hosted the popular Washington, D.C., radio program "Town and Country Time" on WARL-AM, and with his Texas Wildcats became popular in the Mid-Atlantic region. Patsy Cline and Roy Clark got their starts on the show. Although Cline and Dean became good friends, Clark, Dean's lead guitarist, was eventually fired by the singer for his chronic tardiness. Dean replaced Clark with Billy Grammer. In 1955, *Town and Country Time* moved to WMAL-TV on weekday afternoons. Dean and the Texas Wildcats also appeared during 1957 on *Town and Country Jamboree* on WMAL-TV on Saturdays from 10:30 PM TO 1:30 am, which was also carried by TV stations in Maryland and Virginia on a regional network.

Also during 1957, Dean hosted *Country Style* on WTOP-TV on weekday mornings. CBS picked up the show nationally from Washington for eight months in 1957 using the rather generic title, *The Morning Show*. Then from September 14, 1958, to June 1959, CBS carried *The Jimmy Dean Show* on weekday and Saturday afternoons.

Roy Clark, who was born in south-central Virginia in 1933 and moved to Washington, D.C., when his father got a job at the Naval Yard, began playing banjo, guitar, and mandolin in 1947 and within a year placed first in the National Banjo Championships. He juggled a strong interest in baseball and boxing before settling on a career in music. At the age of seventeen, he had his first appearance on the "Grand Ole Opry" and five years later became a regular musician on "Town and Country Time." After Jimmy Dean fired Clark, he never lived in Washington, D.C., again. By 1960 Clark landed in Las Vegas as the guitarist in a band led by former West Coast western swing bandleader-comedian Hank Penny, followed by a stint in a band backing rockabilly legend Wanda Jackson. He then found a home in Hollywood, with recurring roles in *The Beverly Hillbillies* and *Hee Haw* in the late 1960s before opening the Roy Clark Celebrity Theater in Branson, Missouri, in 1983. In 2009 he was inducted into the Country Music Hall of Fame.

Pop Stoneman's second recording career began in 1957 when he was visited by Mike Seeger, a local musician, documentarian, and member of the famous Seeger family that included Pete and that resided in Chevy Chase, Maryland, less than one mile from the line separating the District of Columbia from Maryland. A 1957 Folkways album, *Old Time Tunes Of The South*, marked the first time in more than two decades that Stoneman had recorded and brought him to the attention of people caught up in the late 1950s–1960s folk music boom. In 1962 the Stoneman Family debuted at the "Grand Ole Opry," which brought them a great deal of attention. In 1963 they cut an album for Starday entitled *Ernest V. Stoneman and the Stoneman Family* that included selections such as "In the Sweet Bye and Bye" and "The Sinking of the Titanic" that they'd first recorded back in the 1920s, followed a year later by an album of similar material, entitled *Great Old Timer at the Capitol*. With this emphasis on "old-time" country music and western themes, how does bluegrass figure into the Washington, D.C., music scene?

Bluegrass

It may seem odd, at first blush, that bluegrass music should flourish in Washington, D.C. But, like Chicago and San Antonio, you have to look at the people who made up the population of Washington, D.C., in the years following the close of World War II when bluegrass was developing. Many of these new residents moved from areas where this music initially emerged.

Bluegrass was initially marketed as country music, albeit a fresh form that sounded remarkably brash and innovative. To our twenty-first-century ears it might sound quaint, predictable, and even old-fashioned, but in the immediate post-WW II years bluegrass was new. Like most forms of twentieth century American vernacular music, which drew from existing genres, bluegrass meshed elements of country, blues, jazz (swing, really), and gospel, into a form that emphasized solo musicianship and improvisation.

The term bluegrass was not associated with this music until approximately ten years after the close of WW II, when the music began to be disseminated by way of recordings, radio, and touring musicians. Before the mid-1950s this music came under the rather generic categories of country or hillbilly. But by the late 1950s bluegrass became the term used to describe the music of Lester Flatt and Earl Scruggs, the Stanley Brothers, and Bill Monroe and the Blue Grass Boys.

Bluegrass also was initially associated with southern, rural, or "down-home" music. More specifically this new music was associated with the upland southeast, where Virginia, Kentucky, Tennessee, and North Carolina meet. Bluegrass fermented in small venues in places like the Coeburn, Virginia, VFW and early morning live radio broadcasts over WOPI from Bristol, Tennessee, which provided an early media outlet for the Stanley Brothers.

Due to the migration patterns that followed in the wake of the Great Migration, many (black and white) residents of North Carolina, Virginia, and West Virginia moved toward the Northeast. While many of them stopped in larger cities like Richmond, Virginia, the lure of our nation's capital, with its increasing urbanity and federal jobs, made the District of Columbia and its suburbs a prime destination for migrants from the southeastern states.

Multi-instrumentalist Ernest Stoneman, who moved his wife and family to the Washington, D.C., areas during the Depression, typifies this trend. Not only did he relocate to an urban area, the entire family brought the music of its native Galax County, Virginia, with them. While Stoneman settled near Washington, D.C., others moved on to Baltimore (a much more blue-collar town than D.C.) or southern Pennsylvania or even farther north. This very distinctive migration pattern, one that continues to this day, assured that bluegrass became part of D.C.'s musical vocabulary beginning in the late 1940s. Stoneman's life story serves as the archetype for the transition from the southeastern rural states to Washington, D.C., and the emergence of bluegrass. Because these immigrants often identified with music from Appalachia and the musical roots of their own families, they tended to think of their music as "hillbilly" rather than "country and western."

Fiddle-playing Scotty Stoneman emerged as one of the best of the family musicians and began playing with some of the most impressive local players, including fiddler and (Bill Monroe alumnus) Chubby Wise. In 1955 this ad hoc group played a multi-week gig at the Hotel Charles in Hughesville, Maryland. Guitarist Roy Clark and his band played a successful, extended engagement at The Famous, a club in D.C., which inspired owner Sam Bomstein to suggest that Scotty form a family-based band, **"The Blue Grass Champs."** This name marks the first use by a D.C.-based group of the term "bluegrass."

The Blue Grass Champs also included Jimmy Case in addition to various members of the extended Stoneman Family. Case had been honorably discharged several months earlier at Andrews Air Force Base, after serving four years in the U.S. Air Force and was "discovered" by Scotty while performing at Jo-Dels Supper Club in Washington, D.C. After playing just one gig at The Famous, Sanford Bomstein hired the band and they played there for the next three years.

The initial Blue Grass Champs lineup consisted of Scott Stoneman on fiddle and vocals, Jimmy Case on acoustic guitar and vocals, Ray Cross (a Stoneman cousin by marriage) on electric guitar, and Jimmy Stoneman on upright bass and vocals. Within a month Ray Cross was replaced by Donna Stoneman on mandolin. Porter Church joined the group in the summer of 1956 just prior to the group's audition for the nationally broadcast *Arthur Godfrey Talent Scouts* television show. On July 13, 1956, the Arthur Godfrey show producers sent the group a telegram inviting them to appear on the show on July 30, 1956. The Blue Grass Champs won the *Arthur Godfrey Talent Scouts* show performing "Salty Dog Blues" and enjoyed two weeks of national exposure instead of the usual one.

Appearing on the *Arthur Godfrey Talent Scouts* program opened the door for the group and Jimmy Dean quickly booked them semi-regularly on his local television show, which broadcast from Turner's Arena in Washington. They also appeared locally with Patsy Cline, Roy Clark, Billy Grammer, and Grandpa Jones and on the WWVA Wheeling Jamboree in Wheeling, West Virginia, as well as on WARL radio, Arlington, Virginia, in addition to their weekly radio show on WEAM radio in Fairfax, Virginia.

By the close of 1956 the Bluegrass Champs played six nights a week and won the band contest at the Warrenton National Championships. The elder Stoneman occasionally performed with his children's band but nabbed his own headlines after an appearance on *The $64,000 Question*, a popular TV game show in 1956, where he won $10,000. The group soon earned a regular spot on Arthur Godfrey's daily daytime show, which continued to bring them national recognition. At this time they also played with Charlie Waller, John Duffy, and Bill Emerson, who formed the nucleus of the famous local bluegrass group, Country Gentlemen.

Van (the youngest son) learned to play and sing from "Pop" (Ernest's newly aquired nickname) and eventually joined Scotty in the Blue Grass Champs as a

Perry Westland (guitar) performing live on the air about 1950 at Connie B. Gay's WGAY radio station in Washington, DC with Fiddlin' Curly Smith, Charlie Fetzer on resonator guitar and Don Owens on bass. Owens would go on to become a nationally prominent disc jockey. Courtesy of Perry and Barbara Westland.

lead singer and guitarist. They were regularly featured on WTTG Channel 5 in Washington, D.C., through the mid-1960s. The band played country favorites by Porter Wagoner and Johnny Cash as well as songs by Bill Monroe and other bluegrass bands.

Throughout the late 1940s into the 1950s the nascent country music industry struggled to consolidate the diverse regional styles of rural white folk/commercial music into a more marketable and manageable genre. Even though the industry increasingly looked toward Nashville, which was slowly developing its "Music City" moniker during this same period, the record sales and popularity of "western" groups such as Bob Wills and the Texas Playboys, Ernest Tubb and his Texas Troubadours, and the Sons of the Pioneers continued to fuel the marketing of a more country and western image across the United States.

Western themes and images were not entirely absent in Washington, D.C.'s country music scene in the decade following the end of WW II. The musical interests of native Washingtonian Eddie Nesbit (b. 1919), a local radio announcer, songwriter, and country singer beginning in the late 1930s, typify the local interest in western music. In addition to being greatly impressed by the

In late May, 1948 promoter Connie B. Gay presented this mix of local and national hillbilly acts at a major downtown Washington, D.C. venue. Courtesy of Kip Lornell.

recordings of Jimmie Rodgers and Bradley Kincaid, Nesbitt greatly admired the smooth harmonies of the Sons of the Pioneers, lead in the mid-1930s by Roy Rogers.

Connie B. Gay dominated the marketing of country music in D.C. during the period that bluegrass initially emerged and eventually became a separate genre. Gay also wrestled with these terms as he marketed the music with which he, like so many other Washington residents of similar age, grew up in a small town just east of Raleigh, North Carolina. He knew that the industry needed an encompassing term that it could use for marketing, one that would be universally recognized and understood in the same way that "swing" had captured America's imagination a decade before.

Because Gay grew up in eastern North Carolina, listening to hillbilly music by artists (some local) such as Bill and Charlie Monroe, Three 'Baccer Tags, Ramblin' Tommy Scott, and Wade Mainer, all of whom broadcast over Raleigh's WPTF-AM, he understood the importance of this music to so many Washingtonians. He also knew and understood the importance of branding and marketing. In a 1989 interview with the Country Music Foundation, Gay was reminiscing about the late 1940s and observed that "we were beginning to change the word 'hillbilly' to 'country' and it was becoming known in the Washington area as country music."

Furthermore, this issue of naming provides an interesting example of the "citybilly" phenomenon, which scholars from Charles Seeger to Neal Rosenberg have used since the late 1940s to describe the acculturation process, the

MUSICAL EXAMPLE

One of the national capital's premier bluegrass groups, the Country Gentlemen, formed in 1957 and continued until the death of Charlie Waller in 2004. They were inducted into the Bluegrass Hall of Fame in 1996 and various members continue to perform bluegrass, some in and around Washington, D.C. The hopeful, then sad "Handsome Molly" may have it roots in the British Isle, though it gained more widespread popularity following a 1927 recording by G. B. Grayson and Henry Whitter. Many bluegrass musicians learned it from the Stanley Brothers, who performed it in the 1950s.

Title "Handsome Molly"
Performers The Country Gentlemen
Instruments guitar, dobro, string bass, two voices
Length 2:29

Musical Characteristics
1. The vocals are sung in harmony, one as the lead and the other as the tenor.
2. Dobro (steel) guitar is featured on this selection, the fiddle is absent.
3. The selection opens with the three finger-picked banjo stating the melody twice.
4. You can hear the duple meter made more complex by the underlying rhythms played by the guitar.

Well, I wish I was in London or some other seaport town.
I'd set my foot on a steamship and sail the oceans 'round.
Sailing on the oceans, sailing on the sea.
I think of Handsome Molly, wherever she may be.
Her hair was black as a raven's, her eyes were bright as coal.
Her teeth shone like lillies out in the morning cold.
Oh, don't you remember Molly, when you gave me your right hand.
You said if you ever married that I would be your man.
I saw her in church last Sunday, she passed me on by.
I knew her mind was changing by the roving of her eye.

This selection is from Smithsonian Folkways 40022.

transformation of rural cultural traits to urban settings. Some early "country" music recording artists, most notably Vernon Dahlhart or Carson Robison, traded on a rural image while maintaining an urbane approach to the music that included many composed selections. Their records from the late 1920s traded on a more sophisticated approach to performing and selling country music to a nationwide audience. As a result their recorded legacy is much greater in size and far more generic than any of the down-home, regional groups like Kentucky String Tickers, Freeny's Barn Dance Band (Mississippi), the Shelor Family (Virginia), or Pope's Arkansas Mountaineers.

This survey of country music and bluegrass in our nation's capital stops around 1960 because of the folk revival. Country music became even more commercially viable throughout the 1960s as the Nashville studios began to predominate while regional sounds (while not entirely absent) became less important. Elements of rock and pop music continued to reach into the music as a means of broadening its appeal. The folk revival embraced all sorts of grassroots music and helped to bring bluegrass to a wider, more geographically diverse audience. This was less of an issue in and around Washington, D.C., of course, but for tens of thousands the Newport Folk Festivals began serving up bluegrass as part of its menu. For many the Newport Folk Festivals of the early 1960s served as their introduction to the music of the Lilly Brothers, Flatt and Scruggs, Hylo Brown, and the Stanley Brothers. What was once labeled as hillbilly or bluegrass music was suddenly "folk."

The inclusion of this selection by Country Gentlemen nicely illustrates this point. It comes from a 1961 album, *Folk Songs and Bluegrass* (Smithsonian Folkways SPW 40022), that seems to have been aimed at a bifurcated audience. Perhaps (then Folkways owner) Moses Asch was trying to hit both the hard-core bluegrass audience and the larger and more diverse "folk music" crowd. The albums's title, however, underscores the close associations among folk, hillbilly, and bluegrass made by many music enthusiasts in the early 1960s. In the twenty-first century bluegrass thrives in Washington, D.C., with its own distinctive network of clubs, jam sessions, and bands.

FINAL THOUGHTS

Once you dig below the surface you discover folk, grassroots, and ethnic music throughout the United States, from the grittiest bar on the Southside of Chicago to the grittiest coal mine in West Virginia. In Washington, D.C., West Virginia **senator Robert Byrd** served in the Senate for nine consecutive terms, which ended when he passed away on June 28, 2010. Along with holding the distinction of being the longest-serving senator ever, Byrd was well known for delivering federal dollars back to his home state and for his fiddle playing. In 1977 Byrd recorded an album, "Mountain Fiddle," for County Records that gently mixed old-time and bluegrass standards such as "Cumberland Gap," "Don't Let Your Sweet Love Die," and "There's More Pretty Girls Than One." Accompanied by Doyle Lawson on guitar, James Bailey on banjo, and Spider Gilliam on bass, all of whom were then members of Washington, D.C.'s The Country Gentlemen, Byrd proved to be a proficient fiddler. Like most of the hundreds of "hillbilly" musicians in Washington, D.C. (and elsewhere), however, his music was less about virtuosity than the appreciation and understanding of the music and what it meant to the musicians and their audience.

KEY FIGURES AND TERMS

blues	folk revival
bluegrass	Connie B. Gay
Blue Grass Champs	gospel
Senator Robert Byrd	Hill Billies
citybilly	Ernest V. Stoneman
conjunto	Muddy Waters
Rev. Thomas A. Dorsey	

SUGGESTED LISTENING

Robert Byrd. *Mountain Fiddling*. County 769. A nice blend of bluegrass and old-time fiddling by the West Virginia senator with accompaniment by three of D.C.'s best musicians of the time.

Roy Clark. *Timeless: The Classic Concert Performances*. Varese Fontana B001EC6JZ8. A good sampling of Clark's pre-1975 material currently available.

Bill Clifton. *The Early Years 1957–58*. Rounder CD 011661102125. Maryland born, Clifton was both influential and a fixture on the D.C.-bluegrass scene in the late 1950s into the 1960s.

Country Gentlemen. *Country Songs, Old and New*. Smithsonian/Folkways SFW 40004. Their first album (1959) and one of the first and best from this D.C.-based bluegrass band.

Jimmy Dean. *Big Bad John and Other Fabulous Songs and Tales*. Sony Special Products B000002Y5G. This 1995 compilation, unfortunately, focuses on his post-1960 recordings, but remains the best sampling of his work.

Hazel Dickens and Alice Gerrard. *Pioneering Women of Bluegrass*. Smithsonian Folkways SFW 40065. Lovely recordings from the mid-1960s from two women who were then living and performing around D.C.

Don Santiago Jimenez. *Viva Seguin*. Arhoolie CD 7023. These twenty-seven selections (recorded between 1947 and 1951) illustrate the sound of conjunto and norteno music in San Antonio during the immediate post-WW II era.

Estevan "Steve" Jordan. *Return of El Parche*. Rounder 6019. A representative sampling of this eclectic musician's work from the mid-1970s through the mid-1980s.

Andrew Acosta and the New Old-Time Pickers with Speedy Tolliver. *New Old Time Pickers*. Arlington Cultural Affairs 001. A mix of new recordings with some home discs featuring the fiddling of Tolliver, who moved to the Washington, D.C., in 1939.

Red Allen and Frank Wakefield. *The Smithsonian Years, 1964–1983*. Smithsonian Folkways SFW 40127. Based in D.C. in the mid-1960s, this creative band features two of the genre's most influential instrumentalists.

Muddy Waters. *Definitive Collection*. Geffen Records CD6273. Perhaps not quite definitive, but very close to it and a well-rounded collection that focuses on the late 1940s and 1950s.

Various. *Friends of Old Time Music*. Smithsonian Folkways SFW 40160. New York City was the epicenter for the urban folk revival and between 1961 and 1965 the "Friends of Old Time Music" sponsored concerts by such important "rural" artists as Doc Watson, Mississippi John Hurt, Maybelle Carter, and the Stanley Brothers.

SUGGESTED READING

Thomas Goldsmith. *The Bluegrass Reader*. Urbana: University of Illinois Press, 2006. This well-rounded compendium often touches musicians living in the Mid-Atlantic and the D.C. area.

Robert Gordon. *Can't Be Satisfied: The Life and Times of Muddy Waters*. Boston: Back Bay Books, 2003. The definitive biography of this seminal blues musician.

Michael Harris. *The Rise of Gospel Blues: The Music of Thomas Andrew Dorsey in the Urban Church*. New York: Oxford University Press, 1994. A well-written, thorough biographical and cultural study of perhaps the most influential figure in twentieth-century gospel music.

SUGGESTED VIEWING

Various. *The Best Of Bluegrass: The Legends*. Man-do-lin Productions. This DVD includes a few performances by D.C.-related bluegrass artists Charlie Waller and Bill Harrell.

SELECTED SONG INDEX

"A Ko'olau Au' Ika Ka Ua," 222
"After the Ball," 97
"Alberta," 175
"Allons a Lafayette," 227
"Amazing Grace," 19, 123
"Are You Washed in the Blood?," 132
"Away Over in the Promised Land," 126
"Ay Te Dejo En San Antonio," 256, 358

"Bandit Cole Younger," 91
"Barrel House Blues," 47
"Beer Barrel Polka," 270
"Before You Get to Heaven (I'll Fly Away)," 154
"Big Ten Inch," 340
"Blowin' in the Wind," 301
"Blue Moon of Kentucky," 103, 335
"Born to Lose," 107
"Brighten the Corner Where You Are," 131
"Brownsville Blues," 332
"Bury Me Not in the Lone Prairie," 94
"Butcher's Boy, The," 89

"Carve That Possum," 62–63
"Casey Jones," 183
"Chopping in the New Ground," 174
"Cold Sweat," 327
"Crazy Blues," 51
"Cripple Creek," 364

"Dark Was the Night—Cold Was the Ground," 161
"Death's Black Train Is Coming," 162
"Dices Pescao," 358
"Dig a Hole," 105
"Dixie," 45
"Do-Re-Me," 286
"Downfall of Nebuchednezzar, The," 162
"Drinking Wine Spodee-O-Dee," 337

"Everybody Ought to Treat Their Mother Right," 159
"Eyesight to the Blind," 307

"Farmer's Curst Wife," 83, 186
"Flying Saucer Rock & Roll," 337
"Fox Chase," 22, 62, 328

"Gambler's Doom, The," 162–63
"Georgia Buck Is Dead," 178
"Get Along Home Cindy," 108
"Get on Board, Children," 149
"Give the World a Smile," 131
"God Holds the Future in His Hands," 133
"Going Down the Valley," 132
"Good Night, Irene," 202, 289
"Gospel Boogie," 136
"Gospel Train," 330
"Gregorio Cortez," 259

SELECTED SONG INDEX

"Handsome Molly," 374–75
"Hard Times Killing Floor," 302, 317
"He Will Set Your Fields on Fire," 100
"Hello Central, Give Me Heaven," 98
"His Eye in on the Sparrow," 131
"Hootchie Cootchie Man," 355
"Hound Dog," 338
"House Carpenter, The," 85

"I'll Fly Away," 130, 137
"I'm a Man of Constant Sorrow," 318
"I'm Walking (to New Orleans)," 338
"If the Light Has Gone Out in Your Soul," 135
"If You See My Savior," 156
"In Honor of Kennedy," 259
"In that Great Getting-Up Morning," 146–47
"It's Tight Like That," 156

"Jambalaya," 227
"Jesus Gonna Make Up My Dying Bed," 148
"Job," 163
"John Henry," 178, 181–83
"Jole Blond," 228–29
"Jump Jim Crow," 44

"Kisses Sweeter Than Wine," 289

"La Bonnefemme Robert" ("Old Lady Robert"), 233
"Le Reel de Sherbrooke," 234
"Les Haricots Sont Pas Sales" ("The Snap-beans are Not Salted"), 230
"Let's Do the Cajun Twist," 230
"Like a Rolling Stone," 340
"Listen to the Mockingbird," 330
"Little Old Log Cabin in the Lane," 62, 98
"Little Rosewood Casket, The," 98
"Locomotive Blues," 328
"Love Hides All Faults," 50

"Madre Mia Chote," 269
"Maid Freed from the Gallows, The," 83, 186
"Masters of War," 301
"Midnight Special," 181–82
"Minnesota Polka," 237
"Mother's Only Sleeping," 103
"Mr. Johnson," 181

"Night Cap Blues," 192
"No Depression in Heaven," 345
"Noah," 163
"Nobody Knows the Troubles I've Seen," 148

"Oh, Death," 317
"Old Ship of Zion," 149
"One Nation Under a Groove," 342
"Orange Blossom Special," 102
"Ot azoy," 209
"Our Goodman," 4, 83, 186
"Our Meeting Is Over," 331

"Patty on the Turnpike," 82
"Peace in the Valley," 157
"Pearl Bryant," 90–91
"Peyote Song," 214
"Pistol Packin' Mama," 107
"Poor Boy," 191
"Puff the Magic Dragon," 283

"Rock Around the Clock," 337–38
"Rock Island Line," 184–85
"Rock Lobster," 330
"Roll in My Sweet Baby's Arms," 100
"Rolling and Tumblin'," 13

"Sally Anne," 22
"Sally Goodin," 23, 51
"Shanty Boys, The," 300
"Sign of Judgment," 172

SELECTED SONG INDEX

"Simple Gifts," 128
"Sitting on Top of the World," 108
"So Long, Its Been Good to Know You," 289
"Song from an Outdoor Pow-Wow," 219
"Stack-O-Lee," 183
"Stagger Lee," 338
"Stavin' Chain," 185
"Surely, God Is Able," 165
"Sweet Hour of Prayer," 129
"Sweet Leilani," 223
"Sweeter as the Years Go By," 155
"Swing Down, Chariot," 165

"Take My Hand, Precious Lord," 157
"Take Your Burden to the Lord," 155
"Talkin' about a Good Time," 152
"Tell It to Me," 312
"That's Alright, Mama," 335
"This Land Is Our Land," 294, 350
"Titanic, The," 89, 98
"Tom Dooley," 292
"Try a Little Tenderness," 341

"Try Jesus, He Satisfies," 356
"Turn Your Radio On," 136–37
"Tutlut's Waltz," 241

"Unfortunate Rake, The," 82, 89, 186

"Western Pioneer," 94–95
"What Would You Give in Exchange?," 133
"When the Work's All Done This Fall," 13, 92, 96, 99
"Which Side Are You On?," 285
"White House Blues," 290
"Willow Tree," 128–29
"Wonderful Time Up There, A," 136
"Wondrous Love," 121–22
"Wreck of the Old 97," 56, 362
"Wreck on the C & O," 98

"You Gonna Need Somebody on Your Bond," 161

"Zip Coon," 44

GENERAL INDEX

Abshire, Nathan, 21, 229
Akim, Kawaiokawaawaa, and Hoakalei Kamau'u, 222
Allemand, Tony and Rufus, 228
Allen, Red, 105
Almanac Singers, 285, 287, 303
Andrews, Ed, 47
Ardoin, Alphonse, 231
Ardoin, "Bois Sec," 232, 314
Arhoolie Records, 21, 37, 41, 52, 65, 112, 196–97, 231, 242–46, 277–78, 314–16, 322, 346, 358, 377
Ark-La-Tex, xi
Asch, Moses, 92, 202, 285, 289, 293, 295
Autry, Gene, 43, 61, 82, 91, 93, 94, 109, 264
Azusa Street Revival, 134

Baez, Joan, 283–84, 293, 299, 301–2
Balfa, Dewey, 225, 229, 314, 317
barn dance radio, 54, 93, 101
bembes, 271–72
Benford, Mac, 311
B-52s, 327, 330–31
Big Voodoo Daddy, 340
Bligen, Benjamin, 152
bluegrass, xiii, xx, 11, 20, 27–28, 33, 70, 99–106, 304, 318, 353, 359–60, 368–77
Bluegrass Champs, 370
Bolick, Bill and Earl (The Blue Sky Boys), 33, 100, 133
bomba, 253

Bragg, Billy, xvii, 281–82
Brinkley, Dr. J. R., 59–60
Brown, Chuck, 5, 343
Brown, James, 324–27, 344
Brown, Milton, 108, 357
Brown, Richard "Rabbit," 182–83
Brumley, Albert, 136, 154–55
bullroarer, 217
Burnett, Rev. J. C., 162
Burnette, Johnny, 336
Byrd, Robert, 375–76

Cajun, 5, 8, 13, 16, 20–21, 27–28, 42–43, 52, 108, 205, 224–30, 313–14
California Traditional Music Society, 352
calypso, 275
Cape Cod, xi, xii
Carr, Leroy, 50
Carson, Fiddlin' John, 51, 98
Carter Family, 52, 60, 65, 97, 98–99, 135, 313, 345
CBS Trumpteers, 166, 329–30
Chambers Brothers, 154
Charters, Samuel, 291–92, 301, 307
Chenier, Clifton, 27, 231, 315
Chicago blues, 32, 183, 301, 353, 356
Chicken Scratch, 269
Child, James Francis, 83–84, 89, 292
Child ballads, 83–87
Chuck Wagon Gang, 136, 138
Church of God in Christ, 159

GENERAL INDEX

Clapton, Eric, 307
Clark, Roy, 369–70
Clayton, Paul, 298
Collins, Judy, 25, 299, 351
conjunto, 21–23, 254, 257–58, 357
coritos, 253
Corrales, Frank, 257
corridos, 258–61
Cotton, Libba, 183, 308
Country Gentlemen, 363, 371, 373
Courlander, Harold, 291
cowboy poetry, 93–97, 350
Czech-German music, 357

Dalhart, Vernon, 56, 97, 375
danzas, 266
Davidson, Ananias, 121–22
Dean, Jimmy, 366–69
del la Rose, Tony, 258
Delafose, Geno, & French Rockin' Boogie, 232
Densmore, Francis, 211–12
Dinwiddie Colored Quartette, 51
District of Columbia (Washington, D.C.), xii, xiii, 4, 16, 19, 232, 252, 351, 353, 359–76
Dixie Hummingbird, 165, 325, 329
Domino, Fats, 338, 346
Dorsey, Rev. Thomas, 153, 155–56, 158, 166, 355–56
Doucet, Michael, 225, 230, 232
Dranes, Arizona, 159
Dyer-Bennett, Richard, 284
Dylan, Bob, 3, 20, 25, 39, 202, 283–84, 288, 301–6, 339, 340, 351, 359

Estes, "Sleepy" John, 15, 284, 311, 331–32
ethnomusicologists, 11

Fairfield Four, 164
Falcon, Joseph, 227, 229

fiddle tunes, xi
field holler, 190
Flatt, Lester, and Earl Scruggs, xiii, 56, 103, 105, 375
Fletcher, Alice, 212
Folk Alliance, 352
Folkstreams.com, xii, xiii, 115–17, 142, 170, 199–200, 248–49, 322, 347
Fontenot, Canray, 232, 314
Franklin, Aretha, 324, 334, 341
Fruge, Columbus, 290

Galax, Virginia, 21, 23, 24, 281, 311
Gates, Reverend J. M., 162
Gay, Connie B., 365–68, 372–73
George Washington University, The, xii, xvii
Gluck, Christoph, 15
go-go, xii, xix, 5, 16, 343
Golden Gate Quartet, 101, 153, 163–64, 329
Goldstein, Kenneth, 298–99
Grand Ole Opry, 54, 60, 63, 73, 102, 104, 136, 223, 366
Grandmaster Flash and the Furious Five, 342
Grateful Dead, 14, 183, 339
Great Migration, xix
Greenwich Village, 297
Guthrie, Woody, 281, 284–87, 289, 293–94, 302, 350
Gutierrez, Homero, 273
Gutierrez, Juan, 275–76

Hackberry Ramblers, 227
Haley, Bill, and the Comets, 337
Hall, "Elder" Effie, 160
Hardanger fiddle, 239–40
Harps of Melody, 24
Harris, Charles K., 97–98
Harvesters, 294
Heartbeat, 218, 220

383

GENERAL INDEX

Herman's Hermits, 288
Hillbillies, The (Al Hopkins and the Bucklebusters), 359–61, 363
Hmung, 203–4
Hofner, Adolph, 357–58
Hogan, Ernest, 181
Hopkins, 315
Howington Brothers, 366–68
Howlin' Wolf, 25, 194, 306, 326, 336
Hurt, Mississippi John, 183, 186, 283, 296, 308

Ives, Sandy, 300

Jackson, Aunt Molly, 285
Jackson, Harry, 92
Jackson, Mahalia, 165–66, 325, 352, 355–56
Jarrell, Tommy, 4
Jefferson, Blind Lemon, 48–49, 296
Jenkins, "Snuffy," 101
Jimenez, Flaco, 357–59
Jimenez, Santiago, 21, 23, 258, 357–59
Jimenez, Santiago, Jr., 256, 358
Johnson, Blind Willie, 155, 161, 338
Johnson, Lonnie, 48–49, 50, 193, 335
Johnson, Robert, 25, 65, 194, 306, 308, 324, 327, 339, 355
Jordan, Louis, 282, 324, 346
Jordan, Steve, 359
juke joint, 180

Karl and the Country Dutchman, 237
KDKA, 54
Kentucky String Ticklers, 375
King, B.B., 49, 69, 185, 335, 341
Kingston Trio, 288, 292
Kivi, Erik, 235
Klezmer Plus, 209

Larson, LeRoy, 235, 240
Laws, G. Malcolm, 88, 90

Lead Belly, 25, 61, 181, 184, 186–88, 202, 284–85, 289, 293, 306, 350
Lewis, Furry, 183, 186, 312
Lewis, Jerry Lee, 282, 291, 334, 336–37
lining out (antiphony), 145–46
Little Richard, 324, 334, 338, 346
Lomax, Alan, 90, 179, 229, 285, 291, 308–9, 355
Louisiana Hayride, 107
Love, Hot Shot, 334

Macon, Uncle Dave, 15, 25, 42, 62
Mainer, J. E., and Wade, 33, 101–2, 373
mariachi, 251, 261–65
marimba, 273
Martin, Roberta, 21, 156–57, 165, 356
matachines, 266–67
McAllester, David, 213
McFarrin, Bobby, 327
McTell, Blind Willie, 14
Memphis, Tennessee, 24–25, 47, 53, 70, 76, 150, 159, 166, 186, 195, 335–36, 341–42
Memphis Minnie, 108, 306, 308
Mendoza, Lydia, xiii, 21, 60, 260, 315
Ming, Hoyt, and his Pep Steppers, 290
minstrelsy, 43–45
Monroe, Bill, xxii, 14, 21, 25, 33, 82, 99–106, 133, 283, 335, 358, 368, 370, 372–73
musica tejanos, 255–56

Nashville, Tennessee, 54, 62–63, 82, 102, 106, 136, 164, 344
National Endowment for the Arts (Folk Arts), xii
New Jolly Swiss Boys, 235
New Lost City Ramblers, 293, 297–98, 309–10, 314
New Ulm, Minnesota, xv, 74, 318
Newport Folk Festival, 229, 283, 301, 303–6, 339, 375
Newyorican, 274

GENERAL INDEX

Niles, John Jacob, 284
Norm Dombroski's Happy Notes, 236, 238

Ojibwa, 219
Old Town School of Folk Music, 352–53

Pahinui, "Gabby," 220
Parades, Americo, 255
Parham, Charles Fox, 133
Patterson, Joe, 34–35
Patton, Charlie, 10, 194, 326
Peer, Ralph, 51, 53, 360
Peg-Leg Sam, 326
Perry County Music Makers, 29
Phillips, Sam, 53, 64, 334–35, 346
Phipps Family, 125–26
Pinson, Reverend Leon, 160
plenos, 275
Poole, Charlie, xxii, 61, 100
Presley, Elvis, 63–64, 84, 138, 290, 333–38, 341, 346
Presley, Luther, 130–31
Public Enemy, 325

Queen Ida, 231

Rainey, Gertrude "Ma," 46–47
Red Clay Ramblers, 312
Redding, Otis, 341–42, 346
Reed, Dock, 148
Ritchie, Jean, 85, 87
Roanoke Entertainers, 55
Robertson, Eck, 51
Rodeheaver, Homer, 130–31
Rodgers, Jimmie, 99, 112, 135, 313, 345, 359, 361, 373
Rolling Stones, 25, 304–6, 339, 341
Rounder Records, 21, 38, 41, 52, 112, 139, 140, 197, 242–46, 278, 291, 311, 319–20, 347, 376–77
Ruebush-Kieffer Music Publishers, 129

San Antonio, Texas, 353, 357–59
Sapoznik, Henry, 207, 209–10, 285
Savoy, Marc, 27–28
Scruggs, Earl, 103
Seeger, Mike, xxi, 309–10
Seeger, Pete, 25, 40, 174, 285, 287, 289, 293, 295, 297, 299, 301, 352
Seldom Scene, 363
Severn Foot Dilly, 297
Seymour, William Joesph, 134
shape note (sacred harp) singing, 19, 101, 120–24, 144, 351
Shreveport, Louisiana, xi–xii, 107, 227
Sinatra, Frank, 323, 339
Sing Out!, 292, 294, 301
singing conventions, 129–30
singing schools, 119–20
Six Cylinder Smith, 289
Six Fat Dutchmen, 9
Smith, Bessie, 46–47
Smith, Mamie, 51
Smithsonian Folkways, xii, xiii, xx, 23, 34, 37, 41, 70, 87, 93, 105, 111–13, 122, 139, 148, 153, 155, 160, 167–68, 175, 185, 193, 196, 197, 209, 214, 219, 222, 229, 237, 243–47, 250, 256, 269, 277–78, 287, 295, 301, 313, 316, 319–20, 329, 347, 363, 374–77
son, 272
Son Volt, xvii, 282
Soul Stirrers, 166
Spirit of Memphis Quartette, 165, 166, 329, 336
Spottswood, Dick, xx, 52, 67, 98, 315–16
Sprague, Carl T., 95–96
Stanley Brothers, 104, 318, 375
Stoneman, Ernest V., 64, 97–98, 100, 131–32, 138, 293, 362–65, 369–71
Stoneman, Scotty, 369–70
Strackwitz, Chris, 314–16
Strickland, Napoleon, 179
Sun Records, 53, 63–64, 291, 334, 336–37, 346

GENERAL INDEX

Tarras, David, 208
Taverna, Ben, 257
Terry, Sonny, 328
Thompson, Joe and Odell, xiii, 177
Town and Country Time, 366–68
Travis, Merle, 9
Trouble Funk, xix

Uncle Tupelo, 345
Union Grove, North Carolina, 3, 5
University of North Carolina at Chapel Hill, xiii, xxii, 69

Van Ronk, Dave, 202, 290, 295–99, 350
Vargas, Silvestre, 265
Vaughan Publishers, 130
Viking Accordion Band, 240
vocables, 215
Von Schmidt, Eric, 283–84

waila (chicken scratch), 43, 266–69
Walker, William "Singing Billy," 123
Ward, Wade, 21–24
Washo Indians, 214
Waters, Muddy, 21, 34, 193–94, 306–8, 336, 339, 354–56
Watson, Doc, 303, 305

WBT, 101, 105
WDBJ, 55–56, 288
WDIA, 151, 335
Weavers, the, 285, 303
Wells, Junior, 354
western swing, xix, xx, 43, 227, 357
White, Bukka, 282, 330
White Boy and the Wagon Burners, 220
Wilco, xvii, 281–82
Wilfahrt, "Whoopie" John, xv, 52, 74, 204
Williams, Big Joe, 34, 192, 194, 302, 331–32
Williams, Dewey, 144
Williams, Hank, 107, 138, 227, 335
Williams, Robert Pete, 332–33
Wills, Bob, 43, 82, 107–10, 227, 345, 366, 372
WKYS-FM, xi
Womack, Daniel, 330
WRC, 359–60
WSM, 54, 63, 73, 102

XER, 59–60

Yankovic, Frankie, 9, 27
Youtube.com, xii

Zydeco, 16, 20, 27, 224, 230–33